BESIEGED BEACHHEAD

*The Cold War Battle for Cuba
at the Bay of Pigs*

J. J. VALDÉS

STACKPOLE
BOOKS
Essex, Connecticut
Blue Ridge Summit, Pennsylvania

STACKPOLE BOOKS
An imprint of The Globe Pequot Publishing Group, Inc.
64 South Main Street
Essex, CT 06426
www.globepequot.com

Distributed by NATIONAL BOOK NETWORK

British Library Cataloguing in Publication Information available

Library of Congress Cataloging-in-Publication Data

Names: Valdes, J. J., 1956– author.
Title: Besieged beachhead: the Cold War battle for Cuba at the Bay of Pigs / J.J. Valdés.
Other titles: Cold War battle for Cuba at the Bay of Pigs
Description: Essex, Connecticut : Stackpole Books, [2024] | Includes bibliographical references and index. | Summary: "Decades in the making, Bay of Pigs draws from English and Spanish sources in the United States and Cuba to tell the story of this Cold War debacle as it has never been told before, shedding light on events that have been shrouded in secrecy, myth, and propaganda for six decades"— Provided by publisher.
Identifiers: LCCN 2024003507 | ISBN 9780811776790 (cloth) | ISBN 9780811776806 (epub)
Subjects: LCSH: Cuba—History—Invasion, 1961. | United States—Foreign relations—Cuba. | Cuba—Foreign relations—United States. | Cuba—Foreign relations—1959–1990. | United States—Foreign relations—1953–1961. | Cold War.
Classification: LCC F1788 .V29 2024 | DDC 972.9106/4—dc23/eng/20240403
LC record available at https://lccn.loc.gov/2024003507

*To individual sacrifices made in hopes
of a brighter common future.*

CONTENTS

AUTHOR'S NOTE

Renderings of Spanish surnames in the text merit explanation. Double surnames are typical in Hispanic cultures and commonly consist of the first surname of the father followed by the first surname of the mother. Women customarily retain their birth surnames even after marriage. Usually—but not always—the paternal surname by itself is used in semi-formal appellations. The convention adopted in this work is to refer to individuals by their paternal surnames unless an established preference for the maternal or full double surname exists.

The term "mercenary," widely adopted in Cuba for the Cuban exiles that participated in the battle, is only used herein when part of a direct quote. As recognized in the 1977 Amendment Protocol I to the Geneva Conventions (ratified by Cuba in 1982), only nonnationals in a conflict could possibly be legitimately considered mercenaries.[1]

The reader should also note the following:

- Unless otherwise noted, all times and mile distances refer to Eastern Standard Time (i.e., Cuba and Washington, DC, time) and statute miles, respectively.
- Tide information is derived from the National Oceanographic and Atmospheric Administration's (NOAA) website (https://tidesandcurrents.noaa.gov/tide_predictions.html).
- Information on moon phases and sun/moon rise/set times are from the website of the U.S. Naval Observatory (USNO) (https://aa.usno.navy.mil/data/).
- Ages and unit affiliations stated for brigade members, if not contained in the references cited, are derived from the enlistment lookup database compiled by the *El Nuevo Herald* newspaper (https://c0dzk099.caspio.com/dp/ce401000d69ebaaeb4cb43849383).
- Cuban provinces named refer to those in existence in 1961 and their then corresponding geographic boundaries.
- All translations of passages from Spanish-language sources cited are by the author.

PREFACE

There is a very personal family connection for me with the events narrated in this book. As for many other Cubans, my father's illusions about the democratization of Cuba under Fidel Castro came to an end on April 16, 1961, the eve of the Bay of Pigs invasion. Dad had opposed Castro's dictatorial predecessor, Fulgencio Batista, whose 1952 coup had disrupted the democratic direction of the country. Thus, full of hope for a brighter future, he had welcomed the Revolution's 1959 triumph and early on joined the National Militia, where he attained the rank of sergeant. Steadily, however, he grew wary of the new government's increasingly evident Marxist leanings. All his doubts were removed on that April day when, encamped with his militia unit, he heard Castro's nationally broadcasted speech declaring the Revolution "socialist." During a brief furlough at home hours later, my overwrought father told my equally distraught mother that he would never fight for such a government. When the expected invasion came, he told her, he would go over to the other side if he had the chance. "If I die, tell my children that I wasn't a communist and explain to them the situation that I faced." Dad's unit, as it happened, was kept away from the ensuing battle, so the opportunity for him to switch sides never presented itself.[1] Had he been able to do so, he would later tell me, his life may have ended not in combat but by summary execution after the invasion's defeat. This was the rumored fate of those in the military who had joined the invaders, although Cuban state publications claim that not a single defection occurred.[2]

In 1961 I was just a young child with no real notion of current events or of my father's ordeals. But, during the intervening seven years I lived in Cuba, the invasion relics on display at the local museum were always a source of constant fascination. Placards describing the fight against "mercenary landings" evoked in my adolescent mind fanciful images of humans battling H. G. Wells's Martian invaders. My perceptions, of course, matured with age, but the fascination endured. For, like in the novel, the outcome of the invasion had repercussions that extended beyond the personal to the world at large. It was a conflict that set not only the tone for much of the Cold War but also the stage for its climactic Missile Crisis.

It was just this fascination with the U.S.-sponsored invasion of my former homeland that led me over the decades to amass an extensive collection of publications and documents from both the winning and losing sides. The book you now hold represents the fruition of years of work to interweave this material into a two-sided historical narrative of the battle. Admittedly, the work of synthesizing a coherent narrative from disparate sources spanning more than sixty years has been both daunting and challenging.

As Fidel Castro himself acknowledged in 1986: "I perceive that, although numerous and interesting testimonies exist, an exacting, precise, and overarching history of that battle has not yet been written. At times—as far as we can recollect—there are dates that get confused notwithstanding that it was only three days. Things that occurred on the 19th are attributed to the 18th; some that occurred on the 20th—subsequent events—are attributed to the 19th. Those sorts of things."[3] The vagaries of memory inevitably do take a toll on the accuracy of repeated retellings of events over time. One case in point are the significant discrepancies between the after-action report written in 1961 by Grayston Lynch, a CIA case officer assigned to the invasion fleet, and his book published in 1998. Another poignant example is provided by the recollections of Cuban exile combatants regarding the supposed traffic circle where they fought their "Battle of the Rotonda." In 2008 one of them sketched it out as a circular rotary to which others ascribed widely different diameters.[4] In fact, photographs and accounts by journalists onsite immediately after the battle reveal the presence of a Y-shaped intersection just as exists there today.[5] The "traffic circle" turns out to be a small triangular traffic island at the apex of a larger one known locally as the Caletón Triangle. Even participant testimonies memorialized shortly after an impactful event are not free of stress-induced unintentional distortions as well as manifestly self-serving exaggerations. These issues are compounded by the propagandistic bent of Cuban state-controlled publications and a good number of accounts from the United States. The problem thus becomes one of extricating a "signal" from the "noise."

In this work I have relied on a multiple-lines-of-evidence approach to evaluate the various sources consulted. My aim has been to triangulate and document common threads to derive the most compelling interpretation consistent with the bulk of the evidence. Thus, the resulting versions and timing of events presented are those that reconcile best with the myriad of available information. This process has shone new light on many misunderstandings, misrepresentations, and mysteries that have muddled the Bay of Pigs saga. My overriding guiding principle throughout has been to seek and tell the truth regardless of how it might be perceived on either side of the Straits of Florida. Not everyone will be pleased in all cases with my renderings of people and events, but I have done my utmost to let the evidence guide me and not the reverse. It is my sincere belief and hope that these efforts have distilled into the most in-depth, accurate, and up-to-date history of the Bay of Pigs battle.

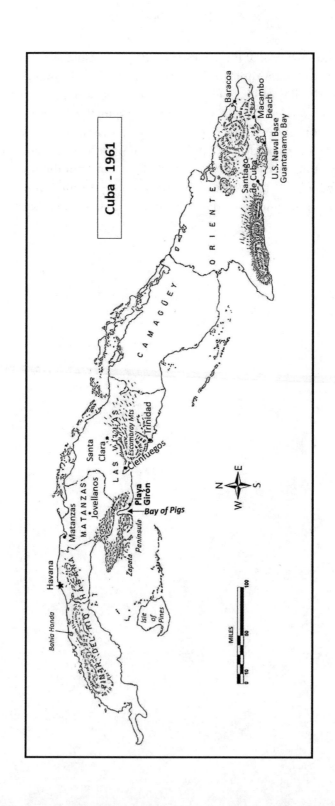

Cuba - 1961

Bay of Pigs Theater of Operations

INTRODUCTION

Thirty-two-year-old lawyer, politician, and revolutionary leader Fidel Castro—*El Comandante*—became de facto ruler of Cuba on New Year's Day, 1959. On that date, the unpopular dictator Fulgencio Batista fled the island having succumbed to a two-year-long guerrilla war undertaken mainly by Castro's 26th of July Movement (M-26-7).[1]

Within months, the young revolutionary made good on his repeated promise of aiding Latin American political refugees in Cuba to start revolutions in their own homelands. Various expeditionary forces, all incorporating Cuban personnel, were launched from the island. The first occurred in April 1959 against Panama, where the invaders landed close to the Atlantic entrance of the U.S.-controlled Panama Canal Zone. This was followed by other expeditions against Nicaragua (June), the Dominican Republic (June), and Haiti (August). All proved unsuccessful but marked the start of Castro's war against American "imperialism" and its perceived collaborators in Latin America.[2] "When this war [against Batista] is over," he had written intimate confidant Celia Sánchez in June 1958, "a much wider and bigger war will begin for me, the war I am going to wage against them [the Americans]. I realize that this is going to be my true destiny."[3]

In 1960 Castro's government nationalized all American properties on the island and began to restructure the economic and political life of the country along Soviet Bloc lines.[4] Ironically enough, the very Americans he so despised had aided his rise to power by refusing to sell weapons to Batista as well as pressuring foreign governments not to do so.[5] Alarmed by events on the island, in March of that year U.S. President Dwight Eisenhower authorized the training of Cuban exiles under a Central Intelligence Agency (CIA) plan to overthrow Castro.[6] By November those exiles were streaming into Florida at a rate of 1,700 per week.[7] The catalyst that would lead to the Bay of Pigs invasion had been created.

PART I

PRELUDE TO BATTLE

1

Assault Brigade 2506

On April 12, 1961, an old rusty cargo ship with a damaged propeller sailed from Puerto Cabezas, Nicaragua, bound for an invasion of Cuba conceived and financed by the CIA. Aboard were the 143 men of the Sixth Battalion of a Cuban exile force calling itself Assault Brigade 2506. Due to its slower speed, the *Río Escondido* had gotten a two-day head start over three other equally unseemly freighters—*Atlántico, Caribe,* and *Houston*—that carried most of the brigade's other troops. Their destination was the Bay of Pigs area on the southern coast of the Caribbean island. The vessels had all been leased at-cost by the CIA from the owners of the García Line Corporation, still operating out of Cuba.[1]

The *Río Escondido, Atlántico,* and *Caribe* were destined for a small coastal town named Playa Girón, commonly shortened to Girón. Codenamed Blue Beach, it lay seven miles east of the entrance to the fifteen-mile-long Bay of Pigs. Aboard the *Atlántico* were brigade headquarters and support personnel as well as the Third Battalion's 179 men and most of the Heavy Weapons Battalion's 127-man complement. Thirteen members of the "Operation 40" counterintelligence unit were also onboard. The unit's remaining 51 members would travel on the *Lake Charles*, due to sail later and arrive (along with additional ordnance and provisions) four days after the initial landings. The *Caribe* carried the 166 soldiers of the Fourth (armored) Battalion and the twenty-six tankers plus support personnel of the brigade's tank company.[2]

The *Houston,* on the other hand, was bound for a landing at the settlement of Playa Larga, code-named Red Beach, on the northern end of the Bay of Pigs. It carried the brigade's deputy commander, Erneido Oliva, plus the 182 troops of the Second Battalion (reinforced by two squads from the Heavy Weapons Battalion). Also aboard were the 159 men of the Fifth Battalion.[3]

No smoking was allowed aboard the crowded ships where men competed for space with fuel drums and combat materiel. The unlikely fleet effectively consisted of floating tinderboxes.[4]

Rounding off the small fleet were two converted LCIs (landing craft infantry) owned by the CIA: the command ship, *Blagar*, and the *Barbara J*.[5] Their crews were a mix of American civil merchant mariners from the Military Sea Transportation Service (MSTS) and well as Cuban sailors. Per maritime tradition, MSTS officer Sven Ryberg, the Swedish-American captain of the command ship, was named naval commander of the invasion fleet and the landing itself.[6] José ("Pepe") Pérez San Román, the brigade's military commander, traveled aboard the *Blagar* along with members of his staff. The two LCIs carried three underwater demolition teams (UDT), totaling eleven frogmen, between them. One of two teams on the *Blagar* would mark the beach at Girón whereas the other would do likewise at another landing site east of it code-named Green Beach. The third team, on the *Barbara J*, would mark the beach at Playa Larga. In total, the brigade troops aboard the six ships amounted to just under 1,200 men.[7]

Assault Brigade 2506 was made up of Cuban exiles from all walks of life, ranging in age from sixteen to sixty-one. Beginning in early 1960, a small cadre had been recruited and trained directly by the CIA to spearhead a guerrilla action program against Fidel Castro's Cuba. Among them had been San Román, a former Cuban army officer under both Castro and Batista. From May of 1960 onward, the CIA was no longer at the forefront of the recruitment effort. That function was undertaken through the Frente Revolucionario Democrático (FRD; Democratic Revolutionary Front), a Cuban-exile political umbrella group sponsored by the agency. Another change occurred in November of that year when the focus of the training changed from guerrilla teams to the formation of an amphibious and airborne assault force.[8] Only a total of sixty exiles (of which only some forty were finally selected) would go on to receive guerrilla training in Panama. They were subsequently infiltrated into Cuba to prepare the way for the invasion.[9]

Most of the brigade men, the majority of whom had no previous military experience, received their training at CIA camps in Guatemala. The U.S.-backed government of that Central American nation owed its existence to PBSUCCESS, a 1954 CIA operation that removed leftist Jacobo Arbenz from power. PBSUCCESS, which had succeeded despite a long series of planning and execution blunders, became the CIA's model for the project to topple Castro in Cuba.[10]

The camps had been secretly built on lands owned by Roberto Alejos, brother of the Guatemalan ambassador to the United States. Base Trax (codename JMTRAV[11]), the main facility, was located within the mountainous confines of Alejos's Helvetia coffee plantation. In late 1960, Lieutenant Colonel Frank Egan of the U.S. Army Special Forces—known to the Cubans only as "Frank"—took charge of Trax. Under Egan, "a florid . . . aggressive and commanding figure," the base quickly changed. The shabby encampment that lacked weapons, equipment, and infrastructure was converted into a true military installation.[12]

Size-wise, the brigade battalions were equivalent to regular U.S. Army companies and its companies to platoons.[13] The expectation was that these units would eventually grow to full strength once the brigade arrived in Cuba and members of the populace joined it.[14] Deceptively, the recruits in Guatemala were assigned serial numbers from a sequence that started with the number 2,501. "That way," explained an early recruit, "we would always project the image of being a force of at least 2,500 men even if we only had a handful of people."[15]

Pepe San Román had chosen the name Assault Brigade 2506 for the small *Ejército de Liberación* (Liberation Army) he commanded. The numeral "2506" was chosen to honor the brigade's first casualty. It had been the serial number of Carlos Santana, a popular young man who had fallen down a cliff to his death during a training exercise.[16] In official American circles, however, the brigade was almost exclusively referred to as the Cuban Expeditionary Force (CEF).[17]

The staggered nature of the recruitments meant that not all recruits had received the same amount of training by the time they sailed to Cuba. Most of the men of the Fifth and Sixth Battalions who were not former military had received barely two weeks of training when they departed Nicaragua. Another 151 trainees slated for the brigade's Seventh Battalion arrived at Base Trax when the brigade ships were already at sea. Still another 220 additional recruits remained in Homestead, Florida.[18]

Of all the brigade units, the 180 paratroopers of the airborne First Battalion were considered the most elite. Their leader was the young and charismatic Alejandro del Valle, another of the cadre of early training recruits. The unit was assigned the task of parachuting into Cuba and establishing advanced blocking positions to secure a perimeter around the beachhead.[19]

An airbase near Retalhuleu, a town on the Pacific plains of Guatemala, was where the crews that would fly both transport and bomber aircraft were initially trained. The base was known by the codename JMADD in official circles but had been nicknamed Rayo Base by the Cuban exiles. Their instructors were personnel pulled from various Air National Guard units, the U.S. Air Force, and CIA affiliates. All the Cuban aviators had prior experience as civil or military pilots. Those with prior military experience were generally assigned to fly the B-26 invader bombers with the others being allotted to fly the transport aircraft.[20] By mid-April 1961, the brigade air force, which called itself the Fuerza Aérea de Liberación (Liberation Air Force), totaled 186 men among aircrews and ground support staff. It was organized into three squadrons as follows:

> B-26 Squadron: nineteen pilots, nineteen navigators/observers
> C-46 Squadron: fourteen pilots/copilots, two nonpilot navigators
> C-54 Squadron: thirteen pilots/copilots, two nonpilot navigators[21]

* * * *

In late March of 1961, at the insistence of the John F. Kennedy administration, the FRD was absorbed into the politically broader Consejo Revolucionario de Cuba (CRC; Cuban Revolutionary Council). The CRC was presided over by José Miró Cardona, a lawyer and law professor who had formerly served as Castro's prime minister. Manuel Artime, founder of an anti-Castro resistance group in Cuba and an influential CIA liaison, was appointed to become the CRC's representative within the brigade.[22]

The final preinvasion phase of the operation began on April 2 when the airbase in Nicaragua that would serve as a strike base for the invasion became operational. Until its identity was disclosed to the Cubans, it had only been known to them as "Trampoline." Officially code-named JMTIDE (but nicknamed "Happy Valley" by its new occupants), it was located on the outskirts of the port town of Puerto Cabezas. The airbase was some 300 miles closer to Cuba than JMADD but still over 575 miles distant. All final advanced training for the pilots was conducted at

JMTIDE. On April 10 the transfer of the brigade soldiers to Puerto Cabe-zas began. Over the course of three days, the troops were taken by truck from Base Trax to JMADD and then airlifted to JMTIDE. From there, all but the paratroopers were transported overland to the nearby port and loaded onto the ships that would to carry them to Cuba.[23]

2

Strategizing the Invasion

On March 17, 1960, outgoing president Dwight Eisenhower authorized the CIA to implement training of Cuban exiles to be infiltrated into the island as small guerrilla forces. The aim was to create "active centers of resistance" against Castro within the country. By the summer of that year, however, the strategy began to transform. It hence became focused on the "development of trained paramilitary ground and air forces of Cuban volunteers" for a full-fledged invasion of Cuba.[1]

Newly installed president J. F. Kennedy received his first official briefing on the CIA's strategic plan for the invasion on January 28, 1961.[2] Among those in attendance were CIA director Allen Dulles and General L. Lemnitzer, chairman of the Joint Chiefs of Staff (JCS). The level of detail offered at the meeting and just how much the new president was able to absorb is uncertain. "After considerable discussion," Kennedy requested that the JCS evaluate the CIA's plan and provide an opinion regarding its chances for success.[3]

The CIA plan reviewed by the JCS proposed a daytime amphibious and airborne assault on the coastal city of Trinidad in southern Cuba.[4] It argued that the nearby Escambray Mountains not only harbored guerrilla units that could aid the invaders but would also provide refuge if retreat became necessary. Airstrikes against Cuban military bases on D–1 and D-Day* were to pave the way for the invasion. The beachhead established would serve as the seat of a provisional government and, it was anticipated, "act as a rallying point for volunteers and a catalyst for uprisings throughout Cuba." On February 3, the JCS issued their evaluation of the

---

* In military usage, D refers to the day on which an operation is to begin. Numbers following a minus or plus after the D indicate a corresponding number of days before or after that date, respectively.

11

Trinidad Plan. They deemed that the operation envisioned had "a fair chance of ultimate success" contingent "upon political factors; i.e., a sizeable popular uprising or substantial follow-on forces." [5]

On March 11, Kennedy was briefed by the CIA's deputy director for plans, Richard Bissell, on a proposed operation somewhat different from the one reviewed by the JCS. The daytime landing at Trinidad would now involve "concurrent (but no prior) tactical air support" as well as a preceding diversionary landing. After a full discussion, the president deemed the operation to be "too spectacular." It resembled a World War II-type of amphibious assault and thus pointed to American involvement. He asked for an alternative plan, to be provided "within the next few days," whereby U.S. assistance would be less obvious.[6]

To address the president's concerns, the CIA men sought to "infer from the comments made on the earlier plan the characteristics which a new plan should possess in order to be politically acceptable." These, they concluded, were:

- An "unspectacular" landing without "prior nor concurrent tactical air support."
- An airstrip capable of supporting tactical operations leading to the establishment of control of the air over Cuba.
- An appreciable period of build up after the initial landing before major offensive action was undertaken and a provisional government recognized.
- A guerrilla warfare alternative ("ideally") if the invasion failed.

The CIA then evaluated five different invasion sites to determine whether they would "permit an operation fitting [these] conditions."

During meetings on March 15–16 at the White House, CIA personnel briefed the president and other officials on their findings. Of the five sites, only one was found to be "eminently suited." It was the Bay of Pigs area, "on the south coast of Cuba," "almost surrounded by swamps," and containing "one and possibly two airstrips adequate to handle B-26s."

The briefing paper Bissell and his staff had prepared detailed the phases of the operation proposed for this location:

- Phase I: A night landing—expected to be accomplished "quite unobtrusively" and "with no serious combat"—during which "the

whole beachhead area including the airstrips" would "be immediately occupied and approach routes defended." Due to the
potential threat from Castro's aircraft, transport ships were to
"put to sea in time to be well offshore by dawn."
- Phase II: "Movement into the beachhead of tactical aircraft and
their prompt commitment for strikes against the Castro Air
Force."
- Phase III: Continue unloading of equipment and supplies as
soon as there was "adequate protection for shipping from enemy
air attack." The provisional government could be installed in
the beachhead "as soon as aircraft can land safely" and be recognized "after a decent interval." This would "prepare the way for
more open and more extensive logistical support if this should
be necessary."
- Phase IV: Breakout from the beachhead, the timing direction of
which would "depend upon the course of events in the island."[7]

Noticeably absent was any mention of a guerrilla warfare fallback to
the Escambray Mountains that had been a key feature of the Trinidad
Plan. Not only were these mountains more than fifty miles east of the Bay
of Pigs but the major city of Cienfuegos lay directly in between.

The JCS (who were represented at the meetings) had already evaluated the new proposed invasion site, which they designated "Alternative
III." On March 15 they produced their findings in writing: "Alternative
III is considered the most feasible and the most likely to accomplish the
objective." They, emphasized, however, that: "None of the alternative
concepts are considered as feasible and likely to accomplish the objective
as the basic para-military plan" (i.e., the original Trinidad Plan).[8]

During the continuing discussions on March 16, it was "emphasized
that the plan was dependent on a general uprising in Cuba." Without
such an uprising, "the entire operation would fail." Paratroop drops at
first light were added to the operation at this meeting, and Kennedy
approved further development of the "Zapata Plan," as it became known
in official circles.[9] Zapata is the name of the extensive wetlands region
that encompasses the Bay of Pigs area.

Additional sessions were held at the White House on March 29 and
April 4, 5, and 6 during which Kennedy's insistence on plausible deniabil-
ity of American involvement was a recurring theme. He wanted "to do

everything possible," as he indicated on the sixth, "to make it appear to be a Cuban operation." This, in his mind, would make it "more plausible for US denial of association . . . although recognizing that we would be accused."[10] It was truly a naive and illogical requirement. As noted by Bissell, albeit some thirty years after the fact: "If the United States was sure to be held responsible, then it made no sense to pay a price in terms of impaired operational capability for a result that could not be obtained. Yet," he notes, "that is exactly what we did."[11] At the March 29 meeting, Kennedy had also raised the question of whether "the force could fade into the brush and not look like a failure" if the operation was unsuccessful. Bissell replied that in such a case "the force would probably have to be withdrawn."[12] Unlike the Trinidad Plan, as previously observed, the Zapata Plan lacked a "turn-guerrilla" outlet.

3

Military Plan for Operation Pluto

With the White House's blessing of the Zapata Plan strategy now in hand, the CIA proceeded to develop the concomitant military plan for the operation. Notably, none of the Cuban exiles involved in the invasion were ever consulted on any part of the strategic or operational planning. Such discussions, even with members of the CRC, were "considered unacceptably dangerous on security grounds." Cuban military leaders who insisted on being included in planning activities were removed or chose to resign upon being ignored. In the eyes of the CIA, the Cubans simply could not be trusted to keep secrets. A long-standing joke within the agency was that Cuba had three forms of communication: telephone, telegraph, and tell-a-Cuban.[1]

When finalized, "Plan de Operación Pluto" (Operation Pluto Plan) and its accompanying "Plan Administrativo" (Administrative Plan) totaled over 150 pages and included seventeen annexes with appendices. In addition to military and logistical directives, the document also provided geographic information about the invasion area as well as intelligence on enemy and friendly forces.[2]

The area of coastal rocky scrubland to be occupied measured about thirty-five miles across and encompassed approximately eighty square miles. It was described as "virtually impenetrable" from the mainland due to the presence of the bordering Zapata Swamp.[3] The accompanying maps and photos[4] showed that three main roads (causeways) extended inland across the swamp from the area. One led to a sugar mill named Central Australia, another to the settlement of Covadonga, and the third to the small rural community of Yaguaramas.

Defending these accessways into the beachhead was a key feature of the Pluto military plan. The task of doing so initially fell to the paratroop

15

companies of the First Battalion, which were to drop down at dawn. Like the ancient Greek defense against superior forces at Thermopylae Pass, the paratroopers were to block the roads where the impassable swampland on either side created restrictive passageways. Small units of about twenty men were to set up defensive strongpoints on the northern entrances into these "bottlenecks." At their southern exits, fallback battle positions would be established. First Battalion headquarters was to occupy the settlement of San Blas, where the two roads south from Covadonga and Yaguaramas intersected.[5]

The shoreline where the amphibious landings would occur was described as "generally rocky but with quite a few little sandy beaches . . . facing deep and clear water."[6] To reach these landing beaches, the brigade ships would follow independent courses until dawn of D–1. At that time, they would come together and proceed as a convoy to rendezvous near Girón (Blue Beach) with a landing ship dock (LSD) carrying the LCVPs (landing craft vehicle personnel) and LCUs (landing craft utility). *Barbara J* and *Houston* would continue on to Playa Larga (Red Beach), at the head of the Bay of Pigs.[7]

A UDT team would mark the approaches to the Girón landing zone with buoy and beach lights. The Fourth Battalion would be the first to land at Girón by means of the LCVPs followed in succession by the Heavy Weapons and Sixth Battalions. At first light the five tanks and other vehicles aboard the LCUs were to be brought ashore there as well.[8]

The Fourth Battalion was charged with the initial occupation of Girón and its airfield. During the first hours of the operation, one of its companies reinforced with heavy weapons and two tanks was to join the paratroopers at San Blas. The rest of the battalion, along with two other tanks, would be held in reserve at Girón.[9]

Responsibility for fortifying and protecting the all-important airfield fell to the Sixth Battalion.[10] "Upon seizing the airstrip," the plan specified, "the Tactical Air Force initiates attacks with the purpose of destroying or neutralizing enemy air, naval and land forces." This "Tactical Air Force" consisted of two B-26s that were to land and operate from the strip plus the other B-26s based in Nicaragua.[11] A list of Cuban installations to be attacked on D-Day was included as an appendix to the invasion plan.[12]

The Third Battalion would proceed aboard the *Blagar* to Caleta Redonda (Green Beach), a small cove nineteen miles east of Girón. At this location, a trail running parallel to the coast intersected another that extended north to Yaguaramas. Reinforced with heavy weapons and a tank from Girón, the battalion was to block this additional access route into the beachhead area.[13] LCIs *Barbara J* and *Blagar*, both outfitted with heavy caliber machine guns and recoilless rifles, were to provide long-shore fire support at the conclusion of the landings.[14]

In Playa Larga, the Second Battalion followed by the Fifth were to hit the beaches using small boats aboard the *Houston*. The Second Battalion and its attached heavy weapons squads were then to head north and join the paratroopers defending the "bottleneck" on the road from Central Australia. The Fifth Battalion was to secure the settlement and on D+1 link up with these units.[15]

* * * *

The planned disposition of brigade forces presumed that the main attacks from Castro's units, when they came, would fall mainly on the northeast and eastern sectors of the beachhead. This tactical premise was evidently based on the projected locations of enemy forces. The CIA planners predicted that, out of a regular army totaling about 32,000 men, the troops closest to the invasion zone were the approximately 6,000 men of the Central Army. These were stationed in Santa Clara, some seventy miles to the northeast. No militia units, estimated to total about 200,000 troops in the whole country, were known to be present in the invasion zone.[16]

To curtail the movement of enemy forces toward the beachhead, the plan envisioned that the main railroad and highway bridges between the beachhead and major regional urban centers (Havana, Matanzas, Jovellanos, Colón, Santa Clara, and Cienfuegos) would be destroyed. The plan ambiguously implied that these actions were to be carried out by the "Tactical Air Force" after the capture of the Girón airstrip. In fact, although not mentioned in the document, the destruction of such bridges was supposed to be spearheaded by brigade operatives infiltrated into Cuba in advance of the landings.[17]

Various sections of the plan discussed the friendly forces that would join the invasion force. The brigade was projected to double its number within twenty days of landing and to double it again within thirty. In addition to disaffected members of the army and navy, the reinforcements would supposedly come from guerrillas, ex-military men, persecuted dissidents, dispossessed landowners, unemployed professionals, and the Catholic clergy. Weapons and supplies to equip up to 4,000 of those joining the brigade supply were loaded onto the two LCIs and the *Lake Charles*. Equipment for an additional 7,000 would be made available by air or sea upon request. Not explained, given that the population of the invasion zone was described as "very sparse," was how such a large influx of people would be able to get through enemy lines to reach the "virtually impenetrable" area. The plan further projected that "an anti-Castro force established on Cuban soil would receive the immediate support of 25% of the population and would face opposition from no more than 20% of the population."[18]

The CIA planners took a dim view of the armament and equipment available to Castro's militia and army, deeming it "more varied . . . than it is possible for a force with little training and organization to absorb." The Cuban air force was characterized as "completely disorganized and having extremely low operational capabilities." According to the agency's intelligence, the service branch "has been left with no qualified pilots and without trained specialists in maintenance and communications. The combat efficacy of the air force is almost non-existent. It has a limited capability to provide early warning to oppose maritime and aerial units and could carry out harassment attacks against lightly armed invaders. However, it is generally limited to the transport of troops and materials, machine gun attacks by flying aircraft, and visual patrols."[19]

Subsequent events would reveal serious flaws in these intelligence assessments, but such a contingency was evidently not seriously considered. The plan provided no exit provision in case things did not turn out as anticipated.

4

Castro's Forces—"Awaiting the Direct Aggression"

The militarization of Cuban society, following a strategy called "the uniformed populace," had begun immediately after Castro assumed power.[1] Whereas on December 31, 1958, Batista's army had numbered approximately 21,000 regular soldiers and 18,000 reservists, by mid-1960 Castro's Rebel Army (as it continued to be called for some time post-1959) had grown to more than 49,000 members.[2] This was over 50 percent larger than estimated by the CIA. In January 1959 the Rebel Army Cadet School was created to train officers for this growing service branch.[3]

To combat antigovernment guerrillas in the Escambray Mountains of central Cuba, in April of 1959 Castro created a combat battalion of some 1,000 men within the National Revolutionary Police (Policía National Revolucionaria or PNR).[4] In October of that same year, he also announced the creation of the National Revolutionary Militias (Milicias Nacionales Revolucionarias or MNR), which would act as a strategic citizen-soldier reserve for the regular army. By March of 1960, the militia had grown to a 500,000-strong national force (i.e., 2.5 times larger than estimated by the CIA) just as military advisers from the Soviet Union began to arrive on the island.[5] First among the new arrivals was a group of former Spanish communist officers who had fled to the Soviet Union after their side lost Spain's civil war. Most notable among them was Francisco Ciutat (alias Ángel Martínez, aka "Angelito"), who had achieved the rank of major general in the Soviet Army. Unofficially acknowledged as "the father of the new Cuban army," Ciutat would play a key role in shaping the ideology, organization, training, and tactics of Castro's forces.[6]

19

The militia became organized into so-called heavy and light battalions. Heavy battalions, consisting of four infantry and one light assault
companies, were deployed in the capital city of Havana and consisted of
some 900–1,000 men each. They were equipped with more machine guns
and heavier weaponry than the light battalions, each of approximately
600 men, established in the rest of the country.[7]

To train the large numbers of officers necessary to lead this militia
force, a Militia Leaders' School was opened in the city of Matanzas in
May 1960. By November, some 550 militia leaders had graduated from
the school while an additional 900 were to enroll in February of the following year.[8]

The second half of 1960 saw the arrival of the first shipments of
Soviet Bloc small arms, artillery, and mortars as well as medium T-34/85
tanks and SU-100 tank destroyers (self-propelled guns). Camps were
established to train more than two thousand militia members under the
age of twenty in the use of the newly arrived antiaircraft artillery. Older
men received field artillery training. Soviet advisers also instructed members of the regular army in the operation of the T-34s and SU-100s, later
also to include heavy IS-2M Stalin tanks.[9]

* * * *

During nightly meetings at Point One (*Punto Uno*), Castro's Havana
headquarters, Ciutat would discuss with *El Comandante* how to distribute
the newly arrived armaments throughout the country. It was a discussion
that was part and parcel of the plans being developed for the defense
not only of the capital but all parts of the island nation.[10] As the CIA presumed, it was known in Cuba that an invasion was coming. Only the time,
place(s), size, and specific makeup of the invasion force were unknown
to Castro and his cohorts. "More than once we occupied our trenches
awaiting the direct aggression," Castro would later say— "direct" imply-
ing the overt involvement of American armed forces.[11]

The existence of the training camps in Guatemala had been disclosed
publicly as early as June 1960 by the Guatemalan Workers' Party. Raúl
Roa, Cuba's representative to the United Nations, denounced before the
General Assembly on October 7, 1960, the "numerous exiles and adven-
turers . . . receiving training under American military personnel" at the
Helvetia plantation. Later that year, the Guatemalan newspaper *La Hora*

published an article containing information on both the Trax and Rayo bases. Information about the existence and location of an invasion force in preparation also reached Castro's intelligence offices from sympathizers and agents in Miami and New York.[12]

On December 31, 1960, fearing that the outgoing Eisenhower administration would launch the invasion during its final days, Castro announced a general military mobilization on the island. Militia battalions, artillery batteries, and other units were entrenched all around the country. Roads and bridges were rigged with explosives. As it had to their CIA counterparts, the Trinidad area stood out to the Point One planners as an ideal area for landing an invasion force. In fact, the previous year Castro and his military had thwarted plans by Dominican dictator and Castro nemesis Rafael Trujillo to land an invasion force there and set up a provisional government. Now, as part of the general mobilization, a wide network of defensive trenches was constructed in the area and considerable forces allocated for its defense. These consisted of six militia battalions supported by mortars, bazookas, artillery, and antiaircraft guns, plus three companies of tanks. Smaller units were also placed on the small cays dotting the entrance to the city's bay.[13]

With the inauguration of John Kennedy on January 20, Castro declared an end to the state of alert. However, the Trinidad area continued to receive special attention.[14] Militia units demobilized from elsewhere in the country were sent to participate in the elimination of an estimated 600–700 anti-Castro guerrillas from the Escambray Mountains. Ironically, many of the leaders of these guerrilla bands had been active in the fight against Batista, and some even came from the ranks of the Rebel Army. Some eighty militia battalions (about 60,000 men) participated in Operación Jaula (Operation Cage), which involved encircling the mountain and sweeping it clean of insurgents. For many of the militiamen involved in the operation, the experience derived from it would far surpass their barely two weeks of formal military training.[15]

A series of reports reaching Cuba between February and early April of 1961 steadily signaled the quickening pace of an approaching invasion. Castro sympathizers in Nicaragua notified Cuban intelligence in February about round-the-clock construction by American crews at the airbase in Puerto Cabezas. On March 10, the Miami-based Spanish-language newspaper *El Avance Criollo* published a front-page banner story under the headline "The Training Has Concluded." The story even

included pictures of the recruits stationed at "one of the Cuban Liberation Army camps." Ironically enough, the pictures had been taken by CIA
case officer E. Howard Hunt during a mid-February trip to the camps in
Guatemala with members of the FRD. Upon his return to Washington,
he had obtained permission from Bissell to distribute them anonymously
to the press. The purpose of the deliberate "leak" was both to "stimulate
recruiting" and to highlight the leadership role of the FRD, members of
which were featured in some of the photos.[16]

On March 29, the Costa Rican newspaper *Adelante* published an
article reporting the arrival at the Puerto Cabezas airbase of notable
amounts of military ordnance. This included 800 tons of explosives that
the writer unequivocally concluded were intended for an imminent invasion of Cuba. Then, on April 7, a front-page article in the *New York Times*
by Latin America correspondent Tad Szulc broke the news to the American public and the world at large. "The recruiting of Cubans," Szulc
wrote, "which has been proceeding since last summer, is being discontinued as the anti-Castro leaders believe that their external forces have
reached the stage of adequate preparation. . . . The Columbia Broadcast-
ing System issued a report last night saying that there were 'unmistakable
signs' that plans for an invasion of Cuba were in their final stages."[17]

The day after the *Times* article appeared, Castro ordered an end to
Operación Jaula and the return of the participating militia battalions to
their respective provinces of origin. By the time the operation ended, 420
of the anti-Castro guerrillas in the Escambray Mountains, representing
60–70 percent of their estimated total, had been captured or killed.[18]
The armed forces of the country were subsequently divided geographi-
cally into the Eastern, Central, and Western Armies. Headquartered in
the provincial capital of Santa Clara, the Central Army encompassed the
Trinidad–Zapata Swamp–Bay of Pigs region. Its general staff consisted of
Chief of Staff Juan Almeida, a veteran commander with Castro's M-26-7
organization, Raúl Menéndez Tomassevich, another early revolutionary
leader, and none other than the ubiquitous Francisco Ciutat.[19]

* * * *

A Cuban intelligence report dated January 12, 1961, predicted that the
invasion would consist of small landings at multiple locations and placed
the size of the Cuban exile force at Helvetia at 6,000 (plus another 5,000

in Florida). Whether this was the result of misinformation planted by the CIA (as some have speculated) or not, Castro evidently believed it. He took steps to deal with multiple landings and on various occasions publicly posited the number of Cuban exiles in training as being on the order of a few thousand. Defensive positions were established at coastal points considered likely landing places, especially those that, like Trinidad, provided access to mountainous areas. In addition, MNR Battalions 112 and 117 were moved from Havana to Santa Clara to be available there for quick deployment to locations within the territory of the Central Army. The coastal city of Baracoa, cloistered by mountains on the eastern end of Cuba, was also of special concern and three militia battalions were sent to reinforce the area.[20]

The same week that Szulc's article appeared, Castro had made one of his now customary trips to the Zapata Swamp. He had taken a special interest in the region since first visiting it shortly after assuming power in 1959. "A world apart within Cuba," as it was described in 1957, the sizable region had less than four thousand inhabitants. This largely peasant population eked out a meager existence from charcoal-making and lived in geographic seclusion from the rest of the country. Under Castro's direction, projects had been undertaken to build tourist centers in Playa Larga along with an airport at Girón—ironically, one of the salient features that made it an attractive invasion site to the CIA planners. Access roads (causeways) had also been built across the swamp to end the region's isolation.[21]

As he inspected a newly constructed concrete pier at Girón during his visit, Castro became pensive. "This would be an ideal place for a landing," he said. Before departing, he issued orders for the residents to be organized into a local militia defense force. Furthermore, he instructed that a militia battalion from Cienfuegos be transferred to the much closer Central Australia.[22]

5

At the Crossroads

Rumors of an imminent invasion of Cuba began swirling around the United States after Tad Szulc's April 7 *Times* article. President Kennedy sought to get ahead of events by preemptively distancing his administration and the U.S. military from future developments in Cuba. "The President has made it clear that in any military moves against the Castro regime, United States forces are not to be used," reported the *Times* on April 11.[1] The point was again made at a press conference on the afternoon of the following day when Kennedy was asked if it had been decided "how far [the U.S.] would be willing to go in helping an anti-Castro uprising or invasion in Cuba." His answer was categorical: "I want to say that there will not be, under any conditions, be [*sic*] an intervention in Cuba by United States armed forces, and this government will do everything it possibly can . . . to make sure that there are no Americans involved in any actions inside Cuba."[2]

Just over an hour after the press conference, a final meeting on the Zapata Plan was held at the White House. The operational strategy had now been revised to incorporate airstrikes prior to as well as concurrent with the landings. However, to address Kennedy's demands for non-association with the United States, these would occur "on a *limited scale* [emphasis added] on D–2 and again on D-Day." As a ruse, a brigade pilot was to land in Miami following the D–2 strikes and claim to be one of the defectors from Castro's air force who had executed the raid. A concurrent diversionary "guerrilla type" landing in eastern Cuba's Oriente Province on D–2 was also planned. Other significant features of the overall invasion strategy as finalized included:

- Transport ships carrying the invasion force would receive unobtrusive U.S. Navy protection up to the time they entered Cuban territorial waters and be escorted to a U.S. port if attacked.
- "Every effort" would be made *after* D-Day to coordinate the operations of internal resistance movements with those of the landing parties.
- One of the six leaders of the CRC (Manuel Artime) would land with the main force. The other members (who would receive "last minute briefings") would follow "as soon as possible after D-Day and . . . announce the establishment of a Provisional Government on Cuban soil."
- The CIA would, "in the early stages at least," exercise the "functions of a general head-quarters . . . with the Cuban brigade commander exercising field command over the units that land on D-Day."

D-Day was to be April 17. The president was told that the deadlines for his "go/no-go" decisions on the D–2 and D-Day phases of the operation were noon on April 14 and April 16, respectively.[3]

* * * *

It was not until 9:00 a.m. on April 14, only hours before they were to sail from Nicaragua, that the site for the invasion was disclosed to the brigade's command staff. The men were handed copies of the Operation Pluto military plan and briefed on it by a CIA intelligence officer and "Frank" (Colonel Egan).[4]

By the time the briefing in Puerto Cabezas ended in the late afternoon, Bissel in Washington had received Kennedy's go-ahead (per the set deadline) for the next day's limited airstrike.[5] The decision as to the number of aircraft to participate in the raid was left to the discretion of the CIA. As of April 12, six aircraft had been scheduled to do so, with two assigned to each of Cuba's three main airbases. Two of these, San Antonio de los Baños (the island's principal military airfield) and Ciudad Libertad, were located near Havana. The third was in Santiago de Cuba, Cuba's second major city, on the eastern side of the island. JMTIDE, however, continued to lobby for the assignment of a third aircraft to both the San Antonio and Ciudad Libertad raids. On April 14, after Kennedy's call, CIA headquarters relented and authorized the use of eight strike bombers. Identical tail numbers were painted on two of the three aircraft assigned to each of the Havana-area fields to create the impression that a total of only four planes were involved in both raids. An additional B-26 was to fly as a backup, ready to take the place of any of the primary bombers that developed mechanical problems. One other bomber was assigned to the "defector" cover-up operation described in the revised Zapata Plan.[6]

* * * *

Sometime before midnight on April 14, five hundred miles east of the Bay of Pigs, the planned diversionary landing at a small beach named Playa Macambo was getting started. Dubbed Operación Marte (Operation Mars), its objective, in conjunction with the dawn airstrikes, was to create the impression that *this* was the site of the invasion. It was hoped that Castro would then divert his forces there, away from what was to be the main landing zone.[7]

The landing force of 156 men had received guerrilla training at a camp in Louisiana and was commanded by a former Revolutionary commander named Higinio "Nino" Díaz. They had sailed from Louisiana aboard a ship named *Santa Ana* (code-named *Perca*) on April 11. After landing, Díaz's unit was to move into the adjacent Sierra del Purial mountains, just southeast of Baracoa, and go on the offensive.[8]

In the dark of night, from boats offshore, men from the *Santa Ana* searched the coastline for the light signal the operation plan specified. The signal, marking the landing location and giving the all-clear, was to come from a squad of insurgents led by Ramón Machado. Machado was a member of the brigade infiltration teams clandestinely operating out of the Guantanamo Naval Base, some twenty-five miles to the west. The signal never came, however, and after two attempts Díaz suspended the operation at 4:00 a.m. Unbeknownst to the landing force, five days earlier Machado and his men had been seriously injured and put out of action while training with explosives. Díaz's men made two more attempts to land during the night of April 15, but of course, the shore signal again failed to appear. Those making the second attempt that night reported having seen vehicles and headlights onshore, which they took to be enemy forces. As stipulated in the operation plan, Díaz then sought instructions from the CIA and was directed to move off. It was the end of the anticipated diversionary landing.[9]

* * * *

At approximately 2:30 a.m. on April 15, the eight B-26 bombers assigned to the raids took off from JMTIDE on their way to Cuba. They were to carry out simultaneous attacks at 5:45 a.m. on all three airbases. The backup B-26 also took off with the other eight but aborted immediately due to engine trouble. Each bomber was equipped with eight nose-mounted .50 caliber machine guns and carried two 500-pound bombs, ten 250-pound fragmentation and eight wing-mounted rockets. They were grouped into three flights. Puma and Linda flights, with three air-craft each, would attack Ciudad Libertad and San Antonio, respectively, whereas the two aircraft of Gorilla flight would attack Santiago. All the aircraft had been painted in the color scheme used by planes of Castro's Fuerza Aérea Revolucionaria (FAR[10]; Revolutionary Air Force) and displayed the corresponding FAR markings and insignia.[11]

Mario Zúñiga, who had been assigned to play the "defector" role, took off half an hour after the other planes. He was to fly to a point about twenty miles off the coast of Cuba and land at Miami International Airport at around 8 a.m. In addition to FAR identifiers, his bomber bore bullet holes to give credence to his story that he and other disaffected Castro pilots had carried out the raids.[12]

By 6:15 a.m. the raids of the three Cuban airfields were over. The ruse of making the planes look like FAR aircraft worked well until the planes let loose their salvos. They were then met with heavy antiair-craft artillery (AAA) fire at both Ciudad Libertad and Santiago. Not so at San Antonio (despite "heavy AAA" reported by the pilots) where all but one of the antiaircraft artillery pieces were disassembled and under-going cleaning when the attack came. One of the bombers attacking Ciudad Libertad suffered heavy damage and crashed into the sea while trying to make it to Key West. Both the pilot, Daniel Fernández Mon, and his crewmate, Gastón Pérez, were killed. Another of the Puma flight planes, piloted by José Crespo, ran low on fuel after staying alongside the doomed bomber and proceeded to land in Key West's Boca Chica Naval Air Station. All the aircraft from Linda flight escaped virtually unscathed, but pilot Alfredo Caballero was forced to make an emergency landing in

Grand Cayman due to low fuel. Caballero had opted not to abort on the way to Cuba despite a malfunction with his plane's droppable fuel tanks. Both Gorilla flight aircraft managed to return to JMTIDE despite sustaining considerable damage.[13]

Zúñiga landed in Miami at 8:21 a.m. and was whisked away by immigration officials. His cover story was subsequently released to reporters who were also allowed to inspect and photograph the plane he had flown. However, the whole charade was met with skeptical eyes by the press. One knowledgeable reporter noted that while Castro's B-26Cs had plexiglass transparent noses and guns mounted on wing pods, the eight guns on the "defector's" B-26B protruded from a metallic nose. In a stormy emergency meeting at the United Nations that afternoon, U.S. Ambassador Adlai Stevenson—unaware of this discrepancy or even the untruth of the cover story—held up a photograph of Zúñiga's B-26 as proof of America's noninvolvement in the attacks. The CIA's ruse was further undermined when reporters noticed that the B-26 in which José Crespo had happened to land in Key West bore the same aircraft identification number (933) as Zúñiga's plane.[14]

* * * *

The airstrikes against the Cuban airbases had resulted in about a half dozen dead and dozens more wounded on the ground. Yet the aim of destroying at least most of Castro's planes on the ground had not been accomplished. At Ciudad Libertad no planes were destroyed. All the aircraft at the base were unserviceable and had been moved away from the airfield operations area. However, nineteen semitrailer trucks loaded with ammunition were there parked close together. Six of them were blown up along with two fuel trucks. One T-33 jet was destroyed at San Antonio and an unserviceable B-26 bomber was damaged. At Santiago, a B-26 was destroyed and another one damaged. In total, the destruction amounted to about a third of the seven or so serviceable combat aircraft that Castro had among all three airfields at the time.[15]

At San Antonio, Alvaro Prendes, one of Castro's T-33 pilots, had personally witnessed the attacks. The out-of-service status of most of the anti-aircraft guns there as well as the presence of ammunition trucks on the tarmac at Ciudad Libertad were, in his words, "unjustifiable." "Our errors during this attack were many," he added. "[S]afeguards, organization, and experience were generally lacking."[16]

As he reviewed the damage, Castro questioned the action of the FAR pilots during the attacks. Addressing senior pilot Enrique Carreras informally, he asked: "So tell me, guy. Just what did the pilots do? Hide?" In fact, as Carreras informed him, a T-33 jet and a Sea Fury prop fighter had managed to take off from San Antonio but too late to do any good. It was a mistake not to be repeated if another attack came. Following Castro's orders, from dusk to dawn an aircraft at San Antonio would be kept manned and ready for immediate takeoff. Four aircraft on different runways would rotate through the night in the "alert" role while the off-duty pilots slept on cots next to their planes. Additional batteries of antiaircraft guns were also sent there and to Ciudad Libertad.[17]

* * * *

Aboard the ships en route to Cuba, the air raid news broadcasted by Radio Swan—the CIA's Caribbean radio station on Swan Island—brought much jubilation. That morning the men of the small invasion fleet had also been elated by the sight of American naval warships on the horizon. The ships belonged to the navy task force charged with shadowing the brigade ships until they entered Cuban territorial waters. It included the aircraft carrier USS *Essex* and a two-destroyer task unit (USS *Eaton* and *Murray*).[18]

Before midday, however, an incident occurred that turned the mood of the invaders decidedly somber. On the *Atlántico* one man was killed and two wounded by stray bullets when the welded plate of a .50 caliber machine gun broke loose during practice firing. The guns had been hastily installed on all the cargo ships at the insistence of ship line owner Eduardo García. García, who was himself on the *Caribe*, failed to be dissuaded by assurances from the Americans that the vessels would not come under air attack.[19]

In the afternoon, the brigade officers finally briefed their respective units on the details of the invasion plan. Aboard the *Houston*, as Second Battalion commander Hugo Sueiro addressed his men, the first hints emerged that there were serious flaws in the CIA's intelligence. According to the Operation Pluto Plan, the only known communications equipment in the area was a telephone located at Covadonga, nineteen miles north of Girón. Sueiro told the group as much and indicated that Castro's forces would hence not soon learn about the landings. "There's something wrong," one of the soldiers interjected. He had been in the area a few months earlier and "there were microwave stations at Playa Larga and Girón." But Sueiro, a former Cuban army lieutenant, had "unshaken confidence in the United States" and was not overly alarmed by the contradictory information. If things did not go as planned, Sueiro was certain, they would "get helped out" by the Americans.[20]

6

Sunday, April 16, 1961—
The Eleventh Hour

On the morning of the sixteenth, in a massive open-air ceremony in front of Havana's Colón Cemetery, the victims of the air raids were eulogized by Castro. He bitterly accused the United States of being behind the previous day's "cowardly attack" by "mercenaries" and, for the first time, openly admitted the Marxist nature of the Revolution. "What [the Americans] cannot forgive of us . . . is our having made a socialist revolution under the very noses of the United States!" *El Comandante* then called the citizenry to arms and exhorted them to heroically face the coming invasion. Privately, as he would later admit, he was surprised that the airstrike had not been followed immediately by troop landings.[1]

Even as Castro spoke, the state security apparatus had already swung into full gear to deal with those who may welcome or support such an invasion. Some twenty thousand people known or suspected to be hostile to the Revolution were arrested in Havana alone, the flood of prisoners necessitating the use of theaters and sports centers to house them. Playing a key role in targeting these undesirables were groups of organized neighborhood watch informers known as Comités de Defensa de la Revolución (CDRs; Committees for the Defense of the Revolution). Established by Castro himself in September 1960, by April 1961 eight thousand CDRs, consisting of ten to a hundred members each, existed around the country.[2]

Sometime around noon, in accordance to the Operation Pluto Plan, U.S. Navy ships engaged in a distraction exercise off the northwestern coast of Cuba. As with the aborted Díaz landing, the aim of the ruse was "to cause the enemy to transfer his land, naval and air forces to said area." It failed to accomplish any of these things.[3]

At JMTIDE, meanwhile, alarm bells started going off when U-2 reconnaissance plane photos showed T-33 jet aircraft on the ground that had survived the airstrikes. The jets presented the greatest potential threat to the brigade's B-26 bombers. Around noon, an urgent message went out from Air Operations Chief Garfield ("Gar") Thorsrud requesting approval from CIA headquarters for a second airstrike that very day against San Antonio and Ciudad Libertad. Not surprisingly, headquarters denied the request, as such action was incompatible with the approved Zapata Plan. However, CIA personnel in Washington were already busily planning the upcoming strike at dawn on D-Day. Throughout the day, the list of targets and number of participating aircraft kept changing. They ranged from as many as eleven total targets (military as well as infrastructure installations) and fifteen aircraft, down to four targets (the two airbases near Havana plus two naval stations) and as few as five aircraft.[4] The CIA planners were clearly torn between military considerations and the "limited" airstrike stipulated in the Zapata Plan.

Out in the Caribbean, the ships of the invasion fleet reached Point Zulu, located forty-seven miles south–southeast of Girón, at about 5:30 p.m. They had traveled the first leg of the trip to Cuba separated from each other along different trajectories so as not to arouse suspicion. All the vessels now formed up in single file behind the *Blagar*, from whose stern flew the Cuban flag Pepe San Román raised during a brief but emotional ceremony.[5] Aboard the *Houston*, following an abbreviated Catholic mass, Oliva delivered an impassioned speech. Perhaps many would die in the coming battle, he told the men, but "that blood would serve to return freedom to the oppressed and enslaved homeland." They all began to sing the Cuban national anthem.[6] For the first time during the crossing, the soldiers donned their camouflage combat uniforms, which prominently displayed the Brigade 2506 emblem over the left shoulder.[7]

The formation proceeded to an expected rendezvous with the LSD USS *San Marcos* some three miles from Girón. The *San Marcos*, which had departed from Vieques Island, Puerto Rico, carried all the landing crafts for the operation. In addition to four LCVPs, there were three much larger LCUs. The latter were combat-loaded with five M-41 tanks, seven M-35 armored gun trucks (an additional five were aboard the *Río Escondido*), jeeps, other support vehicles, and heavy equipment.[8]

* * * *

In one of the many twists of fate that would characterize the Bay of Pigs affair, that very afternoon Central Army chief of staff Juan Almeida was visiting Playa Larga. While there, he ordered that a militia company be dispersed to key locations along the Bay of Pigs coastline. The men were to come from MNR Battalion 339, stationed at Central Australia following Castro's orders of earlier that month.[9]

Fate again played its hand when General C. P. Cabell, acting CIA director while Allen Dulles was away on travel, learned by happenstance of the planning going on for the D-Day airstrikes. "Do we have approval for the mission?" he asked the project staff assembled at CIA headquarters; in their estimation, there definitely was. The plan for Operation Pluto called for commencing tactical air operations against targets within Cuba "upon seizing the airfield within the objective zone." As the Girón airstrip was due to be seized before dawn on April 17, project staff reasoned that the D-Day strikes had been implicitly approved by the president's endorsement of the Zapata Plan. Cabell, however, was a by-the-book disciplinarian not given to taking chances and, over the objections of those present, telephoned Secretary of State Dean Rusk for clarification. His phone call opened a Pandora's box of second-guessing among Kennedy's staff.[10] At 9:30 p.m. National Security Adviser McGeorge Bundy called Cabell to inform him that the CIA "would not be permitted to launch air strikes the next morning until they could be conducted from a strip within the beachhead."[11] In other words, possession of a demonstrably operating air field would have to be a *fait accompli* before the D-Day aerial attacks could take place. Bundy had good reason to doubt the actual urgency for the follow-up airstrikes. Just a month earlier he had echoed the CIA's poor assessment of Castro's air force in a memo to Kennedy. It was such "a very sketchy force," the memo said, that "Colonel Hawkins (Bissell's military brain) thinks it can be removed by six to eight simultaneous sorties of B-26s."[12]

After informing headquarters personnel of the development, Cabell and Bissell quickly went to meet with Rusk in person and appealed for a reversal of the decision. The two CIA men warned the secretary of the danger that attacks by FAR aircraft presented to the brigade's transport ships and B-26 support bombers (which were devoid of tail guns[13]). Given their agency's belittling assessment of the efficacy of Castro's air force, apparently the pair either distrusted the accuracy of their own intelligence or perhaps were simply hedging their bet. Rusk then phoned the

president and "with accuracy," according to Cabell, reported the position
of the CIA followed by his own concerns regarding the situation at the
United Nations. Kennedy, through Rusk, reaffirmed the cancellation
order and both Cabell and Bissell refused Rusk's offer to let them talk
directly to the president. Rusk did make the concession, however, that
strikes could be made in "the immediate beachhead area," as Cabell had
argued that failing to do so "first thing in the morning (D-Day) would
clearly be disastrous."[14] The implication that the landings would encounter heavy resistance "first thing in the morning" is again at odds with the
CIA's own assessments. Given the supposed lack of troops in the area,[15]
the invading force should not have been expected to face significant initial opposition.

* * * *

That evening Radio Swan broadcasted "nonsense messages" to Cuba that
"could, conceivably, confuse and misdirect Castro's G-2 [intelligence ser-
vices]." The messages had been drafted by E. Howard Hunt and David
Phillips, CIA propaganda chief for the Cuba project, and approved by
Bissell's assistant Tracy Barnes. "*Alert! Alert! Look well to the rainbow. The fish
will rise very soon. Chico is in the house . . .*" the transmissions droned on in
Spanish. However, no direct instructions went out to the brigade infiltration operatives inside Cuba to undertake the tactical sabotage missions
for which they had been placed there. Although Hunt would later claim
that this was a last-minute decision, his assertion is patently disingenuous.[16] In the agency's view, the timing and area of the invasion "could not
be revealed to them in view of the propensity of all Cubans to tell secrets"
and the possibility there might be double agents among the infiltrators.[17]

* * * *

By 11:00 p.m. the *Blagar* and the other ships were met by the *San Marcos* about three miles from Girón as planned. Now, within sight of the
settlement on this dark night (the crescent moon had set almost three
hours earlier), they were surprised to see how brightly lit the place was.
It was an unexpected development given the "very sparse population"
ascribed to the area in the CIA plan.[18] Over the next hour, the Cuban

crews for the LCVPs and LCUs were transferred over to them along with the personnel that would man the M-35 gun trucks and M-41 tanks.[19] As the *Blagar* closed within two miles of Girón to launch the first UDT team, the *Barbara J* followed by the *Houston* proceeded to Playa Larga.

At 11:45 a.m. five Cuban frogmen, armed with Browning automatic rifles (BARs) and Thomson submachine guns, headed from the *Blagar* toward the beach aboard a rubber boat powered by a 16-horsepower silent motor.[20] Aboard were the lighting sets for marking the approaches to the beach and a portable radio transceiver for communicating with the ships. Also aboard was the American CIA operations officer Grayston ("Gray") Lynch. Lynch, a twenty-one-year veteran of the U.S. Army, had risen to the rank of captain in the Green Berets and had seen action in World War II, Korea, and Laos before joining the CIA in 1960.[21]

The *Blagar*'s radio-equipped 20-foot catamaran, armed with two high-caliber machine guns, escorted the frogmen on the way to shore. Some 100 yards from the beach the group encountered a barrier reef—not once mentioned in the operation plan—that ran opposite the landing area one foot below the surface. The rubber boat crossed it and continued shoreward while the catamaran remained seaward of the unexpected obstacle.[22]

* * * *

In Girón, local militia chief Mariano Mustelier in his jeep was making the rounds of the six key locations around town, including the electrical plant, water tower, and airport, where militiamen were stationed. The local militia unit consisted of a total of twenty-three townsmen, mostly charcoal burners by trade. Aside from Mustelier, who had been issued a Belgian-made FAL automatic rifle, their armament was rudimentary. It mostly consisted of Czech-made M-52 semiautomatic rifles and vintage American-made bolt-action Springfields. Accompanying Mustelier on his rounds that night was thirteen-year-old volunteer literacy teacher Valerio Rodríguez. A smooth talker, the precocious teen had persuaded the militia leader to let him ride along sporting a cartridge belt and a rifle in hand.[23]

The pair reached the public works office at 11:45 p.m. and talked with the guard there who offered to brew them some coffee. During the conversation, Mustelier pointed out a blinking light in front of the beach. Rodríguez at first could not make it out, but a few moments later he did; it was a ship, they agreed. Surmising that the vessel must have become lost on its way to Cienfuegos, the two headed toward it in the jeep.[24]

PART II

BATTLE

7

Monday, April 17, 1961

MIDNIGHT—6:00 AM

General Cabell and Bissell returned to CIA headquarters around midnight and confirmed to project staff that the planned airstrikes against Cuban airfields had been cancelled. Operations chiefs Richard Drain and Colonel Jack Hawkins (U.S. Marine Corps) were joined by project director Jake Esterline in pointing out that the change of plans could well jeopardize the whole enterprise. But Cabell was blunt: "the Agency had been given its marching orders"; it would comply.[1]

* * * *

From their rubber boat some fifty yards from the shore of Girón, Lynch and the frogmen could see the headlights of a jeep approaching down the beach road. Oblivious to the danger, Mustelier and Rodríguez pulled up close to the shoreline from where they could more clearly make out the ship—probably the *Blagar* anchored just offshore—and its blinking light. Mustelier turned the jeep's headlights toward the ship and started flashing them, trying to catch the attention of what he still supposed was a wayward vessel. But to Lynch and the frogmen out in the water the lights shining toward them were a sign they had been discovered. Immediately they opened fire in the direction of the two beams. Mustelier jumped out of the jeep and began shooting back with his automatic rifle. "Mariano, I have lost an eye!" he heard Rodríguez cry out from inside the vehicle. He leaped over to the boy and could feel blood flowing from a

41

graze wound near his eye. "Climb down from the jeep and follow me!" he instructed Rodríguez. They both then ran to the militia command post in town.[2]

Lynch reached the beach and immediately raised the *Blagar* on the radio to report what had happened. The element of surprise was lost. As the frogmen began to place the shore marker lights, he called for an immediate landing of troops before enemy forces could be rushed in.[3]

"Boys, the Americans have landed!" Mustelier called out upon arriving at the militia post. Aware that the radio transmitter there was inoperable (although the CIA was indeed totally unaware even of its existence), he quickly dispatched a messenger to Covadonga, nineteen miles away, to report what was happening. It was the nearest place with a phone. The available weapons were handed out, and some of the men were ordered to take up positions in town and at the seawall. Then the militia leader and five others headed out in a truck for the beach as the town went into a complete blackout.[4]

The frogmen on the beach saw the militia truck approaching. Mustelier and his men were soon upon them, and a fierce gun battle broke out. The *Blagar* moved in to provide fire support and from a position 400 yards from shore began to pour fire on the militia with its battery of heavy caliber machine guns and dual 75 mm recoilless rifles. Ten minutes later it was all over. Mustelier and one of his men were wounded and the small band of militiamen retreated. The only casualty on the brigade side was a crewman on the *Blagar* who was wounded by a lone machine gun firing from shore.[5]

Preparations for the landings were soon in full swing throughout the small fleet. The *Blagar* backed away following the brief engagement and the first two LCVPs, according to plan, made for shore. Between them they carried a few dozen men from the Fourth Battalion that had clambered onto the crafts from the *Caribe*.[6]

After a rocky start, it may have seemed briefly that things were starting to run smoothly, but the first logistical snag soon surfaced. Around 1:00 a.m. messages in Spanish started to pour into the *Blagar*'s bridge from the different vessels with questions about various aspects of the landings. However, the ship's radio operator, Rolando Moya, who did not speak English, could not easily convey these messages or get answers from Captain Ryberg—in charge of the landing—who did not speak Spanish. Fortuitously, Blas Casares, a frogman on the UDT team slated for Green Beach, happened to be on the bridge and was bilingual. At first, he merely acted as an interpreter between Moya and Ryberg but then quickly realized that Ryberg took time consulting the landing plan before replying to each question. Casares had taken it upon himself to study and become familiar with the plan beforehand, so he began to answer Moya's questions directly, and Ryberg turned his attention elsewhere.[7]

* * * *

In Playa Larga, where a five-man militia squad from MNR Battalion 339 was posted, strange flashes of light could be seen coming from the direction of Girón, nineteen miles to the southeast.[8] At 12:30 a.m. squad leader Ramón González Suco relayed this information via the post's radio transmitter to battalion headquarters at the Central Australia sugar mill, some sixteen miles north.[9] The existence of the transmitter at Playa Larga, which (unlike the one at Girón) *was* working, had also not been suspected by the CIA planners.[10]

The flashes over Girón were also seen by the men aboard the *Barbara J* and the *Houston* as they lay off Playa Larga at the end of their journey into the Bay of Pigs. They immediately recognized the red and orange streaks of light piercing the night sky as tracer ammunition. It was, as described by Oliva, "a very emotional moment because they were the first shots fired toward Cuba."[11]

The light show in the sky also caught the attention of the crew of Cuban navy patrol boat SV-3 docked at the small inlet of Buenaventura just east of Playa Larga. They cast off to investigate and near the mouth of the inlet the sailors could make out the dark shapes of ships in the water. However, the feeder mechanism on the boat's .50 caliber machine gun was not working, and the crew headed back to port. (One version of events purports that SV-3 exchanged fire with the invasion ships before turning back.) SV-3 radioed a short message at 12:20 a.m. regarding the situation at the Bay of Pigs, but, due to the transmitter's weak battery, only garbled words reached the naval station at Batabanó, seventy-five miles away.[12]

As in Girón, a UDT team set out from the *Barbara J* to mark the beach at Playa Larga and, here as well, the American CIA operations officer aboard the LCI joined the frogmen going ashore.[13] William ("Rip")

Robertson had seen combat in World II and risen to the rank of captain in the U.S. Marine Corps (USMC) before joining the CIA in 1950. In 1954 he had played a major role in the CIA's PBSUCCESS operation in Guatemala.[14]

Robertson and the three Cuban frogmen reached the right side of the landing beach in one of the *Barbara J*'s two launches equipped with a pair of heavy caliber machine guns fore and aft. While he and one of the frogmen reconnoitered about, the other two began deploying the marker lights and a sign with large luminous letters that read: WELCOME LIBERATORS—COURTESY OF THE BARBARA J FROGMEN.[15]

By 1:00 a.m. the ten small (fourteen- and nineteen-foot) aluminum motorboats to be used for landing the troops were being lowered into the water from the *Houston*.[16] Seeing them aboard for the first time at Puerto Cabezas, Fifth Battalion soldier Luis Iglesias thought to himself: "No! That's impossible. If those little aluminum boats are what we are to land in, I would return right now if I could."[17] But indeed, they were. The few landing crafts available for the invasion had been procured by the CIA with Trinidad—and its essentially one landing beach—in mind. Given the switch to the Zapata Plan and its three landing beaches, each some twenty miles from the other, there were simply not enough of them on hand. The agency had purchased the boats as stand-ins for the missing landing crafts and shipped them to Nicaragua where they were put onboard ship.[18]

To the men on the *Houston*, the noise made by the ship's screeching lowering winches seemed loud enough to be heard, as one put it, "maybe in Havana."[19] But onshore Suco and his militia squad heard nothing; the noise of the waves crashing against the jagged coastal rocks drowned out all other sounds from the sea.[20] What did catch the attention of the militiamen was what seemed to be a dark shape inside the bay. Suco reported the strange sighting to his headquarters and requested permission to blackout the town but was refused.[21]

Second Battalion soldiers soon began climbing down the cargo nets placed over the side of the *Houston* into the small boats below. Each of the eight boats could hold six to eight men carrying weapons and equipment. Then, as they made ready to head to shore, the repercussions of another logistical snafu began to surface. The outboard motors noisily coughed and sputtered and refused to tun over.[22] As it happened, the fuel for the motors had been prepared in Puerto Cabezas using the wrong oil-to-gasoline ratio at the insistence of a Department of Defense "logistical expert." Lynch and Robertson, who knew better, had told the "expert" that this was the wrong mixture to use; however, their protestations had done no good.[23] Initially, only the engine on one of the boats would turn over. Eventually five more were started but this was just the beginning of the woes that the literal "mix-up" would cause.[24]

The boat carrying Second Battalion commander Hugo Sueiro was the first to get under way close to 1:00 a.m. As it approached the shore, the men aboard watched with concern as the lights of Playa Larga went off. They took it as a sign that the enemy was waiting for them.[25] In actuality, Sueiro's boat had not been detected, but Suco, wary of the large black shape in the bay, had decided to disobey his orders and blackout the town after all. "Whoever is on the other side, whoever it may be, has no business looking in on us," he reasoned.

At one point the militiamen did hear an approaching motorboat, but it was that of Robertson and the frogmen. Having been informed that the troops were on their way, the team had gone to mark the left side of the beach. Suco, uncertain as to who might be in the boat, shouted for it to stop and was answered with a burst of tracer bullets flying in his direction. The militiamen fired back and the motorboat sped away. The fast-developing situation was indeed alarming for Suco's militia squad. Other than their one Czech-made .30 caliber (ZB-30) light machine gun, their only weapons were short-barreled automatic carbines.[26]

* * * *

Contrary to the CIA's expectations, reports of the attack at Girón started to filter out in short order. Just before 1:00 a.m. a radio post located seven miles to the west at Punta Perdiz—also unknown to the CIA planners— had transmitted a message to Central Army headquarters in Santa Clara. "Shots, apparently canon fire, can be heard in the direction of Playa Girón," the message said.[27] Confirmation of what was happening at Girón would soon follow. The messenger sent by Mustelier to Covadonga arrived there just as the report from Punta Perdiz was being transmitted.[28]

Offshore, the two LCVPs carrying the first troops to the beach started to sustain damage when their wood bottoms hit the recently discovered reef some 100 yards from the coast.[29] The pilots of the loaded landing crafts tried their best to ride them over the sharp rocks, to no avail. Thus, the bow ramps were lowered right where they were and the Fourth Battalion soldiers aboard, carrying their weapons and equipment, waded ashore.[30] It was one more major and unexpected problem with serious repercussions beyond delaying the landing. As the disembarking troops waded through 300 feet of fairly deep water, most of the portable radios they carried got wet and would fail to function afterward.[31]

Brigade commander San Román, accompanied by his staff and Manuel Artime (as representative of the CRC), arrived ashore at 1:15 a.m. on the *Blagar*'s catamaran.[32] Moved by the occasion, the normally stoic San Román knelt, picked up a handful of his native soil and kissed it.[33] José Alonso, lead frogman at Girón, met San Román on the beach and gave him a report on the ongoing search for a channel through the reef that the LCUs could use at dawn. Unless such a channel could be found, the unloading of the crucial vehicles they carried would be in serious jeopardy.[34] These vehicles included not only the tanks but also a bulldozer and other heavy equipment to deal with what CIA photo analysts had identified as a mound of sand or gravel on the Girón airstrip.[35] The two B-26 bombers that were to operate from there could not do so until these supposed obstacles were eliminated.[36]

Unable to do anything about the alarming news, San Román turned his attention to the pressing matter of occupying Girón and its airfield. He ordered Valentín Bacallao, commander of the Fourth Battalion, to do so with however many of his men had landed so far. As they went house to house, Bacallao's soldiers warned the townspeople to stay indoors and remain calm. They would not be hurt, the invaders told them, "We are all Cubans, and we have come to liberate Cuba."[37] The occupying force only met with sporadic firing from scattered members of the local militia.[38] Recognizing that they were outmatched, the militiamen opted for fleeing rather than fighting. Four of them had taken up positions near the center of Girón inside pits for an unfinished gasoline station. But with the enemy getting closer, the small group quickly dispersed when one of them said, "Let's go, we are surrounded."[39] At the small militia command post, the brigade soldiers found only a group of visiting literacy teachers, among them teenager Valerio Rodríguez, who had been wounded in the face earlier. There was also a roster of local militia members and a few weapons, which were confiscated.[40]

* * * *

At Playa Larga, small groups of Second Battalion men managed to trickle ashore under sporadic firing.[41] Many others, however, drifted helplessly in the bay inside their small boats as the outboard motors cut out one after the other.[42] Robertson and the frogmen team became aware of the situation and headed out to find and tow the strays to the beach.[43] On their return they received fire from shore, and the *Barbara J* responded with its .50 caliber guns. The soldier steering the boat in tow was hit in the crossfire and became the invasion's first casualty killed in action. He was thirty-six-year-old Marcelo Carmenates of the brigade's Fifth Battalion.[44] Lead frogman Andy Pruna urgently radioed the *Barbara J* to stop firing. As he would later remark: "There's no telling where the bullet [that killed Carmenates] came from, but if the [*Barbara J*'s] line of fire had dipped just slightly, everyone would have been wiped out."[45]

In the face of growing enemy pressure and low on ammunition, at approximately 1:30 a.m. Suco and his men retreated inland after updating battalion headquarters at Central Australia by radio.[46] A phone call also arrived at the residence there of Abraham Masiques, the government official in charge of development for the area. La Boca, two-thirds of the way between the sugar mill and Playa Larga, was reporting gunfire sounds coming from the coast. Masiques immediately tasked his wife with raising Castro on the phone while he rushed off to rouse Battalion 339 at the mill as well as the local militia in nearby Jagüey Grande.[47] From nearby Buenaventura the word also went out. Upon returning to the inlet, the crew of SV-3 replaced the boat's bad transmitter battery with one from a construction winch and sent out a message to the Batabanó naval station: "We are fighting. They are landing troops." The sailors also fixed their malfunctioning .50 caliber machine gun and emplaced it along the shoreline of the bay.[48] Thus, in Playa Larga as in Girón, the CIA had seriously misjudged just how fast news of the landings would spread outside the invasion area.

* * * *

From the taxiway at JMTIDE, C-46 pilot Eduardo Ferrer could see the B-26s still being readied for the supposed dawn airstrikes against Cuban installations. His was the first of five C-46s and one C-54 to take off at 2:00 a.m. to deliver a total of 172 paratroopers to their drop zones north of Playa Larga and Girón at dawn.[49]

At Girón, even as the transport planes set off on the nearly five-hour journey, Gray Lynch boarded the catamaran and returned to the *Blagar* where an urgent message from CIA headquarters awaited him.[50] All of Castro's aircraft had not been destroyed, the message began. The unloading of troops and essential cargo from the *Houston, Caribe,* and *Atlántico* was to be expedited and these ships moved out to sea before daylight. The *Río Escondido* was to remain and continue unloading its vital supplies while the *Blagar* and *Barbara J* provided air defense alongside the B-26s that would fly cover over the beachhead.[51] "How bad it would be and what had gone wrong," Lynch reflected at the time, "were things that we now had no time to speculate on."[52]

A few minutes later, at 2:15 a.m., JMTIDE received a corresponding cable announcing the cancellation of the airstrikes. "COMPLETE PLAN AMENDED TO PLACE ALL B-26 AIRCRAFT AT DISPOSAL OF BRIGADE COMMANDER, AND TASK FORCE PROTECTION," read the message. The twelve bombers that had ultimately been assigned to the dawn strike mission had been scheduled for takeoff between 2:30 and 3:00 a.m.[53] To Air Operations Chief Thorsrud it was unwelcome news indeed: "There were only two people in that commo shack [when the message was received], the sergeant who was my commo officer and myself. . . . I couldn't believe it, neither could he."[54]

* * * *

Drifting helplessly in the Bay of Pigs since 1:45 a.m., Brigade Deputy Commander Erneido Oliva may have also found his credulity strained. In overall charge of military operations at Playa Larga, Oliva had decided to land early with his staff given the unexpected opposition encountered. But his boat's outboard motor had refused to start, and the seven men aboard found themselves adrift in the bay.[55] One hour into the landing, only one of the engines still worked. The two launches from the *Barbara J* were kept busy searching for the boats drifting in the darkness and towing them to shore. A pair of inflatables from the LCI had been taken to the *Houston* to help replace the missing boats, but they too required being towed to the coast.[56]

Oliva's boat finally reached the beach in tow at 2:30 a.m., whereupon he went to find Hugo Sueiro. Compared to the boat situation, things on land seemed to be relatively under control. Sueiro had set up the available men in defensive positions.[57] Some trucks, moving in from a nearby construction site at Caletón to the west, had been stopped with fire support from the *Barbara J* and prisoners taken.[58] However, what Oliva learned next truly added to his worries. A radio transmitter, still warm to the touch, had been found not far from the beach. Clearly it meant that Castro's forces elsewhere had been alerted, but just how close "elsewhere" was Oliva had no inkling.[59]

At Central Australia the militiamen of Battalion 339 were about to get under way. The unit did not have its own vehicles, so the men had had to unload sugar sacks from two trucks parked at the mill before they could board them.[60] It was less than an ideal situation; of the approximately five hundred men in the battalion, each truck could only carry less than thirty. A jeep carrying Captain Ramón Cordero, the battalion commander, led the small convoy headed toward Playa Larga to confront the incipient invasion.[61]

* * * *

In Havana, Fidel Castro was spending the night at the swanky Vedado neighborhood apartment of Celia Sánchez, his reputed lover and close associate since their shared guerrilla days. Suspecting he would be there and knowing Sánchez personally, Masiques's wife had been unsuccessfully ringing her for close to an hour. Thoroughly frustrated, at 2:30 a.m. she had called the emergency contact number that Sánchez had given her and left an urgent message. When Sánchez called back five minutes later and learned of the fighting at Playa Larga, she was not entirely surprised. They knew, she said as Castro listened in on the call, that something was happening in that area because some garbled communications had been received from a patrol boat there.[62]

As soon as the call ended Castro sprang into action. Right from Sánchez's apartment, with her in the role of administrative assistant, he began issuing orders to various commands and relaying them to headquarters at Point One. "They have landed and just where I supposed they would" he said into the phone, as witnessed by one of his bodyguards who was there. "But it doesn't matter; we're going to bust them up!" he continued, "although using a stronger word," the eyewitness noted.[63]

As Castro was receiving the news about Playa Larga, the news about Girón was also spreading out from Covadonga like an expanding ripple in a pond. From the sugar mill at Covadonga there was only a direct telephone link to Cienfuegos so it required several intermediaries before the "ripple" reached Central Army headquarters in Santa Clara. When general staff officer Raúl Tomassevich received the report there at 2:30 a.m., he immediately informed Chief of Staff Almeida and Point One in Havana. Almeida posthaste ordered Tomassevich to lead MNR Battalion 117 to Yaguaramas and on to Covadonga. The battalion had been sent to Santa Clara from Havana the week before and garrisoned at the city's airport in anticipation of just such a development.[64] News of the landing also reached army commander Evelio Saborit near Aguada de Pasajeros, some nine miles north of Covadonga. The unit under Saborit's command, totaling less than twenty men armed only with small arms, was soon also on its way to Girón.[65]

* * * *

At JMTIDE the B-26s prepared for their restructured mission of flying air cover for the beachhead and offshore ships starting at dawn. The bombers, each carrying a pilot and another crewman, were to fly out in pairs on their almost three-hour trip to Cuba.[66] René García and Mario Cortina were the first to take off at 2:45 a.m. In a small compromise, before heading to the beachhead area, García and Cortina were to seek out military vessels near the Isle of Pines naval station at Nueva Gerona. It had been one of the targets for the cancelled airstrike. Two more flights would take off at half-hour intervals over the ensuing hour.[67]

* * * *

By 3:00 a.m. the remainder of the Fourth Battalion aboard *Caribe* had made it into Girón. The men had again been forced to wade ashore from 100 yards out where the unrelenting reef continued to tear away at the wood hulls of the LCVPs.

Offshore, the UDT teams had been searching for about two hours without success for a cross-reef channel that would permit bringing in and unloading the bulky LCUs close to shore.[68] If one were not found, the operation would become even more dire than it was already proving to be.

* * * *

The single roads southward from Central Australia, westward from Playa Larga, and eastward from Buenaventura intersect at a three-sided traffic island near the northernmost extent of the Bay of Pigs. It is named the Caletón Triangle after the settlement where it is situated, barely half a mile northwest of Playa Larga.[69] By 3:30 a.m., events were quickly unfolding in every direction marked by the three corners of this triangle.

E and F Companies of the Second Battalion, less than a hundred men altogether, were moving toward the triangle's southeast corner. Except for one of F Company's squads, which remained adrift in the bay, all the battalion's approximately 180 men, reinforced by two squads from the Heavy Weapons Battalion, had made it into Playa Larga by then. E Company, commanded by Luis Acevedo, had been ordered to block the road from Buenaventura while F Company, under Máximo Cruz, was to block the road from Central Australia.[70] As the two companies were under way, sailors from SV-3 in Buenaventura began firing their shore-emplaced machine gun at the *Barbara J,* 500 yards offshore, and the ship returned fire.[71] The sounds of shooting caught the attention of the militiamen from Battalion 339 whose trucks were just then arriving at the northeast corner of the Caletón Triangle. For a moment they thought about heading down to Buenaventura, but then they saw lights and heard a vehicle engine coming up the way from Playa Larga. Captain Cordero ordered the men off the trucks, and they marched forward in two columns on either side of the road toward the group they now saw approaching. Luis Clemente, leading the column on the left, was the first to call out:

"—Who goes there?"

"—And who are you?" the response came back.

"—We are Battalion 339."

"—And we are E Company of the Second Battalion. We are the Liberation Army. Surrender."

"—Fatherland or Death!" Clemente shouted back as he opened fire.[72]

The defiant attitude of the militiamen was a rude awakening for many of the brigade soldiers now hitting the ground under the stream of bullets that flew in their direction. They had been assured that Castro's militia would eagerly join them, but the reality of the situation was proving quite different. José Gutiérrez of F Company captured what many were thinking: "We have been lied to . . . deceived! Now we must bear whatever comes because we've been deceived."[73]

The brigade forces, supported by .50 caliber machine guns as well as 75 mm and 57 mm recoilless rifles, were soon pouring heavy fire on the militia whose heaviest weapons were .30 caliber (ZB-30) light machine guns.[74] Captain Cordero concentrated his machine gun fire on an enemy position inadvertently illuminated by an overhead street light. But soon the light was shot out, and within minutes mortar shells began falling around Cordero and his men. He ordered them to retreat a few hundred feet back to the northeast corner of the Caletón Triangle, where an excavation pit offered a better defensive position. The two brigade companies then proceeded to occupy the triangle's southeast corner.[75]

* * * *

Even as the battle for Cuba escalated, Celia Sánchez's Vedado apartment remained the country's de facto key command center. Orders issued forth from there for various of Havana's militia battalions, each numbering over 900 men, to be made ready to move out.[76] The same directive also went out to Harold Ferrer, commander of the 600-man First Column of the Rebel Army.[77] Tank battalion commander Néstor López Cuba was likewise instructed to proceed with fifteen of his armored vehicles toward the site of the invasion.[78]

At 3:40 a.m. Castro phoned Rebel Army Captain José R. Fernández, who was sleeping at the army cadet center inside the Managua Military Camp just south of Havana.[79] Fernández had served as an artillery instructor under Batista[80] and currently directed different military training centers around the country, including the Militia Leaders' School in Matanzas.[81] Castro knew that the 900 men at the school, just short of graduating,[82] represented the best trained unit closest to the beachhead, and he wanted Fernández to lead them there posthaste. "They have landed at Playa Girón," a groggy Fernández heard *El Comandante* say on the other end of the line. "Take a car and leave with all speed for Matanzas. You are to head out with the Militia Leaders' Battalion and oppose the landings. Don't concern yourself with calling [the school]; we'll take care of that." Alacrity was of the utmost importance in Castro's mind. It was too late to prevent the enemy from landing, but he was intent on "quickly exterminating the invaders" and removing whatever foothold they had on Cuban soil.[83]

* * * *

At Girón, thanks to the assistance of a local fisherman, a channel through the reef for bringing in the LCUs had finally been found. The passageway was narrow and would only allow one vessel to come in at a time, but it was still a godsend.

As the frogmen finished marking the vital channel with buoys, San Román faced a difficult dilemma. The time was 4:00 a.m.; low tide and sunrise would both occur in approximately two hours. Waiting to bring in the LCUs at low tide was advisable because the reef would be exposed then, allowing the crafts to navigate through it more safely. Daylight would also allow the safer unloading of the vehicles onboard. But still, what weighed on the brigade commander's mind most was the forewarned risk of dawn air attacks. After pondering the matter, he decided to bring in the LCUs immediately and so informed Captain Ryberg. Gray Lynch strongly disagreed with the decision, however. He talked to San Román directly and diplomatically advised him against so doing. "Pepe, you are the commander and you make the decisions, but I think it is better to wait until daylight. . . . This beach is very difficult and at night . . . you might lose one or two tanks." San Román reluctantly agreed.[84] It was, after all, what was called for in the operation plan.

* * * *

"There will be no more landings," Castro assured Almeida when they spoke on the phone around 4:00 a.m. Given the absence at the time of any firm basis for such a statement, it was clearly born out of wishful thinking rather than insight. An invasion limited to the Bay of Pigs would offer him the advantage of being able to concentrate his forces at essentially one spot on the island. Moreover, from his many trips there, Castro "knew the place perfectly," including its hidden backtrails. It was a tactical prospect that undoubtedly delighted him, as must have Almeida's estimate of the number of invaders that had landed: "no less than 1500 and no more than 3000." Castro ordered that Tomassevich proceed with Battalion 117 to Covadonga and there turn it over to army commander Filiberto Olivera, who he was sending to that location.[85]

At Managua, Captain Fernández was busy breaking into the center's storage room when Castro called again about half an hour after their initial conversation. The key keeper could not be located, and the captain was not about to depart for Matanzas without retrieving maps of the invasion area from the room. "Fernández, how it is possible!" the unmistakable, scolding voice said on the other end of the line. "Call me from Matanzas," he commanded at the end of their brief conversation.[86]

It was approximately 4:30 a.m. when *El Comandante* finally decided to leave Celia Sánchez's apartment. Bienvenido Pérez, one of his personal bodyguards, became alarmed when Castro abruptly stood up and shouted, "Long live free Cuba!" Then, wildly gesturing with his hands, he said, "Let's go!" "We are screwed now!" thought Pérez. "The Americans are landing and this man has gone crazy!" The impression was in keeping with Castro's nickname as a youth: *El Loco* (the crazy one). They quickly departed for Point One, only a short drive away.[87]

* * * *

At 4:22 a.m. the JCS transmitted the Rules of Engagement (ROE) to the naval task force assigned to the invasion operation. Among other stipulations, the ROE specified that air cover was to be provided to the brigade ships outside of Cuban territorial waters.[88]

General Cabell once again confounded matters by broaching the question of ship air cover with the White House. At 4:30 a.m. he phoned Secretary of State Rusk at his Sheraton Park Apartments residence and asked to see him at once. Rusk acceded to the meeting and Cabell drove over immediately. But even the urgency which he viewed the matter was not enough to override Cabell's by-the-book mindset. Seeing "No Parking" signs all over the apartment complex, he opted for parking a few blocks away and walking back to his destination.

Rusk met him in his robe and, "gracious and businesslike," listened as Cabell pleaded the case for navy air cover over the brigade ships to compensate for the loss of the airstrikes. Considering this a request that should be made directly to the president, Rusk got Kennedy on the line and handed the phone to Cabell. The general presented the president with three options, in order of preference, for the extent of air protection: all the way up to shore, outside of Cuban territorial waters, and outside of Cuban territorial but with no authority to engage. The president made no comment after Cabell had finished talking and merely asked him to hand the phone back to Rusk. In short order the secretary gave Cabell the president's decision: the request for *any* sort of air cover was not approved.[89]

At 5:50 a.m., after learning of Kennedy's decision from Bissell, the JCS transmitted a revised ROE to the task force removing all air cover for the brigade ships.[90]

* * * *

With dawn fast approaching, Castro's first call upon reaching Point One was to veteran pilot Luis Silva at the San Antonio airbase. Silva had achieved revolutionary fame when on December 7, 1959, flying a captured Cuban navy Kingfisher, he had undertaken the first rebel air mission (memorialized as "FAR Operation A-001") against Batista's forces. The government soldiers were lured out into the open by Silva's aircraft which bore naval markings and rocked its wings in salute on the first pass. Then, as the men below gleefully waved and called out to the "friendly" plane, Silva dropped his bombs on them. He employed the same decoy on several other occasions, including one in which he set off a huge fire by dropping napalm on a town hall square.[91]

"There are three [*sic*] enemy ships at Playa Larga . . . and there's ground fighting there," Castro informed Silva when he phoned him at 4:45 a.m. He ordered two Sea Furies and two B-26s to take off just before dawn, attack the ships inside the Bay of Pigs, then quickly return to San Antonio and report. A T-33 jet was to be on standby ready to take off and help defend the base. Less than thirty minutes later, Castro called Silva again and revised his earlier instructions. The content of the call reflected the still uncertain and rapidly changing understanding of the tactical situation. "We are assured that Playa Girón has been taken but not Playa Larga," Silva was told. Castro described the features of the Girón–Playa Larga area then enumerated the order of attack priorities for the pilot: airfield (if planes present), ships, trucks, and personnel.[92]

Castro's was counting on his small air force to play a critical role in fending off the invasion. So much so that within an hour of his last call to Silva he replaced the FAR chief at San Antonio with Communications Minister Raúl Curbelo.[93] Castro had been jarred over the previous months by the defections of veteran military leaders of the Revolution, including air force chief Pedro Díaz Lanz who had later fled to the United States. In responding to the invasion, he would assign key positions to trusted men such as Curbelo from the top leadership of his M-26-7 organization.[94]

The FAR was in about as rough a shape as the CIA's intelligence assessment had estimated—even more so after the damage inflicted during the April 15 air attacks. Its T-33, Sea Fury, and B-26 combat planes had been inherited from the Batista government, and spare parts as well as ordnance for them were limited due to the embargoes imposed first on Batista then on Castro.[95] However, Castro held two trump cards that the CIA's assessment had not foreseen. The first was the ingenuity of his aviation mechanics who became "miracle workers" at jerry-rigging unavailable replacement parts. Worn out T-33 fuel injector orifices were "repaired" by filling them with silver from melted coins then employing a miniature bit to ream out the small holes.[96] Truck tires and brake pads were put to work on the Sea Furies.[97] Old parts on one airplane were replaced with slightly less-old parts from other airplanes.[98] These "Fatherland or Death" planes, as they were christened,[99] took to the air "practically at pilot's risk," remarked one of the aviators.[100] The point was driven home when, on April 15, a T-33 on a night reconnaissance mission out of Santiago de Cuba exploded in midair, killing pilot Orestes Acosta.[101] That the handful of airmen available were, for the most part, disposed to fly in such hairy machines was Castro's other surprise trump card. The few of whom much was expected totaled four T-33, four Sea Fury, and three B-26 pilots, in addition to senior aviator Enrique Carreras, who could fly all three types of aircraft.[102]

At twilight, a flight of aircraft took off from San Antonio bound for the invasion area. It consisted of two Sea Furies but only one of the two B-26s Castro had called for, as no other could be made flyable by then.[103]

* * * *

The reef had been taking a heavy toll on the LCVPs. By 5:30 a.m., with only the Fourth Battalion on land, only two of the four crafts remained in service. One had sunk and the other reluctantly been abandoned. As a result, the Girón landing was seriously behind schedule as the arrival of daybreak became imminent.[104]

Onboard the *Río Escondido*, Sixth Battalion commander Francisco Montiel became concerned. The operation plan called for his battalion to be taken off the ship by the first LCU to be unloaded of its cargo. However, the prospect of doing so in broad daylight was now fraught with danger of air attacks. Montiel thus decided to start landing his men immediately using the ship's spare aluminum boats. However, his improvised plan soon, and quite literally, stalled out. In a farcical encore of what had occurred at Playa Larga, the outboard motors on the boats began to fail.[105]

* * * *

The outboard motor problems hampering the Playa Larga landing were being compounded by cold feet on the part of the Fifth Battalion's commander, Ricardo Montero. As future events suggest, his reticence was likely shared by many of his men. Montero and most of those in his battalion were Batista loyalists not generally popular with the rest of the brigade.[106] He had served as an officer in Batista's army until his discharge in December 1958 for "defeatist conduct" in the fight against Castro's guerrillas.[107] Now, faced with the unexpected fighting at the beach, Montero simply refused to go ashore.

At 5:30 a.m., noticing that the Fifth Battalion remained on the *Houston*, Robertson went there in person and was appalled at the complete inaction he encountered. Quickly he took it upon himself to begin loading men into the small boats. But Montero quickly stepped in and adamantly demanded that he stop. Following what may be presumed was a heated exchange between the two men, Robertson gave up and left.[108]

6:00 AM—7:00 AM

The sun's disk grazed the horizon as brigade B-26 pilots René García and Mario Cortina reconnoitered the waters northeast of the Isle of Pines, just over one hundred miles from the Bay of Pigs. Below them, illuminated by the nascent rays of light, they spotted Cuban patrol boat PT 203 *Baire* at anchor some four miles from the Nueva Gerona naval station. It was one of three Cuban navy vessels stationed in those waters. The *Baire*, built in the United States before World War II, had a crew of thirty-nine and a single 76 mm cannon as its main armament. It was also equipped with four 20 mm antiaircraft guns, but they were in poor condition and supplied with aged ammunition.

Spotting the two bombers, and in a state of high alert since the April 15 air raids, the vessel's commander sounded general quarters. His crew rushed to their combat stations. The first bomber began its strafing run flying barely above mast height, and *Baire*'s antiaircraft guns opened fire. Quickly the one engine of the boat's two that worked was started. The vessel weighed anchor and moved to stern, avoiding hits by most of the 250-pound bombs dropped by the B-26s as they passed over. However, the underpowered *Baire* was sluggish, and its shabby antiaircraft guns started jamming. Over the course of ten to fifteen minutes, the planes made five to six passes over the vessel spraying it with .50 caliber bullets and scoring several hits with 5-inch rockets. The two bombers then headed for the Bay of Pigs area. They had not sustained significant damage or any crew casualties but left behind an unsalvageable Cuban patrol boat with two dead and seventeen wounded sailors aboard.[109]

* * * *

It was daybreak when the first FAR planes arrived over the beachhead. The B-26 piloted by Silva carried a crew of four, including a rear gunner. Unlike their brigade counterparts, the FAR bombers were equipped with a tail gun turret.[110] Carreras flew one of the two Sea Furies in the formation and rookie pilot Gustavo Bourzac the other. The spectacle that now unfolded before Carreras made him feel as if he "were watching a movie, a World War II documentary; a mockup of Normandy on a small scale."[111] Silva chose as his target a small boat being towed to shore by Robertson's launch while Carreras went after the *Houston* with Bourzac in the wing-man role.

The first pass of the B-26 on the boat, carrying the missing F Company squad, caused no casualties, but one man was wounded on the plane's second pass. The bomber then headed for Girón, and at this point Robertson decided to abort the trip to shore and make for the *Barbara J* with the boat in tow.[112]

Carreras, meanwhile, with Bourzac remaining at altitude on lookout, made a bombing dive on the *Houston*. The machine gunners on the freighter as well as the circling *Barbara J* frantically fired at the small target swooping down toward the *Houston* at over 400 miles per hour. Carreras released his two bombs just before pulling his plane up into a steep climb. Looking back, he saw that they had both fallen short of the ship.[113]

Responding to a distress call from the ships, brigade pilot Gonzalo Herrera arrived on the scene just in time to see Carrera's bombs miss. His and another B-26 piloted by Joaquín Varela were escorting a C-46 transport headed for a paratroop drop south of Central Australia and had just reached the beachhead. The Sea Fury whizzed past the nose of Herrera's plane, climbing to 10,000 feet and becoming lost in the glare of the rising sun. A quick-thinking Herrera then decided to pull a ruse. Switching to the radio frequency he knew the FAR used, he transmitted a call for U.S. Navy jet support. Either the ruse and/or the presence of Herrera's plane itself proved effective because both Sea Furies went away.

With the imminent danger over, the *Barbara J* instructed Herrera to attack any ground targets approaching the beachhead from Central Australia or the east.[114] Both ships then quickly headed away from Playa Larga hoping to avoid further attacks until there was better control of the air.[115] The entire Fifth Battalion remained aboard the *Houston* along with ammunition and vehicle fuel that had not made it ashore. The freighter, which was slated to serve as an interim hospital, also carried equipment and supplies for setting up a fifty-bed field medical facility on land.[116]

Herrera flew north and rejoined Varela in patrolling the area as the paratroopers they had escorted to the beachhead prepared to jump. Some thirty paratroopers and their equipment were to be dropped near the settlement of Pálpite, three miles north of Caletón, along the road to Central Australia. The place marked the southern end of the "bottleneck" along the westernmost accessway to the beachhead. A smaller paratroop unit was to temporarily block the northern entrance into this bottleneck and then fall back toward Pálpite, where the paratroopers were to be joined by the Second Battalion.[117] The men about to drop down had no inkling that a militia force at Caletón blocked the way north for the Second Battalion.

* * * *

The first LCU started making its way up the narrow channel across the reef in front of Girón at 6:00 a.m. Aboard were three tanks, two jeeps, and one M-35 gun truck.[118]

The LCU discharged the vehicles in somewhat deep water, forcing Jorge Álvarez to ram his tank roughly through jagged rocks and surf to get ashore. The tank's gun elevation mechanism was damaged as a result, but the other tanks managed to land without mishap.[119]

Meanwhile, the two remaining LCVPs took turns pulling up alongside the *Atlántico* to take on the men of the Heavy Weapons Battalion who were aboard. The men clambered down the nets over the side of the ship as the landing craft's pilot struggled to keep it steady. Lowering down the component parts of the brigade's seven M30 4.2-inch mortars was an especially painstaking process. Some of them weighed as much as 193 pounds (with a combined weight of 640 pounds when assembled). "They treated those mortars as if they were made of glass," remarked a soldier on deck as he watched the disassembled weapons being lowered like "a months-old baby." The 4.2-inch mortars were the closest the brigade would have to land-based heavy artillery support.[120]

* * * *

Captain Fernández was greeted by what "looked like an open market" when he arrived at the Militia Leaders' School in Matanzas. As Castro had promised, the school had been notified prior to his arrival. The facility lacked means of transportation, so every passing truck was being requisitioned and unloaded of its cargo—mainly animals, vegetables, and other foodstuff items. These in turn were being piled up onto the school's parade ground creating a marketplace atmosphere.

Fernández rushed to the phone where Castro was on hold awaiting his arrival. The first question from *El Comandante* was about the morale of the troop at the school. "Excellent," Fernández answered. After verifying that the captain remembered the area where he was going (they had visited it together some weeks prior), Castro explained that, although the number of invaders remained uncertain, it was confirmed that they had landed at both Playa Larga and Girón. The battalion of militia leaders was the nearest major unit available, so it was crucial that they moved there to beat back the enemy forces. Fernández was to set up his command post at Central Australia, where a direct telephone line to Point One had been installed. A few minutes after the call ended, Castro was on the phone again. Typical of his micromanagement style, this time he wanted to know the exact route that Fernández planned to follow to his assigned destination.[121]

Fernández immediately departed to take up his post, taking with him only a handful of assistants. The battalion itself was to follow as soon as there were enough trucks to transport the entire troop.[122]

* * * *

The militiamen fighting at the Caletón Triangle had received reinforcements since their early morning retreat to the traffic island's northern corner. But their ammunition was mostly gone, spent on constant running skirmishes with the brigade units situated less than 200 yards away.[123]

The stalemate that had lasted for over two hours ended suddenly at six o'clock when a flatbed truck moved east down the southern side of the triangle toward the brigade positions. When shouts of "*Águila*" (Eagle)—the password challenge used by the invaders—went unanswered (the correct response was *Negra* [Black]), they opened fire and the truck exploded.[124] Simultaneously, thinking this was the start of a coordinated militia assault, a hail of machine gun and recoilless rifle fire erupted toward the militiamen to the north. Thirteen militia combatants were wounded and six killed, including twenty-two-year-old Jesús Villafuerte, who had been fighting alongside his father. Panic-stricken, the men of Battalion 339 scattered in different directions.[125]

Several brigade soldiers subsequently went over to inspect the knocked-out truck. Its occupants turned out to be four men, four women, and four girls. The group had left Buenaventura to escape the shooting there and all but one of the men belonged to two local families. Amparo Ortiz lost her sister, her husband, and her fourteen-year-old niece, Dulce Martín. Cira García, who was accompanied by her husband and two young daughters, received severe injuries. As a militia member and local head of the Revolutionary women's association, García wore the bright blue shirt of the militia uniform. The sight of distinctive shirt, according to the brigade men, had sealed the fate of the truck occupants.[126]

A brigade truck came to pick up the survivors but not the bodies of the dead. Sixteen-year-old Nora Martín, Dulce's sister, would not have it. "Bring my sister!" she shouted. "I'm sorry but she is dead; we are at war," one of the soldiers told her. As she sat crying inside the truck, another soldier tried to hand the distraught girl a $10 bill. "I don't want money, what I want is my sister!" she screamed at him.[127]

The group was taken back to one of the resort buildings under construction at Playa Larga where they joined the more than thirty prisoners, including militia members, already there. From among the captives, two local mechanics had volunteered their services. A few militiamen also had offered to fight with the brigade, but there were no weapons to give them. Lacking as well were medical supplies for treating Cira García's injuries or those of anyone else.[128] The inability to unload the *Houston*'s cargo was already having consequences ashore.

* * * *

Paratrooper Waldo de Castroverde could hear the bullets zip by as soon as he jumped out of his C-46 transport close to Pálpite. Gonzalo Herrera, flying his B-26 nearby, heard the urgent call from the cockpit reporting that ground fire was being directed at the aircraft as well as the men and equipment parachuting down. The firing, it seems, came not only from the militiamen of Battalion 339 retreating from Caletón but also from others mobilized from Jagüey Grande, some fifteen miles north of Pálpite.[129]

Herrera's B-26 arrived in mere seconds over the cluster of huts from which the firing originated and proceeded to bomb and strafe them. Then, some three miles to the north, he spotted two trucks speeding toward the tourist center at La Boca. He was on them in an instant and set both vehicles ablaze with .50 caliber machine gun fire. Seeing several men running away from the burning wrecks, he mowed them down with both bullets and a rocket that exploded in their midst. A second rocket blew up the filling station at the facility. The pilot became ecstatic at "the sight of the filthy militiamen running from one side to the other, abandoning their combat posts and leaving our boys in peace for a while." Such was his excitement that he literally jumped out of his seat and hit the overhead canopy, almost crashing into the B-26 accompanying him in the process.[130]

Upon reaching the ground, the paratroopers found that one of them was dead and another missing (also killed, as it turned out). Moreover, many of their supply boxes were lost. Due to the ground fire, the boxes had been dropped first and the men had not been able to see where they had landed. Tomás Cruz, the group's commander, ordered his small unit of just over two dozen men to enter Pálpite, from which militiamen continued to shoot in their direction. The first paratrooper to go in cradled a .30 caliber machine gun on his hip: "[like] John Wayne," thought De Castroverde. A couple of militia resistors were taken prisoners, but the rest managed to escape.[131]

* * * *

A few minutes after his Playa Larga attack, Luis Silva's B-26 was approaching the ships off the coast of Girón. There the first LCU to unload its cargo was now on its way to the *Río Escondido* to finish offloading the Sixth Battalion. A second LCU had moved into the cross-reef channel as the third waited its turn outside the reef. The two LCVPs still afloat had finished offloading the men and 4.2-inch mortars of the Heavy Weapons Battalion from the *Atlántico* and were now landward bound. Aboard one of them was Roberto San Román, the battalion's commander and younger brother of brigade commander Pepe San Román.[132]

Those aboard the various vessels could see the silhouette of a distant plane closing in from the east but were unable to identify it as friend or foe. All doubts about the aircraft's identity were dispelled when it suddenly opened fire and dove down on the LCVPs. Plumes of water shot up from the water as the .50 caliber bullets zeroed in on the barges. Unthinkingly, many of the remaining men on the *Atlántico* sought cover among the fuel drums and ammunition boxes that cluttered the deck. "Fire on it with everything, dammit!" Manuel Penabaz shouted at them. Penabaz, a lawyer by profession who had fought Batista's military alongside Castro, harbored since that time a deep resentment of cowering in the face of air attacks. Intense firing was soon spewing out of every gun on every vessel toward the bomber and its offending crew. "We shot back with everything we had," said one of the *Blagar*'s sailors. "The men in the little boats fired at them; the tanks in the barges shot at them; we shot at them with our machine guns and rifles. We went *papapapa* . . .—just like in the movies."[133]

The hail of projectiles must have dissuaded Silva from pressing his attack for it was limited to the LCVPs. He made three strafing passes over the barges damaging the motor on one of them, but, fortuitously, there were no casualties although indeed some close calls. One lucky man used his combat jacket to plug the large hole made by a bullet that ripped through the hull mere inches away from him.[134]

Silva's B-26 soon departed the area, but the consternation it had caused only grew when more aircraft were seen approaching. Although some confusion exists as to the number of incoming planes, this time they were immediately fired upon by the vessels. As it happened, however, these new arrivals were not FAR planes but a C-46 carrying paratroopers being escorted by a brigade B-26. "What the hell's going on? They've gone crazy," a paratrooper yelled out when bullets started ripping through the plane's fuselage. The firing finally ceased after the pilots identified who they were.[135] From the *Blagar* an urgent message was sent to JMTIDE: friendly aircraft were not to approach the ships unannounced, as they could not be distinguished from enemy aircraft. All the brigade B-26s were painted with identical makings and color schemes to their FAR counterparts but bore a light blue stripe around both wings. In practice, however, the stripes were not visible unless the plane was directly overhead.[136]

When the LCVPs finally reached the reef line, the men of the Heavy Weapons Battalion had their work cut out for them. Wading 300 feet to shore carrying the heavy mortar parts and shell boxes proved an arduous task that, as described by Roberto San Román, "took a while."[137]

* * * *

In the early morning light, from their entrenched position just north of Girón, Rebel Army Commander Evelio Saborit and his small band of soldiers could see an enemy tank approaching followed by infantry. Hours earlier Saborit's group had arrived at San Blas from the vicinity of Aguada de Pasajeros, twenty-four miles away. Leaving their vehicles at San Blas, they had walked some eight miles to their current position and dug the shallow foxholes they now occupied. The advancing brigade force, apparently a patrol, spotted the men but did not open fire. "Come over to our side!" one of the invaders called out. "We have come to free you from communism!" As in Playa Larga, the response they received was a shout of "Fatherland or Death!" followed by a burst of bullets. To the surprise of the Castro loyalists, the enemy quickly retreated.[138]

Their elation over this easy success was to be short-lived, however, because from overhead came the rumble of engines followed by the sight of planes traveling north in the direction of San Blas. Soon the sky was filled with what looked like blooming mushrooms slowly falling through the air. The men immediately understood that paratroopers were being dropped to their rear. Without thinking, some in the group began firing at the drifting shapes in the distance, but Saborit yelled for them to stop as they were just wasting their scarce ammunition. Turning to William Selva, with whom he had been active in the anti-Batista underground, he issued an order. Selva and a driver were to use Saborit's personal Toyota, which had been brought down from San Blas earlier, to speed past the developing encirclement. Their mission was to reach Covadonga with news of what was happening. "You cannot fall prisoner or get killed. Understood?" were the commander's parting words. Selva got in the car, turned to the driver and said, "Floor it, friend!"[139]

* * * *

The paratroopers descending north of Girón were assigned three separate drop zones. One was near Jocuma, on the road from Covadonga, and another near Horquita, on the road from Yaguaramas. As with their counterparts north of Playa Larga, the paratroopers in the eastern sector of the beachhead were to defend the "bottlenecks" where these roads crossed the swamp. The north end of one such bottleneck was at the intersection of the road from Covadonga with a waterway called the Muñoz Canal. There, some two miles south of Jocuma, a paratroop detachment was to set up a defensive strongpoint. South of Horquita another paratroop contingent was to do likewise at Babiney, the north end of the bottleneck on the road from Yaguaramas. Both units would eventually fall back to battle positions at the other (southern) end of each bottleneck. A third drop zone was located immediately to the north of San Blas. The paratroop headquarters company was to parachute there then proceed to occupy the key settlement wherein the roads from Covadonga and Yaguaramas intersected.[140]

Airdropping all the men and equipment over every zone required several passes for each plane. Unlike the airdrops north of Playa Larga, the ones here did not have to contend with ground fire or any immediate opposition on land. In fact, the only casualties during the drops were due to an accident on one of the C-46s. As the last paratrooper onboard made his jump, the static line running the length of the aircraft snapped. The recoiling cable broke the leg of a parachute drop officer and jammed the plane's tail controls. Two crewmen managed to pull in the paratrooper who had been left dangling outside the plane wounded and with a torn parachute. Weeping, the man insisted on jumping. "Please turn back and drop me. It's the invasion!" he pleaded fruitlessly with the pilot, who stayed on course back to Nicaragua.[141]

Over San Blas, just before jumping, paratroop commander Alejandro del Valle gave pilot Eduardo Ferrer a bear hug and affectionately told him: "Country boy, all I ask of you is not to drop me in the wrong place. I don't want the war to end for me so early. We'll get together for a beer soon." Twenty-two years old and "strong as an oak," Del Valle, as described by Ferrer, "had quite a reputation for being tough with the men under his command during training, yet they all liked and trusted him."[142]

Even though the drops went smoothly for the most part, several issues cropped up nonetheless. North of San Blas, a considerable number of ammunition boxes were lost in the dense woods. On the road to Yaguaramas, Ricardo Sánchez, one of about twenty paratroopers assigned to the strongpoint at Babiney, found that the telescopic sight for his 57 mm recoilless rifle was missing. Moreover, he had only been supplied with antipersonnel rounds and lacked antitank ones. To make matters worse, the paratroopers were out of communication with Pepe San Román in Girón as the communications trailer destined for his command post was still aboard the *Río Escondido*.[143]

At San Blas, the paratroopers found that, although at first timid, most of the locals quickly became friendly and offered to help. A few even asked for brigade uniforms and volunteered to fight with them. Not all were so welcoming, however. One woman was bold enough to walk up to the invaders and shout insults at them. She was quickly told off by another resident who yelled back at her: "Shut up already, you whore without clients. You no longer rule here." Del Valle himself took on the job of screening the inhabitants, and anyone arousing suspicion was confined inside a dilapidated cowshed that became a provisional jail. The paratroopers requisitioned all the working vehicles in the settlement, including a convertible that Del Valle took for himself.[144]

* * * *

"They are telling me that paratroopers are dropping down," Fidel Castro heard militiaman Gonzalo Rodríguez say from Covadonga on the other end of the line. A direct telephone connection had been established between Point One and the sugar mill there just a few minutes before. Rodríguez came back on the line after going to verify the report and informed Castro that he had counted twenty-four parachutes descending just over a mile away. It was a correct estimate of the distance to the drop zone near Jocuma where men and equipment were coming down. Although the mission for these paratroopers was not to attack Covadonga but to head south to the Muñoz Canal, Castro feared the airborne force would soon advance on the sugar mill. "Are they advancing or falling back?" he asked Rodríguez. "I don't know. It looks like they're not advancing," came the reply. Rodríguez then pleaded for Castro to send more weapons as they lacked enough of them to fight off an attack. The conversation between the two intensified at that point.

"—And just how many weapons do you have there?"

"—We have eleven weapons . . . eight M-52 rifles, two Springfields, and an old Brazilian carbine."

"—For balls' sake! With those weapons I'd stand my ground there and not let those people take a step forward. You're all just scared stiff."

Castro grew more exasperated when Rodríguez denied that this was the case and again reiterated his request for weapons.

"—Listen, I don't want to hear any more complaints about weapons. Arm yourselves with machetes, clubs, and stones, but don't let those people take the sugar mill, damn it!"[145]

* * * *

The *Houston* and *Barbara J* had continued sailing south away from Playa Larga since Carrera's 6:00 a.m. attack. They had traveled more than five miles down the Bay of Pigs when, at around 6:30 a.m., a brigade B-26 piloted by Matías Farías appeared overhead and requested instructions from the *Barbara J.* Farías's and another B-26 flown by Mario Zúñiga were the latest pair of support bombers to arrive from JMTIDE. Farías was instructed to engage any enemy forces on the road to Playa Larga, and he headed off in that direction. He and Zúñiga would split the task of supporting the Girón and Playa Larga sectors between them. Thereupon, perhaps reassured by the arrival of this additional air power, the two-ship convoy reversed course and started back north toward the head of the bay.[146]

Suddenly and without warning, Carreras in his Sea Fury reappeared out of the blue, closing in fast on the *Houston*'s stern. At close range he fired all eight of his underwing rockets. Plumes of smoke and oil spewed out of the ship as the pilot made a second pass, strafing the ship with all four of his 20 mm cannons. One of the rockets from his first pass had penetrated the ship's hull astern and started a fire below decks. The water rushing in through the gaping hole near the water line quickly extinguished the flames. However, as Captain Luis Morse on the bridge soon realized, the ship had lost all steering control. The *Houston* ended up oriented crosswise to the axis of the bay and could only go forward or backward. Morse decided to move it backward away from the rocky shoreline, but this caused water to rush in faster through the breach and the stern began to sink. As this was happening, the Sea Fury piloted by Bourzac launched a second rocket attack. Immediately Captain Morse called for full speed ahead and the stricken vessel lurched forward for a few moments then ground to a stop with a loud crash. Five miles south of Playa Larga, opposite a small headland named Punta Cazones, the *Hous-ton* was now stranded on reefs. Three hundred yards of water separated it from the western shore of the Bay of Pigs.[147]

Panic seized those aboard when they saw steam shooting out from the stern section. "We are sinking! The boilers are going to explode!" the frenzied horde cried out. Fifth Battalion men stampeded to one side of the ship and plunged into the water below, even though many of them could not swim. Unable to control the mad onslaught, battalion commander Montero grabbed an M-3 submachine gun and threatened to shoot anyone who jumped overboard. A lifeboat was put in the water under orders that only wounded men were to go into it. Only two of the injured managed to board before a throng of frenzied men rushed the boat. This time Montero just looked down from the bridge and said nothing.[148] Any hope the men on the stranded ship held for assistance from the nearby *Barbara J* quickly vanished. The LCI, which was itself taking on water due to damage it sustained in the attacks, started out of the bay at best possible speed. They were "leaving us to our fate," reckoned one of the stranded Fifth Battalion soldiers as he watched the *Barbara J* recede in the distance.[149]

None of the B-26s in the area had been able to intervene during the FAR raids. Gonzalo Herrera, who had continued to patrol the area for close to an hour, heard the distress calls from the ships and flew toward them. His fuel situation became critical while en route, however, and reluctantly the frustrated pilot aborted the attempt. Desperately he radioed a request for immediate navy jet support from the nearby American carrier but received no reply. "I started to feel," Herrera found, "that we had been deceived; betrayed."[150]

* * * *

Abraham Masiques and Captain Cordero, accompanied by a newsman, made their way in a jeep to Central Australia with news of Battalion 339's rout near Playa Larga. Masiques had gone to see Cordero earlier that morning with orders from Castro that the invaders must not be allowed to advance beyond Pálpite; reinforcements were on the way.

Some distance north of the La Boca, they heard a loud rumble before seeing a B-26 pass over them almost at tree-top level. "It's ours; it says 'FAR!'" Cordero said gleefully. Masiques, however, suspected something was not right when the plane turned in the distance and came back toward them. "Captain, jump; jump into the roadside ditch!" he yelled. Seconds later, a torrent of bullets rained down right next to where the men hid. The plane—undoubtedly the one flown by Matías Farías—made two more strafing passes before disappearing. Happy to find that none of them had been hit, the men climbed back onto the road and into the jeep. It still worked.[151]

Less fortunate were thirteen-year-old Nemesia Rodríguez and her family traveling in a pickup truck just a few miles to the north. Their destination was Jagüey Grande, where they sought to escape the fighting around Playa Larga. Some seven miles away from their destination, they had just crossed paths with a car traveling in the opposite direction when the B-26 appeared overhead. It made two passes over both vehicles with no sign of hostility but opened fire as it came around a third time. The truck and car immediately stopped, and their occupants quickly ran into the thicket. Not all of them did, however. The car's driver, news photographer Ernesto Fernández, could see from the ditch where he hid that a woman remained standing on the back of the truck. In her hands was a white sheet that she waved in the air toward the plane. The B-26 kept shooting, however, and the bullets violently ripped through the woman's abdomen. She was Nemesia Rodríguez's mother. Even decades later the then-teenager vividly recalled the horrible sight: "Everything was coming out of her." The girl's grandmother too, who had remained sitting in the truck's cab, had been hit. Miraculously she was alive, although seriously wounded.[152]

A few miles south of the grim scene, as Masiques and Cordero continued on their way to Central Australia, they saw "dots" falling from the sky ahead of them. "Paratroopers!" the men exclaimed, estimating that there were one or two hundred of them. In fact, these were the approximately twenty paratroopers commanded by Pedro Vera (the First Battalion's second-in-command) that were to set up the strongpoint north of Pálpite. The drop of Vera and his men was off target. Instead of landing near the road as planned, the paratroopers plopped down into the swamp and became lost.[153]

In a few minutes the jeep reached the place where the truck carrying the Rodríguez family had been attacked. The wounded grandmother, still sitting in the cabin of the pickup, was utterly distraught. "I only regret that my young daughter was killed and not me," she repeated inconsolably. Her dead daughter's body lay on the bed of the truck covered with the now blood-soaked white sheet she had been waving. A truck then came by with forty militiamen from Jagüey Grande aboard. They were led by Lieutenant Antero Fernández, head of the army post there. Captain Cordero ordered the lieutenant to proceed to La Boca where he was to take up defensive positions until reinforcements arrived. The captain and Masiques then placed the injured old woman in the jeep and resumed their journey north.[154]

* * * *

The *New York Times* hit the streets before dawn with news of the Cuba invasion. Radio Swan had reported it at 1:15 a.m. in the form of CRC Bulletin Number 1, which began with the following statement: *Before dawn*

Cuban patriots in the cities and in the hills began the battle to liberate our home-land from the despotic rule of Fidel Castro.

Another bulletin followed at 4:00 a.m. This one announced *a successful landing of military supplies and equipment in the Cochinos Bay [Bay of Pigs] area . . . [that] reached elements of internal resistance engaged in active combat.* The views of the CRC, it added, would be conveyed to the press only through a spokesman as its members were *totally occupied with the dramatic events unfolding in Cuba.*[155]

In actuality, the bulletins were entirely CIA creations. After perfunctory approval by second-tier CRC representatives, the statements were issued to the media through the Lem Jones public relations agency in New York. The six stateside CRC members (the seventh, Manuel Artime, was with the invasion force) were themselves completely unaware that the invasion had even begun. CIA operatives had taken them into custody the previous day in New York where the group had been holding a meeting. They were subsequently flown to Florida and ensconced in a deserted airbase in Opa-locka, near Miami. It was at 6:30 a.m. when the members of the provisional-government-to-be heard of the Cuba landings on the small transistor radios the CIA had provided them.[156]

7:00 AM—NOON

Following the first air attacks on Girón, Lynch called San Román around 7:00 a.m. to recommend canceling the scheduled landing of the Third Battalion at Green Beach (Caleta Redonda). Lynch argued that only one serviceable LCVP remained and that it should not be diverted elsewhere. Moreover, the departure of the *Blagar* with the Third Battalion would leave the cargo ships without their main antiaircraft defense. As an alternative, he proposed that the battalion be put ashore at Girón then moved overland the nineteen miles east to Green Beach. San Román agreed.[157]

While the last LCU unloaded its cargo at the beach, the other two got busy picking up Third Battalion personnel and others still on the ships. Suddenly, the roar of plane engines made all eyes turn to a spectacle unfolding in the sky. A C-46 returning from an airdrop was being chased by a Sea Fury which kept trying to close in on the transport's tail for a kill shot. Endeavoring to reach the ships and the protection of their guns, Captain Mario Tellechea skimmed the surface of the water and reduced the C-46's airspeed to a minimum. The Sea Fury could not stay in the air at such low speeds, so it kept overshooting the transport and circling around seeking a firing position behind it. Every gun on every ship opened fired on the obstinate predator as it came within range. The cause of what happened next is uncertain. Whether due to the antiaircraft fire or to stalling out so close to the water, the Sea Fury crashed into the sea killing its pilot. He was Carlos Ulloa, a Nicaraguan national flying with the FAR.[158] Ulloa had been accompanied on his flight by a T-33 flown by Guillermo "Willy" Figueroa. However, all the eyewitness reports mention only seeing the Sea Fury, and Figueroa was, in fact, arrested upon his return to base for desertion in the face of the enemy.[159]

* * * *

"Like greased lightning," the Toyota with Selva and his driver had raced up the road toward Covadonga since departing Saborit's group on the outskirts of Girón. They had taken some fire at San Blas and along the rest of the way but finally managed to reach the sugar mill at Covadonga. Speaking directly to Castro on the phone, he informed him about Saborit's situation and the paratroop drops, some as close as half a mile from the mill.

Castro was nonchalant about Saborit, whom he knew personally. He told Selva not to worry about him because "that one knows what he's doing." Concerning the need to defend the Covadonga mill, however, Castro was unequivocally emphatic. "Listen, you know that that sugar mill cannot fall into enemy hands, right!" he barked out. "To take it they must go over your dead bodies! You hear me!" Selva protested that there were not sufficient men or weapons there to mount an effective defense and offered to go to Aguada de Pasajeros to look for reinforcements. "Do whatever you want," Castro replied, "but remember, the only way they can take that sugar mill is over your dead bodies!"[160]

* * * *

Since retreating from Caletón, Carlos Cepero and a wounded comrade from Battalion 339 he was carrying had been heading north. Cepero was intent on reaching Jagüey Grande to get the man medical care. At Pálpite the pair had found a truck and driven it to La Boca, where Cepero was told that paratroopers might be blocking the way farther north. He was advised to follow a van about to depart for his destination; it was their best chance for getting through. Aboard the van were the lieutenant from Jagüey Grande, Antero Fernández, and a public official. Lieutenant Fernández was apparently returning to his army post after dropping off the militiamen at La Boca per Captain Cordero's orders.

Cepero had followed Fernández's vehicle for about three miles when a group of five or six men appeared ahead wearing what looked like olive-green Rebel Army uniforms. The van in front stopped, and Cepero realized as he got closer that the uniforms were actually the camouflage ones worn by the invaders. Indeed, these were not Rebel Army soldiers at all but some of Pedro Vera's paratroopers who had become lost after missing their drop zone. When the brigade men started shooting, Cepero quickly crawled out of his truck, but Fernández ahead stood behind the van and returned fire. Within moments the lieutenant lay on the ground motionless and bleeding profusely from the head. The small band of paratroopers then disappeared into the thicket.[161]

The gunfight that killed Lieutenant Fernández would be Vera's unit's only noteworthy involvement in the battle. The road from Central Australia to Pálpite lay open to Castro's forces.

* * * *

Just before 8:00 a.m. Captain Fernández reached Central Australia, where he found less than a dozen militiamen and learned about the presence of paratroopers in the area. The instructions he received from Castro when Fernández phoned him at 8:05 a.m. were explicit: "You should first eliminate the paratroopers and then advance on the enemy and keep on advancing."

Fernández immediately sent out a patrol to determine if there were any paratroopers near the mill.[162] Sitting in a jeep nearby he saw Captain Cordero, who identified himself as the commander of Battalion 339. "We fought the landing since early morning," Cordero said. "All my people are dead or captured." In reality, most of the battalion's men lay scattered in small groups across the region west and north of Caletón.[163]

Elements of MRN Battalions 219, 223, and 225, made up mainly of peasants from various towns within Matanzas Province, arrived at Central Australia around 8:30 a.m. They amounted to some 300 militiamen, albeit poorly armed and trained. Still, Fernández ordered them to advance and take Pálpite.[164]

The paratroopers at Pálpite became alarmed when scouts reported a large enemy force moving toward them. Not only had they been unable to raise the Second Battalion on the radio, but they took the approach of Castro's men to mean that the supposed strongpoint to their north had been readily eliminated. Their anxiety eased a bit when the B-26 flown by Matías Farías appeared and attacked the enemy column coming toward them, stopping its advance.[165] The air support was a testament to the dedication of the brigade pilots. By this time the only pair of B-26s patrolling the beachhead, flown by Farías and Mario Zúñiga, had reached their nominal maximum loiter time of two hours.[166]

When Fernández got word of the attack, he rescinded the order for the peasant militiamen to take Pálpite. They were instead reassigned to guard the culverts along the causeway lest the enemy try to blow them up to impede further counteroffensives.[167] Ironically, unbeknownst to Fernández, at that very moment the enemy force at Pálpite was pulling out. Paratroop commander Tomás Cruz told his men following the aborted militia advance that their unit was totally inadequate to defend their position. They would therefore abandon it and seek to link up with the Second Battalion at Playa Larga. Cruz's paratroopers then hastily boarded two confiscated trucks and headed south.[168]

* * * *

By early morning, a general plan of attack had been formulated at Point One to counter the invasion. Fernández was to lead an advance toward Playa Larga from Central Australia and Filiberto Olivera would do likewise toward Girón from Covadonga. Castro also wanted units to advance along the coastal trail that extended west from Juraguá, across the bay from Cienfuegos. At 8:13 a.m. he called Central Army headquarters in Santa Clara and instructed Almeida to arrange for the coastal advance. While on the phone Castro was informed of reports of yet another paratroop drop near Horquita, on the road to Yaguaramas. "Go out and fight those isolated paratroopers because they are condemned to die. The paratroopers at Horquita are condemned to die!" Castro hollered. "Use whatever militia forces you have against them." Almeida, as it turned out, had already sent Rebel Army commander René de los Santos to take charge at Yaguaramas and direct the offensive south of there.[169]

Following the phone call, Captain Orlando Pupo was summoned to Santa Clara headquarters and ordered to lead a militia battalion from Cienfuegos along the coast toward Girón. Francisco Ciutat, the Spanish-Soviet adviser on Almeida's general staff, explained to Pupo the objective of his assignment. "Your mission is not to attack the mercenaries," he said, using the officially sanctioned term for the invaders, "but to tickle them from that direction so that they know we have forces on that front."[170]

* * * *

Fernández would not allow the men from the Militia Leaders' School to dismount from their trucks when they arrived at Central Australia around 9:00 a.m. He ordered them to keep going and take Pálpite.[171] The trucks had gone less than three miles when they were attacked by Faría's B-26. At least one man was killed: thinking the plane was friendly, he stood in the middle of the road waving skyward just before the B-26 opened fire.[172] Somewhere south of Pálpite, Tomás Cruz's paratroopers had seen the unknown plane pass overhead and jumped off their trucks into the thicket. Cruz then decided that they would not continue to Playa Larga without knowing what was happening there. He therefore sent two volunteers to scout ahead while the rest of the unit stayed hidden in the brush.[173]

At 9:18 a.m. Fernández called Castro and informed him about the latest thwarted attempt to capture Pálpite. "In thirty to forty minutes a jet will arrive to protect that road there," Fernández heard when Castro called him back ten minutes later. He had personally ordered that the jet be sent to deal with, in his words, "a B-26 really fucking things up" along the route of advance.[174]

* * * *

Since daybreak, FAR pilots had pressed their attacks on the invasion fleet. At 8:26 a.m. Castro had reiterated his high expectations for them during a phone call to Curbelo at the San Antonio airbase. "Attack the ships without letup," he enjoined his personally appointed air operations director. "Tomorrow we will shoot down planes, but today we are going to sink ships. Sink ships!"[175]

With the *Houston* out of commission, the aerial attacks now concentrated on the vessels off the coast of Girón. The landing of the last remaining troops was in progress at 9:00 a.m. when a T-33 flown by Álvaro Prendes arrived.

Prendes selected one of the LCUs nearing shore and dove on the unwary vessel at full throttle from 3,000 feet up. At close range he unleashed his four underwing rockets and then leveled off and skimmed the surface of the water for some distance before climbing back up to altitude. With the rockets now expended, he positioned the T-33 for a follow up strafing attack. A stream of bullets rushed up toward him this time as he made the power dive, surprise no longer on his side. Prendes unleashed "an interminable burst" of machine gun fire and again levelled off over the water. By his own reckoning, however, "overconfidence had now set in," and he initiated his second vertical climb within range of the LCU's antiaircraft fire. A sudden sharp blow made his plane shudder and, realizing it had been hit, he immediately set course for San Antonio. Luckily for him, the projectile that struck the aircraft had only disabled its right brake, and he managed to make a safe landing.[176]

The LCU Prendes attacked did not sustain significant damage, and to those aboard the sight of the retreating damaged plane—which they were sure had "exploded in the distance"—brought great cheerfulness. "An incredible, unbounded, indescribable, delirious joy came over us," remarked Manuel Penabaz, who was on the vessel. "We seemed like children, many rolling on the floor like crazy men. It was revenge." They reached Girón "[f]ull of optimism" shortly after 9:00 a.m. along with the rest of the soldiers who had been on the cargo ships.[177]

With the landing of the troops finally at an end, all three LCUs started to converge on the *Río Escondido*, about a mile offshore, to begin unloading it. Still aboard the freighter was most of the cargo intended to supply the invasion force during its first ten days ashore as well as the vitally important primary communications trailer. The trailer's radio equipment was to be the main means for San Román to communicate with his field units as well as JMTIDE and CIA headquarters in the United States. So crucial for communications was the equipment that a backup trailer was also carried aboard the *Atlántico*.[178] Castro's pilots, however, were about to deal another decisive blow to the invasion plans.

Two Sea Furies and a B-26 had taken off from San Antonio at approximately 9:00 a.m. headed for the area along different paths.[179] Carreras, in one of the Sea Furies, was first to arrive. From on high he could see the stranded *Houston* looking "like a mortally wounded great fish" and, in front of Girón, an even larger ship that he chose as his target. Unbeknownst to the pilot, it was the *Río Escondido*. Diving down on his prey, Carreras fired all eight rockets under the plane's wings dead center into the middle of the large vessel.[180] A fire erupted among the two hundred barrels of vehicle and aviation fuel stored on deck and began to spread quickly. Unable to do anything, the crew of the stricken ship jumped into the water to escape the fast-developing inferno. Within minutes the ship exploded with a thunderous roar, releasing a huge fireball and mushroom cloud that rose high into the sky. To Oliva in Playa Larga, it seemed as if an atomic bomb had exploded over Girón.[181] The *Blagar* rushed to rescue the men in the water, as did the frogmen and others ashore, using whatever boats were available. Amazingly, none of the ship's crew was killed.[182]

Carreras overhead became so embroiled "enjoying the spectacle" that he was oblivious to Mario Zúñiga's B-26 closing in on him from behind. When a hail of bullets struck the Sea Fury, Carreras immediately took evasive action and headed for San Antonio. Just then Gustavo Bourzac appeared in the other Sea Fury and began attacking the ships. Matías Farías, who had now arrived on the scene, took off after Carreras's damaged fighter and Zúñiga turned his attention to Bourzac.[183] Zúñiga and Bourzac proceeded to engaged in a series of "scissor" maneuvers, each trying to get behind the other. Despite the much greater maneuverability of the Sea Fury, Zúñiga's greater experience as a pilot got the better of his rookie rival. Bourzac eventually opted for pulling out of the dogfight and setting course for San Antonio.[184]

The violent maneuvers had critically taxed Zúñiga's fuel reserves. He thus informed Farías, who had returned to the area after fruitlessly pursuing Carreras, of his immediate departure. So critical was Zúñiga's fuel situation that he was forced to make an emergency landing in Grand Cayman Island.[185] Farías fuel situation must also have been dire by then, but he opted to stay anyway, perhaps planning to divert elsewhere at the last possible moment.

A FAR B-26 flown by Jacques Lagas, a Chilean pilot flying for Castro, was the third aircraft to arrive over the waters off the coast off Girón and begin attacking the ships. Farías claims he spotted the enemy bomber and went after it while Lagas claims the opposite happened. Whatever the case, both aircraft became embroiled in a fierce dogfight in which Farías ended up getting the upper hand by seizing a position on his opponent's tail. Despite unsubstantiated claims by both pilots—Farías claiming to have shot down Lagas and Lagas to have mortally damaged Farías's plane—both agree that the intervention of a T-33 concluded the episode. The T-33, flown by Alberto Fernández, scored several hits on the brigade bomber, forcing Farías to attempt an emergency landing on the Girón airstrip. Out of control, the stricken plane hit the left side of the runway at more than 140 miles per hour and broke apart. Farías miraculously survived, but crewman Eddy Gónzalez died in the crash.[186]

What was left of the *Río Escondido* disappeared beneath the sea at 9:30 a.m., just as San Román was reporting that the airstrip at Girón was ready for use.[187] The sinking marked a pivotal point for the invasion. Shortly before 10:00 a.m., Captain Ryberg aboard the *Blagar* ordered all the remaining ships out to sea, including the damaged *Barbara J*, which was still sailing away from the Bay of Pigs.[188] None of the cargo aboard the freighters had made it ashore.[189] What had been offloaded from the LCUs represented (tonnage wise) only about 25 percent of the seaborne materiel—including vital radio equipment, ammunition, and medical supplies—earmarked to initially go ashore.[190] Ryberg informed San Román by radio of the decision to leave but assured him that they would come back that night to unload supplies.[191]

* * * *

By 9:00 a.m., William Selva and the ten other men with him had set up a defensive position near Jocuma, about a mile south of the Covadonga sugar mill that Castro had ordered him to defend at all costs. Their heaviest weapon consisted of a Browning automatic rifle. The small contingent of army, police, and militia volunteers was all that Selva had been able to wrest from Aguada de Pasajeros, where preparations for the town's own defense were in full swing. Now, determined to carry out Castros order, they took cover as best they could just north of the curve where paratroopers had landed.[192] In fact, however, as previously mentioned, the paratroopers had no intention of advancing on Covadonga; their aim was to proceed south and establish a strong point at Muñoz Canal.[193]

By midmorning, according to plan, Roberto San Román arrived at San Blas from Girón with reinforcements. He had brought with him two of the M-41 tanks and one company from the Fourth Battalion plus a battery of the highly prized 4.2-inch mortars. One of the M-35 gun trucks that had carried the reinforcements to San Blas subsequently went north to assist the paratroopers at the drop zone near Jocuma.[194]

Selva and his men heard the loud engine of the approaching truck just before a torrent of incoming fire started hitting their position. The paratroopers, aware of their presence, took advantage of the arriving reinforcement to rake them with machine gun and recoilless rifle salvos. Before long, a Rebel Army soldier on the other side lay dying, and Selva's small band retreated.[195]

* * * *

Interrogations of the 150 prisoners being held at Girón had yielded little by way of useful military intelligence. Nevertheless, more than 50 of them, including militia members, had volunteered to help in whatever way they could. Valerio Rodríguez was not one of them. Rodríguez, wearing his militia-style literacy teacher's uniform, was defiant when Manuel Artime spoke to him about their coming to free Cuba from communism. "I'm a communist," the boy brazenly stated. He listened as Artime expounded on the wrongs of communism but remained steadfast. "My teachers and my father tell me different. I believe them. You are mistaken," he told his dejected would-be persuader.[196]

Out of radio communication with his units, San Román was in the
dark about the situation in the different sectors of the beachhead. He
had dispatched messengers to his various field commanders and could
do nothing but await their return. At 10:00 a.m., however, a weak radio
connection was established with Playa Larga, and the brigade commander
got his first news of the situation there. Oliva informed him that they had
been in combat with the enemy since landing. The report surprised San
Román. The CIA's intelligence information, on which the deployment of
his forces was predicated, suggested that attacks from enemy forces—when
they *eventually* came—would fall on the northeast and eastern sectors of
the beachhead. Yet he was now being told that substantial resistance had
been encountered immediately where it had been least expected. It was
still one more inauspicious development. Oliva added that he had had
no communication with the Fifth Battalion or the paratroopers to the
north and requested reinforcements, including a tank, and ammunition.
San Román assured his second-in-command that they would be sent but
advised him that the surviving ships with their supplies had all left, supposedly to return that night. After the conversation ended, San Román
ordered a tank with a squad from the Fourth Battalion and two M-35 gun
trucks loaded with ammunition to go to Oliva by way of the coastal road.[197]

* * * *

Fidel Castro was oblivious to the military expectations of the CIA. The
militia force he had placed near Playa Larga shortly before the invasion
had given him a tactical edge not foreseen by the agency planners. He
now intended to maintain "at all costs," as he told Fernández, a foothold
on the side of the swamp the enemy sought to occupy.[198]

Eager to get on with the mission of taking Pálpite, Fernández grew
increasingly impatient waiting for the arrival of the jet Castro had promised him. When ten o'clock came and went with no T-33 in sight, the captain decided to wait no longer. He ordered Lieutenant Nelson González,
in charge of the battalion of militia leaders, to move his men south by
truck and seize the settlement. The few hundred men of MNR Battalion
227 who had just recently arrived marched on foot behind them. This
time no brigade aircraft intervened, and with no paratroopers to oppose
them, Castro's men entered Pálpite without resistance.[199]

Fernández communicated the news to Castro just before 11:00 a.m., much to the elation of *El Comandante.* "We have already won!" Castro cried out. "We have already won the war! We have sunk two [*sic*] of their ships . . . and if they did not realize that they had to defend Pálpite they are lost."[200] As recorded in the Point One transcriptions, he then ordered Fernández to "continue advancing toward Soplillar," a settlement about three and a half miles southeast of Pálpite. Soplillar featured a small airstrip, but its main tactical importance was the backtrail that extended southeasterly from there. Five miles away, the path intersected another going southwest that led to Caleta del Rosario, a location on the coastal road between Playa Larga and Girón. The circuit thus offered a potential way to circumvent Playa Larga and divide the brigade forces.[201]

Fernández immediately dispatched one company from the Militia Leaders' Battalion to occupy Soplillar in unison with the men of Battalion 227. The latter battalion was to continue on to Caleta del Rosario by way of the backtrails and set up a blocking position there.[202]

* * * *

Anticipating a strong attack from the direction of Cienfuegos, San Román had sent the Third Battalion overland to the vicinity of Playa Morena, about a mile east of Girón. It was nowhere near the position the battalion had been intended to occupy at Caleta Redonda (Green Beach), nineteen miles farther to the east, but San Román feared that the unit would be out of radio contact at that distance.[203]

Meanwhile, at the airport in Cienfuegos, Orlando Pupo was busy organizing the 400 men of MNR Battalion 326 that he was to lead toward Girón by way of the coastal trail. Suddenly, at approximately 11:00 a.m., the operation ground to a halt when a B-26 bomber flew over and dropped bombs, setting some of the awaiting trucks on fire. The militiamen scattered wide and far seeking cover, and Pupo had his work cut out regrouping them afterward.[204] Ironically, the strike had not even been planned. The bomber, flown by Ignacio Rojas, was one of a pair of B-26s that had arrived over the retreating ships more than an hour earlier. One of Rojas's wing tanks had failed to fully release and, despite several attempts to eject it, continued to hang nose down from the plane's right wing. The increased drag significantly impacted the plane's

maneuverability, and flight leader Gustavo Ponzoa ordered his companion aircraft to return to JMTIDE. Rojas, however, was intent on making
use of his bombload before heading back to Nicaragua, so he asked and
received permission from the *Blagar* to bomb the Cienfuegos airport.[205]

* * * *

Commander René de los Santos and his four-man staff arrived at Yaguaramas around 11:00 a.m. only to find no forces there to command. Unbeknownst to him, the arrival of Tomassevich and the men of Battalion 117
had been delayed by reports (all of which eventually proved false) of paratroop landings near towns along the way. Suddenly, as De los Santos was
on the phone to Almeida, a red Chrysler sped by and kept going despite
attempts to flag it down. The car's eager driver was Captain Victor Dreke,
a veteran of the war against Batista's army and later the anti-Castro insurgents in the Escambray Mountains. He had been on his way to a new post-
ing in Oriente Province but, upon hearing about landings at Girón, had
driven to the area on his own initiative. Dreke drove south past Yaguaramas until he came across a small group of militiamen who had skirmished
with the paratroopers nearby and assumed command of the men.[206]

An equally unlikely arrival showed up south of Jocuma about an hour
later. Félix Duque had risen to the rank of commander during the war
against Batista but had since been put in charge of a large state farm fifty
miles north of Girón. After learning of the invasion, he had rushed to
the area carrying the bazooka and some shells he had stored since his
guerrilla days.[207] "Where are they?" Duque asked Selva when the two met
near the position now occupied by the small band of defenders. "There,
behind that curve," Selva told him, glad to see the bazooka-wielding
Duque and the few other men he had brought along. "Well, let's go find
them!" came the reply. Joined by the others, they made their way down
the center of the road when suddenly the M-35 truck that had come
from San Blas appeared and opened up with its .50 caliber machine gun.
The other men took shelter in the ditches paralleling the causeway, but
Duque stood behind an old concrete wall, pointed his bazooka up as if
it were a mortar, and fired. The weapon's rocket hit with a tremendous
explosion five or six yards from the truck, which immediately made a
hasty U-turn and disappeared behind the curve.[208]

NOON—4:00 PM

By noon, still lacking reinforcements, Oliva must have been growing increasingly weary. Without such reinforcements and additional ammunition, an attack from the north by a sizable force could prove disastrous. Able finally to communicate with the *Houston,* grounded five miles away, he ordered Montero to reorganize his men and lead them to Playa Larga as soon as possible.[209] As it happened, however, many of the surviving men of the Fifth Battalion (a total of nine died during the air attacks or drowned trying to swim ashore[210]) were as disinclined to fight as their commander. Desertions, a common practice among Batista's soldiers during the anti-guerrilla war,[211] started almost immediately after the battalion reached shore. Such was the case with Luis Iglesias who had been corporal in the former army. Ordered to man a machine gun position against possible enemy attack, Iglesias decided that he had had enough and chose to flee accompanied by twelve to fifteen others. By late afternoon his group of deserters had grown to some two dozen men.[212]

Meanwhile, the brigade reinforcements sent from Girón had been held up seven miles from Playa Larga by a militia platoon from Battalion 339 stationed at Caleta del Rosario. The platoon members, who had been there since before the landings, initially mistook the approaching tank at the head of the column for one of theirs. They soon realized their mistake when the tank blasted a small building next to the road. In the ensuing firefight, two militiamen were cut down by .50 caliber machine gun fire from one of the convoy's gun trucks. Several others in the platoon were wounded, and when the skirmish finally ended, those who had not managed to escape by boat or on foot were taken prisoner.[213]

Fortunately for Oliva and his men, the brigade bombers continued to hinder the enemy forces north of Playa Larga. When two B-26s arrived over the area at about 12:15 p.m., the pair split up. Pilot Raúl Vianello flew toward Central Australia and blasted a roadside machine gun nest on the way there. Near the sugar mill, he and crewmate Demetrio Pérez spotted a four-vehicle convoy moving south. An ambulance with a red cross painted on its roof led the pack.[214] The militiamen with the vehicles stood on the road waving their caps and guns in the air when the plane they mistook as friendly swooped over them on its first pass. They continued to wave as it started to make a second pass until the B-26 opened fire with its .50 caliber machine guns and let off two rockets, causing the ambulance to explode.[215] Simultaneously, just a few miles to the south, the other B-26 flown by Antonio Soto attacked the troops in Pálpite and Soplillar and put an 85 mm field artillery gun out of action.[216]

FAR pilot Álvaro Prendes could see columns of smoke rising as he approached Soplillar in his T-33. Spotting Soto's B-26 turning away from the area, he set off after it. Soto also spotted the approaching jet and, as Prendes feared, sped toward a bank of low clouds. The outcome of the encounter now hinged on whether Soto could duck into the clouds before Prendes could close within firing range. At the last possible second before the B-26 disappeared, a burst of machine gun fire from the T-33 found its mark, and the bomber's left engine caught fire. Prendes continued to circle the cloud bank for a while but was unable to find what he presumed was a mortally wounded prey.[217] Soto, in fact, managed to fly on despite his damaged engine and reached Grand Cayman, where he made an emergency landing.[218]

Not far away another air chase was taking place. Vianello's B-26 was heading south following his ground attack when Rafael del Pino arrived in a T-33 and saw the bomber fly by in the distance. Del Pino radioed Luis Silva, whose B-26 was also in the area, and determined that the bomber in front of him was not Silva's. At that point a single thought possessed his mind: "shoot it down." Stealthily, Del Pino sneaked up behind the B-26 and slowly closed in for the kill. At 800 yards he could make out the blue stripes on the wings that unequivocally identified it as an enemy aircraft. Then, with "shaky legs and sweaty palms," he fired at point blank range. The bullets ripped into his victim, tearing off pieces that flew back and struck the T-33. Del Pino immediately pulled back hard on the plane's control stick to gain altitude. As he came around for a second pass, he could see that the B-26 was on fire and beginning to break up.[219] Struggling to control the stricken plane as smoke poured into the cockpit, Vianello spotted a destroyer nearby and steered toward it. "Bail out!" he ordered Pérez. "We'll meet down there," the pilot told his crewmate pointing toward the water then wishing him "good luck." Seconds later, as Pérez watched floating down on his parachute, the flaming bomber crashed into the sea. The USS *Murray* subsequently rescued Pérez, but Vianello was lost and presumed dead.[220]

* * * *

The fleeing invasion ships south of Girón had been instructed to stop and regroup seventeen miles out. However, only the *Blagar*, the three LCUs following it, and the *Barbara J* did so. The *Atlántico* and *Caribe* continued moving south as fast as their engines could take them and would not respond to radio calls.[221]

Silva, flying a B-26 along the coast, spotted the two LCIs in the distance sometime past noon. The forty-six-year-old, nicknamed *Abuelo* (Grandpa) by the younger pilots, was not in good health and told Del Pino before taking off that this would be his last mission. Even though the vessels were now in international waters, the senior pilot and Bourzac, flying a Sea Fury as his wingman, went after them. Del Pino, still in the area after shooting down Vianello, also rushed to the scene after Silva informed him about the ships.[222]

The machine guns on both LCIs opened fire on the B-26 approaching them at low altitude. Silva fired two rockets at the *Blagar*, both of which fell short of the target, then sought to gain altitude. But as the bomber rose in the air it was caught in the crossfire between the two vessels and exploded. The B-26 became a fireball from which pieces of metal flew violently in all directions then rained down onto the surface of the water and the deck of the *Blagar*. Silva and three other crewmen on the plane were killed. Bourzac, having witnessed the macabre spectacle, did not press his luck. He departed the area quickly after making a short strafing pass at the *Barbara J* and unsuccessfully firing his rockets at the LCUs from high altitude.[223] Del Pino claims that he also attacked one of the ships and scored a hit with a rocket.[224] However, no other account substantiates that claim.

If Castro was informed of the loss of Silva and his crew when he spoke to Curbelo at 12:47 p.m., it certainly provoked no expression of sympathy from him. His only concern, as indicated by the phone call transcription, was to press Curbelo for assurances that the vessels attacked were not American navy ships. He then ordered that another raid be launched against them.[225] By then, however, the two LCIs along with the LCUs had renewed their journey south seeking safety from air attacks farther out to sea.[226]

* * * *

At half past noon the paratroopers defending the Babiney strongpoint, eight miles south of Yaguaramas, were under attack by two companies of militia from Battalion 117. Less than an hour earlier, the battalion (minus one of its companies) had reached Yaguaramas on the way to Covadonga. Tomassevich had decided to turn the First and Second Companies over to De los Santos and Dreke to deal with these paratroopers while he continued to Covadonga with the rest of the troop.[227]

Now, as 200 militiamen advanced down the road from Yaguaramas, a fierce firefight broke out between them and the eighteen men manning the strongpoint. Repeated shots from paratrooper Ricardo Sánchez's recoilless rifle—the sight for which had somehow not been included with the weapon—kept missing, seriously reducing the effective firepower of the outnumbered defenders. To complicate matters further, the unit's radio was hit, and the men were out of radio communication with Del Valle in San Blas. A runner was thus sent there to request immediate reinforcements.[228]

Unbeknownst to the paratroopers, however, a brigade tank and eighteen infantrymen equipped with an M-20 "super bazooka" were already on the way to Babiney from San Blas. When the tank suddenly appeared behind the strongpoint and fired in the direction of the militia, the paratroopers mistakenly thought they had been outflanked and turned on it. One of them took aim at the vehicle with a bazooka, but the weapon failed to fire. Sánchez, although he lacked antitank shells, then shot at it with his recoilless rifle and missed. It was only when the brigade uniforms of the arriving men were spotted that the friendly fire standoff ended. The combined force then went on the attack. Faced with a concerted counteroffensive by the tank and reinforced paratroopers, the militia force retreated.[229]

* * * *

By early afternoon Castro had made the decision to go in person to the theater of operations. His last phone conversation before departing Havana was at 1:48 p.m. when he spoke to commander Filiberto Olivera at Covadonga. Olivera had arrived there to take charge just a few minutes prior to the call, having previously gone to Central Australia by mistake and told Fernández he had come to relieve him. Upon learning of the mix-up, Castro had set Olivera straight about his destination and assignment. From Covadonga, Olivera reported that there were no forces in the settlement to command. He was assured that troops, including a battery of mortars and another of 85 mm field guns, were on their way. It was only after the conversation ended that Olivera learned from the locals about Duque and the other men already fighting south of his location.[230]

Before midafternoon, with Chief of Staff Sergio del Valle (another member of M-26-7's leadership core) left in charge at Point One, Castro and his entourage were headed for the Zapata region. An odd caravan of ex-guerrillas in green fatigues aboard appropriated Oldsmobile deluxe cars wound its way through the streets of Havana toward the island's main highway. Castro traveled in a white 1960 sedan accompanied by General Staff Chief of Operations Flavio Bravo (also one of the M-26-7 elite) and others. The rest of the group rode in a blue 1959 model with distinctive fins and oval-shaped taillights.[231]

* * * *

The Fourth and Light Infantry Companies of Battalion 117, along with a 120 mm mortar battery, reached Covadonga at around 2:30 p.m. Tomassevich turned the force over to Olivera, then, as he had been ordered, headed to Cienfuegos to take charge of defensive preparations there.[232]

News of the arrival of reinforcements brought great joy to William Selva and his small band of defenders near Jocuma. Selva's joy became all the greater when he learned that Evelio Saborit, whom he had last seen on the outskirts of Girón, had made it back to Covadonga along with the rest of his platoon. As Saborit later recounted, they had managed to elude capture by making their way through the swamp past enemy-held positions, including a well-entrenched one around the Muñoz Canal.[233]

When the new units reached Jocuma, the work of setting up the mortar battery quickly got under way. Soon the Light Infantry Company was ordered to continue moving south toward the enemy. Its members formed up in double file and started down the roadway behind a jeep driven by the company's commander. The sight of a plane overhead, which had been circling the area for several minutes, comforted the men as they marched. On the aircraft's tail was painted a Cuban flag, and the troop supposed that it had been sent there to protect them.[234] In was, in fact, a brigade B-26 flown by pilot Crispín García. García had departed JMTIDE along with another B-26 flown by Miguel Carro at 11:30 a.m. Although the available evidence is muddled, it appears that both García and Carro had been assigned to protect a C-46 that was to land at Girón and deliver ammunition. The bombers were armed only with their nose-mounted machine guns in the hope that making them lighter would improve their chances if engaged in air combat. Although Carro had aborted in flight due to mechanical problems, García had flown on alone to await the arrival of the C-46 being piloted by Eduardo Ferrer.[235]

The militiamen were taken completely by surprise when García's plane dove down on them, all eight of its machine guns blasting away. "Like a strong downpour coming toward you," is how one of them described the torrent of bullets that swept along the ground in their direction. Even as others sought to take cover, the company commander remained seated in the jeep utterly transfixed by the shocking spectacle, his hands tightly gripping the steering wheel. Someone got to the petrified man just before the bullets did and pulled him out. In the mayhem, those seeking to duck into one of the roadside ditches found their way blocked by a barbed wire fence. Fortunately for them, the attack did not last long because García evidently wanted to save his ammunition for the C-46's arrival. Four or five of the men in the company were wounded, one of whom later died.[236]

Following the air attack, a truck carrying ammunition moved ahead of the column and was spotted by a nearby brigade picket. A shell fired from a recoilless rifle hit the vehicle and it instantly burst into flames. Of the three men inside two managed to escape, but Sergeant Marcelino Gutiérrez became trapped and could not be rescued. William Selva, who witnessed the event, described how Gutiérrez begged, screaming, to be put out of his misery as he burned alive. Whether anyone did, Selva does not say.[237]

Mortar fire began hitting the brigade strongpoint at Muñoz Canal around 3:00 p.m. The explosions from the 120 mm rounds could be heard back at San Blas. Huddled in their foxholes, some of the twenty or so men manning the position began to pray. Requests from the defenders for air support went unanswered.[238] Although García in his B-26 continued to loiter for at least two hours awaiting the arrival of the C-46, he did not engage in any more ground attacks. Finally, almost out of fuel and with Ferrer's plane nowhere in sight, he set course for the Naval Air Station in Key West to make an emergency landing.[239] His wait, as it turned out, had been futile. The course of events at Playa Larga would ensure that the C-46 would never make it to Girón.

* * * *

Under orders from Fernández—who would forever after insist it was what Castro wanted—around 2:00 p.m. the Militia Leaders' Battalion set out from Pálpite to take Playa Larga.[240] The move, as Castro would later observe, "came as a surprise" to him when he learned about it. "It never even crossed my mind," he said about the matter fifty years later, "to order those people to advance at that time because neither the tanks nor the antiaircraft artillery had yet arrived."[241] Indeed, his assertion is supported by the record. Despite Fernández's statements to the contrary, Castro, as recorded in the Point One transcriptions, clearly ordered him to move on Soplillar when the two spoke at 10:53 a.m. after the capture of Pálpite. Playa Larga was not even mentioned. Perhaps Fernández became confused when at 12:37 p.m. Castro told him, "Let's see if we can be in possession of everything there by dawn." If so, he failed to heed Castro's words when the two again spoke less than an hour later at 1:11 p.m. "Don't worry about Playa Larga. Install the 120 [mm heavy mortars] as soon as they arrive."[242]

Whether due to confusion or overeagerness on the part of Fernández, the convoy carrying several hundred of the militia leaders was ordered to advance. Before 2:30 p.m. the head of the column halted near Caletón, and the men aboard the vehicles started getting out. They were completely unaware that well-camouflaged brigade positions were just a few hundred yards away.[243]

Máximo Cruz had seen the convoy approaching and informed Oliva, who immediately called off his plan of sending a squad with two trucks to pick up men of the Fifth Battalion. A tank commanded by Fernando Torres Mena and the other reinforcements from Girón had finally arrived by then and were in position when the militiamen appeared. Cruz waited until the enemy troops had assembled around their mortars and other weapons before giving the order to open fire. Recoilless rifles, heavy machine guns, and the 76 mm tank cannon then ripped into Castro's men. "[Y]ou could see them flying up in the air," Cruz recalled.[244] At some point, the shell loading mechanism of the tank cannon failed, and the crew had to use a knife to pry out the spent round before they could reload. That slowed down the gun's firing rate, but it continued to take a toll on the militia huddling and firing back from within the thicket on either side of the road.[245] As was characteristic of the whole area, even outside the limits of the swamp, the thick vegetation bounding the road-way made it impossible for a larger force to bring its full strength to bear. Direct ground combat was essentially limited to those in the front ranks.[246]

The fighting had been raging for some thirty minutes when two brigade B-26s flown by José Crespo and Osvaldo Piedra arrived and made radio contact with Oliva. After making an initial pass over the enemy column, one of the pilots reported back that it appeared to consist of some 700 men in sixty to seventy vehicles. "Give it to them!" Oliva told the airmen.[247]

"It was terrible, terrible," said militiaman Félix Borrego of the ensuing aerial attack, which lasted over twenty minutes and, in the words of Fernández, "caused numerous casualties."[248] Many of those casualties were no doubt the result of the deception used by the brigade bombers which rocked their wings at the men below on their first pass. The faux salute, in combination with the aircraft's FAR markings, lured the militiamen to stand on the open road waving back.[249] They were completely caught by surprise when the bombers turned back and opened fire. Castro's press later called it a "dirty tactic."[250] The characterization conveniently ignored that just such a ruse had been used by the Revolution's Luis Silva when he had attacked Batista soldiers from a plane bearing Cuban navy markings

As the planes continued their attack, "the most despairing thing," militiaman Borrego noted, "was that we had nothing [in the way of anti-aircraft weapons] with which to shoot back, and our planes were nowhere to be seen."[251] The battered militia was beating a retreat to Pálpite when FAR planes finally arrived: Prendes and Del Pino in T-33s and Douglas Rudd in a Sea Fury. Crespo and Piedra, their ammunition spent, were just then departing the area.

Prendes went off in pursuit of Piedra's plane. Positioning himself behind the B-26, he made at least three firing passes past the slower bomber, each time either missing or failing to critically damage it. With only enough ammunition remaining for one more attempt, the FAR pilot closed in on his target and fired. The bomber's left engine ignited and quickly flared up into a huge blaze that engulfed the whole aircraft. Although the accounts of Prendes and Del Pino differ in several respects, both agree that, seconds before the flaming bomber hit the water, the plane's navigator/observer (José Fernández) jumped out in a parachute.[252] Whether he survived the jump is not known, but he was never seen again and was presumed dead.[253]

Del Pino, in pursuit of Crespo's B-26, was less successful than Prendes. At one point he almost crashed into the sea trying to shoot down the enemy plane, which desperately darted about, skimming the surface of the water. When the T-33 ran out of ammunition, Rudd in his Sea Fury took up the chase. The prop fighter, equipped with 20 mm cannon, made three passes on Crespo's plane, managing on the third pass to hit one of its engines, which began to smolder.[254]

Essex pilot Jim Forgy spotted the smoke from his A4D Skyhawk some twenty miles away and raced toward it followed by his wingman. Closing in, he saw the Sea Fury sitting on the tail of the damaged bomber and decided to take action. He radioed a request to the carrier for permission to engage and, while awaiting a response, made his presence known to Rudd by flying near the Sea Fury. When the *Essex* radioed back denying his request, the wily navy man did more than just curse. He brought his right wing within a few feet of the Rudd's left wing and, for some two minutes, resorted to "flying formation on him."[255] Rudd, exercising the better part of valor—albeit alleging that his ammunition had run out—broke off and, flying low over the water, headed back to San Antonio.[256]

About thirty miles south of Cuba, Eduardo Ferrer's C-46 was on course to Girón when a mayday call came over the radio. Ferrer recognized the voice as that of Lorenzo Pérez, Crespo's crewmate. "Do not enter the area," Crespo himself told Ferrer when the latter reached out on the radio. "Two fighters jumped me. Only a few seconds ago a Sea Fury shot up my left engine, and many of my navigation systems aren't working." One of the B-26's fuel tanks had apparently also been hit, for Crespo also reported that he was losing fuel fast as he headed south. Deciding to abort the landing at Girón, Ferrer also turned south and attempted to fall into formation with the B-26, but neither crew could spot the other's plane. Less than three hours later, still out of sight and now out of fuel, the B-26 ditched into the sea. Neither the aircraft nor its crew was ever seen again.[257]

4:00 PM—8:00 PM

With the invasion clearly floundering from the toll inflicted by FAR planes, at 4:15 p.m. CIA headquarters ordered JMTIDE to "bomb as many airfields as possible at night with fragmentation bombs."[258] The previously unacceptable repeat attack on Cuban airfields was now permissible since the origin of the bombers could "plausibly" be attributed to the captured Girón strip.[259]

At 5:07 p.m. the first of five bombers to be launched over the coming hours took off from JMTIDE headed for the Havana area. Navigator/observer Tomás Afont once again joined pilot Joaquín Varela on the flight, even though they had both flown a combat mission to the beachhead early that morning.[260]

* * * *

Castro's intermediate destination as he headed for the theater of operations was the town of Jovellanos, ninety-five miles from Havana, which was being used as a staging area for the movement of troops. Twice along the way there his two-car motorcade had stopped to give the antiaircraft artillery trailing it a chance to catch up.[261] Ever since his guerrilla days, *El Comandante* had harbored a deep-seated fear of air raids. As told by José Pardo Llada, an old friend and fellow revolutionary from the time, "Fidel Castro was terrified of aerial bombings. Every time a warning cry of 'Airplane!' rang out, the first to run to the air shelter was Castro."[262]

When he finally arrived in Jovellanos at approximately 4:00 p.m., Harold Ferrer, along with the 600 men of the army's First Column (minus its mortar battery, which had gone to the wrong place) were already there.[263] Néstor López Cuba and five T-34/85 tanks were also there waiting. Not enough flatbed trailers had been found in Havana to transport the fifteen armored vehicles López Cuba had been ordered to bring. Thus, another five T-34s and five SU-100 tank destroyers were en route traveling under their own power.[264] The tank battalion commander used the idle time at Jovellanos to drill his inexperienced crews, three-fifths of whom lacked even basic tank operation skills.[265]

In a meeting with both commanders, Castro laid out his plan for artillery-supported offensives along the three roads that ultimately converged at Girón. The principal thrust was to be made from the direction of Pálpite. At 5:00 p.m. Ferrer and López Cuba were to move with their units toward that locality. Jovellanos, some forty miles from the theater of operations, would continue to serve as a staging area for the forces to be used in the assaults. From there they would move out late in the day to avoid air attacks.[266]

By 4:30 p.m. Castro was on the road again. At Jagüey Grande, some thirty road miles south of Jovellanos, he stopped to drink coffee while again waiting for the antiaircraft artillery to catch up.[267] The caravan then traveled the remaining two and a half miles to Central Australia where it arrived sometime around 5:00 p.m. At the sugar mill Castro briefed Captain Fernández on the tanks, infantry, and artillery guns on the way. That very night the captain was to launch a concerted attack to take Playa Larga.[268]

* * * *

Vultures circled above the dead and wounded militiamen on the stretch of road between Pálpite and Caletón. Oliva ordered his men to withhold their fire when around 4:00 p.m. two ambulances followed by a white truck bearing a red cross was seen approaching, ostensibly to pick up the injured. But when troop trucks were spotted in the rear of the convoy, he ordered his men to open fire. The vehicles quickly retreated.[269]

This incursion, along with information he had gleaned from prisoners, must have added to Oliva's wariness that a larger attack on his position was imminent. The deputy brigade commander dispatched a messenger to Girón requesting reinforcements, including more tanks and ammunition, then spoke again on the radio to Montero. He ordered the Fifth Battalion commander to bring his men posthaste to Playa Larga. The only opposition possibly standing in their way, Oliva told him, was a small militia group at Buenaventura armed with a .50 caliber machine gun. In about three hours, Oliva emphasized, he expected the battalion to arrive and be in position to help meet the anticipated enemy attack. Montero replied that they had already "started walking" and "would be there early." However, according to Luis Gónzalez Lalondry, the Fifth Battalion's chief radioman, Montero was still aboard the *Houston* when he spoke to Oliva. In a brief address to his troop after he finally went ashore, Montero briefly explained the situation and asked for their "utmost cooperation" in accomplishing the objective of linking up with the Second Battalion. None of the men said anything when he finished talking, and Lalondry deemed the exhortation uninspired. What the demoralized and bedraggled men desperately needed, the radioman thought, was "an emboldened speech that would restore the lost hopes of those men [and] raise the spirits of that troop." A patrol was sent to scout ahead as the battalion, followed by the crew of the *Houston*, started on the approximately six-and-a-half-mile overland march. They had not gone far, however, when they encountered a battalion soldier who had been wandering around by himself. The man alarmingly reported that a great number of militia and tanks were making their way toward them from Buenaventura. Taking the report at face value and without informing Oliva, Montero halted the march and ordered the men to take up defensive positions.[270]

Oliva, meanwhile, had gone scouting for the best place to set up a defensive position while he waited for reinforcements to arrive. He settled on the northernmost part of the Caletón Triangle where the road from Central Australia splits into two branches. A billboard from INRA (the Spanish acronym for National Institute for Agrarian Reform) on that very spot hailed the construction of the new causeway as one of its achievements. It was the same spot to which the militiamen of Battalion 339 had retreated after their initial firefight with brigade forces. A five-foot deep excavation pit near the junction provided a ready-made trench. The site, a smaller triangular traffic island within the larger Caletón Triangle, became nominally known among the brigade men as "la rotonda" (the traffic circle—a short "turnaround" byway connects the two road branches some fifty yards beyond the point where they diverge). Oliva recognized that the position offered a great tactical advantage. Fire could be concentrated on the spearhead of any force advancing down the narrow road bordered on either side by almost impassable vegetation.[271]

* * * *

By 6:00 p.m. a recently arrived battery of 85 mm field artillery had joined the 120 mm mortars in pounding the area around Muñoz Canal. "In a few minutes, it became an incessant roar; the blasts of our artillery shook everything all around," remarked William Selva. "The crabs . . . believing that the thunder presaged a downpour, came out of their dark burrows by the hundreds."[272]

The two companies from Battalion 117 already at Jocuma were reinforced by the arrival of Third Company, which had been diverted to deal with alleged paratroop drops elsewhere. As evening set in, the three companies began their advance toward the enemy position to the south. The men traveled by truck unaware of the exact location of the brigade forces. It was a tactical mistake underscoring the lack of proficiency that prevailed among Castro's troops. The paratroopers, who had also received reinforcements that included a tank, were waiting for them. "They let [the militiamen] approach to within a distance our enemies considered prudent and then opened fire on them with every weapon they had," said Selva of the ill-considered advance. A jeep carrying mortar ammunition that had overtaken the column received a direct hit from a recoilless rifle and instantly exploded, killing its occupants. Frenzied men scrambled to get off the trucks. "The gunfire was brutal," said one of them who for a time found himself pinned down by the human stampede. "Bazooka shots darted past the sides of the truck. I have never seen so many bullets fly out like that. It took me aback for a moment, but I quickly got a hold of myself, took cover in the roadside ditch and started firing back." As their casualties mounted, including among those in charge, the militia pulled back. The blundering attempt to overrun the Muñoz Canal strongpoint had failed.[273]

* * * *

Throughout the afternoon, the two companies of Battalion 117 facing the strongpoint at Babiney had kept up their attacks. "They just kept coming down the road in waves—the way the Chinese did in Korea. They were easy targets," said one of the brigade soldiers.[274] By early evening the strongpoint defenders received support from the 4.2-inch mortars. The heavy mortar fire convinced Victor Dreke, in field command of the militia force, to hold off on any more infantry assaults for a time. While the rest of the troop rested, he had his own mortars open fire to soften up the enemy position.[275] Paratroop company commander Néstor Pino realized that the preparatory shelling presaged another infantry attack but had no way of knowing when it would come. When the tank that had been supporting the strongpoint announced it had to leave,[276] Pino decided to pull his men back to the other side of the "bottleneck" south of the swamp. Unaware of the fact, however, Dreke's mortars continued for hours to shell the abandoned position.[277]

* * * *

At 7:00 p.m., as night set in, anxious expectation rose among the men in Girón over the return of the ships. "We knew," said Pepe San Román, "that without the ships we could not make it." The *Blagar* could not be raised on the radio, but San Román had faith that it and the other vessels would return after dark as promised. Marker lights were placed on the beach, and a large group stood by, ready to unload the vital supplies.[278]

As it happened, however, the ships had kept sailing south *away* from Girón right up to nightfall. *Blagar*, along with *Barbara J* and three LCUs, were over sixty-three miles from Girón—well beyond the forty-seven-mile limit for shore-ship communication—when they finally stopped. The *Atlántico* and *Caribe*, on the other hand, steadfastly continued moving south.[279]

* * * *

The reinforcements from Girón arrived at Playa Larga shortly before 7:00 p.m. They consisted of two additional M-41 tanks plus the three available companies of the Fourth Battalion. The men of the armored battalion—nicknamed "Bon-Blin," short for *Batallón Blindado*—had a personal connection with Oliva, who had trained and led them in the Guatemala camps. "I am very happy to have you," he fondly told the troop, "because this is going to be a strong fight."[280]

To defend against a possible rear attack on Playa Larga from the east, one of the newly arrived companies and a squad from Pedro Ávila's G Company were positioned on the coastal road facing Girón. The rest of the force, with nothing held in reserve, was assigned to the defenses against the expected enemy push from the north. Oliva deployed his units in an inverted wedge configuration anchored on the excavation pit 150 feet behind the northeast corner of the Caletón Triangle. The remaining three squads from Ávila's company, with machine gun and recoilless rifle reinforcements from the Heavy Weapons Battalion, were entrenched inside the pit. Luis Acevedo's E Company, along with one of the Fourth Battalion's companies and a tank, was placed on the left wing of the inverted wedge, blocking the road toward Buenaventura. On the right wing, blocking the road toward Playa Larga, Oliva positioned Máximo Cruz's F Company as well as two tanks and the other Bon-Blin company. The Second Battalion's 81 mm mortars, positioned 150 yards behind the front line, were the final piece of the area defense plan. "Don't fire until I give the word," Oliva told the mortar crews.[281]

From the Fifth Battalion, no reinforcements came. The troop had not moved from the spot where three hours earlier the stray soldier had reported to Montero the approach of a large enemy force. It was not until about 7:30 p.m., the time by which they had been expected to arrive in Playa Larga, that the battalion started moving again. The scouting patrol sent out earlier had returned with the news that not a single militiaman stood between them and Buenaventura.[282]

Oliva's force at Caletón totaled less than 370 men.[283] In the coming hours they would be put to a harrowing trial-by-fire against the first major onslaught of Castro's ground forces.

8:00 PM—MIDNIGHT

It was close to 8:00 p.m. when Joaquín Varela's B-26 entered the airspace around San Antonio, shrouded somewhere below in mist and darkness. The sound of muffled explosions and the noise of plane engines instantly created pandemonium among the FAR pilots gathered in the mess hall at the airbase. Just seconds before, the group had been cheerfully gloating over dinner about the toll they had inflicted on the enemy that day. Now, "as if every chair in the mess hall had turned into an ejection seat," they leapt out of them. The blasts of an antiaircraft gun firing from the roof made some think they were under rocket attack. Although the base and surrounding towns were under a blackout, the overhead lights in the room became a source of concern. Unable to find the off switches, the men reached for their side arms and started shooting at the bulbs from under the tables where they had taken cover. To Rafael del Pino, "it looked like a western movie." The hot shell expelled from the gun that put out the last bulb struck the back of a doctor who was also sheltering under the table. His shirt had become wet from a falling water pitcher, and as he screamed that he had been hit, Gustavo Bourzac ran his hands over him in the dark. "Doctor, they've killed you," Bourzac told him, thinking that the wetness came from a hemorrhaging terminal wound. The medical man passed out.

The "misdiagnosis" was corrected following the attack, when it was also discovered that the explosions heard had come from bombs falling on an illuminated chicken farm nearby. Low clouds and the blackout conditions conspired to make even the outlines of the airbase invisible from the air. Another bomber flown by Mario Cortina that arrived a few minutes later had no better luck. Two other pilots assigned to the night operation had aborted and never even reached Cuba. Only one last mission, to be flown by Gonzalo Herrera after midnight, remained.[284]

Not lost on Castro's airmen was the desperation conveyed by the attempted night attacks. "The enemy had felt the brunt of our aerial superiority," Del Pino summarized. "Now they wanted by any means to try to destroy our worn-out airplanes."[285]

* * * *

By 8:00 p.m., the buildup of Castro's forces in and around Pálpite for the offensive to take Playa Larga was reaching a climax. In addition to men from the Militia Leaders' Battalion, they would include 600 troops from the army's First Column, five tanks, four 122 mm artillery batteries, two or three batteries of 85 mm guns and one of 120 mm mortars. A total of fourteen antiaircraft batteries were also allocated to the endeavor.[286] Castro had initially held back two batteries of 122 mm artillery and three of antiaircraft guns at Central Australia, but at 7:00 p.m. he had dispatched them all to Fernández. "I have decided to send the other twelve artillery guns," he wrote Fernández in a note, "because I consider it of the utmost importance to unleash an infernal barrage [on the enemy]."[287]

Castro himself set off for Pálpite about an hour after sending the note. While on the way there, an urgent communication from Point One was delivered to him. It had been couriered over from Central Australia by Bienvenido Pérez, one of Castro's personal bodyguards, who had rushed out to find him. Point One was reporting a possible second landing at Bahía Honda (in Pinar del Río Province), some fifty miles west of Havana. Castro read the message, but continued on to Pálpite nonetheless.[288]

In a green-colored wooden shack next to Palpite's general store, *El Comandante* held court with his field commanders. Leaning over an unfurled map, he laid out his plans for the upcoming battle. The ground assault toward Playa Larga was to begin at midnight following an intense period of artillery fire preparation. This offensive was to be coupled with a thrust along a backtrail deep into enemy-held territory toward the settlement of Cayo Ramona. A short byway that extends east from Cayo Ramona intersects the road linking Girón and San Blas near the small hamlet of Helechal. Castro planned to block this road and thus divide the enemy forces. Undertaking the "backdoor" mission would be the 995 men of MNR Battalion 111 (under way from Havana) commanded by a man Castro affectionately called *Dentista* (dentist). He was Luis Borges, a professional dentist, who during the fight against Batista had joined Castro's guerrillas in the mountains. Administrator Masiques, who had knowledge of the local terrain, was to guide Borges and his men along the tortuous network of backtrails.[289]

With the conference over, Castro did not linger at Pálpite for long. Some forty minutes after arriving, he and his entourage headed back to Central Australia.[290] From there he called Sergio del Valle at Point One to check on the previously reported landing at Bahía Honda. The phone conversation between the two was witnessed by Cuban journalist Luis Báez who was shadowing *El Comandante* on his travels through the area. Del Valle, as reported by Báez, was explicit in reassuring Castro: "there's nothing."[291]

* * * *

More than sixty-three miles south of Girón, with neither the *Caribe* nor the *Atlántico* anywhere in sight, the crew of the *Barbara J* was busy transferring its cargo into one of the LCUs for an anticipated run to the beach that night. The ordnance and other supplies aboard both LCIs (as well as the *Atlántico*) had been intended to equip guerrillas and other friendly forces expected to join the brigade. But now, with most of the mainstay supplies never making it ashore, this secondary cache became vital for the survival of the first-line brigade combatants.[292]

The transfer of cargo was two-thirds complete when an order arrived from CIA headquarters around 9:00 p.m. It directed the *Barbara J* to take supplies to the beach under cover of darkness. However, the *Barbara J* was still taking on water due to the damage it had sustained that morning, and the assignment passed to the *Blagar*.[293]

Even as the *Blagar* started up its engines, it informed headquarters that, given the slow speed of the accompanying LCU and the distance involved, they could not make landfall before daybreak. It was a prospect that did not sit well with the rescued *Río Escondido* survivors aboard. Taking matters into their own hands, with support from some of the *Blagar's* crewmen, they shut down the engines. The mutineers would not hear of going back. "We are lost. This is a disaster. We have been betrayed," they said when Cuban crew chief Juan Cosculluela appealed to their patriotism and sense of duty. "I told them they should be ashamed," Cosculluela later recalled. He reminded the reluctant men that "our brothers were fighting and dying and needed the ammunition." The Americans, he noted, were willing to go back, but they, fellow Cubans, shamefully did not. Not many of the unnerved crewmen were persuaded by the harangue, however. While a few expressed their readiness to return, the majority remained silent. Ultimately, it was the arrival of a reply from CIA headquarters to abort the run that brought the standoff to an end.[294]

* * * *

It must have been around 8:30 p.m. when Rebel Army artillery chief Roberto Milián set out in a radio-equipped jeep from Pálpite to direct the fire of his heavy guns. He only had a rudimentary map of the area and no clear idea of the enemy's location. The jeep continued south through the darkness until the driver spotted the outlines of the INRA billboard at Caletón less than 200 feet away. "Turn around. We have gone too far," Milián told him. Then, from a point some two and a half miles south of his artillery guns, the chief radioed for them to fire spotting rounds. Unsure of his location, however, and without illuminating shells on even parachute flares, he could not readily ascertain the layout of the terrain or where the shells were landing. After radioing back a series of best-guess adjustments, he gave the order to fire for effect and all twenty-four 122 mm guns opened up. By 9:30 p.m., a curtain of exploding shells was systematically sweeping across the area. Batteries of 120 mm mortars and 85 mm field guns also partook in the bombardment.[295]

Along the path to Buenaventura, the men of the Fifth Battalion could hear the explosions just a few miles to the north. From the bay also came the noise of a boat engine moving slowly along the shore. An hour went by before it was discovered that the boat had been sent by Oliva to locate Montero's men and carry away those seriously wounded. One of the two brigade soldiers aboard provided a status report on the situation at Playa Larga. The Second Battalion, he said, had been engaged in battle since landing and was expecting a strong ground attack following the artillery bombardment now under way. Listening to the emissary, radioman Lalondry felt it was incumbent on them "to arrive as soon as possible, given the need to replace the men who had been fighting [there] since early morning."[296] It was a sense of duty clearly not shared by Montero himself judging by his subsequent actions.

* * * *

Since their earlier push on the strongpoint at Muñoz Canal, Castro's forces had been launching probing attacks against the paratroopers and infantrymen there. The multiple attacks had been successfully repelled, but in doing so the brigade men had depleted much of their ammunition.[297]

As the night wore on and the stalemate continued, Castro's forces opted for unleashing an intense preparatory artillery and mortar bombardment before undertaking an all-out ground assault. "I am going to turn the Muñoz Canal into . . . the 'Muñoz Pit,'" Evelio Saborit boasted, as tons of high explosives began flying toward the enemy position at 11:30 p.m.[298]

A runner arrived at San Blas to inform Del Valle about the desperate situation at the strongpoint. José Miguel Battle, a company commander with the Fourth Battalion, heard the grim news and stepped forward to go to the rescue of the beleaguered men. Battle and two of his men—brothers Fidel and Ramón Fuentes—boarded an M-35 truck and headed into the fiery hell. Peering out from inside a ditch, paratrooper Raúl Martínez marveled at the sight of the truck coming from the direction of San Blas with its lights on. "I'm telling you, those guys had balls," he would later say, thankful to Battle and the Fuentes brothers for saving his life. Altogether, some twenty men, including the wounded ones, were evacuated. As of midnight, the Muñoz Canal strongpoint had ceased to be.[299]

8

Tuesday, April 18, 1961

MIDNIGHT—7:00 AM

The artillery fire in preparation for the ground assault toward Playa Larga ceased at midnight. As it turned out, the imprecise spotting for the 122 mm artillery fire had deprived Castro's "infernal barrage" of much of its hellishness. With no clear idea of where the enemy defenses were, Milián had tried to concentrate the bombardment on the beach itself.[1] However, most of the rounds fired over the previous hours had fallen harmlessly into the sea.[2] The smaller caliber shelling did not fare much better. Fernández was dumbfounded when he realized that a battery of 120 mm mortars had been firing unfused rounds, which thus failed to explode.[3] The shelling by a battery of 85 mm field guns emplaced at Soplillar was nullified because a local peasant had given its artillerymen the wrong distance to target. Instead of the three to four miles that separate Soplillar from Playa Larga, the man (who reportedly had escaped from the invaders) told them it was six. Consequently, close to seventy boxes worth of shells ended up being fired into the sea before the crews learned of the error. "I don't know if the peasant became nervous or what his intentions were," one of the frustrated gunners remarked afterward.[4] In total, the brigade casualties from the shelling amounted to three wounded, one seriously enough to require a subsequent leg amputation.[5]

For the brigade men entrenched at Caletón, the cacophony of explosions was soon replaced by the din of mechanized armor growing louder with each passing minute. "The blood chilled in my body upon hearing

103

the rumble of the approaching tanks," recalled infantryman Orlando Atienza of the Second Battalion's E Company. "I asked God to give me courage to face those steel monsters."[6] The realization that tanks were now joining the battle against them deepened the general sense of disillusionment among the would-be liberators. As described by another Second Battalion soldier: "The men would look at each other and say, 'What is happening here? Where are the militia that were going to cross over to our side. Where are the peasants that were supposed to come?'"[7] Down the road in single file came four of López Cuba's T-34s. He himself commanded the lead tank; Castro's chief of operations, Flavio Bravo, took the commander's place in the fourth one. The platoon's fifth tank had been left in Pálpite to maintain radio communications with the advancing units. Behind the tanks marched an infantry formation of some 900 men made up of the First and Third Companies of the Militia Leaders' Battalion and the First Column of the Rebel Army.[8]

In the dark of night, the opposing forces could not see each other. López Cuba's lead tank moved forward slowly, occasionally turning on its headlights to illuminate the way. The lights immediately attracted fusillades of fire from the brigade positions, and the tank responded by firing back at the muzzle flashes. As the T-34 continued to move forward, the clanking inside the tank from the projectiles hitting its exterior intensified. Fortunate for the occupants, none penetrated inside as they were not armor-piercing rounds. However, as the tank closed to within twenty yards of the pit occupied by Ávila's men, a hit from an exploding shell tore off its right track. The thirty-one-ton vehicle became intractable and slipped sideways into a depression along the right side of the road where it lay immobilized at a steep angle. Unable to communicate via the radio, López Cuba clambered out and headed toward the second tank coming down the road. He climbed onto its turret and pounded on the hatch trying to get in, but the hatch remained close. Darting back onto the road, he climbed onto the turret of the third tank and did as before. This time the hatch opened and he was let inside.[9]

The second tank, which continued to move forward, came under heavy fire when its headlights were turned on momentarily. It then lurched into the thicket and down the embankment on the east side of the road where it remained motionless.[10] The third and fourth tanks remained in the rear and did not press the attack.[11]

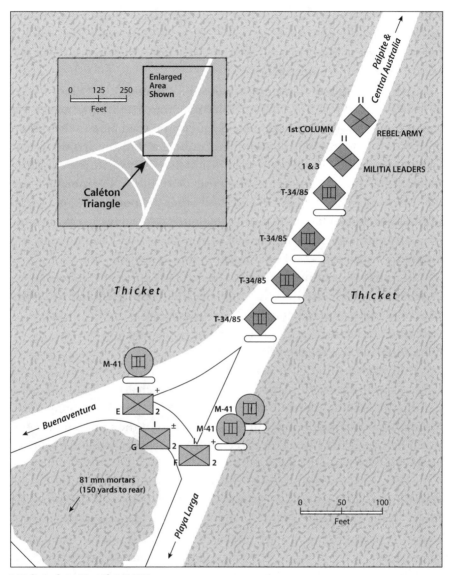

Midnight, April 17/18

The weight of the battle now fell on the infantry slogging their way down the shooting gallery. Lieutenant Juan Díaz led the Third Company of militia leaders that spearheaded the attack. "Forward! I have never commanded a gutsier troop," he called out to his men, spurring them on. Moments later he lay dead on the ground, cut down along with others around him just a few yards from the brigade lines.[12] "The enemy was really close in front of us," recalled Rafael Montalvo, one of the Second Battalion defenders. Unable to "see shit" in the dark, Montalvo and his fellow brigade soldiers blasted away at every noise they heard. "You saw people when something exploded."[13]

Even in complete darkness, the position taken up by Oliva offered an excellent field of fire. A .50 caliber machine gun emplaced on the rim of the excavation pit systematically swept the road bare inches above ground level. Scores of militiamen seeking safety by lying flat on its surface were wounded or killed by the grazing fire. "[E]ven at [two or three miles] away," noted Fernández, "the enfilade of fire from [their] .50 caliber machine guns, shell-firing guns and other weapons . . . would hit us without our being able to do anything about it."[14] The restrictive, narrow road also ensured that—like an encased python—only the head of the assaulting formation was able to strike.[15]

As casualties mounted and the attackers sought cover helter-skelter along the roadside ditches, the units became comingled and lost their cohesion and command control.[16] Castro's troops along the entire road were thrown into further disarray when at 1:00 a.m. Oliva ordered his 81 mm mortars to fire for the first time.[17]

To the men of the Fifth Battalion, still a few miles southwest of Playa Larga, "the firing of different types of weapons clearly told of the hard fighting happening there." But, true to character, battalion commander Montero was not inclined to hurry to the sound of the guns. He had the troop halt for what became a three-hour sleep break while he sent yet another patrol to scout ahead.[18]

At Central Australia, sixteen miles north of the front, Fidel Castro could also hear the blasts of gunfire. At 1:00 a.m. he penned a note to Flavio Bravo (addressing him as "Julio," his nom de guerre in the anti-Batista resistance), apparently unaware that Bravo was aboard a tank somewhere south of Pálpite. "I think it may take you at least two or three more hours to take Playa Larga and Buenaventura," he smugly prognosticated. "In that case, there would be no time left to advance on Girón." After a slew of tactical suggestions, Castro enumerated additional troops and armament he was prepared to send upon being informed "that the beach has been taken." "Fatherland or Death," the note closed. "We shall triumph."[19]

* * * *

At midnight, "mad as hell" that the ships had failed to return, Pepe San Román set out from Girón in a radio-equipped boat to find them. With him were his radio operator and a staff officer. From as far as six miles out, they tried to raise the *Blagar* but received no reply and saw nothing of the vessels. Only the flashes of explosions from the direction of Playa Larga penetrated the darkness. Still fuming, he returned to shore at approximately 1:15 a.m. An aid took his place in the boat, and once again it headed out to continue the futile search.[20]

The brigade commander soon received a visit from Enrique ("Harry") Ruiz Williams, second in command of the Heavy Weapons Battalion. The manifest fury of the not-so-distant battle to the northwest was too much for Williams to ignore. He was as certain that the failure of the ships to return assured their defeat as he was that they were all doomed to die. It was thus his goal to kill as many of Castro's men as possible. If each brigade man killed fifteen of the enemy, he figured, "we are going to kill a hell of a lot of people in here and even if we die something is going to happen." To that end, Williams asked permission from San Román to take thirty volunteers along with 4.2-inch mortars to go help Oliva. San Román approved the request, and William's group headed for Playa Larga in a truck loaded with the weapons and boxes of ammunition.[21]

* * * *

Tomás Cruz and his unit of paratroopers had been hiding in the thicket somewhere between Pálpite and Playa Larga since the previous morning. The scouts he had sent to reconnoiter south had not yet returned, but the incessant gunfire from that direction left no doubt that the brigade force there was under attack. Waldo de Castroverde, remorseful about having refused to join his friend Roberto de los Heros on the scouting mission, now sought to redeem himself. He proposed that the group launch a surprise, commando-style attack on the rear of the enemy units assaulting Playa Larga. Abruptly, another paratrooper cut him off. "Waldo, shut your mouth and don't talk any more bullshit. Your chance to be a hero has passed, and what you're proposing is crazy." Cruz also dismissed the suggestion and opted for staying put and waiting—just for what was not entirely clear.[22]

Bad luck rather than timidity ensured that the men defending Playa Larga would also get no help from the heavy mortars headed there with

Williams from Girón. In the dark of night, as it neared its destination, the truck carrying the relief ordnance and personnel hit an artillery shell crater and flipped over. "Nobody died because God is great," said one of the soldiers riding in the truck. "Just imagine all that equipment— the mortars alone weighed six hundred pounds." Accompanied by the cacophony of battle filling the air, the small group set to work recovering the mortars and boxes of ammunition from the overturned vehicle.[23]

* * * *

The forces under commander Filiberto Olivera had continued to shell the former brigade strongpoint at Muñoz Canal, unaware that it had been vacated hours earlier. Finally, at 3:00 a.m., the militia and army troops lurking in the dark advanced to take the position. What they found there, along with numerous scattered weapons, was a scene of carnage. About half a dozen horribly mutilated dead bodies lay about but not a single living individual.[24] The evacuation of surviving defenders carried out by José Miguel Battle and the Fuentes brothers had indeed been thorough.

Thinking that they had the enemy on the run, Castro's men continued down the road in full pursuit. It was just what paratroop commander Alejandro del Valle had anticipated hours earlier while the defenders of the strongpoint were being evacuated. He had ordered that the 4.2-inch mortar battery defending Babiney be brought west to defend the road from Covadonga. Before long, Roberto San Román's forward observers spotted the enemy advancing down the "bottleneck" on foot, clearly outlined by the truck headlights behind them that illuminated the way. Without realizing it, they marched right into the pre-ranged target zone for the heavy mortars and immediately came under fire. Among screams and explosions, the entire formation beat a hasty retreat toward the Muñoz Canal.[25] The impetuous advance thus halted, Olivera decided to hold off on any further ground attacks for the rest of the night. He did, however, order his mortar crews to subject the enemy to harassing fire over the coming hours. This they attempted to do, but, lacking forward observers, they had no way of determining where their shells were landing on the other side of the swamp five miles away.[26]

* * * *

Back at Central Australia, three hours into the offensive toward Playa Larga that had begun at midnight, Castro had grown impatient at the lack of news from the front. He had received no word about what was happening since an earlier note from Fernández, apparently sent around 2:00 a.m., reporting a decrease in the enemy's volume of fire. It had become clear to *El Comandante*, however, that the quick victory he had anticipated a couple of hours earlier was not to be. So now, at 3:00 a.m., Castro had just finished composing a note to Fernández. He was working on getting the artillery ammunition the captain had requested, the note said, and additional tanks would arrive at dawn. However, he himself would not be there by then. "I have to leave for Havana within the hour [but] will be in constant communication regarding the course of the operation." Commander Augusto Martínez—another member of M-26-7's leadership cadre—was designated to be his personal liaison at Central Australia in his absence.[27]

Castro did not give the reason for his departure in the note, although he would resolutely claim afterward that it was due to the supposed landing near Havana. That claim has become accepted as fact in essentially every retelling of the invasion story.[28] Its validity, however, is negated by what was conveyed to him on the phone ("there's nothing") from Havana as witnessed by journalist (and lifelong Castro loyalist) Luis Báez.[29] The claim is also incompatible with Castro's more than seven-hour delay in departing for Havana after receiving the report of the supposed landing. To obfuscate that telltale fact, he would disingenuously later assert publicly that the report had reached him at "around 1:30 in the morning,"[30] despite substantive evidence to the contrary. A good excuse for his departure was no doubt essential for the sake of his image. That *El Comandante* would leave the theater of operations otherwise was unfathomable to Fernández: "If it hadn't been [on account of the reported landing], I'm convinced that Fidel would not have left the Australia–Playa Larga region."[31] The truth, however, is compellingly quite different. Given Castro's dread of aerial attacks,[32] the approach of dawn and the dangers from the air it would bring may well have been foremost on his mind when he left the area.

* * * *

Just as Castro was finishing his note to Fernández, sixteen miles away Erneido Oliva ordered his mortars to employ white phosphorus shells against the enemy infantry edging closer. The highly flammable substance ignited fiercely on contact with air and rapidly started numerous brush fires. Castro's men were driven out of the burning brush and became illuminated targets for the brigade gunners. The swarm of flying projectiles made Enrique Salazar, a platoon leader with the army's First Column, regret choosing the cap he wore instead of a heavy, albeit uncomfortable, steel helmet. "Even a small stone will pass through these caps," he woefully reflected. Other soldiers shouted out practical advice to their comrades-in-arms, "Stick your head deep into the ground; your buttocks can go to hell!"[33]

Nearby crews manning Czech-made Vz.53 antiaircraft artillery pieces, each comprising four .50 caliber machine guns, were desperately ordered to shoot toward the brigade positions. However, in the prevailing darkness, the bright stream of tracer bullets fired by the weapons made them easy targets. When one of the quad guns was hit by a mortar shell that killed its crew, the others were ordered back to Pálpite.[34]

With the assault now decidedly at a standstill, Fernández deemed it was time to relay the disappointing news to Castro, not having yet received his 3:00 a.m. note. By messenger, he dispatched the following report to Central Australia:

> Comandante Fidel Castro:
>   Thus far Playa Larga has not fallen. Julio [Flavio Bravo] is there. The enemy is putting up resistance against the battalion from the Militia Leaders' School and the First Column.
>   All my [artillery] pieces are hitched up [ready to move,] but if Playa Larga is not taken within a few minutes I will have to emplace them again.
>   *J. Fernández* [35]

The interrelation of subsequent events at the Caletón Triangle during the early morning hours becomes particularly muddled by dubious, conflated, and divergent accounts (some stemming from the same individual). What follows is proposed as the most plausible interpretation of the available evidence. Special consideration has been given to parallel elements across accounts that align too closely for mere coincidence.

Sometime around 4:00 a.m., López Cuba, intent on rescuing the crew of the disabled tank he had commanded, went toward the front line

aboard the T-34 he now occupied. As the tank moved toward the junction, the T-34 that had been "playing possum" for hours at the foot of
the embankment on the east side of the road came to life. Up the slope
the T-34 went in reverse, but, in so doing, backed into López Cuba's
tank coming down the road. López Cuba took to the radio and curtly
instructed the other crew to get out of his way, so down the embankment
the "possum" went again.[36]

The battered militia and army men on the front line received a welcome respite from the gunfire trained on them when López Cuba's T-34
burst onto the scene. The tank lunged toward the enemy blasting away
with its main gun and drawing the fire of the brigade defenders. Seizing
the opportunity, one of Castro's infantrymen launched a rifle grenade at
the troublesome .50 caliber machine gun emplaced in the excavation pit
and took it out.[37]

By then, the brigade's own M-41 tanks were low on ammunition. One
of them, commanded by Fernando Torres Mena, had pulled out of formation and gone to the rear. Oliva went over and asked Torres Mena his reason for retreating. The tank commander told him that they were almost
out of rounds and the main gun's shell-loading mechanism needed repair
(it was the same issue the gun had experienced the previous afternoon).[38]
As this conversation was going on, López Cuba's T-34 continued to speed
toward the brigade's front lines. One of the two M-41s that remained
there, commanded by Daniel Carmenate, blasted it with its last shell—
likely a high explosive round—but failed to stop it. Oliva and Torres Mena
watched as the enemy tank approached them then halted. López Cuba
climbed out of a hatch and came running toward them, assuming that the
M-41 there was the disabled T-34 he had vacated hours earlier. Suddenly
realizing his mistake, he froze, yelled, "It's the enemy!" and then scurried
back to his own tank. A trail of bullets followed him, one striking his arm
before he made it back inside and the tank quickly retreated.[39]

Back on the front line, meanwhile, Carmenate had spotted an enemy
tank climbing up the embankment that bordered the road. It was the
"possum" T-34 once again coming to life. With no ammunition left, Carmenate's driver, Jorge Álvarez, did the only thing possible—he hurled
the tank at the T-34 and repeatedly rammed it. "We kept butting into
each other like a couple of prehistoric monsters," Álvarez later said. "He
tried to turn his gun toward me, but I wouldn't let him." Giving up, the
"possum" retreated down the embankment to play dead once again.[40]

* * * *

Like his fellow brigade pilots before him, Gonzalo Herrera saw only darkness below him where the airfield he was to bomb was supposedly located. His would be the third and final attempt that night to strike back at Castro's scant but pestilent air force which was so seriously jeopardizing the invasion. The fact that his target was José Martí International Airport, twelve miles northeast of the San Antonio airbase, bespeaks a lack of certainty by the CIA planners as to just where the FAR planes were located. There was no doubt, however, that Castro's forces were effectively remaining loyal to him. At 3:44 a.m., Radio Swan had transmitted an impassioned appeal urging them to rise up. It contained a direct exhortation to all FAR personnel: "Comrades of the Air Force! Listen closely! All planes must stay on the ground. See that no Fidelista plane takes off. Destroy its radios; destroy its tail; break its instruments; and puncture its fuel tanks! Refuse to give service!"[41]

Herrera's mission was now proving as ineffective as the Radio Swan broadcasts. He had spent half an hour looking for the airport he was to bomb without so much as a glimpse of it. Dropping his bombs blindly was out of the question lest they fall on the surrounding residential neighborhoods. As his frustration grew, he cursed the fact that no alternate target had been assigned to him and decided to pick one on his own. At 4:30 a.m. he headed for the Batabanó naval station and proceeded to drop his entire bomb load there. Doing so at least made him feel better.[42] Still, the night attempts to destroy at least some of the offending FAR planes had ended in complete failure.

* * * *

The attack on the road from Yaguaramas that Néstor Pino had been anticipating came at 4:00 a.m. North of Babiney, the two companies from Militia Battalion 117 commanded by Victor Dreke formed up and started south.

Pino radioed for support from the 4.2 mortars, supposedly located a mile back from his new position on the southern edge of the swamp but received no answer. No one had informed him of the mortar battery's redeployment hours earlier to defend the road from Covadonga.[43] With the head of the advancing column now 150 yards away, the camouflaged paratroopers opened fire on the surprised militiamen. "We were stopped right in the middle of the roadway," said Dreke. "They shot at us from a curve to the right on the road. That was [their] favorite tactic; they would hide behind curves and open fire when our vanguard came around them."

On the brigade side "[e]veryone fired pretty good. It was amazing the quantity of people we could hit," commented Pino. The fact that he himself was doing so much shooting surprised him. "[I]n a war, I didn't think an officer could fire so much." With only swamp on either side of the advancing column, the roadside ditches provided the only practicable cover available to the militiamen. Some of them, taking advantage of blind spots in the enemy's field of fire, crawled in close and hurled grenades at the defenders.[44]

As the fighting continued, the paratrooper commander sent a runner to see what was happening with the mortars. "No one is there," the messenger reported back. Pino, wary his men would not take the news well, admonished him, "[D]on't repeat it to anyone else."[45]

* * * *

With dawn barely an hour away, the night-long battle for Playa Larga was beginning to abate. It was quiet except for the cries of the wounded, drowned out now and then by occasional brief exchanges of fire between the weary enemies.[46]

The brigade tanks, their ammunition used up, had all retreated to the rear. Oliva had been out of radio communication with San Román in Girón since the previous evening. At 5:00 a.m., he dispatched a messenger to the brigade commander reporting that the situation of the Playa Larga defenders was desperate. Without reinforcements plus ammunition and other supplies, the message indicated, his men could not face another attack.[47]

At around the same time, a message from Castro was being delivered to Fernández. It was a reply to the report Fernández had sent him about the situation at the front. The reply gave the time of its writing as 4:40 a.m. and had evidently been phoned into Central Australia by Castro on his way back to Havana. "From Augusto [Martínez] to Fernández," it read. "Fidel received your message and informs me to give you the following instructions." The instructions consisted of eight numbered directives. Clearly, the danger of enemy air attacks at daybreak was fore-most on Castro's mind because directives one *and* three concerned making ready all the available antiaircraft guns. The second direc-tive instructed that the tanks continue attacking and that the 122 mm artillery guns be emplaced again. Directives four through seven urged Fernández to use newly arriving infantry and/or tanks to flank the enemy by way of backtrails. "Lastly," read the eighth and final directive, "Fidel says that Playa Larga must be taken without excuses."[48]

The T-34 carrying general staff officer Flavio Bravo had stayed out of the fray until—perhaps "motivated" by *El Comandante*'s directives—it suddenly went on the attack. The charging tank took the brigade soldiers by surprise and managed to penetrate deep into the rear of their lines. Company commander Máximo Cruz saw what was happening and sprang into action. The steel hulk was difficult for the bazooka men to discern in the still prevailing darkness, so Cruz stood up and began peppering it with tracer bullets to outline its position. At that point, the T-34 fired back with its 85 mm main gun then beat a speedy retreat out of the area. The exploding shell seriously wounded Cruz and radioman Adalberto Sánchez who had been standing next to him. Cruz was carried back to Playa Larga with severe multiple wounds, but Sánchez lost consciousness and was left for dead as he lay motionless covered in blood.[49]

Dawn finally broke over the battlefield, yet, in the coolness of the nascent morning, the carnage littering the ground remained concealed by a carpet of opaque fog.[50]

With Castro's troops now in full retreat to Pálpite, most of the exhausted brigade units were sent back to Playa Larga. Only a small detachment was assigned to a blocking position along the road leading to the settlement.[51]

Pandemonium suddenly erupted in Playa Larga when the men assigned to the blocking position came running down the road scream-ing about an approaching tank. Such was the men's panic that they ignored all shouted commands from Oliva and Second Battalion com-mander Hugo Sueiro to get back into position. It was a potential rout that required drastic action. Without exchanging a word between them, Oliva grabbed a 57 mm recoilless rifle lying nearby while Sueiro picked up a shell for the weapon. Both men then sprinted toward the curve around which the tank was expected to come. As Oliva knelt aiming the gun, Sueiro loaded the shell into it and stood by. It was a brilliant display of leadership by example that had the intended effect. The rest of the men now also picked up their weapons and prepared to meet the threat encroaching on them. Soon an enemy T-34 became visible some fifty yards away as it turned the bend in the road. Just as Oliva was about fire, the tank stopped and remained motionless for a few moments. A tank hatch opened and out came one of the crew waving a dirty handkerchief that he held high in the air. The man walked toward Oliva and then halted and spoke to him from a few feet away.

"—Are you the commander of these men?" he asked.

"—Yes."

"—Mister, I congratulate you because these men are truly heroes. They were never afraid of our tanks. We would like to have the privilege of fighting with you if the opportunity arises."[52]

The tank men were undoubtedly none other than the crew of the "possum" T-34 that had spent most of the battle down the embankment on the east side of the road. They were the only prisoners taken during the hours-long engagement.[53] Per their account to Oliva, they had realized that their tank was inside the brigade's defensive perimeter and had decided not to fire on his men. The tank had no machine gun ammunition left anyway. Oliva had serious reservations about the sincerity of these alleged defectors. He had them kept away from the prisoners he already had from the previous day lest they try to incite some kind of rebellion.[54] Whatever the crew's true intentions may have been, the military information they offered was certainly grossly inaccurate. The tankers reportedly claimed that over 2,000 of Castro's men and dozens of his tanks had participated in the overnight battle.[55]

The reply from San Román to Oliva's 5:00 a.m. dispatch arrived via messenger at 6:15 a.m. *Resist until the last moment—the moment of death. No ammunition is available. Our supplies are almost depleted.* "How in the hell does he expect me to fight a war without ammunition and supplies!" Oliva shouted to the aide who stood next to him as he read the message. The deputy brigade commander wondered out loud if San Román really intended for them "to be massacred at this beach without having the means to defend ourselves." Ostensibly lost in the exchange of hand-carried messages between the two commanders was the fact that the reinforcements and ammunition traveling with Harry Williams had met with a mishap. San Román was seemingly unaware that Williams had not made it to Playa Larga, and Oliva did not know that he had been sent from Girón.

In a meeting with his officers, Oliva explained his concerns: (1) a new attack with fresh troops and hardware was inevitable, and (2) the enemy would try to encircle them. Given their situation, he told them, he had decided to abandon Playa Larga and withdraw to Girón.[56] Not only the officers but also the common soldiers of the Second Battalion and attached units trusted Oliva implicitly. Among the close to 400 brigade men under his command during the battle, casualties had been relatively few: ten to twenty killed and some forty to fifty wounded. With everything else about the invasion going wrong, Oliva's unwavering leadership and valor remained the one thing they could count on. Such was their respect and admiration for the twenty-eight-year-old Afro-Cuban that they affectionately dubbed him "Maceo." The name was an allusion to the historical figure of General Antonio Maceo, also a black man, who is revered among Cubans for his bravery during the country's war of independence.[57]

Oliva next dealt with the problem of what to do with the approximately two hundred prisoners being held at Playa Larga. There was no way to take this many people to Girón, so the only choice was to release them. Rather than admitting this to his captives, however, he decided to try to bluff them. The invaders were moving elsewhere on their way to Havana, Oliva proclaimed. They were so strong and had won such a decisive victory that they no longer needed to take prisoners and were setting them free.[58] Given the frenzied eagerness of the brigade men to depart,[59] probably few if any believed him.

During the withdrawal preparations a radio call came in from the Fifth Battalion's Ricardo Montero. They had been unable to come to his aide, he blatantly told Oliva, because the battalion had been attacked and become disorganized. In truth, no enemy forces had stood between Montero's men and Playa Larga for hours. The fifty or so militiamen and sailors that had occupied Buenaventura earlier on the seventeenth had grown alarmed by that evening's artillery shelling. At midnight they had gone to Santo Tomás, a small cluster of houses seventeen miles west of there. Oliva knew he was being lied to and would not have it. He rebuked Montero sharply and, by one account, attempted to relieve him of command on the radio, but the wily ex-Batista army officer just cut him off.[60]

More than twelve hours after setting out, the men of the Fifth Battalion had covered less than five miles and had not even entered Buenaventura in force. "It must be admitted" concluded the battalion's Luis Lalondry, "that [Montero] hesitated much in meeting the responsibility before him."[61]

* * * *

"I see the combatants returning from the front," a journalist with the Cuban state press reported from Pálpite. "Their faces and hands are blackened from the gunpowder and the expression of their countenance is tense."[62]

The casualties among Castro's forces totaled twenty to thirty dead and over fifty wounded. Most of these were among the men of the Militia Leaders' Battalion who had been at the forefront of the assault.[63]

In a report written five months after the event, Fernández displayed a candor he would never again demonstrate. "Due to the indecisiveness of some tanks in advancing, the lack of efficient subordinate leaders and the volume and effectiveness of the enemy's fire, [our] firepower . . . proved of little efficacy against the enemy's armaments." He faulted the pullback of the troops to Pálpite as "a blunder, because they did not continue to engage the enemy." "Thus," the report continued, "we immediately reorganized some units and prepared for a new attack, sending the rest of the units to the rear."[64] In fact, *all* the infantry units that had fought in the engagement were taken out of action and replaced with newly arrived fresh troops. The Sixth Company of the Militia Leaders' Battalion, which had been held back, was sent along backtrails with a tank and mortars to try to reach Buenaventura. Fernández, unaware that the brigade forces had abandoned their previous positions at the apex of the Caletón Triangle, hoped by so doing to flank them as Castro had directed.[65]

The newly arrived troops included MNR Battalions 144 and 180, each composed of 1,200 men. Fernández sent Battalion 144 to Caleta del Rosario by way of backtrails to cut off Playa Larga itself from Girón. It was the same mission that had been assigned the previous morning to Battalion 227, but Fernández did not know its whereabouts. The additional men would at least serve to reinforce that earlier force if it had managed to reach its ordained destination. A local man was to guide Battalion 144 on its trek through the complex maze of indistinct backtrails to ensure it would not get lost.[66] Already making their way through that maze on the even longer trek to Cayo Ramona were the men of Battalion 111. The battalion had arrived at Central Australia at 1:00 a.m. and within hours set out to carry out the order issued by Castro to *Dentista* Borges the previous evening.[67]

The task of launching a renewed frontal attack toward Playa Larga fell on Battalion 180. As members of the battalion's light infantry company scouted ahead, they came under air attack. A ricocheting bullet entered the groin of fourteen-year-old Juanito Rodríguez and exited though his hip. The teen, whose birthday fell on that day, was serving alongside his father.[68] Ironically, the attack had come not from the enemy but their own air force. Only FAR aircraft were in the air at the time, including a B-26 flown by Jacques Lagas that was heading to the Girón area for a bombing run. Lagas himself would only admit afterward to ordering his rear gunner to "test the machine guns" while "north of the Bay of Pigs . . . in enemy territory."[69] Enrique Oropesa, an army officer overseeing the ground air defense units, went a bit further in admitting the friendly fire incident. "At dawn on the 18th, one of our planes showed up," Oropesa would obliquely state later. "We learned that [it was ours] years later, because the enemy [also] used [FAR] insignia." Oropesa quickly ordered his antiaircraft gunners to open fire on the presumptive enemy plane, which they did enthusiastically. They all wanted to "give the mercenary air force what it deserved," but "fortunately [the plane] pulled away in time."[70]

Also in the area were a T-33 flown by Alberto Fernández and two Sea Furies, one piloted by Carreras and the other by Ernesto Guerrero. Carreras was assigned to bomb the stranded *Houston*, fearing that supplies were still being unloaded from the disabled ship.[71] Fernández and Guerrero, on the other hand, were ordered to attack the location of the enemy units "resisting the advance of our forces at Playa Larga." Exactly what location they took this to mean when they dropped their bombs is as uncertain as the origin of the ground fire that hit Guerrero's Sea Fury after the attack. With smoke filling his cockpit and the aircraft losing hydraulic fluid, a panicked Guerrero called out on the radio for help. Carreras heard the frantic calls and came to Guerreros's rescue. He escorted the terrified pilot back to base and talked him through the procedure for dealing with a stuck landing gear. Guerrero did manage to land safely, but the experienced caused him a nervous breakdown, and he was relieved from further duty.[72]

For the militiamen scouting the way toward Playa Larga, the calamities of the air attack were immediately followed by artillery shells exploding near them. They detonated "right in front of our noses" according to American journalist and Castro sympathizer Robert Taber, who was traveling with the scouts. The rounds came from behind them. Back at Pálpite, Fernández had boastfully described the shelling to reporters gathered around him as "the merceneries' breakfast." Taber and his Cuban photographer rushed there and proceeded to "photograph the gun batteries . . . being fired with formidable enthusiasm and disciplined precision."[73]

Upon resuming their reconnaissance, the light infantrymen caught sight of dozens of men, women, and children walking toward them waving a white sheet in the air. They were the civilians and militiamen that had been released from Playa Larga. From them, Fernández would finally obtain some hard information about the makeup of the enemy force opposing him. "There were no foreigners," he learned, "and it consisted of young men, properly uniformed and armed, that behaved as an army of occupation."[74]

* * * *

The official Soviet reaction to the invasion reached Washington at 6:00 a.m. in the form of a letter from Chairman Nikita Khrushchev to President Kennedy.[75]

As Khrushchev later recollected, "We first heard on the radio that a counterrevolutionary invasion had been launched against Cuba. We didn't even know who the invaders were: were they Cuban conspirators or Americans? However, we knew that no matter under whose banner the invasion was launched, it had to have the backing of the Americans."[76]

One day later, the Soviet premier explicitly laid out his position not only to Kennedy but to the world at large. His letter had been delivered to the U.S. Moscow embassy at 4:15 a.m. (Washington time; 12:15 p.m. local time) and simultaneously released to the press.

Mr. President, I send you this message in an hour of alarm, fraught with danger for the peace of the whole world. Armed aggression has begun against Cuba. It is a secret to no one that the armed bands invading this country were trained, equipped and armed in the United States of America. The planes which are bombing Cuban cities belong to the United States of America, the bombs they are dropping are being supplied by the American Government. . . . As far as the Soviet Union is concerned, there should be no mistake about our position: We will render the Cuban people and their government all necessary help to repel armed attack on Cuba. We are sincerely interested in a relaxation of international tension, but if others proceed toward sharpening, we will answer them in full measure. . . . I hope that the Government of the USA will consider our views dictated by the sole concern not to allow steps which could lead the world to military catastrophe.[77]

7:00 AM—NOON

"3 Beachheads Secured, Cuba Invaders Push On"; "Giant Pincer Drives to Cut Cuba in Two" screamed the heady, if highly inaccurate, front-page headlines of the *Miami Herald*'s April 18 street edition. The articles under the headlines fared no better in accuracy and, like a fairy tale come true, seemed the fulfillment of the CIA's and the Cuban exiles' wishful expectations. "Reports filtering back to exile leaders in the United States," said one article, "indicate that Cuban underground fighters have joined the assault." "Acts of sabotage and explosions, damaging strategic military installations were timed to coincide with the three-pronged invasion. Segments of the Cuban navy . . . were reported in revolt. And thousands of Castro's 300,000-member militia . . . were defecting to the rebels."[78]

As "joyful pandemonium" grew among Miami's 40,000-strong Cuban émigré community, thousands were reported to be flocking to local churches. Hundreds of male exiles continued to swamp the local CRC recruitment offices just as they had done the previous day. Planes carrying new recruits to the training camps in Central America had started taking off at dawn "with almost airline regularity." Ten men who wanted to join the fighting immediately had been unable to find a charter boat in the Florida Keys willing to take them to Cuba. A 173-foot former navy subchaser bought by an exile businessman was being readied at a pier in Miami to go help the anti-Castro fighters. The vessel had been stripped of its three-inch main gun and other armaments for delivery, as required by government regulations, but the owner openly intended to reoutfit it for action. "If the Castro regime is overthrown," the paper quoted U.S. United Nations representative Adlai Stevenson as declaring the previous day, "it will be overthrown by Cubans and not Americans. I do not see that it is the obligation of the United States to protect Dr. Castro." An editorial cartoon echoed the official American government position of noninvolvement. From across the Florida Straits, a poised Uncle Sam detachedly observed the fighting in Cuba through a spyglass.[79]

On the other side of those straits, the general population of Havana and the rest of Cuba were largely being kept in the dark about the progress of the invasion. Since the first day of the landings, Castro's government had cut off all forms of incoming and outgoing communications, including for foreign correspondents. Two official government communiques had been issued so far, but they only described the fighting in broad terms.[80] Furthermore, the arrests that had started on the fifteenth of those known or suspected to be hostile to the Revolution continued.[81]

As the second day of the invasion began with still no sign of open dissent within the country, Radio Swan kept trying to make it erupt. At approximately 7:00 a.m., the station went on the air with an urgent appeal:

> *People of Havana; attention, people of Havana. Help the brave soldiers of the liberation army. . . . Electrical plants must not supply power today to the few industries that the regime is trying to keep in operation. Today at 7:45 A.M., when we give the signal on this station, all the lights in your house should be turned on; all electrical appliances should be connected. Increase the load on the generators of the electric company! . . . But do not worry, people of Havana, the liberation forces will recover the electrical plants and they can be placed in operation rapidly.*[82]

The entreaty bore no fruit. Throughout the day, as reported by the *New York Times* from information that managed to filter out of Cuba, "Havana and Santiago [its second largest city] were calm."[83]

* * * *

A scene of carnage awaited the vanguard of Battalion 180 when, around 7:00 a.m., it reached the northern junction of the Caletón Triangle. Gone was the morning fog that had veiled the ground, but the pungent smell of gunpowder permeated the air and gave it a bitter taste. Two of Castro's soldiers lay dead with their heads resting on their arms, looking as if they were fast asleep. Not so the five bodies nearby riddled with holes and grime, victims of a mortar shell explosion. What remained of another militiaman—a goo of flesh, blood, and mud bearing the impression of tank treads—awaited discovery among the thicket bordering the road. Coming across the remains proved, for the corporal who found them, "one of the hardest moments I experienced during the whole of the operations." Inside the pit by the junction, the bodies of dead brigade soldiers were strewn behind the deadly .50 caliber machine gun emplaced there. They were joined in death by some of the very men who had so adamantly refused to do so in life. The militia fighters who had charged the position under Lieutenant Díaz lay dead practically at the very edge of the pit, Díaz's corpse mere yards behind them.[84]

As the rest of Battalion 180 arrived at the road junction, the light infantry company was ordered to press ahead and locate the enemy lines. About a quarter mile from Playa Larga, they took fire from the brigade's advanced positions blocking the road eastward. The militiamen quickly retreated, and a request went out from their battalion commander for artillery support against the enemy position.[85]

Back at Pálpite, the men of Battalion 144 had already spent an hour fruitlessly waiting for the peasant who was to guide them along the back-trails to Caleta del Rosario. Fernández finally concluded that coward-ice had gotten the better of the man and decided to send the battalion ahead on its own. Based on his estimation of the speed its trucks could make, he instructed the battalion's commander to go east for forty-five minutes to an hour then turn south toward the coast.[86]

* * * *

The shelling of the brigade's new position some five miles south of the Muñoz Canal had continued throughout the night and presaged a com-ing ground attack. Around 7:30 a.m. Roberto San Román returned to Girón to inform his brother and request reinforcements.[87]

The atmosphere in Girón was tense. Not only had the ships failed to return during the night, but Castro's planes had been launching attacks concentrated on the airfield there since daybreak. The brigade commander informed his younger sibling that the news from Playa Larga was not good. Francisco Montiel's Sixth Battalion had been ordered to guard the western approaches into town in case of an enemy break-through from that direction. No attacks had yet come from the east, but as one could materialize at any moment, the Third Battalion remained in place on Girón's eastern outskirts.[88] With the situation such as it was, the bottom line was there were no reinforcements to send the men fighting in the north. All the units in Girón were needed there pending further developments.

* * * *

Despite having decided to withdraw from Playa Larga more than an hour earlier, Oliva delayed doing so hoping he might yet be able to avoid it. Although out of radio communication with Girón, he presumed that the American navy task force offshore might be able to intercept a transmission from him. At 7:30 a.m. he radioed a message stating that the position at Playa Larga could not be maintained for more than thirty minutes without air support. The message was indeed immediately received by the Americans but prompted no reaction from them.[89] For half an hour the deputy brigade commander futilely waited for the requested air support. When none arrived, he decided it was time to go. A mortar squad, which had remained in place to cover the withdrawal, was the last to board the caravan of departing trucks.[90]

After traveling a short distance down the coastal road, the group spotted the overturned truck that had been carrying Harry Williams and his contingent of volunteers. With tears welling up in his eyes, Williams walked up to Oliva and expressed his sorrow for not being able to come and help in the fighting.[91] The stranded men along with their heavy mortars and ammunition boxes were picked up by the convoy, and the journey to Girón resumed.[92]

Passing by Caleta del Rosario, no one in the caravan realized that they were now in the sights of militia hiding in the brush bordering the road. They were the men of Battalion 227, sent there the previous morning for the specific purpose of preventing what was now occurring before them. The militiamen did nothing, however. "We watched as the mercenaries withdrawing from Playa Larga passed us by," said their commander, "but did not open fire on them. . . . [O]ur battalion only had light infantry weapons, and they were withdrawing aboard tanks and gun trucks."[93] Commenting on the incident years later, Fernández took a dim view of their inaction. "The battalion could have cut off the [enemy's] withdrawal but did not do so and allowed them to continue on toward Playa Girón."[94]

* * * *

The roughly 10:1 numerical advantage of the militia over the brigade defenders south of Babiney increased fourfold after 8:00 a.m. when—entirely fortuitously—MNR Battalion 113 arrived there from Havana. The battalion had been destined to go to Covadonga but, due to confusion on the road, ended up in Yaguaramas instead. Now the unexpected reinforcements joined the two companies from Battalion 117 that had been fighting Néstor Pino's men since before dawn.[95]

For the new arrivals, the stream of wounded militiamen headed for the rear was a sobering sight.[96] The brigade defenses straddling the curve where the road exited the swamp continued to prove a formidable obstacle for the attackers. Their numerical advantage did not mean much when only those in the front ranks were able to directly engage the enemy.[97]

Victor Dreke ordered the newly arrived troop to emplace their mortars and asked for ten volunteers to go scout for the location of the enemy's machine gun nests.[98] Fred Salazar, nicknamed *Elegante* ("the Elegant One"), was one of the ten who stepped forward to carry out the mission. As he recounted:

> We fanned out as we advanced. The ground there was a bit swampy and the mud and black fetid dark water came up to our knees. We kept moving toward our assigned objective and, as we got close, we heard someone calling out to us, "Come closer, communists, we are waiting for you." . . . There were some of them that were a bit boastful and this was one of those guys. We shouted back "Fatherland or Death. We shall triumph!" and fired. . . . I shot twice at him [to test his firepower]. He fired back across a wide arc with a .50 [caliber machine gun], and I said to myself, "Dammit, *Elegante*! I think your life ends here for sure." In an instant, a thousand memories flashed before me. I thought about my children, about everything else. . . . [W]e all shot blindly because you could see nothing among the tangled thicket. The only thing visible was the muzzle flash of the .50 whose song the dammed guy played for us unrelentingly. . . . Luckily for us, being in the swamp allowed us to sink down, otherwise we would have been finished. . . . I thought it would never end."[99]

* * * *

Oliva and his aide sped ahead in their jeep and arrived at Girón before the rest of the convoy.[100] Understandably, Pepe San Román was greatly alarmed by his deputy's arrival and the information he brought back from Playa Larga. Still out of communication with the *Blagar*, the brigade commander sent out a radio message at 8:24 a.m. He hoped, as Oliva had done, that it would be intercepted by the U.S. Navy task force stationed offshore. Anticipating an imminent assault on Girón, the message reported that Blue Beach was "UNDER ATTACK BY TWELVE TANKS AND FOUR JET AIRCRAFT." It also reiterated the need for ammunition and supplies.[101]

Indeed, the transmission was again intercepted by the Americans but again failed to elicit any support. However, shortly after the report was received, CIA headquarters was moved to authorize the use of napalm over the beachhead area for the first time.[102] Up to then, the agency had been reluctant to allow its use during the operation as it "would cause concern and public outcry."[103]

* * * *

The first day of the invasion had taken a heavy toll on the brigade aircrews. Ten B-26 crewmen, including five pilots (i.e., 28 percent of the aviators available on April 17), were either dead or missing. The most recent casualties had been pilot Crispín García and his crewmate Juan Gónzalez, who had disappeared on the way to JMTIDE. They had not been seen since 9:48 p.m. the previous day when their B-26 had taken off from Key West after diverting there hours earlier due to low fuel.[104]

The failure of the attempted night strikes to curtail Castro's air power may well have been the final straw leading to a drastic decision. It came down from the brigade air force's Cuban chief, Manuel Villafaña, and its chief of operations, Luis Cosme. They decreed that any further participation by Cuban personnel in air missions would be on a strictly voluntary basis.[105]

* * * *

At 8:45 a.m. San Román, his chief of staff, Oliva, and Artime met to discuss the overall situation in the concrete house that served as brigade headquarters. As they pored over maps of the area, Oliva argued that their defenses could not hold out against the large force soon expected to descend on Girón from Playa Larga. He therefore proposed concentrating all their forces there and then striking out along the coastal trail toward Cienfuegos and on to the Escambray Mountains. San Román was not receptive to the proposal, however. He countered that as Cienfuegos was a large, important city, the enemy would surely have substantial forces there. In fact, he still expected that a third offensive toward Girón would be launched from that direction. There were also the logistical problems of not having the means to transport the entire brigade on such a journey or ammunition to fight their way through. But above all, San Román had faith that the Americans would not abandon them if they stuck to the plan. "If we could hold this position for two or three days everything was going to be alright," he reasoned. "I knew that we were in a very rough situation, very dangerous, but I felt optimistic about everything."[106]

Faced with a looming offensive on his position, at 10:09 a.m. San Román sent another overstated message into the ether hoping the Americans he so trusted were listening: UNDER HEAVY ATTACK SUPPORTED BY 12 TANKS. NEED AIR SUPPORT IMMEDIATELY. RED BEACH WIPED OUT. REQUEST AIR SUPPORT IMMEDIATELY.[107]

* * * *

As San Román expected, by late morning Castro's forces had advanced within five miles east of Girón along the coastal trail. However, their express mission was not to attack the town but merely to make their presence known.[108]

Battalion 326 under Orlando Pupo reached the small settlement of Caleta Buena some twenty hours after setting out the previous afternoon. It was a location fourteen miles inside the eastern perimeter of the beachhead, as originally planned. A local peasant who had managed to escape from Girón informed Pupo about the weapons he had seen there but could only describe them in nonmilitary terms. "A bulldozer with five wheels on each side, no tires, tracks like a tractor, and a long tube with a club hammer at the end," Pupo understood was a tank. "Two tubes that they join together and hold on their shoulder" was clearly a bazooka.[109]

Guided by the peasant, the battalion eventually resumed its westward march. The troop had gone barely a mile when a B-26 appeared that bore FAR markings. "Hide, hide!" the peasant yelled out. Seeing the plane's markings, however, Pupo thought there was nothing to fear and rebuked the man. "You're nothing but a coward. That plane says 'FAR' on it," he told him. But the peasant protested, "'FAR' is also painted on the crashed plane at the Girón airport and it's not ours." The debate became moot when the plane began to fire on them, prompting Pupo to seek cover under a nearby mastic tree.[110] In fact, there were no brigade planes in the air at the time, and this was undoubtedly another friendly fire incident by a FAR B-26.[111]

* * * *

By midmorning, Néstor Pino and his men south of Babiney faced a desperate situation. They had been resisting against repeated ground assaults since 4:00 a.m. without heavy mortar support. The attacks had grown in strength over the last couple of hours with the arrival of Battalion 113. Castro's forces had taken significant casualties but kept coming.[112]

Pino thought the reinforcements he had requested from San Blas had finally arrived when a brigade M-35 gun truck appeared firing its .50 caliber machine gun toward the enemy. As it turned out, however, the truck carried orders from Del Valle for Pino and his men to retreat. In the confusion, many took the orders to mean they were to pull back to Girón. They went all the way there only to be sent back to San Blas.[113]

With resistance at an end, the militia was finally able to occupy the last advanced blocking position between Yaguaramas and San Blas. Not all the brigade defenders had been able to make it out. As they entered the area, a group of militiamen came across a pair of bloodied pants and then, a short distance away, blood-soaked undershorts. They followed a set of footprints to a small stand of palmettos and found an enemy soldier, naked from the waist down, bleeding from a buttock wound. "It made me laugh," one of his captors recollected. "I called him a faggot, I called him a son of a bitch, I called him a coward." The wounded man was eventually taken away in a jeep.[114]

* * * *

Badly wounded brigade soldier Adalberto Sánchez, left for dead at the Caletón Triangle, found himself surrounded by militiamen when they finally streamed into Playa Larga by midmorning. After being forcefully picked up and thrown into the back of a truck, he was driven to a nearby town, which must have been Jagüey Grande. A large crowd of civilians congregated around the truck when it stopped at a public square. They began spitting on Sánchez to chants of "*Paredón, paredón!*"—the Revolution's way of calling for execution in front of a firing wall.[115]

The only opposition to the occupation of Playa Larga had ostensibly come from Castro's own planes. "There is no enemy activity in this zone, [but] apparently some jets around 10:15 a.m. strafed our advanced forces." Thus reported Captain Fernández in the message he dispatched to Central Australia at 10:30 a.m. with news of the enemy's withdrawal from the settlement. "Please inform the FAR (Air Force) that Playa Larga is in our possession," the captain implored.[116] Immediately he also sent orders for the units making their way to Buenaventura along backtrails to halt their march lest another friendly fire incident occur.[117]

Swiftly the occupiers went house to house around Playa Larga searching for enemy stragglers. A militiaman entering a room in one of them found that his boots stuck to the floor. Looking down, he saw that it was caked over with congealed blood. The room had been the brigade's improvised infirmary. Presumably it was where Cira García, the dying militiawoman from the Buenaventura truck incident, had been taken. It was certainly where a mortally wounded brigade soldier had lain. His rasping, blood-spurting breathing sounded to the radio operator in the adjoining room "the way it does when you blow under water." At one point, when the radioman had gone over to comfort him, the suffering man asked for a gun to shoot himself. Alternatively, he requested, his visitor should do it for him. The radioman refused both requests and walked away. García's body was later recovered from a sandy lot where her husband buried it after she died. The identity and fate of the doomed soldier are unknown.[118]

* * * *

Sometime before 10:30 a.m., San Román got word that communication had been reestablished with the *Blagar*. Joined by his chief of staff along with Oliva and Artime, he ran to the radio. A faint voice that grew louder by the minute was coming through the device. Frustrated and in no mood for proprieties, San Román's opening remarks when he spoke to Captain Ryberg were blunt. "Where have you been, you son of a bitch? Where the hell have you been? You have abandoned us."[119]

The full answer to the question was convoluted. Following the previous night's aborted supply run, the *Blagar* and *Barbara J* had waited for the return of *Atlántico* and *Caribe*. Just before 5 a.m., with neither freighter in sight, the two LCIs and slow-moving LCUs had started sailing north toward Point Zulu, forty-seven miles from Girón.[120] It was at that distance that the *Blagar* was able to establish radio communications with the beach.[121] Ryberg chose not to elaborate. "I know that you have your problems, but I've had mine," he simply said.

Lynch spoke to San Román next and assured him that the ships would "go in tonight" with the supplies he needed. That was certainly welcome news to the brigade commander; however, it was overshadowed by what he was told next: "Jets are coming." According to San Román, Lynch informed him that six jets and several B-26s would be arriving within two hours.[122] However, the information was inaccurate. The CIA *hoped* that the navy would be allowed to provide air cover for a B-26 mission to be flown that afternoon, but it was mere wishful thinking.[123] If Lynch did, in fact, give San Román a two-hour time frame for the arrival of jets, he may have been uninformed. Or perhaps it was desperate attempt to boost morale served with a helping of exaggeration.

San Román, of course, was oblivious to what was really going on behind the scenes. "Now we will hit them!" he joyfully exclaimed to those around him after hearing Lynch's words. Oliva, however, felt remorseful. He now began to doubt his decision to withdraw from Playa Larga and to regret having suggested abandoning the invasion plan altogether and heading east.[124]

The deputy brigade commander's mood no doubt brightened when he visited the men of the Second Battalion resting in Girón. Oliva dropped in on them after inspecting the Sixth Battalion's defenses west of town. The veterans of Playa Larga welcomed "Maceo" with cheers and genuine affection. After sharing the good news about the coming jets, he told them to rest because perhaps that afternoon they would have to fight again. "Oliva, with leaders like you, we would fight to the ends of the world," eighteen-year-old Humberto Díaz told him. In spite of himself, Oliva became visibly moved.[125]

* * * *

By midmorning, the anticipated advance by Castro's forces south from the Muñoz Canal was under way. As was their standard tactic, the brigade defenders were camouflaged on either side of a curve where the road from Covadonga exited the swamp. A majestic ceiba tree with luxuriant foliage marked the deceptively peaceful spot where hell was about to be unleashed.[126]

As soon as the vanguard of the advancing columns came into view, they were met with a flurry of projectiles. Interlocking fields of fire from two .50 caliber machine guns straddling the road cut across it like dual scythes. When the brigade mortars opened up, the frontal advance down the causeway ground to a stop. Small groups of militiamen were then sent slogging through the swamp to try to flank the enemy, but the going was slow and difficult. Explosive shells and grenades plunged into the mud all around them.[127] The 120 mm mortars of the advancing force joined the fray trying to soften up the defender's well-emplaced positions.[128]

An army bazooka man named Arteaga was making his way back to the road through the brush when mortar shells began falling near him. He had ventured into the bordering swampland minutes before when he heard voices coming from there. The voices turned out to be from a transistor radio left behind by some brigade soldier. Now, back on the causeway, he was met by a gruesome spectacle. Three of his fellow army mates lay on the ground, horribly mutilated.[129] "My God, what is this!" exclaimed Félix Duque from nearby, stunned by the ghastly scene. Evelio Saborit beside him urged medic Luis Posada to do something for one of the injured men who was still conscious despite losing all four of his limbs. "Look at the comrade!" the frustrated medic shouted back. "Even putting four tourniquets on him would not save his life. His injuries are horrendous, and he has already almost bled dry. For reasons of humanity, of mercy, in cases like this sometimes it would be preferable to . . ." Posada "did not complete his thought," noted William Selva, who recorded the event. "It was [something] impossible for a Revolutionary to carry out, more so under the circumstances."[130] Selva's denial notwithstanding, Arteaga tells a different story that suggests the mercy killing of at least one of the victims, Diógenes Jiménez.[131] "All of Diógenes's intestines and insides had spilled out, and he had a gunshot here, in the head. When we put him on the pickup truck, I looked at him. He was already dead."

"To boot," according to Arteaga, "the firing came from behind us; it was our own fire. That makes it even harder to take; it pisses you off even more."[132] "The mortar fire caused turmoil," he recalled. "[Our] lieutenant faltered and we faltered too. . . . He ordered us to retreat, to go back a ways. . . . [He] became nervous because the incoming fire was from our own people." The spooked men only started moving forward again when an army commander showed up and ordered them to do so.[133] By then the mortars to their rear had finally found their mark and were hitting the brigade position. Further supported by .30 caliber ZB-30 machine guns, the infantry push continued.[134]

Sometime before 11:00 a.m., Alejandro del Valle dispatched an urgent message to San Román in Girón: the last remaining stronghold north of San Blas was under heavy attack, and reinforcements were needed.[135]

* * * *

At 10:30 a.m., back in Havana, Castro had just concluded an hour-long meeting with some of his army commanders. He intended, they were told, to take San Blas as soon as possible and push toward Girón from the north as well as from the west. René de los Santos, appointed by Almeida to lead the Yaguaramas–San Blas offensive, would be replaced by Captain Emilio Aragonés, a member of M-26-7's inner circle. Castro's cheeky pet name for the plump Aragonés was *Gordo* (Fatman) and, in typical Cuban fashion, he would rarely refer to him any other way.[136]

In addition to Santo's forces, Aragonés was to assume command of four other battalions and fifteen tanks, including ten IS-2 Stalin tanks, that would be dispatched from Managua. Chief of Artillery Pedro Miret, also present at the meeting, was ordered to personally lead twelve 122 mm artillery guns to the area. They would be used to heavily bombard the enemy-held territory around San Blas.[137]

After the meeting ended, unaware that Playa Larga had just been occupied, Castro again returned to his planned encirclement of the forces there. Three hours earlier, he had summoned commander Efigenio Ameijeiras, head of the PNR, and ordered him to prepare to take his combat battalion from Havana to Soplillar. From there, they were to reach the coastal road and cut off the Playa Larga defenders from Girón.[138] It was the same mission that Fernández had already previously assigned to Battalions 227 and 144 separately. Castro did not know that Battalion 227, although in place at Caleta del Rosario, had failed to interfere with the pullout of Oliva's forces. Neither was he aware that Battalion 144—after getting lost for lack of a guide—had not arrived there until 9:00 a.m. when it was too late to block the enemy's withdrawal.[139]

At 11:10 a.m. Castro issued orders for Ameijeiras to be at Soplillar with his troop by dawn of the next day. Just thirty-two minutes later, however, *El Comandante*'s plan evaporated when Martínez called from Central Australia to inform him that the enemy had withdrawn from Playa Larga. "It is shameful that those characters were able to withdraw to Playa Girón, shameful!" Castro irately shouted into the phone. "It's utterly negligent that not even one company was sent to block their way. A company should have already been on that road! Setting out from Soplillar we should have already reached the coast. . . . You must see how simple it would have been to place a company on the coast to block the withdrawal of those gents, who will fight on otherwise. So now you will tell Fernández for me that he must advance! Tell him to do as he was told." He then asked Martínez to put Chief of Operations Flavio "Julio" Bravo on the phone.[140] Castro dressed him down for not ensuring that his orders were followed. "Julio, how is it that that those people's withdrawal was not blocked? . . . I ordered that some infantry troops be sent to cut off their withdrawal. Why was this not done, given that it is also elementary?" Bravo's response is not recorded, but Castro was in no mood for excuses. "The least you can do [now] is to pursue those people with tanks, those six [*sic*] tanks there! . . . Are they not pursuing the enemy? Tell me if you have a pact of non-aggression with the mercenaries!" Briefly interrupting the conversation, he instructed Chief of Staff Del Valle to order the FAR to immediately launch an air attack on the withdrawing forces. Then, back on the phone with Bravo, he continued his tirade. "I'm sending in the air force given that you have let them escape when you should have pursued them. What concept of war is that? What are you doing with so many artillery guns and so many tanks! It is shameful! Julio, order them to pursue those people immediately. . . . Find a way to pursue them into Girón, lest a ship goes in to pick them up. . . . Mark my words, the mercenaries are going to get away!" For over fifteen minutes Castro gave vent to his frustration at the turn of events in Playa Larga.[141] His fear that the invaders would reboard the ships and escape would be a recurring theme of his ongoing harangues.

* * * *

CIA headquarters received the bad news from JMTIDE at 11:23 a.m. about the failure of the previous night's airstrike attempts on Cuban air-fields. The cable from Nicaragua requested approval for another strike against San Antonio at dusk or just before dawn. Although not specifi-cally mentioning the situation with the Cuban exile pilots, JMTIDE also requested permission to use American contract pilots.[142]

With the invasion now on the brink of collapse, CIA headquarters knew that gaining control of the air was imperative for averting, or at least postponing, disaster. Clearly, the best option was to convince Wash-ington to allow U.S. Navy jets to enter the fray, something the CIA men still hoped would happen soon. As a fallback, however, a number of single-seat, piston-engine Mustang F-51 (a.k.a. P-51) fighters had been obtained from the Nicaraguan government. The plan was to fly these fighters to Girón and operate them from there.[143] To make up for the B-26 lost during the previous day, arrangements were made for four replacements to be flown to Nicaragua from Eglin Air Force Base.[144]

The reply from headquarters to JMTIDE's cable was not long in coming. At 11:26 a.m. the airbase was instructed to deploy the F-51s and informed that the Americans could fly B-26 missions but only over the beachhead. The cable spelled out explicitly the restrictions to be placed on the American airmen and what they could expect from their govern-ment if captured:

AMERICAN CONTRACT CREWS CAN BE USED B-26 STRIKES BEACH-HEAD AREA AND APPROACHES ONLY. EMPHASIZE BEACHHEAD AREA ONLY. CAN NOT ATTACH SUFFICIENT IMPORTANCE TO FACT AMER-ICAN CREWS MUST NOT FALL INTO HANDS ENEMY. IN EVENT THIS HAPPENS DESPITE ALL PRECAUTIONS CREWS MUST STATE HIRED MERCENARIES, FIGHTING COMMUNISM, ETC; US WILL DENY ANY KNOWLEDGE.[145]

Within minutes, another cable from arrived at JMTIDE from headquarters:

IMMEDIATELY UPON RECEIPT THIS MESSAGE, LAUNCH FIFTY PER-CENT B-26 STRIKE[.] AIRCRAFT ARMED YOUR DISCRETION[.] DESTROY TANKS AND VEHICLES ON APPROACHES BEACHHEAD.

CONSERVE CUBAN CREWS FOR MAX EFFORT NIGHT ATTACKS TAR-GET ONE [i.e., San Antonio airbase].[146]

Lynch soon after relayed the news to San Román of the scheduled arrival of F-51s at Girón that night alongside a C-46 carrying ammunition and other supplies.[147] Although headquarters urged the "USE OF F-51'S IN SUPPORT OF GROUND FORCES FROM PLAYA GIRON [*sic*]," the plan had a major flaw: None of the Cuban exile pilots at JMTIDE had any experience flying that type of plane.[148]

NOON—4:00 PM

By noon, the pressure on the last remaining brigade position north of San Blas had become unbearable. Hence, the evacuation of its seventy to eighty defenders into San Blas itself, two miles to the south, was under way. Only a single 4.2-inch mortar and its crew were left in place to cover the pullout. "At that time we were in the hands of God," recalled Roberto San Román, "because we had only one gun protecting the road."[149]

Castro's men, however, were not inclined to rush the enemy position. Their attempts to seize it had cost them as many as six dead and an untold number of wounded. "It was there," remarked Félix Duque, "that we suffered the most serious losses up to that moment."[150] When they finally occupied the site after the brigade units had retreated, assorted weapons, food articles, and personal items were discovered. Infantryman William Selva came across "bottles of clear nail polish and some underwear" that to him "seemed more like panties than athletic underpants." "It is very possible," he surmised, "that among that group of unscrupulous people there may have been some homosexuals."[151] Alongside ration packs and boxes of Corn Flakes, there were also orange bars wrapped in black nylon. One of the men, convinced that they were orange paste bars, bit into one and was immediately sickened by its terrible taste. Only later did he find out, much to his embarrassment and the amusement of the others, that the "orange paste" was actually plastic explosive.[152]

* * * *

Sometime around half past noon, the Third Battalion, escorted by a tank, set out from Girón to reinforce Del Valle. Pepe San Román still anticipated an attack on Girón from the east, but with the situation in the north quickly deteriorating, he had to engage in operational triage. He sent the Fourth Battalion unit that had returned from Playa Larga to take up the positions vacated by the Third Battalion on the trail to Cienfuegos.[153]

The convoy heading to San Blas had gone less than two miles when it was attacked by a FAR fighter. It was one of a pair of Sea Furies being flown over the area by Gustavo Bourzac and Douglas Rudd. As the trucks zigzagged to avoid the bullets streaming down from the sky, a melee developed among the frenzied men onboard seeking to jump off. Some got hurt when others landed violently on top of them. On its second pass, the plane was met by .50 caliber machine gun fire from both the trucks and tank. Thinking better of it, the pilot broke off the attack.[154]

One the Sea Furies (flown by Douglas Rudd) also attacked a stray brigade truck north of San Blas. A rocket fired from the plane found its mark and the vehicle, which carried munitions, blew up. The lone driver aboard managed to open the door and started to crawl out of the burning hulk but got no farther. As it happened, two of Castro's men were nearby and witnessed the spectacle. One of them went over and, grabbing the hair on the dead man's head, pulled his body out of the fiery cab. "I couldn't just leave him there to burn!" he snapped back at his companion who silently stood by staring at him in disbelief.[155]

Both pilots afterward proceeded to Girón.[156] One likely victim of their raid on the town was six-year-old Alberto Cordova. The boy, who had been playing outdoors, received a serious wound to his leg that bled profusely. Little in the way of medical help was available, so the brigade's Catholic priests (three had landed[157]) apparently led a group of imprisoned locals in praying a rosary for him. As the child's condition continued to worsen, his father—a local man who had joined the brigade and wore its uniform—became increasingly desperate. Cradling his son in his arms, he set off on foot for the rural hospital at Cayo Ramona, seven miles away.[158]

The existence of the medical facility, whose construction had begun under Batista and included a small operating room, was not identified in the invasion plan. Brigade surgeon Juan Sordo had first heard of it hours earlier that very day. He had gone there, escorted by an infantry squad, with a group of wounded men needing surgery. One of the two doctors at the facility had agreed to cooperate but not the other. Pointing to the uncooperative one, Dr. Sordo told the infantrymen accompanying him, "Sit this man down. If he moves, put a bullet through his head."[159]

For young Alberto Cordova none of that mattered, however. He died from blood loss in his father's arms before reaching the hospital.[160]

* * * *

Since learning of the invaders' withdrawal from Playa Larga, Castro had become concerned that they might try to flee en masse toward Cienfuegos along the coastal trail. Thus, he planned to land troops east of

Girón by helicopter, unaware that, per his order of the previous day, Battalion 326 had already been sent there.[161]

His mind was changed when he spoke on the phone to Almeida in Santa Clara at 12:45 p.m. Almeida informed him that a militia battalion under Orlando Pupo was already approaching Girón from the east. Moreover, commander Tomassevich in Cienfuegos was preparing to follow behind Pupo with another battalion. *El Comandante* was very pleased at the news. "What matters to me," he told Almeida, "is that we be in possession of the coast east of Girón. That is of primary importance because they are going to flee in that direction . . . and they are going to fall into the hands of whomever is advancing down the coast. . . . We mean to capture them all." He ordered Almeida to send Pupo a message "by horseback or whatever means" instructing him to advance at night and take up a position three miles from Girón.[162] Castro's aim was to lure the enemy into a trap by making them think they could escape eastward unopposed. Thus, he was adamant that Pupo's force not attack the brigade forces.[163] At 1:10 p.m. he again telephoned Almeida to reiterate his directive. "[Pupo] is not to take Girón. . . . Listen carefully, Almeida. Make sure that he receives that order."[164]

But even as Castro and Almeida spoke, Captain Pupo and Battalion 326 were already less than a mile from the eastern outskirts of Girón. Although his orders from Ciutat had been to merely "tickle" the enemy, Pupo evidently felt that he had to draw close to do any tickling. He now arranged his men in a wedge-shaped assault formation, like an arrowhead pointed at Girón. From its tip on the coastal trail, the wings of the wedge extended to the shoreline on one side and to the thicket on the other. Onward toward Girón they thus marched.[165]

* * * *

Peasants, workers and militia are joining the freedom front and aiding the rapidly expanding area already liberated by the Revolutionary Command.

So proclaimed the latest "CRC bulletin" issued at 1:20 p.m. by the CIA through Lem Jones.[166] The situation described was far from truthful, but as Mark Twain had said, "Lying is a necessity of our circumstances." And indeed the circumstances in which the invasion found itself were dire and growing more so.

At 1:25 p.m. the *Blagar* relayed a cable message "from brigade Commander to Colonel Mallard," which read:

UNDER HEAVY ATTACK SUPPORTED BY 12 TANKS. NEED AIR SUPPORT IMMEDIATELY. RED BEACH WIPED OUT. REQUEST AIR STRIKES. NEED AMMO OF ALL TYPES IMMEDIATELY. 4 B-26 ETA BEACH HEAD [*sic*] 181900Z [4:00 PM]. REQUEST NAVY AIR [COVER] FOR BEACHHEAD. IF NOT PROVIDED EXPECT LOSS 4 B-26. CONFIDENT YOU CAN PROVIDE. ADVISE.[167]

Notwithstanding its stated source, the cable unquestionably did not come from San Román, although it did rehash information from his earlier messages. "Colonel Mallard" was Marine Colonel John F. Mallard, the CIA's liaison aboard the *Essex*,[168] of whom San Román would have had no knowledge. The communication was, in effect, an appeal from JMTIDE for air support.

The B-26s strike ordered by headquarters just before noon departed Nicaragua shortly after 2:00 p.m. Despite the directives received from Washington, the ground support mission was initially set to be flown entirely by Cubans. Eight of them, including the brigade's Cuban air force chief, Manuel Villafaña, had volunteered to fly in four B-26s. The voluntary-basis-only rule that he and his chief of operations had set down for Cuban participation was now in effect. American pilots Connie Seigrist and Doug Price, both with a CIA front company in the Far East, were subsequently allowed to join the flight as they had requested. Air Operations Chief Gar Thorsrud agreed to let them fly if each could find a Cuban crewmate willing to accompany him, which they were able to do.[169]

* * * *

A stream of phone messages from Castro to be delivered to Fernández kept arriving at Central Australia.

12:10 p.m. *Tell Fernández . . . to grab the tanks and whatever else and go pursue those men because they are going to get away. . . . Those people are falling back, they are demoralized and must be pursued. It fills me with shame that a damned defeated enemy may get away!*[170]

12:26 p.m. Send another message to Fernández. Tell him from me that in my opinion the enemy is retreating completely demoralized overall. . . . That this is the moment to pursue them relentlessly. We have to try to take Girón because if not they will leave. . . . Tell him he has to understand that this is the psychological moment to pursue them. . . . He should take advantage of the eight tanks [sic] that we can get under way and pursue them without respite. [Tell him] that Girón must be taken this afternoon; to make a supreme effort.

The "eight tanks" Castro referred to apparently included the three T-34s that had survived the overnight fighting plus five, actually SU-100 tank destroyers, that he had been informed had arrived from Managua.[171]

1:27 p.m. Tell [Fernández] that the enemy is defeated . . . [and] to pursue them with utmost tenacity . . . for this is the psychological moment to do so. You tell him again to pursue [them] without letup. Tell him that Pupo is [one mile] from Playa Girón on the east; that he needs to hurry up or Pupo is going to take Girón away from him.

Castro, in fact, did not know the whereabouts of Captain Pupo and Battalion 326. Moreover, he had issued express orders twice within the previous hour for the captain *not* to attempt to take Girón, so the bluff was merely intended to egg Fernández on. Castro did not even think that Pupo's force had the necessary strength to take Girón in any case. "What the fuck is Pupo going to attack Playa Girón with?" he snarled at Martínez on the phone at 1:56 p.m. The latter, taken in by the bluff, had brought up Pupo's supposed competing offensive.

It was during that very call that *El Comandante*, in no uncertain terms, threw down the gauntlet for Fernández:

Look, if with eight tanks [sic] Fernández doesn't take Playa Girón before six in the evening . . . he should retire. Write it down and send it to him by motorcycle messenger. [Tell him] that if with eight tanks [sic], 24 artillery guns, a mortar battery and 5,000 men following behind he doesn't take Girón before six in the evening., he will have embarrassed himself before a fleeing enemy.[172]

* * * *

On the northern outskirts of San Blas, Castro's forces were making a determined push. "They are fucked and that position is lost," he declared when told at 1:51 p.m. of the offensive toward the settlement and the many weapons captured along the way.[173] But the pronouncement was to prove hasty. The brigade forces defending San Blas, now reinforced by the Third Battalion, were putting their all into the fight from well-placed positions. "It was the most intense combat since the first night," deemed one of the militia fighters partaking in the assault.[174] Using a Soviet-style tactic apparently passed down by advisers like Ciutat, the militiamen were ordered to rush the enemy in waves. Headlong they charged repeatedly into the concentrated fire from the brigade infantry and two tanks, suffering heavy casualties in the process. When their frontal assaults failed and they pulled back, ranged fire from the brigade's 4.2-inch mortars took an additional toll on them.[175]

As the casualties mounted, by 3:00 p.m. it became evident that San Blas would not fall as readily as Castro had hoped. The infantry assaults were halted and replaced by artillery fire. Even more artillery was just then arriving at Covadonga. Two batteries of 122 mm guns had come from Havana with Pedro Miret.[176]

Paratroop commander Del Valle in San Blas was not about to sit and take the pounding. Without the enemy taking notice, he ordered the withdrawal of his entire force to the western outskirts of the settlement, on the side closest to Girón. Booby traps were rigged around the place before abandoning it.[177] Using land mines was not an option as they had gone down with the *Río Escondido*.[178]

* * * *

To spearhead the advance on Girón, Captain Fernández in Playa Larga chose a militia battalion that had arrived from Havana aboard new Leyland buses just after noon, some two hours earlier. The approximately 1,000 men of MNR Battalion 123 were taken off the buses and formed up behind the five available SU-100s to begin twenty-one-mile march to Girón. Fernández realized that the journey there on foot would take eight to nine hours. Doing otherwise, however, would make the troop highly vulnerable to surprise air or land attack, as previous experience had shown.[179]

Just as the column was about to get on its way, Castro's ultimatum reached Fernández through Martínez at Central Australia.

Fidel says to go after those people quickly with whatever tanks and artillery you have on hand. You are not to waste time, nor the opportunity to finish those people off. Girón must be taken before six in the evening. Death to the invader.[180]

The order put the captain in a quandary. Regardless of the inherent dangers, only by transporting the infantry troops forward would he stand a chance of achieving what *El Comandante* demanded. A reconnaissance patrol had found no enemy forces within nine miles of Playa Larga, so at least there was no apparent ambush danger within said distance. Moreover, Fernández had earlier been told to expect air support and cover between 3:00 and 4:00 p.m. However reluctantly, therefore, he ordered one of his officers to put the men of Battalion 123 back aboard the buses that would now carry them on the road to Girón.[181]

* * * *

Trying to advance in wedge-shaped formation toward Girón from the east had not gone as Pupo had anticipated. Those trudging off-trail on the flanks were unable to make much headway due to the difficult terrain. Gradually they gravitated onto the longshore track and began to bunch up. It thus became apparent that the entire battalion would not be able to advance as a unit. Pupo thence placed a single platoon on each side of the path and hastened forward with the smaller force. The rest of the battalion trailed behind.

Within 400 yards of enemy positions near Playa Morena, a mile from Girón, the advancing force was spotted and came under mortar and machine gun fire. As the militiamen got closer to the enemy lines—at times by crawling on their stomachs—the fire from the brigade defenders intensified. Before long, three of Pupo's men lay wounded, one of them fatally. The advance ground to a halt and a stalemate punctuated by intermittent skirmishes set in between the opposing forces east of Girón.[182]

* * * *

That Oliva's force had long before fully withdrawn to Girón was not known to Castro or those trying to follow his orders. Insofar as FAR chief Curbelo in San Antonio was concerned, the order from Castro he had received just after noon still stood. His pilots were to locate the enemy force that had pulled out of Playa Larga and "give them hell."[183] However, the lack of accurate information on the location of their own troops made the job difficult for the pilots and perilous for friendly forces. Already, seeking to flush out the enemy, Prendes had strafed the area around Soplillar from a T-33.[184] He was evidently unaware that the place had been occupied by Castro's forces since the previous day.

As 3:00 p.m. rolled around, the air support and cover that Fernández had been promised was indeed overhead. From the air, the FAR pilots spotted a troop concentration at Caleta del Rosario. They had no idea that these were the militiamen of Battalion 144 who had arrived there too late that morning to stop the withdrawal of Oliva's force. Manuel Torreiro and the other members of the battalion were not concerned when they spotted a plane bearing FAR insignia pass overhead. Their sense of ease quickly dissipated when the plane looped back and started firing on them. There was nowhere to take shelter except for some water-filled rock cavities that the men crammed into.[185] In the midst of the mayhem, a comedic counterpoint played out to the amazement of all who witnessed it. One of the militiamen seeking cover stepped over someone lying on the ground and then turned around and repeated the maneuver in the opposite direction. Not to have done so, he explained afterward, "would have brought him bad luck."[186]

As is often the case with men under stress, the reports about the types of aircraft involved in the attack are inconsistent.[187] A B-26 was reported by one of the men. It flew so low, he said, that he could see the rear gunner firing his .50 caliber machine gun. The bullets ripped through Sandalio Díaz, throwing him three feet in the air and leaving him bleeding from everywhere when he hit the ground. Militiaman Torreiro was wounded by a bullet from the other aircraft (identified by him as a Sea Fury) that pierced his chest clear through.[188]

There were positively no brigade planes in the air at the time and the attack was undoubtedly carried out by FAR pilots. By the time the friendly fire incident ended, as many as thirty-nine had been wounded and one killed.[189]

4:00 PM—8:00 PM

The FAR planes that Fernández had counted on were gone by the time Battalion 123 finished reboarding the buses and set out for Girón after 4:00 p.m.[190] Two B-26s that were to follow aborted shortly after takeoff.[191]

Regardless of the situation in the air, however, Fernández had received an explicit order from Castro and he was not about to disregard it.[192] To defend against enemy planes, he would rely on truck-towed anti-aircraft guns sent ahead to be deployed along the route.[193]

The five SU-100s, commanded by Fermín Tobar, led the column of vehicles leaving Playa Larga. Groups of six or seven men from Battalion 123's first and light infantry companies sat atop each of the tank destroyers. Behind them, in single file, came the dozen buses filled with men and munitions.[194] The bus parade sent chills down the spines of a group of artillerymen who stood dumbfounded watching it. "We commented to each other that this was extremely dangerous," one of them said. "That type of transportation afforded the men aboard practically no way of escaping."[195] Before long, their apprehension would prove to be wholly justified.

* * * *

Against the original wishes and intentions of John F. Kennedy, U.S. Navy jets took to the skies over Cuba on the afternoon of April 18'. However, their strictly nonaggressive mission over the country (although they were authorized to "protect themselves from attack") was to determine the situation on the beachhead. Even at this juncture, maintaining the ridiculous pretense of American noninvolvement continued to be a concern. The navy airmen flew unmarked aircraft and were instructed to "take all possible precautions to avoid having operations identified as US."[196] "All possible precautions" included flying without dog tags or ID cards.[197]

The mission had been hastily approved in the wake of a chaotic noon meeting that had concluded just before 1:30 p.m. In attendance were the president and key members of his staff along with CIA and Pentagon officials, including Admiral Arleigh Burke, the chief of naval operations. As Burke summarized the chaos afterward, "Nobody knew what to do nor did the CIA . . . know what to do or what was happening."

So disquieting was the state of affairs that shortly after the meeting the president called on Admiral Burke to "advise him on the situation." "[B]ypassing Lemnitzer . . . CIA and the whole works and putting me in charge of the operation" was "a helluva thing," thought Burke.[198] Still, however reluctantly, he picked up the gauntlet and dispatched a telegram to Admiral Robert Dennison, commander in chief of the Atlantic Fleet.

THERE IS LITTLE INFORMATION HERE ON STATUS OF OPERATION. FEW REPORTS AVAILABLE INDICATE OPERATION MAY BE IN DESPERATE STRAITS. NO GENERAL UPRISING IN CUBA YET.

WHAT IS MOST URGENTLY NEEDED HERE IS INFORMATION ON WHICH TO MAKE AN ASSESSMENT OF THE SITUATION OR A JUDGMENT ON WHAT TO DO AT HIGH LEVELS.[199]

The eyeball reconnaissance flown from the *Essex* that afternoon in response to Burke's cable was, by all indications, an improvised undertaking assigned to airmen not trained for it. Reportedly, a "tattered Esso roadmap" was the only means the Skyhawk pilots had to orient themselves as they reconnoitered the terrain below. No less disconcerting, however, was their assigned air-to-air combat role aboard the carrier. The aviators admittedly lacked the necessary experience for such duty because the Skyhawks they flew were primarily light ground attack aircraft.[200]

More than nineteen miles east of Girón the jets whizzed over militia-laden trucks carrying the men of MNR Battalion 345 (formerly designated as 303). It was the additional battalion, led by Tomassevich, that Almeida had earlier told Castro would follow behind Pupo. Everyone immediately jumped off the trucks and scattered so far and wide that it took considerable time to regroup them all.[201]

When they overflew Girón, the sight of the unmistakably American planes brought a moment of jubilation to the brigade soldiers there. They leaped out of their prepared positions to wave and cheer wildly.[202] The same occurred on the western outskirts of San Blas when the formation flew over the settlement headed north. Surely, they thought, the arriving jets signaled the start of the long-awaited U.S. air support and would now strike the enemy forces facing them. However, no explosions came, and soon the jets returned and soared away from the expectant men. "Watch for them, they'll be back," someone shouted out, as if making an act of faith.[203]

West of Girón the navy pilots spotted the line of vehicles making their way southeast from Playa Larga. Their subsequent reconnaissance report mentioned it but was glaringly inaccurate. Not only did the aviators err regarding key aspects of the caravan; they failed to note the enemy units east and north of Girón.

> *Large Castro <u>tanks (10 to 14)</u> with trucks and <u>lorries</u> on road from <u>Galli-</u> <u>nas</u> [? sic] extending to point about three miles south moving south and east. Only a few troops seen with convoy. <u>No others sighted</u>.* [Emphasis added.][204]

Still, these inaccuracies paled in comparison to another inconceivable deficiency. The inbound brigade bombers were passing over the *Essex* at 4:20 p.m. just as the carrier jets flew above the vehicles headed for Girón.[205] Notwithstanding their proximity, however, it was impossible for one set of pilots to pass on information to the other because their radios operated on different frequencies.[206]

* * * *

The six B-26s arrived over Cuba at 4:50 p.m. and spotted the long line of SU-100s followed by buses halfway between Playa Larga and Girón. Americans Seigrist and Price were the first to peel off from the group and head for the target.[207]

"Here come the sons of bitches!" came a yell from the front of one of the buses carrying the men of Battalion 123. Ironically, the alert did not come from anyone in charge but from a lowly cook. From his front row seat, despite taunts from the others, he had been keeping a close eye on the sky. At the sight of the two diving planes, the driver of the bus brought it to a stop, opened the front door and made a run for it. The back door remained closed, so a stampede of men surged forward for the one available exit. Nelson Domínguez was one of those who managed to make it out. As he stood by the side of road watching, the FAR insignias visible on the closest plane momentarily assuaged his fears. Officers aboard the lead buses also saw the insignia and ordered their drivers to keep going. Then, suddenly, the planes opened fire.[208]

Seigrist and Price passed over the convoy at low altitude. Each plane unleashed a torrent of .50 caliber bullets from its eight nose-mounted machine guns and fired off underwing rockets.[209] The five SU-100s in the lead, as well as the men riding on top of them, scrambled to get off the road and into the bordering thicket. They managed to do so but not before one man was killed and the tracks on two of the tank destroyers were blown off.[210]

Some 200 feet behind the armored vehicles, bullets started ripping through the bodies of the buses and into the bodies of the men inside. On one of the coaches a rocket burst through a windshield, slid down the center aisle, and impacted the back seat without exploding. Those who managed to escape, some by climbing out the windows, hunkered down by the sides of the road unable to do much but watch. For one unhinged individual, however, even watching proved too much. To "protect" himself from the sight of the planes, the man draped a plastic rain sheet over his head. Some futilely fired at the bombers with their rifles and the few complete .30 caliber machine guns that had made it out of the buses. The strain on the men rose even further when rumors went around that the airstrike was a precursor to an infantry counterattack.[211]

As the two planes disappeared in the distance toward Playa Larga, many thought the worst was over. But then another pair came at the convoy and more explosions followed, each accompanied by an expanding wave of all-consuming fire. "They're dropping napalm!" someone shouted. A militiaman alongside the road found himself engulfed by flames which set his uniform and backpack on fire. He tore off everything that was burning and got down to his underwear and boots. The extensive burns over most of his body made him feel ill, but he had no pain, although periodically patches of flesh would reignite. Lying on the ground, he thought of his loved ones and prepared for what seemed inevitable: "I took off my boots, ready to die." Others quickly learned the futility of jumping into the nearby sea hoping to extinguish the flames. They emerged from the water still burning, and those standing around desperate to help compelled them to roll around in the sand.[212]

The antiaircraft artillery sent ahead of the column did not do much good. One gun crew suffered several casualties, two of them fatal, when one of the B-26s attacked the truck towing their weapon.[213] Another team, with no time to fully deploy and level their gun, resorted to haphazardly propping it up manually while firing.[214] None of the attacking planes apparently suffered any significant damage from ground fire and all made it back to JMTIDE.[215]

Although the airstrike lasted fifteen minutes,[216] to the men on the ground it surely must have seemed to go on forever. Each of the six planes made a total of three passes over the caravan. Altogether they unleashed 9,000 rounds of .50 caliber ammunition, fifty rockets, twenty fragmentation and eight napalm bombs.[217]

"A Dantesque spectacle," said militiaman Domínguez of the raid's shocking aftermath. "What moments before had been a defiant caravan of Leyland buses were now twisted and smoking hunks of metal. Inside and outside of them were carbonized bodies that gave off a peculiar stench, and chilling moans could be heard everywhere."[218] Wrecked vehicles strewn about in helter-skelter fashion completely blocked the road.[219] "One hell of a mess," is how the sight struck T-33 pilot Alberto Fernández when he arrived over the area minutes after the attacking bombers had already left.[220]

Estimates of the total number of casualties vary widely. The more than eight hundred figure offered by one of the exile pilots[221] is almost certainly too high; the "almost one hundred" alleged by the other side[222] is likely too low. The official Cuban government figure of militiamen from Battalion 123 who died during or as a result of the airstrike is fourteen plus one bus driver.[223] Whatever the actual number, some of those who were there think it could have been much worse. "If they had concentrated their fire on the thicket [where we hid alongside the road], they would have killed a whole bunch of comrades." Thus opined the burned militiaman who had taken off his boots expecting to die but managed to survive the ordeal.[224]

In the wake of the attack, any means of transport available was pressed into service carrying the injured to the closest medical facilities at Jagüey Grande, thirty miles away. The number of arrivals set off a wave of panic among the residents of the small town. "I began to think that we were losing the battle," recalled a local woman. "Dozens of wounded were arriving one after the other, covered with blood, horribly burned. Never have I seen anything like it. Many of us women were crying. . . . At that moment I thought that our side had suffered a great defeat and that the mercenaries were advancing on Jagüey."[225]

Even as Fernández arrived at the scene of the attack and became embroiled in the chaos,[226] Castro, oblivious to what had occurred, kept peremptorily messaging him through Central Australia.

5:25 p.m. *Fidel says: . . . Advance quickly with the tanks, guns, the mortar battery and the troop to Girón. . . . The enemy is on the run; the moment is now or never. Girón must be taken by six in the evening. . . . Death to the invader.*

6:15 p.m. *Fidel says: . . . Let me know the position of your advancing force. . . . I again tell you that we must take Girón before nightfall. I hope the planes have sufficiently softened up the position for you. . . . Death to the invader.*[227]

* * * *

That "desperate times call for desperate measures" appears to have been the prevailing mindset on Tuesday afternoon at CIA headquarters. Even as the first authorized use of napalm around the beachhead was taking place, the restrictions on its employment against Castro's military bases were being lifted. The telegram sent to JMTIDE at 5:01 p.m. read:

AUTHORITY NOW GRANTED FOR USE CARGO AIRCRAFT TO DELIVER IMPROVISED NAPALM BOMBS TO ISOLATED AIRSTRIPS. TARGETS SHOULD BE IN ORDER SAN JULIAN AB [AIRBASE], SANTIAGO AB, SAN ANTONIO AB, MANAGUA, NUEVA GERONA AB[.] CAUTION CREWS TO AVOID RESIDENTIAL AREAS.[228]

The "improvised napalm bombs" would consist of napalm-filled 55-gallon drums.[229] Headquarters was apparently unaware that earlier experiments at both JMADD and JMTIDE with pushing these home-made devices out of cargo planes had been unsuccessful.[230] No less dumbfounding than the crudeness of the scheme is the third-place priority assigned to attacks on San Antonio, where the offending FAR planes were based.

The napalm bombing of Cuban military installations was to take place around 2:00 a.m. on April 20.[231] Clearly, the CIA's last-ditch efforts to forestall defeat had moved into the realm of the desperately inane.

* * * *

The boom of the 85 mm field guns, which had seemed so deafening to the militiamen nearby, was dwarfed by the roar of the 122 mm artillery that began firing on San Blas after 5:00 p.m. "It was something like comparing the bark of a Pekingese with that of a Bulldog," one of them said.[232]

The twelve 122 mm guns that had arrived with Pedro Miret at Covadonga hours earlier were now emplaced near the Muñoz Canal. "That same night, we started shelling the zone occupied by the enemy," Miret would recall years later. Even then, he was apparently unaware that San Blas had been vacated by Del Valle and his men earlier that afternoon.[233]

Despite the bombardment, small groups of brigade soldiers sheltering on the outskirts of the settlement would periodically reenter it to obtain water from a well there. Over the coming hours, they would become numb to the incessant whistling of shells and nearby explosions that shook the ground around them.[234]

* * * *

President Kennedy had spent the afternoon deliberating with Secretary of State Rusk and other key figures on a reply to Khrushchev's ominous missive from that morning.[235] By 6:50 p.m. the official response letter signed by the president had been personally delivered by Rusk to Soviet ambassador Mikhail A. Menshov in Washington. Its key parts read:

> It cannot be surprising that, as resistance within Cuba grows, refugees have been using whatever means are available to return and support their countrymen in the continuing struggle for freedom. Where people are denied the right of choice, recourse to such struggle is the only means of achieving their liberties.
>
> I have previously stated, and I repeat now, that the United States intends no military intervention in Cuba. In the event of any military intervention by outside force we will immediately honor our obligations under the inter-American system to protect this hemisphere against external aggression. While refraining from military intervention in Cuba, the people of the United States do not conceal their admiration for Cuban patriots who wish to see a democratic system in an independent Cuba. The United States Government can take no action to stifle the spirit of liberty.[236]

In the coming hours, Kennedy would find it increasingly difficult to draw the tenuous line between overt and covert involvement in the Cuban operation.

* * * *

At Girón, San Román was becoming increasingly concerned by the escalating artillery bombardment to his north and the skirmishing on the east. He was sorely unaware that the navy jets seen earlier had merely been conducting reconnaissance and was puzzled by their inaction. With night nearing, he transmitted the following telegram at 6:00 p.m.:

FIRST BT. [BATTALION] UNDER HEAVY ARTILLERY ATTACK ALSO BLUE BEACH FROM EAST. REQUEST AIR KNOCK OUT ARTILLERY AS SOON AS POSSIBLE. WHERE IS OUR JET COVER GONE TO[?] PEPE.[237]

The brigade commander's attention then turned to the upcoming airdrops of desperately needed supplies that Lynch had told him would be made that night. He had marker lights placed on the airstrip over which C-54 planes, each carrying about 12,000 pounds of ammunition, were to make staggered airdrops before daybreak.[238]

Just before sunset, the first C-54 made its drop. However, the boxes were carried away by the wind as they parachuted down. Most ended up landing in the thicket to the north, and brigade soldiers accompanied by peasant volunteers set out with flashlights to search for them.[239] When the boxes recovered were opened, another of the snafus that came to characterize the whole invasion became apparent. The rifle ammunition clips delivered were for Springfield rifles rather than the M-1 Garands the brigade soldiers had. Making use of the bullets required finding empty M-1 clips and reloading them with the rounds extracted from the unusable ones.[240]

At 7:47 p.m., the beleaguered San Román again appealed to the Americans:

WILL BLUE BEACH HAVE JET COVER TONIGHT AND TOMORROW? REQUEST AIR COVER STAY LOWER DOWN AS ENEMY PLANES COME IN LOW. WAS ATTACKED BY JETS AFTER OUR OWN COVER ARRIVED. DID NOT RECEIVE HELP FROM AIR COVER. PEPE.[241]

A few minutes later, militia scouts began probing the defensive lines west of Girón. Francisco Montiel, commander of the Sixth Battalion positioned there, was slightly wounded in a skirmish. Fearing that this was the beginning of the anticipated assault from Playa Larga, San Román sent the Second Battalion to reinforce the Sixth. Oliva, who had volunteered, was put in overall command of the western defenses.[242]

8:00 PM—MIDNIGHT

Militiaman José León had been traveling westward along the coastal trail for hours looking for Captain Pupo and Battalion 326 to deliver the orders he carried. The deepening night added to the tension and fear he felt as he drove on alone down the ragged track with no sign of the men. At one point, sometime round 8:00 p.m., he heard someone shout out from the dark, "Get down or they'll kill you!" León, with his jeep's headlights blazing, was unknowingly driving past the militia lines facing Playa Morena toward the brigade positions nearby. Instantly the startled driver faced a flurry of gunfire that lit up the night like "a carnival." "Luckily, they shot high," he said, which enabled him to turn the jeep around and escape unharmed.[243]

Pupo did not much care for the orders León finally delivered to him. He was to pull his men back some four miles to Caleta Buena and set up a blocking position there to prevent any enemy movement toward Cienfuegos. The captain did not see the sense in abandoning what he considered an excellent advanced position.[244]

When the shooting and moving lights to the east were reported to San Román, he surmised that they heralded the major thrust he had long anticipated from that direction. The frogmen team, which had elected to remain ashore when the *Blagar* departed, was sent to defend the eastern fringes of Girón against possible infiltration raids from the east.[245] At 8:17 p.m., the worried Brigade Commander transmitted the following urgent message:

MANY VEHICLES LIGHTS APPROACHING BLUE BEACH FROM EAST ON COAST ROAD. REQUEST AIR OR NAVAL STRIKE WITH THEM. PEPE.[246]

Come morning, the mistaken belief that had prompted the request would have deadly—and pointless—consequences.

* * * *

Sorting out the chaos left in the wake of the airstrike on Battalion 123 took Fernández more than three hours. Sometime after 8:00 p.m. what was left of the troop was sent on foot toward Girón. However, the mission assigned to the haggard men was no longer to assault that enemy strong-hold. Instead, they were to secure a backtrail that ran north from a point three miles west of the all-important town.[247] It was a peripheral role and the unit would play no part in the coming fight.

By then, the PNR Battalion, along with the light infantry company of MNR Battalion 116, had arrived at Playa Larga. It was a combined force of some 1,000 men. Standing next to López Cuba's disabled T-34, Fernández informed battalion Commander Ameijeiras and his second-in-command, Samuel Rodiles, that their mission would now be to take Girón. The PNR men were to occupy the third echelon of the advance behind the men of Battalion 180 and a tank vanguard.[248] Only about half of Battalion 180 would be available to partake in the assault, however. The rest, Fernández had decided, would remain in Playa Larga in case of a surprise attack by the battalion reportedly left behind with the *Houston*.[249] He was referring to Montero's Fifth Battalion. This unintended distraction, resulting from their mere presence miles away, would be the only—if indirect—contribution that Montero and his men would make to the invasion.

At 9:00 p.m. Fernández dispatched a message to Martínez at Central Australia hoping, no doubt, that the attack plan it described would mollify Castro in Havana:

1. *We plan to advance until we make contact with the enemy in Girón. We believe we can move our lines forward to within [one or two miles] of Girón.*

2. *We are getting the 122 [mm artillery guns] into position and also the mortars. I ask you to send me two more batteries of 120 [mm] mortars now. . . . With them all, I will shell the enemy during the night.*

3. *At dawn, we plan to attack with artillery, infantry, tanks, and to advance with infantry on Girón.*

4. *Based on past experience, we think a tow truck will be needed to remove disabled tanks. Urgently request tank tracks from Managua.*[250]

* * * *

Just over half an hour after San Román's message inquiring if he would "HAVE JET COVER TONIGHT AND TOMORROW," CIA headquarters opted for giving the brigade commander a measured dose of reality. At 8:24 p.m. he was sent a message informing him that ships would be sent in on the night of April 19 for evacuation if he so recommended. It was the first time since the invasion began that such as prospect had been raised. In the interim, the cable added, a C-46 would land on the airstrip to deliver ammunition and evacuate the wounded.[251]

San Román did not immediately respond to the oblique implications of the message. His next transmission at 9:31 p.m. advised that the aircraft that would land needed to do so before morning. He also reported that the wind had carried away the supplies from the first airdrop and asked that the next one take place "on roads in town from low altitude."[252] Only a few of the packs that had parachuted down over the airstrip had been found and recovered.[253]

Half an hour later, however, not even bothering to use encryption, an exasperated San Román gave his reply to the insinuative message from headquarters.

DO YOU PEOPLE REALIZE HOW DESPERATE THE SITUATION IS? DO YOU BACK US UP OR QUIT? ALL WE WANT IS LOW JET COVER AND JET CLOSE SUPPORT. ENEMY HAS THIS SUPPORT. I NEED IT BADLY OR CANNOT SURVIVE. PLEASE DON'T DESERT US. AM OUT OF TANK AND BAZOOKA AMMO. TANKS WILL HIT ME AT DAWN. I WILL NOT BE EVACUATED. WILL FIGHT TO THE END IF WE HAVE TO. NEED MEDICAL SUPPLIES URGENTLY.[254]

Ironically enough, San Román was rejecting the very scenario that Castro feared would deprive him of total victory over the enemy—a naval evacuation of the invasion force.

* * * *

At Point Zulu, forty-seven miles from Girón out in the Caribbean, another attempt at a supply run to the beach was getting under way by 11:00 p.m.[255]

The *Atlántico* had rejoined the *Blagar* and *Barbara J* at Point Zulu by early evening. Some ten hours earlier, the freighter had been located by the U.S. Navy 127 miles out to sea and its captain "encouraged" to return. The *Caribe,* 124 miles farther out, had not been found until almost half past noon. Its captain, who stated his radio equipment had been shot up, was likewise "persuaded" by the navy to head back.[256] However, even at a sustained top speed of 10 knots (11.5 mph), there was no chance that the *Caribe* could reach Point Zulu until the next morning.[257]

Anticipating the *Atlántico*'s arrival, CIA headquarters had issued orders in the afternoon to transfer its cargo, as well as all the ammunition aboard the *Blagar* and *Barbara J,* into the three LCUs and make a night run to the beach. The plan was for the vessels to finish unloading and be off the beach by daylight.[258]

Transferring the materiel into the LCUs proved a grueling task. All the more so because, as described by frogmen Andy Pruna aboard the *Barbara J,* "a lot of the crew didn't want to help in the loading."[259] It became clear from the start that the arduous undertaking would take hours. Even longer would be required for the trip to the beach given that the speed of the LCUs was only 6 knots (7 mph).[260] At 6:55 p.m., a message from the *Blagar* had gone out to headquarters:

BARRACUDA [*BLAGAR*], MARSOPA [*BARBARA J*] AND LCU CANNOT ARRIVE BLUE BEACH DISCHARGE AND LEAVE BY DAYLIGHT. REQUEST JET COVER FOR US IN THE BEACH HEAD [*sic*] AREA.[261]

Another message from the ship had followed at 9:02 p.m. requesting a navy destroyer escort and yet another thirty-six minutes later warning that "IF LOW JET COVER NOT FURNISHED AT FIRST LIGHT WE WILL LOOSE [*sic*] ALL SHIPS."[262] By then, it had been decided that only the *Blagar* would accompany the LCUs to the beach, leaving the damaged *Barbara J* to await the arrival of the *Caribe*. Rip Robertson, however, rather than remaining aboard the *Barbara J,* went over to the *Blagar* to assist in the run and lend a hand with communications.[263]

The response from headquarters regarding the requested destroyer escort did not bring good news to the men preparing to head back to the beach: not possible.[264] The recalcitrant crewmen from the *Río Escondido,* who had spearheaded the earlier near-mutiny, had been consigned to the *Atlántico* to avoid their causing further trouble.[265] However, the *Blagar*'s own crewmen were apparently not much more inclined to put themselves back into harm's way without direct American support.

Sometime before midnight, another foreboding message went out from the *Blagar*:

IF WE CANNOT GET SANTIAGO [USS *EATON*] TO COVER US ON WAY IN AND OUT AND LOW JET COVER FEEL CUBAN CREW WILL MUTINY. CREW READY TO MUTINY NOW. REQUEST IMMED[IATE] ANSWER.[266]

* * * *

Jet cover was also foremost on the mind of Gar Thorsrud at JMTIDE as midnight approached.

Of the remaining Cuban B-26 pilots, only Gonzalo Herrera—fittingly nicknamed *El Tigre* (the Tiger) by the other Cubans—was "not only willing but anxious to fly." Thus, earlier that evening, Thorsrud had sought help from the five pilots of the Alabama Air National Guard (AANG) present at the base. "Fellas, this thing is going to hell," he told them. "A lot of Cubans have quit and we need volunteers for a mission in the morning." All five pilots offered to fly.[267]

Thorsrud was well aware that without air cover the coming missions faced almost certain doom. At 11:28 p.m. he sent the following cable to CIA headquarters:

1. . . . TWO B-26'S SCHEDULE OUT EVERY TWO HOURS TO WORK ALL ROADS LEADING INTO BEACHHEAD. C-54 BEING LOADED WITH 55 GALLON DRUMS OF NAPALM. ALSO TO HIT BEACHROADS [*sic*] AND MSR'S [MAIN SUPPLY ROADS] APPROACHING BEACH.
2. ALL ABOVE CREWS WILL BE AMERICAN. CUBAN CREWS NEARLY BROKEN WITHOUT AT LEAST 12 TO 24 HRS OFF.
3. ABOVE EFFORTS WILL CONTINUE THROUGH TOMORROW BUT VERY CONCERNED RE[GARDING] LACK OF EFFECTIVE NAVY AIR COVER. TONITE[']S B-26 MISSION WERE MET AT THE 12 [NAUTI-CAL] MILE LIMIT INBOUND AND OUTBOUND. BEACH REP[OR]TS ENEMY AIRCRAFT MADE PASSES ON BEACH WHILE NAVY A/C [AIR-CRAFT] REMAINED AT HIGH ALTITUDE. IF THIS PROCEDURE USED IN THE MORNING HQTRS CAN EXPECT TO LOSE SOME AMERICAN CREWS.[268]

The twelve-mile limit mentioned in the cable referred to the distance from the coast, in nautical miles (fourteen statute miles), that delimited Cuban territory. In actuality, the CAP had remained even farther out than Thorsrud stated, having been ordered to "operate no closer than 15 [nautical] miles [17 statute miles] to Cuban territory." This followed from the navy's Rules of Engagement (ROE) in place on the afternoon of April 17. Also, per the ROE, the naval pilots were authorized to attack enemy aircraft *only* if they made an "aggressive move" toward a navy ship. To constitute such a move, a plane would have to either approach the ship with open bomb bay doors or make a strafing run on it. "Attacks will not be made by US aircraft under any other condition," the ROE firmly specified.[269]

Thorsrud's message stretched the truth by intimating that only Americans would be imperiled if the navy did not change its procedures relative to this limit. In addition to pilot Herrera, two Cubans had volunteered to fly in the B-26s as observers.[270] Other Cubans would supposedly also have been aboard the C-54 dropping improvised napalm bombs on beachhead approaches (apparently prior to their deployment against miliary facilities).[271] In pleading on behalf of fellow Americans, however, Thorsrud may have been playing what he considered was his best trump card.

The Cuban flag is raised at the stern of the *Blagar* in an emotional
ceremony as the invasion fleet arrives within 50 miles of the main
landing beach at Girón. Standing in salute to the right of the flag are
Cuban Revolutionary Council representative Manuel Artime and Assault
Brigade 2506 Commander (in Stetson hat) Pepe San Román.
(Courtesy Brigade 2506 Museum and Library.)

Deputy Brigade Commander Erneido Oliva (left) brilliantly led the defense of the beachhead on the west against the main thrusts of Castro's forces. Alejandro del Valle (right) and his paratroopers bore the brunt of counterattacks from the north. *(Courtesy Brigade 2506 Museum and Library.)*

Although scraggy and undermanned, Castro's air force proved its effectiveness right from the start of the invasion. A Sea Fury (above) flown by Enrique Carreras put the *Houston* (below) out of action while supplies and troops remained aboard. Subsequently, again in a Sea Fury, he sunk the *Río Escondido*, depriving the invaders of vital communication equipment and ammunition aboard. *(Cuban press photos.)*

Sitting in front of this T-33 (top) is Enrique Carreras, the only one of Castro's pilots who could fly the jet as well as Sea Fury and B-26 aircraft. The T-33s, although in disrepair and subject to breakdowns, took a heavy toll on the brigade's B-26 bombers. Exile pilot Matías Farías was forced to make a crash landing at the Girón airstrip after his bomber was jumped by a T-33. Farías was pulled alive from the wreck (below), but his crewmate was killed. *(Cuban press photos.)*

The B-26s used by the invaders were painted to resemble those of Castro's air force. To aid in their identification by friendly forces, a light blue stripe was painted around each wing. The stripe (see arrows) is visible on this otherwise yet unpainted bomber and on the crashed one above. *(CIA photo.)*

Captain José R. Fernández (center) was Castro's point man for the main counterattacks against the beachhead, which focused on its western reaches. *(Cuban press photo.)*

From midnight to sunup on April 18, Fernández's superior forces tried but failed to seize this road junction at the hamlet of Caletón. The defenses prepared by Erneido Oliva centered on the pit seen below the billboard. The disabled T-34 tank in the foreground had led the assault and carried tank battalion commander Néstor López Cuba (inset). *(Cuban press photos.)*

Czech-made Vz. 53 quad guns were the mainstay of Castro's antiaircraft defenses. Their crews consisted of young militiamen under the age of twenty. *(Cuban press photo.)*

Wreck of the B-26 flown by American airmen Thomas "Pete" Ray (inset, left) and Leo Baker (inset, right) on the last day of the invasion. It crash-landed near the Central Australia sugar mill after being hit by antiaircraft fire from Vz. 53 quad guns. Incredibly, both men survived the crash and managed to escape the wreck before it exploded but were shot dead by arriving militiamen. *(Cuban press photos. Airmen photos courtesy Brigade 2506 Museum and Library.)*

Militiamen of Battalion 123 prepare to board the bus caravan that would take them into battle behind SU-100 tank destroyers. Although ill advised, Fernández was under time pressure from Castro to seize the key town of Girón. *(Cuban press photo.)*

A smoldering hulk bears witness to the relentless attack by six B-26 bombers on the bus caravan carrying the men of Battalion 123. The attack, which included the use of napalm, eliminated the unit as a frontal fighting force. *(Ernesto Fernández/Cuban press photo.)*

The heaviest artillery weapons available to the brigade fighters were 4.2-inch mortars (above). They were greatly outmatched by Castro's preeminent 122 mm field guns (below). *(Cuban press photos.)*

Brigade M-41 Walker Bulldog light tank (above) and soldiers (below) captured after the end of the battle. *(Cuban press photos.)*

9

Wednesday, April 19, 1961

MIDNIGHT–7:30 AM

Fernández's forces for the morning attack on Girón were building up six miles west of there at a small settlement named Punta Perdiz. The captain himself had arrived there the previous evening but, lacking maps (which Castro ordered remain at Central Australia[1]), did not know the settlement's name or exactly how far it was from the enemy-held objective. Fortunately for Fernández, a German-born resident carpenter "possessing some culture" had, unlike his neighbors, opted to remain behind. From this man, the captain learned about their location as well as the size of the enemy forces that had passed by earlier to and from Playa Larga. Punta Perdiz, he then decided, was a good place from which to stage the coming attack.[2]

For a time, as men and equipment piled up in and around the darkness-cloaked hamlet, Fernández thought that it would be impossible to impose order on the chaos. As he later recalled, "There were overturned water trucks, shot-up vehicles . . . [and] you couldn't walk on the road; you had to do it over the people . . . that were sleeping [on it]." After establishing a defensive perimeter some 500 feet east of Punta Perdiz, he began taking stock of the units already there and those just arriving.[3]

* * * *

An uneasy calm had set in at Girón. When the all-out attack expected the night before failed to materialize, Oliva and the Second Battalion

159

had been ordered back into town to await further developments. However, San Román knew well that this was the proverbial calm before the storm that was sure to come. At some point he again lost all contact with the *Blagar*. "Maybe they turned the radio off in order not to hear my complaints."[4] It was an insightful and, from all indications, accurate inference. The brigade commander was evidently being kept in the dark about the disheartening exchanges between CIA headquarters and the ship begrudgingly headed for shore.

Out at sea, unbeknownst to those in such dire straits on land, the forlorn hope ultimately came to naught. Unable to meet the *Blagar*'s demands for air or destroyer cover, some hours past midnight headquarters cabled the ship to return with the LCUs to Point Zulu.[5]

* * * *

"It was a session in the Oval Office no one present is likely to forget," wrote Walt Rostow of the meeting that had begun just before midnight and ended at 2:46 a.m.[6] Beside Rostow, an academic and close Kennedy adviser, also in attendance were McGeorge Bundy, historian-adviser Arthur Schlesinger, Defense Secretary R. McNamara, Admiral Burke, and Bissell. All agreed that, although there was a lack of concrete information available, the dispatches from the beachhead indicated that things were going badly. Bissell and Burke argued for employing unmarked navy jets to provide full air support, up to and including a strike to knock out the T-33s. President Kennedy, however, opted for a compromise: he authorized six jets from the *Essex* to fly incognito cover for the brigade planes for a one-hour period that morning. The navy fliers were not to seek air combat or go after ground targets but could defend the brigade planes from attack.

Bissell was greatly disappointed with Kennedy's compromise decision. Rusk, on the other hand, thought allowing the jet cover would more deeply involve the United States and said as much to the president. "We're already in it up to here," Kennedy replied, raising his hand to a point just below his nose.[7]

Almost immediately, the implementation of the decision taken at the meeting started to go awry.

Bissell carried the news of the presidential directive back to CIA headquarters and by 3:04 a.m. a FLASH-precedence cable was on its way to JMTIDE. (FLASH is the highest priority available for official communications and is reserved for "an emergency situation of vital proportions."[8]) The principal portions of the cable read:

1. POSITIVE AGGRESSIVE NAVY AIR SUPPORT AND COVER GRANTED FOR ONE HOUR 11:30Z[9] [6:30 A.M.] TO 12:30Z [7:30 A.M.] 19 APRIL.

2. ALL ENEMY FORCES ON APPROACHES LEADING INTO PLAYA GIRON [*sic*] AIRFIELD SHOULD BE ATTACKED.

3. SUPPLY AIRCRAFT WILL ALSO RECEIVE ESCORT FOR THIS PERIOD.

4. MAIN PURPOSE IS HOPE TO CATCH ENEMY AIRCRAFT IN AREA.

5. FOLLOW ON AIR STRIKES [. . .] DESIRED.

6. PLEASE ADVISE PLAN.

7. ESSENTIAL MAKE BEST USE OPPORTUNITY THIS ONE HOUR PERIOD.

The message originated with Stanley Beerli, one of Bissell's subordinate chiefs.[10] One wonders if Bissell misrepresented or Beerli misunderstood the scope of Kennedy's directive given the mention of "navy air support." Air support, meaning aerial attacks on ground targets, was explicitly outside the scope of the president's authorized mission for the navy jets.

Inconceivably, the cable from headquarters did not result in any immediate changes at JMTIDE to the planned B-26 takeoff schedule. The first pair of them took off from the base at approximately 3:15 a.m. Aboard one of them was an all-American crew: pilot Thomas "Pete" Ray and crewmate Leo Baker. The pilot of the other bomber was American Dalton Livingston, who was accompanied by a Cuban volunteer. As the evidence clearly shows, they arrived over Cuba at 6:00 a.m., half an hour before the scheduled air cover.[11] Yet another B-26 flight evidently took off about fifteen minutes later—again too early to arrive within the air cover window. One of the planes was piloted by *El Tigre* Herrera, who flew on alone because his Cuban crewmate jumped out as he was taxiing. Aboard the other was pilot Billy Goodwin along with another American.[12] No one in either of the two flights was told anything about air cover.[13]

It seems, however inconceivable, that it took some time for JMTIDE to acknowledge the FLASH message sent by headquarters. In his history of air operations during the invasion, CIA historian Jack Pfeiffer glosses over this incongruity (although he interviewed Thorsrud for the project). At 3:15 a.m., oblivious to the top-priority cable, Thorsrud dispatched a message to Rear Admiral John A. Clark, commanding officer of the *Essex*. It was in the same vein as his telegram to headquarters the previous night but used the naval acronym for air cover: CAP (combat air patrol).

B-26'S FLYING CONTINUAL SORTIES FOR CLOSE SUPPORT BEACH-HEAD. IMPERATIVE CONTINUAL AIR CAP BE PROVIDED AT REPEAT AT BLUE BEACH NOT REPEAT NOT AT THE 12 [NAUTICAL] MILE LIMIT. YOUR PILOTS SHOULD STAND BY 121.5 [MEGAHERTZ RADIO FREQUENCY]. ALSO C-46'S AIR LANDING AT AIRFIELD. WILL BE SITTING DUCKS WITHOUT YOUR HELP . . . THESE ARE AMERICAN BOYS. RESPECTFULLY, AIR COMMANDER, [JM]TIDE.[14]

Thorsrud's message would have lacked any special significance for Clark. As far as the admiral was concerned, he had no authority to override the standing ROE which forbade navy planes from flying closer than 15 nautical miles to Cuba. It was not until 3:37 a.m. that the JCS informed him and Admiral Dennison of the orders resulting from Kennedy's decision. The parts of the cable pertaining to the CAP read as follows:

1. TG 81.8 TO FURNISH AIR COVER OF 6 UNMARKED AIRCRAFT OVER CEF [Cuban Expeditionary Force] FORCES [*sic*] DURING PERIOD 0630 [6:30 A.M.] TO 0730 [7:30 A.M.] LOCAL TIME 19 APRIL TO DEFEND CEF AGAINST AIR ATTACK FROM CASTRO FORCES. DO NOT SEEK AIR COMBAT BUT DEFEND CEF FORCES FROM AIR ATTACK. DO NOT ATTACK GROUND TARGETS. PILOTS CARRY AS LITTLE IDENTIFICATION AS PRACTICABLE. IF NECESSARY TO DITCH, DITCH AT SEA.

2. CEF TRANSPORT AIRCRAFT, TO INCLUDE C-46, C-54 AND POSSIBLY C-130 TYPES, ARE SCHEDULED TO AIR DROP SUPPLIES TO CEF FORCES IN BEACHHEAD FROM 190630R TO 190730R [APRIL 19, 6:30 TO 7:30 A.M. LOCAL TIME]. FRIENDLY B-26'S ARE SCHEDULED TO ATTACK CASTRO TANKS AND FORCES IN VICINITY OF BEACH-HEAD DURING SAME PERIOD.

[. . .]

NEW SUBJECT. FURNISH AIR COVER TO CEF SHIPS MORE THAN 15 MILES FROM COAST AS PRACTICABLE.[15]

Despite the ambiguous "over CEF" qualifier, there was no explicit mention that the fifteen-nautical-mile exclusion zone specified in the standing ROE had been rescinded. The matter was further confounded by the inclusion of CEF ships *outside* of this zone within the umbrella of air protection.

Clearly, the scope and tone of the orders issued by the JCS were decidedly more restrained than the contents of the cable from CIA headquarters. The disconnect between the two is not surprising as no attempt was made to coordinate the directives to their respective field personnel.[16] One point is clear, however: there was no ambiguity regarding the time window for the navy operation. This utterly invalidates the often-repeated assertion by various authors,[17] including Bissel,[18] that differences in time zones between Cuba and Nicaragua led to confusion in implementation.[19]

* * * *

At 5:25 a.m., with sunrise just over half an hour away, Fernández messaged Martínez at Central Australia about the makeup and disposition of his assault force:

> *1. Tanks, protected by infantry, 120 [mm] mortars, 122 [mm artillery] guns, the PNR Battalion, 400 men of [Battalion 227] and Battalion 180 (500 men), all poised to attack except the latter.*
>
> *2. Six quad-gun and one 37 [mm antiaircraft] batteries protect the aforementioned units. All in position. Two quad-gun [antiaircraft] batteries protect Playa Larga.*
>
> *3. We need support from our Rebel Air Force [FAR]. PS: [Three miles] from Girón [are located] our tanks and infantry; behind [them], all the rest. Alert our FAR of same.*[20]

In truth, the actual situation on the ground was considerably more muddled. Rodiles, who had been put in operational command of the PNR Battalion by Ameijeiras, had started out in complete darkness from Punta Perdiz about half an hour prior to Fernández's message. But not only had the troops from Battalion 180 not arrived by then, the tanks were not there either. So instead of occupying the third echelon of the advance, as planned, Rodiles's PNR combatants, reinforced by the light infantry company from Battalion 116, were in the lead. Men from Battalion 227 followed behind them as the march on Girón commenced.[21]

* * * *

As San Román had requested after the first ineffectual airdrop of supplies, the second one took place before dawn directly over the town. The boxes dropped from the C-54 landed in the streets and were quickly recovered.[22]

Attention now shifted to the C-46 and accompanying F-51 fighters that were to land within the hour. At 5:00 a.m. Oliva, who had only been asleep for an hour, was awakened and ordered to report to the brigade commander. When he arrived at the command post, San Román instructed him to compile a map of the military situation over what remained of the beachhead. Oliva was to get on the cargo plane due to land soon and return to JMTIDE with the map. Back in Nicaragua, he was to personally brief "Frank," the American officer who had overseen Base Trax in Guatemala. Only the first name of Colonel Egan was known to them even now. "If any person could get Frank to support us, that person was Oliva," San Román thought. "He would have raised hell at the rear base." The deputy brigade commander was adamant in his refusal to leave Girón given the predicament faced by the other brigade men there, but San Román would not consider sending anybody else. At Oliva's request, he put the order in writing: *Frank, Oliva presents himself to you to tell you that our situation is desperate and we need your help badly. Pepe.*[23] The idea that "Frank" would have been able to "send in the cavalry," as it were, is revealingly naive. Clearly, the workings of the wheels of power that had set the invasion in motion were a mystery even to its top Cuban military leader.

Fifty minutes later, just at the cusp of dawn, a C-46 piloted by Manuel Navarro (with an American as navigator) touched down at the airstrip.[24] However, none of the promised Mustang F-51 fighters that were to operate from Girón accompanied the cargo plane. The job of stripping Nicaraguan Air Force markings from the F-51s delivered to JMTIDE on the eighteenth had taken the entire day rather than the estimated fifty minutes. Consequently, the training of the Cuban pilots that were supposed to fly them had not even begun by the time they should have been heading to Cuba.[25]

The unloading of the 8,000–10,000 pounds of ammunition and other cargo aboard the C-46 quickly got under way.[26] When it was nearly complete, wounded B-26 pilot Matías Farías, who had crashed-landed at Girón two days earlier, was put aboard the plane. Oliva soon pulled up in a jeep and spoke to Navarro, informing him that he had been ordered to fly back with him to Nicaragua. The pilot replied that he had his own orders to take back only wounded but was agreeable to taking Oliva under the circumstances. Oliva would not have it, however. As he figured it, "I had an excuse not to go." He handed Navarro the documents he had prepared along with the note from San Román to "Frank" and told him to deliver them back at the base.

With daylight upon him, and only the injured Farías aboard, Navarro decided that he could not delay taking off any longer. Brigade surgeon Juan Sordo arrived just as the C-46 was preparing to take off and demanded that the pilot wait for some forty other wounded men. Navarro firmly told him that there was no time. As he later recounted, "I took the decision, as the captain of the plane, that it was too much risk to stay any longer."[27] Indeed, a FAR B-26 flown by Lagas was in the area at dawn to attack the road leading north from Girón. He carried out the airstrike but apparently did not sight the C-46.[28]

* * * *

As the noose on the beachhead tightened, the lack of actionable intelligence on enemy movements became critically consequential. Without it, the obscene risks assumed by B-26 crews flying support missions grew increasingly more senseless.

Castro's assault forces (including artillery) were concentrated just west of Girón and north of San Blas. When the B-26s flown by Livingston and Ray arrived at 6:00 a.m., Livingston headed to San Blas, but Ray set off for the immediately less important Central Australia area.

Benigno Miranda was on guard duty at Central Australia when, against the pale blue sky, he spotted a small black dot that gradually became larger. "Airplane in sight!" he shouted, setting in motion an onslaught of fellow blue-shirted militiamen seeking cover in a nearby cane field. Quickly the small dot in the sky transformed into a large aircraft from whose nose erupted a brilliant stream of fire.[29] The time of the plane's appearance is beyond doubt for Castro happened to be on a call with Central Australia at that very moment. It was 6:02 a.m., as recorded in the Point One transcripts. "Are the antiaircraft guns firing back?" he asked when told of the attack. "I think you should be able to shoot it down easily."[30]

Sixteen-year-old Carlos (his full name is not recorded) was defecating near the antiaircraft gun he commanded when the shouts of alarm rang out. He rushed back to his crew without bothering to clean himself. The display of pink tracers raining down from the plane struck him as "something really beautiful." Although his gun team fired furiously at the intruder, they failed to score any hits. It seemed that the attack was over when the bomber receded into the distance, but the plane turned and came back. This time it released three 250-pound bombs along with two rockets. Several militiamen around the sugar mill were wounded by the explosions, and Carlos's gun loader scampered for cover behind a metal tank. Insults and menacing orders for the man to return to his post proved fruitless. It was only after Carlos pointed a rifle at him that the reluctant loader, pale as a ghost, finally obeyed.[31] The loader's act of cowardice stood in stark contrast to the courage displayed by the daring attacker overhead. "The pilot was one badass guy; a gangster type, for sure," deemed Carlos. "We remarked among ourselves that what the guy had between his legs were two huge sacks that he had to carry around in a wheelbarrow. Because he made one pass, then made a second pass and yet a third pass."[32]

During its third pass, the B-26 was mortally wounded. "We're going in," Ray said over the radio as heard by Billy Goodwin, whose own B-26 was now nearing the coast.[33] Billowing smoke and losing altitude, the stricken bomber headed for a field in the vicinity of the mill. It slid along the ground for some 700 feet before finally coming to rest, after which it exploded into pieces.[34] Despite the violent crash, Ray and crewmate Leo Baker managed to exit the wreck before the explosion and sought cover among the foliage. Exactly how events subsequently unfolded is not clear, but, in an apparent standoff with the militiamen that descended on them, both Americans were shot dead.[35]

No identification was found on Ray, but Baker carried fake documents (bearing the surname "Berliss") that appeared to identify him as a U.S. national. Unable to parade live captured Americans before the cameras, Castro did the next best thing; he publicized the seized credentials as evidence of American participation in the invasion.[36] One of the bodies was even preserved as proof. Ironically, it was not the Latin-looking body of Baker but that of unidentified Ray, who was fair complexioned and had American looks.[37]

* * * *

Artillery firing on San Blas had continued into the dawn hours oblivious to the fact that no brigade forces remained there. The sight of Livingston's B-26 passing overhead in the direction of Covadonga was a welcome one to Del Valle's men holed up on the western outskirts of the settlement.[38] In hopeful expectation of air support, they had already placed panels marking their front line and the direction of the enemy, now less than half a mile away.[39]

Coming in at low altitude, Livingston strafed the concentration of Castro's forces on the northern side of the small hamlet and dropped napalm. A huge ball of flame ignited and set the surrounding brush on fire. However, the air attack did not last long and only caused a few casualties. The militiamen from Battalion 117 soon pressed on.[40]

With Castro's infantry about to enter San Blas, Del Valle made the daring decision to launch a counterattack. It was the type of impetuous move that was entirely in character for the cocky and self-assured twenty-two-year-old natural leader. "We came here not to retreat but to die in the fulfillment of our duty," he told his men. "We are going to push back those chickenshit militiamen. Soldiers of Free Cuba, we are going to retake San Blas."[41] On Del Valle's signal, the two tanks, on one of which he stood, moved forward; the paratroopers and infantrymen from the Third and Fourth Battalions followed behind. They pushed through San Blas under the still-falling artillery fire and clashed with the front ranks of the enemy infantry. Shocked by the unexpected offensive, the militiamen fell back in panic and some attempted to surrender. However, the brigade attackers were stretched thin and could give no quarter. "We had no orders to take it easy on them," recalled Adolfo Padrón of the Fourth Battalion, "so we kept right on firing at them."[42]

Militia mortars some distance to the rear were ordered to open fire to try and stop the onslaught, but the inexperienced men directing their fire ended up making things worse. It was a near repeat of the friendly fire incident that had occurred on that same road the previous day. "You cannot fire at such a high angle because it's going to come down on us," mortarman Julio Hernández argued to the captain commanding his team. "Fire as I say, dammit!" the captain replied. In the front lines, Castro's men heard a shell whistling over their heads and watched it explode a few yards away." "Fucking hell, it's from our side!" someone yelled. The suggestion of sending someone back to notify the mortar crews of their mistake was brought up, but there were no takers. So fierce was the incoming machine gun fire from the brigade side that no one dared so much as lift his head off the ground.[43]

Before long, with their ammunition running out, the intense firing from Del Valle's men ceased and the counterattack ground to a halt. Somehow, for some fifteen or twenty minutes, silence descended over the battlefield. Del Valle and his men, now in control of the northern entrance to San Blas, took a respite and congratulated themselves on their feat. "We accomplished it with our rifles, with our hands, but above all with our hearts," said one of the paratroopers.[44]

"We were driven back with great losses," admitted Félix Duque of the unexpected enemy offensive.[45] Olivera, upon learning of the counterattack, had Duque order the men to pull back just over a mile so that the artillery could safely shell the enemy position. Some of the troops, thinking it signaled a general retreat, at first refused to comply. They did so after Duque sternly told them that they would be in the barrage zone if they stayed.[46]

Del Valle and his men waited in vain for follow-up air support to consolidate their unlikely victory but none came. Instead, artillery shells started exploding around them. To their bitter disappointment, the dashing offensive then turned into a hurried retreat to where it had started.[47]

* * * *

Herrera and Goodwin arrived over the beachhead by 6:15 a.m.[48] Where they headed upon their arrival again demonstrates how the lack of actionable intelligence further emasculated what precious little air support was available. While Herrera set off to attack west of Girón,[49] Goodwin targeted the eastern approach to the town. This evidently was in response to San Román's message from the previous night requesting an airstrike on the enemy force "APPROACHING BLUE BEACH FROM EAST ON COAST ROAD." Aerial surveillance would have revealed that Pupo's militia battalion had backed away from Girón and was now entrenching itself at Caleta Buena.[50] Still, even if such intelligence had been available, there was no mechanism for relaying it to the brigade bombers in real time.

Goodwin had discovered on the way to Cuba that his plane's machine guns were not working but decided to continue on anyway and do what he could with his eight wing rockets. He spotted a number of trucks down the trail east of Girón and proceeded to make several attack passes on the scattered vehicles and personnel below. As it was, only seven of the rockets fired. Unbeknownst to the two men in the cockpit, one had malfunctioned and hung straight down from the plane's right wing.[51] Whatever damage the airstrike inflicted on the enemy force was inconsequential in any case. As Castro had ordered, Pupo and the men of Battalion 326 under his command would play no part in assaulting Girón.

Herrera, several miles northwest of Goodwin, made his initial attack on artillery gun emplacements west of Girón. He was immediately met with intense antiaircraft fire as he dropped his bomb load from 800 feet up. The plane's right engine was hit and began to lose oil pressure. After skimming the surface of the swamp to avoid the antiaircraft shells, he climbed to 1,000 feet to check his engines. From that height he saw a line of trucks rolling down the road and dove on them with machines guns blazing.[52] Onboard the trucks were the men of Battalion 180 making their way to Girón from Playa Larga. An alert whistle blared at the sight of the incoming plane, and the militiamen quickly leaped off the vehicles and dispersed into the bordering thicket. Disaster loomed, however, when one of the fuel containers on a truck loaded with them and grenade boxes was set ablaze. Springing into action, the battalion's commander jumped onto the vehicle and pushed off the burning container with his foot, thus narrowly averting a dire catastrophe.[53]

* * * *

The plan to drop improvised napalm bombs from a C-54 to support the beachhead came to naught. JMTIDE informed headquarters that there were "NO SPOTTING CHARGES FOR IGNITERS" to carry out the mission.[54] According to one of the Americans at the base, however, "The only thing that stopped us was that we couldn't figure out a way to get the [napalm] drums out of the aircraft in flight."[55]

The third of the C-54s scheduled to make airdrops over Girón did reach its destination approximately half an hour after sunup. It was just about the time when the promised air cover was supposed to start, but no navy jets were around. Aboard the plane, in the role of PDO (parachute dispatch officer), was forty-seven-year-old René Leyva. A journalist by profession, he had joined the brigade along with his seventeen-year-old son, Eduardo, and they had trained together in Guatemala. Despite the danger of the mission, the senior Leyva was glad to be doing something to help his son, now serving with Second Battalion, and the rest of the brigade.

Streams of antiaircraft shells immediately rose toward the distant plane. "We received fire. It's a miracle we escaped," Leyva said of the hair-raising experience.[56] Those on the ground as well were imperiled by the firing. Shooting at the distant target had to be done at such a low elevation angle that a PNR soldier in the vicinity of one of the guns was struck by its bullets.[57]

The intense ground fire, as well as the threat of enemy aircraft, made the drop a hurried affair. The boxes were hastily dropped close to shore, and most ended up drifting out to sea. It thus became necessary for the frogmen to go after them. San Román was especially grateful for the diligent service of these men. "Those frogmen did a good job. They were very brave," he acknowledged. Still, for all the UDT team's efforts, only some of the boxes were able to be recovered.[58]

Samuel Rodiles, who was advancing with his troop in the direction of Girón, had no clear idea of how far they were from the town until he saw the parachutes falling from the sky. As he later said, "Knowing now where the enemy was, we moved on in that direction."[59]

* * * *

"At 1128Z [6:28 a.m.] on the 19th a FLASH message to [JM]TIDE from the Task Force (via headquarters) reported that the *Essex* aircraft had been launched." So reveals CIA historian Jack Pfeiffer in his formerly classified *Air Operations* history. Because the carrier was too embroiled with air support activities, the quoted cable added, JMTIDE should "NOT ANTICIPATE [A] FORMAL REPLY" to Thorsrud's 3:15 a.m. cable to Clark.

The message went on to clarify that radio communications between naval and B-26 pilots would not be possible, as the navy planes were "UNABLE TO OPERATE" on the 121.5-megahertz frequency used by brigade bombers. This revelation regarding radio frequency incompatibilities stands out as yet another serious indictment of the CIA's operational planning. Commenting on it eighteen years later, however, Pfeiffer saw it differently. In his view, the late discovery "would seem to indicate a degree of carelessness not generally associated with the operation of a United States aircraft carrier."[60] Pfeiffer's finger-pointing at the navy seems particularly sanctimonious given the degree of carelessness apparent in the CIA's own handling of flight operations that very morning. As previously indicated, although JMTIDE had been notified of the CAP time frame at 3:04 a.m., two pairs of B-26s had somehow taken off too early to arrive within this window. Neither of those missions, as it happened, encountered enemy aircraft and Ray's B-26 was shot down by antiaircraft fire, but this had been entirely fortuitous.

Riley Shamburger and Joe Shannon, whose B-26s had departed Nicaragua at 4:00 a.m., were the first who could possibly make landfall within the allotted CAP window.[61] They were also the first to be told about the air cover. Reid Doster, the AANG general appointed as JMTIDE's B-26 tactical air chief, had climbed up on Shamburger's wing just prior to his takeoff and given him the news.[62] "Now we'll crush them," the pilot is said to have replied.[63]

As Shamburger and Shannon neared the Cuban coastline just before 6:45 a.m., their radio conversation was picked up by Goodwin, who by then was on his way back to Nicaragua. Goodwin broke in and reported the group of trucks east of Girón that he had only been able to attack with rockets due to his malfunctioning machine guns. The two inbound Americans decided that this would be their target and headed there, thus compounding the error of going after a militia unit that posed no offensive threat. "How about our little friends? See any of them?" Shamburger asked Goodwin after the latter informed him that he had not encountered any enemy aircraft in the area. By "little friends," Shamburger meant the navy jets that he, but not Goodwin, had been told about. "We're supposed to have some little friends with us at the beach. You know, the good guys," he clarified for Goodwin. "I didn't see anybody," the departing pilot replied.[64]

Arriving at the coastline, Shannon and Shamburger positioned their aircraft for the attack. Shannon took the lead and performed an east to west strafing run along the coastal trail on the trucks below.[65] Having completed the run, he began a tight turn for another pass in the opposite direction. Now facing east, he saw that Shamburger was initiating his own pass down the track but was being trailed by tracer bullets streaming from one of a pair of T-33s closing in on him.[66]

The T-33s, piloted by Prendes and Carreras, had taken off some twenty minutes earlier from San Antonio after sitting for a while on the tarmac waiting for ground fog to lift. During their preflight briefing, Curbelo had foreseen the possibility that they might encounter American jets during the mission. "If they attack you or strike our troops on the ground, you will have to engage them in combat," he had admonished the two pilots. "Victory is only hours away. No one can violate our waters!"[67]

Speeding toward the three oncoming planes, Shannon watched horrified as one of the engines on Shamburger's B-26 burst into flames. "Hit, hit!" Shamburger shouted into the radio before his plane pitched sharply to one side and plummeted into the waters some distance offshore. The time was 6:50 a.m., more than twenty minutes after the reported launch of the nowhere-to-be-seen navy CAP.[68]

Whether Prendes or Carreras was responsible for the kill cannot be determined as they would later claim to have shot down both bombers between them.[69] In actuality, after shooting down Shamburger and his crewmate, Wade Gray, the two T-33s sped by Shannon in a steep climb. "T-Birds! They got Riley," Goodwin heard Shannon say, followed by repeated mayday calls hoping for the promised air cover to come to his aid. Gonzalo Herrera, still flying in the area at the time, heard the calls too. Shannon desperately made a series of quick, steep turns trying to spot the enemy fighters but did not see them again.[70] Ironically, although the navy jets were unable to pick up Shannon's transmissions, Carreras did. It was yet another of the many incongruous twists that punctuated the entire saga. The FAR pilot heard the maydays from the B-26 followed by cries in American-accented English: "We're being attacked by Castro's planes." He thought the whole thing "very strange" and grew worried at the prospect that American jets would arrive. Notwithstanding Curbelo's patriotic admonishments, Carreras excitedly informed Prendes that they were in imminent peril and needed to return to base. Thereupon he proceeded posthaste to make good his getaway, and Prendes followed suit after briefly searching the waters for crash survivors and spotting none.[71]

Despite having heard the mayday transmissions, *El Tigre* Herrera, still over land a few miles away, was determined to spend all his remaining rockets and machine gun ammunition before leaving. Seeing no enemy aircraft approaching, he decided to attack "a town"—no doubt Punta Perdiz—that was "full of trucks and antiaircraft guns." Heavy ground fire tore into the bomber's nose and the cockpit began to fill with smoke. Still the courageous pilot managed to fly on. His plane, as it turned out, bore thirty-seven bullet holes. Herrera, who lacked any military background prior to the invasion, had a well-earned reputation for being someone not easily deterred by danger. "If there was one man in the whole operation who I believe deserved to be called *El Tigre*," wrote Eduardo Ferrer, "it was Captain Gonzalo Herrera."[72]

Joe Shannon, meanwhile, unaware that he was out of danger and not seeing the American jets appear, called out to Goodwin again. "Hey, [Billy]. Can you get back here and give me a hand?" "I can come back, [Joe]," replied Goodwin, who was dealing with a rough-running engine and a hung rocket, "but I'm already twenty [nautical] miles out and don't have any ammo."[73] What happened next—well over fifteen nautical miles from the coast—points to the whereabouts of the CAP during the allotted time window. Three unmarked navy jets materialized around Goodwin's bomber and began flying in formation with him.

Goodwin tried unsuccessfully to communicate via radio with the jet on his wing; when that failed, he motioned the pilot toward the beach. Getting the message, the three jets sped off in that direction.[74] Continuing his journey back to Nicaragua, just south of Grand Cayman Goodwin picked up Doug Price and Connie Seigrist engaged in radio conversation on their way to Cuba. The two CIA contract pilots had been the last to leave JMTIDE at 5:30 a.m. and would not have arrived over the island before 8:00 a.m. This would clearly have been outside the CAP window. However, as had been expressed in the 3:04 a.m. cable from headquarters, it was hoped that by then the navy jets would have been able to "CATCH ENEMY AIRCRAFT IN AREA" and eliminate them. Goodwin cut in on the radio and informed his compatriots of Shamburger's shootdown by T-33s and of his encounter with "some of our little friends" that he had sent after Shannon. "They'll be gone by the time we get there," Price said, alluding to the elusive "friends." "We're pressing our luck, Connie.

We'd better do a 180 and head back." Seigrist agreed, and both B-26s changed course to return to JMTIDE.[75]

The incredible but compelling conclusion from these events is that the CAP was not where it should have been during the specified time window. Clearly, the intended modification to the ROE temporarily eliminating the fifteen-nautical-mile air protection exclusion limit had not been implemented. Admiral Clark had not understood that jet cover within the allotted time was to be provided *over the beachhead.* The JCS order, presumably originating with Admiral Burke, was indeed ambiguous about where the CAP was to be located, but Clark had not sought clarification. He, it appears, subsequently engaged in a deliberate attempt to cover up his and, by wider implication, the navy's snafu. In postinvasion testimony, Clark stated that "the CEF aircraft came over [the *Essex*] an hour early," that is, at 5:30 a.m. His account is undoubtedly the basis for the standard notion that the April 19 sorties arrived too early and that this led to the deaths of four Americans. To be sure, only the B-26s flown by Ray and Livingston could possibly account for the planes reported by Clark. According to the admiral, the navy jets were immediately launched thereupon and arrived "over the beach area forty minutes before 0630 Romeo," meaning 5:50 a.m., local time. "However," he added, "by that time the CEF aircraft had already made their strikes and left."[76] These assertions are patently contradicted by the *Essex*'s 6:28 a.m. cable reporting the launching of the CAP.[77] Moreover, if the aircraft reportedly spotted by the carrier had indeed been those of Ray and Livingston, they would still have been inbound at 5:50 a.m. That Clark's representations constitute deliberate subterfuge is reinforced by the cable he sent to Dennison at 6:30 on the morning of the nineteenth: "WILL DEVOTE MY ENTIRE RESOURCES TO EXECUTION OF JCS 190833Z" (i.e., the 3:37 a.m. order from the JCS).[78] Such a cable would be moot if events had transpired as the admiral described later. The fact that all the records from the *Essex*—and only the *Essex*—were subsequently ordered destroyed (while the ship was still out at sea)[79] enhances the suspicion of a premeditated coverup.

As Sun Tzu would have predicted, in the midst of chaos the FAR pilots found opportunity. Still, they marveled to themselves about the absurdity of the situation. "Given [the Americans'] military prowess, it is inconceivable that that would happen," reflected Alberto Fernández. "Carreras and Prendes got away. . . . But had they run into [the American jets] they would have been mowed down."[80]

7:30 AM—NOON

Commander René de los Santos, put in overall charge of the Yaguaramas sector by Almeida, must have been at least somewhat irked to be relieved by a captain. If so, he apparently disguised it well when Emilio Aragonés arrived from Havana with the news. Castro, Aragonés explained, had put him in command of the armored offensive to be launched on San Blas along the road from Yaguaramas.[81]

At 7:32 a.m., the "Fatman"—Castro's customary moniker for Aragonés—spoke on the phone with *El Comandante* back in Havana. He had been told by Castro the previous day that fifteen tanks, including ten IS-2 heavy Stalin tanks, would be available for the offensive. However, the IS-2s were too massive to be transported on flatbed trailers, so instead five T-34 tanks and five SU-100 tank destroyers had been sent by that means. Five of the IS-2s were to follow by train later. Aragonés reported that eight of the trailer-carried vehicles were already there.[82] Fresh militia troops, Battalions 114 and 115, had also arrived from Havana overnight, although Castro had promised a total of four.[83] Still, along with the previous troops present, the infantry force that would follow behind the tanks probably totaled no fewer than 3,000 men.

Castro immediately set about coordinating air cover and artillery preparation for Aragonés's assault. Ten minutes after their initial conversation, he was back on the phone with the captain. "Fatman, starting at 9:00 o'clock you'll have in the air . . . a pair of our planes, at about 2000 feet, on the lookout." However, Castro added, "[t]hose planes are not going to attack [ground targets] because they tell me it is difficult to coordinate with the people on the ground." Evidently, the FAR was by now wary of its past friendly fire mishaps. Notwithstanding the lack of any air support, Aragonés was told, "[t]he tanks you have should be enough. . . . [The enemy forces] are not expecting an attack from that direction; hit them hard."[84] By the time Castro again called from Havana at 8:30 a.m., Aragonés had already left Yaguaramas for Horquita, five miles to the south, which would be the jumping-off point for the attack. "Let the Fatman know," he instructed the lieutenant on the phone, "that at 8:45 [a.m.] the 122 [mm] artillery will stop bombarding San Blas so they may advance." Castro ended the message on a confident note, certain of the inevitable success of his planned assault. "When he arrives at San Blas, when he takes San Blas, he must coordinate with [Pedro] Miret regarding the use of the artillery."[85]

* * * *

By 7:30 a.m., with the enemy closing in from the west within two miles of Girón,[86] Oliva had assumed command of the defenses there. Based on his experience at Caletón, he deployed his forces so as to take advantage of a Y-junction where the road from Playa Larga forked into two branches. One branch curved sharply northeast toward the airfield and the other ran eastward and intersected the main roads inside Girón. The location was covered by seagrape foliage that provided good cover. Oliva arranged the Sixth Battalion, numbering less than 200 men, in an inverted-wedge configuration that extended across the fork to the road branches on either side. Some seven bazookas and a number of heavy machine guns with overlapping fields of fire commanded the roadway down which the enemy would come. The 4.2-inch and 81 mm mortars, emplaced to the rear of the front lines, had been pre-ranged to concentrate their fire on a curve just ahead of the fork. Finally, the three M-41 tanks on hand were positioned in stepwise fashion on the left flank of the inverted wedge, pointing toward this curve. The men of the Second Battalion, still exhausted from the previous day's fighting, were held nearby in reserve.[87]

Close to 8:00 a.m., Rodiles's advancing troop came within sight of the brigade position and started receiving heavy fire. Continuing on down the center of the road was clearly not feasible, so the column halted. Battalion 116's light infantry company, attached to the PNR Battalion, then received orders to scout ahead and feel out the enemy. The company's ninety-six men were split into two detachments, each led by a PNR captain. One group, under José Sandino, crept through the thicket bordering the road on the north while the other, commanded by Luis Carbó, trudged up the jagged coastal fringe on the opposite side. Carbó sighted the enemy position ahead first and relayed the information to a 120 mm mortar battery which began shelling it.[88]

Confronted with Castro's infantry now at the doorstep of Girón and air attacks that commenced around 8:30 a.m.,[89] San Román's radio messages became increasingly desperate.

8:15 a.m. SITUATION CRITICAL LEFT FLANK WEST BLUE BEACH. NEED URGENTLY SUPPORT. PEPE.[90]

8:40 a.m. BLUE BEACH IS UNDER AIR ATTACK. PEPE.[91]

Just over a half hour later, artillery fire also began falling on San Román's position, further adding to his frustration.

9:14 a.m. BLUE BEACH UNDER ATTACK BY TWO T-33[s] AND ARTILLERY. WHERE IN HELL IS JET COVER[?]. PEPE.[92]

With little comforting news to offer him, CIA headquarters decided to lay the cards on the table. At 9:34 a.m., a cable with EMERGENCY-level priority was sent to JMTIDE to be forwarded to the brigade commander.

1. WE CAN CONTINUE TO FURNISH LOGISTIC SUPPORT BY AIR.

2. CANNOT FURNISH JET AIR COVER NOW.

3. WE PLAN TO PROVIDE T–33 JET FIGHTER SUPPORT WITHIN ESTIMATED TWO DAYS.

4. IF YOU FEEL YOU CANNOT HOLD POSITION, LET US KNOW NOW SO WE CAN EVACUATE BRIGADE TONIGHT. SHIPS MOVING INTO POSITION FOR POSSIBLE EVACUATION[.] WE AWAIT YOUR DECISION.[93]

The T-33s mentioned in the cable had been requested by the CIA from the U.S. Air Force. It was expected that they would be flown (sans identifying insignia) by agency contract pilots either from JMTIDE or an airbase in central Florida.[94] In any case, to San Román the message spelled doom. With imminent defeat closing in around him and the intercession of navy jets being ruled out, he wondered just what support, if any, he could count on. His next communication bespoke his perplexed desperation.

9:55 a.m. CAN YOU THROW SOMETHING INTO THIS VITAL POINT IN THE BATTLE[?] ANYTHING. JUST LET PILOTS CHOOSE. PEPE.[95]

* * * *

As the tide of bad news about the invasion flooded across the Florida Straits, a somber gloom descended over the expectant Cuban exile community. Recruiting centers in Miami that had been overrun by cheerful new applicants just twenty-four hours prior now lay silent and shuttered.[96]

Equally dismal was the mood that prevailed among the six members of the CRC, sequestered under armed guard at the Opa-locka airbase twelve miles from Miami. Arthur Schlesinger and Adolf Berle, Kennedy's adviser on Latin America, were not looking forward to the mission thrusted on them by the president. They were to go meet with the embittered Cuban leaders.[97]

The arrival of the two high-level Americans at just about 8:15 a.m. invigorated the council members. All six took turns speaking out as the group sat around a plain wooden table. Miró Cardona, looking to Schlesinger ten years older than when he had seen him a week before, was the first to do so. It was not too late to turn the tide in what was a life-and-death struggle, he said, then asked that they be allowed to join the men on the beachhead. "It is this which I request, this which I beg," he declared somberly. Miró's own son, as well as six other relatives of CRC members, were among the men fighting with the brigade in Cuba.[98]

The other council members followed with a slew of recriminations. They had not been consulted or allowed to coordinate with resistance groups on the island. Actions had been taken in their name without their control, approval, or knowledge. Letting the invasion fail would be an unconscionable defeat for democracy. Manuel de Varona, the feisty veteran politician who was to be secretary of war for the provisional government, decried the way they were being detained. "We don't know whether we are your allies or your prisoners." He then declared that at noon he planned to bypass the armed guards around the house and leave for Miami to hold a press conference. "Let them shoot me down if they dare." De Varona subsequently read a list of requests that boiled down to immediately transferring the entire CRC to the beachhead, carrying out immediate air strikes, and sending in reinforcements. American planes, he said, should enter the battle and, if that was not sufficient, the marines as well. "Someone placed us in this position, that person will have to get us out of it," De Varona declared. Carlos Hevia, the eldest member of the group, pleaded that "if these boys are to be wiped out on the beachhead, our place is to die with them." "But we are not defeatist," he added. "If we have massive air attacks, we can still perhaps convert defeat into victory."[99]

Some two hours into the meeting, Schlesinger and Berle stepped out to confer and call the White House. Dean Rusk took the call and agreed with Berle's suggestion that the Cubans should be brought to Washington and perhaps meet with the president. Having been so informed, the council members changed from their khaki uniforms meant for Cuba into civilian clothes for the trip to the U.S. capital.[100] Perhaps they still held out hope of wrangling a last-minute reprieve for their cause. If so, they were woefully misguided. During the morning, McGeorge Bundy met with Cabell, Bissell, and other CIA personnel to discuss the dire situation. Bundy, on behalf of the group, then apparently called the president to request that navy jets be allowed to engage ground targets as well as FAR aircraft. Kennedy rejected the idea, refusing to go beyond the one-hour CAP he had previously authorized.[101]

* * * *

As yet unaware of the fate of that day's earlier flights, back at JMTIDE Thorsrud was readying additional sorties to the beachhead to be flown by three Cuban volunteers. That all changed when returning pilots brought news about the enemy air activity still present in the area.[102] "WHERE IS YOUR AGGRESSIVE AIR SUPPORT?" a frustrated Thorsrud demanded of the *Essex* when he cabled the carrier at 9:14 a.m. with news of Shamburger's shootdown.[103]

Things reached a breaking point at 9:45 a.m. when the Cuban chief of operations, Luis Cosme, addressed his countrymen and forbade them from even volunteering to fly. "I think we've had enough losses," he told the assembled men. "I believe this operation is a failure. I don't see any reason to continue the flights. Either they appoint another operations officer or no airplane takes off from Happy Valley [JMTIDE] with Cubans aboard."[104]

Goodwin's late arrival at the base marked the closing act of the invasion's air operations. He had limped back to Nicaragua nursing a failing engine, and his hair-raising landing provided a dramatically fitting end to the whole three-day daredevil episode. A low pass over the control tower confirmed that the rocket that had misfired hung straight down by its tail from one of the plane's wings. For thirty minutes Goodwin tried fruitlessly to shake the rocket loose by executing different maneuvers over the nearby sea. He was then advised to fly over the field at 4,000 feet and for him and his crewmate to bail out. But the men decided that their best chance was to try to land the plane, hanging rocket and all. Goodwin finally came in for a landing after allowing time for the control tower to be evacuated, as the personnel there had requested. With great skill, and much luck, he managed to set the aircraft down without causing an explosion.[105]

In Cuba, meanwhile, unaware of the goings-on behind the scenes, the brigade men obstinately—if not quixotically—fought on as the beachhead was reduced to a small pocket of resistance.

* * * *

So certain was Castro that the assault on San Blas by Aragonés would be successful that at 8:07 a.m. he had joked about it on the phone with Martínez at Central Australia. "I think that if Fernández does not take Girón he is going to become the biggest laughingstock in the world because the Fatman is going to take it instead."[106] Blocking the escape route from San Blas to Girón was a concomitant part of his plan. He therefore ordered the Second Column of the army, under Captain Roger García, to link up with Battalion 111 already slogging its way east along a backtrail. The combined force was to reach the key road junction near Helechal by way of Cayo Ramona and block the road connecting San Blas and Girón.[107]

For all of Castro's fastidious planning for the Aragonés offensive, he had overlooked one critical aspect: Olivera, moving down the other road toward San Blas from Covadonga, was not told to halt his own infantry advance. Unaware that Del Valle's force had abandoned San Blas, Olivera's men made themselves ready to "pounce on the enemy." When no enemy appeared, however, they moved forward and entered the settlement unopposed at about 10:00 a.m.[108] The only casualties among the occupiers resulted from the booby traps left behind by the paratroopers. In one instance, a militiaman lost both his hands and feet when the "abandoned" Garand rifle he tried to pick up off the ground set off an explosion.[109]

The advance of Aragonés's force from Horquita to San Blas, thirteen miles away, got started at 9:00 a.m.[110] Three T-34s of the eight armored vehicles that had arrived by then spearheaded the offensive.[111] Before 10:20 a.m., as the column neared its objective, commander Joel Pardo in the lead tank spotted some men a short distance ahead crossing the road. Neither side—neither the San Blas occupiers nor those in the approaching force—was aware that they were facing their own troops.[112]

Pardo's tank fired first at the supposed enemy, then, as per his previous instructions, the other two tanks flanking him took up positions and fired as well. As described by bazooka man Arteaga in San Blas, the unidentified tanks "let loose some god-awful blasts" as they approached the hamlet. Two hut houses on either side of the road were instantly blown to smithereens.[113] A running gun battle quickly developed between the two sides. The supposed enemy fire emanating from the brush around San Blas was answered by the tanks' machine guns and various weapons of the infantry behind them. Near a small rise, Arteaga was intent on knocking out the armored beasts with his bazooka but found himself snared in a fence that blocked his way. "Dammit, this is really fucked up!" he said inwardly as bullets hit close to where he was stuck. Suddenly, a man wearing an olive-green army uniform hopped onto the road and started walking toward the lead tank shouting, "Don't shoot!" It turned out to be Evelio Saborit, who, realizing that the tanks were T-34s, surmised that they must be friendlies. Pardo recognized Saborit as he approached and quickly called out to his men to stop firing.[114]

"You have killed ten comrades!" Saborit told a stunned Pardo when the two spoke afterward. According to Pardo, Saborit told him later that "he had said that to me in jest." Pardo admitted, however, that he would not have been surprised if the deaths had indeed occurred, as "no less was to be expected" given the high explosive shells they had fired. In fact, a number of deaths did result from the friendly fire encounter. "It cost us several lives," said Félix Duque.[115] Militiaman Mario Gutiérrez also witnessed the deadly consequences first hand. "It was during that fighting that I saw the first dead men from our own side; something truly unforgettable. A truck arrived and started picking them up."[116] Whatever toll the friendly fire incident caused, it could have been worse had Arteaga not become ensnared by the fence. "[I]f I had been able to get into position, it would have been a damned mess because I was going . . . to fire with the bazooka to get them off me. They were three frightful tanks."[117]

When Castro in Havana was later informed about the fall of San Blas, he was miffed that it had not been as a result of the dashing armored assault he had planned. "[The infantrymen] say the tanks fired on them, but they should not have been the ones to take San Blas, it should have been the tanks."[118] Apparently, no one dared point out to *El Comandante* that what had transpired was due to his failure to inform Olivera of Aragonés's offensive.

* * * *

The mortar shelling of the brigade position west of Girón did not last long. Most of the Soviet-made 120 mm mortars were soon reported to be out of action.[119] Still, the two light infantry detachments from Battalion 116 continued slowly making their way toward the enemy along the margins of the road to Girón.

The men under Sandino plodding through the thicket on the north side found that the dense growth made it difficult to see each other and where they were going. Gradually and unintentionally, the men became separated into small, isolated groups.[120] Slowly they reached the Y-junction and came into the open where the sharp curve to the northeast cut across their path.[121] When Arístides Cordoví got there with two other militiamen, he assumed that the tank less than 100 feet away and "painted just like ours" was indeed theirs. "Friends. What's happening? Friends," Oliva heard the shouts coming from militia soldiers peering out of the brush from the other side of a fence. He was perplexed. "We were dressed in camouflage and standing in the open and they . . . saw us and shouted at us." Playing along, Oliva waved and called for them to come over. Cordoví crawled under the fence and approached. "Don't shoot, we're comrades!" he yelled out when a machine gun opened up on his two companions as they crossed the fence behind him. Even when the brigade men began trying to obtain information from the trio, it did not dawn on Cordoví that they had fallen into enemy hands. He began answering in earnest until one of the other captives told him, "Shut up, dammit! We're prisoners!"[122]

On the opposite side of the road, Carbó and his men came under heavy fire as they neared brigade foxholes on the coastal flank. From across the way, Sandino and the men around him could clearly hear the exchange of shouts that preceded the firing. "Surrender, militiamen!" was followed by shouts of "Fatherland or Death!" The dug-in brigade defenders opened up at close range and were soon joined by their 4.2-inch mortars in pouring fire on the advancing troop.[123] Around twelve of Carbó's troop were killed in short order.[124]

Even as the firing intensified on their right, the militiamen advancing on the opposite side of the road kept mistaking the brigade units at the junction for their own forces. A small group was lured to go across by a brigade soldier atop a tank some forty yards away. "Cross the road," he told them, "your comrades on the other side are in danger." They took the bait and were machined-gunned as they crossed. One of the militia prisoners watching the mayhem noted how the blue uniform shirt worn by his mates stood out "like a neon sign" and made them easy targets.[125]

Throughout the ordeal, it was the fewer than 100 men of the light infantry company from Battalion 116 who bore the brunt of the enemy defenses. The PNR Battalion itself had remained firmly in the rear. Realizing that they were seriously outgunned, both Sandino and Carbó sent runners back asking for PNR grenadiers.[126] Suddenly, to the elation of the men in the line of fire, T-34 tanks were seen coming up the road with PNR soldiers following behind them. Captain Carbó rallied his men shouting, "Comrades, on your feet! Everybody on their feet! Follow the tanks!"[127]

Quickly the brigade M-41 tanks and bazooka men camouflaged among the seagrape took aim at the approaching vehicles. The time was now 10:00 o'clock.[128] A shell pierced the armor of the first tank that entered the junction. Three of its five occupants bolted out of the burning wreck, their coveralls on fire. The second T-34 moved up and was also struck by an armor-piercing round. "A red ball of flames whirled around inside," said one of the tankers aboard. "I went down, seriously wounded. The guts of one of my comrades were hanging out . . . the others were unconscious." Another T-34 moved forward and it too was hit.[129]

Bullets buzzed by—"like the sound of cicadas," someone thought—over the heads of the men following behind the destroyed tanks. Carbó, who stood over six feet tall, received a wound to the shoulder and fell to the ground. But just moments later he got up, picked up his rifle, and again began rallying the men forward. A bullet then ripped through his forehead and finished him off for good. "He," said Rodiles afterward of the courageous captain, "was the most outstanding of all our comrades, the most determined."[130]

A disorganized retreat ensued by the remaining T-34s as well as the men following behind them. Such was the haste of the retreating tanks that the infantrymen had to jump out of their way to avoid getting crushed. A PNR officer heard from a tank crewman that they were pulling back because of an oil problem. Unconvinced, the officer pressed him: "How come it works to retreat? Why doesn't it work to advance?" When the tanker ignored him and closed the hatch, the livid officer had to be restrained from shooting inside the tank through a slit.[131] Commander Ameijeiras, who remained in the rear, had to personally intervene to stop the headlong rout.[132]

Those who did not retreat piled up along the narrow coastal fringe bordering the road. Shoulder to shoulder, the men were so bunched together that they could hardly move or shoot and became easy targets for the brigade mortars. Among the casualties were five PNR soldiers killed simultaneously when a mortar shell exploded in their midst.[133] The huddled men watched in amazement when "ambulances"—all manner of vehicles, including a bakery truck, painted with red crosses—came racing down the road to pick up wounded and dead alike. "They ventured right into the line of fire," noted one of the awestruck militiamen. "Those people are risking their lives," he said to the man next to him. To Ameijeiras, the volunteer orderlies were manifestly "braver men than we."[134]

* * * *

By 11:00 a.m., Castro's forces in San Blas were ready to resume their advance toward Girón.[135] As indicated by Castro's phone conversations from Point One, a total of fifteen armored vehicles (T-34s and SU-100s) were available in and around San Blas by then. At least three heavy IS-2 Stalin tanks had also arrived at Yaguaramas, but Castro ordered that they be held there in reserve.[136]

Castro's men did not know that Del Valle had prepared a position at the far end of a curve a few hundred yards west of the settlement. There he waited with his two tanks, heavy machine guns, bazookas, and mortars.[137] When a peasant who had escaped his captors informed Commander Saborit about the nearby enemy force, Joel Pardo sent out a tank to explore the way ahead.[138]

The brigade defenders spotted the T-34 as it approached and opened fire. The tank immediately returned to San Blas, whereupon three T-34s, including one commanded by Pardo himself, formed up and got under way toward the enemy position. Pardo's tank, flanked by the other two, led the way down the narrow road. Suddenly, as described by tank commander Ramón Martínez, "a deluge of shrapnel, a tremendous barrage of fire," was unleashed on them. Over his headset Martínez could clearly hear Nelson Sánchez, in command of the tank on Pardo's right, ordering his gunner to fire. Sánchez had evidently set his radio to external rather than internal communications, so the gunner was unable to hear the order. Just then, Miguel Zequeira, a bazooka man with the brigade's Third Battalion, took aim at Sánchez's T-34 and fired his weapon. The bazooka rocket did not penetrate the hull but exploded with such force that it broke off one of the tank treads and shattered the optical equipment inside. Sharp pieces of glass were violently sent flying around the tank's interior, inflicting severe wounds on the crew. Sánchez, still not realizing his error, went on berating his gunner. "You see dammit! Now I'm wounded . . . because you didn't shoot in time, dammit!"[139]

As soon as Pardo learned that Sánchez's tank was immobilized and its crew wounded, he backed up his own tank and went to their aid. Using the disabled T-34 as cover, he helped the injured tankers climb out then drove them away in a nearby jeep that had been abandoned by its driver. "The [crew] was fortunate," thought Martínez, "that . . . instead of a penetrating round, a high explosive one had been used."[140]

The tank advance halted at that point, and the militia infantry took up the offensive. However, "no one could move forward," recalled a militiaman named Puente, due to two machine gun nests with overlapping fields of fire.[141] Puente decided to take matters into his own hands after an army bazooka man next to him failed three times to take out the one closest to them with his weapon. Carrying six grenades, the determined militia fighter slithered along the ditch bordering the road. Upon reaching a spot almost in front of the machine gun, hemmed in by sandbags and palmetto palms, he grabbed one of his grenades. "I almost lost my teeth," said Puente, when he tried to bite the pin off "like the Americans in the movies." On his next attempt, he grasped the grenade firmly in one hand and nervously pulled out the pin with the other. Then, as the army man had instructed him, he lobbed it at the enemy emplacement. The machine gun immediately fell silent after the ensuing explosion, and Puente ventured over for a look. Among the fallen palmettos, three mangled bodies were all that remained of the men who had been firing the weapon. It was a gruesome, unsettling spectacle, and the shaken militiaman did not linger there long. "When you kill like that, directly . . . your human consciousness makes you think. You must get it out of your head quickly, but your human consciousness is there. Those are men, after all."[142]

With renewed vigor, the frontal militia attacks continued. "It is a lie if anyone says that the militiamen were cowardly," remarked one of the paratroopers who was there. "It is a lie if anyone denies that they were thrown forward in waves trying to crush us with their numerical superiority."[143]

The brigade defenders started to crack under the continuing onslaught. Third Battalion squad leader Oscar García had to act quickly when one of his men, seized with panic, began to scream and shake. Afraid that hysteria would spread to the rest of the squad, García took out his pistol and held it to the overwrought soldier's head. "Either you continue fighting and shooting at the enemy or I will blow your brains out right here. You choose," he told him sternly. The threat worked and the man regained his composure.[144] But what happened in García's squad was not an isolated case. Other men of the Third Battalion who lost their nerve broke formation and headed for the rear. Some paratroopers joined them and a runaway rout seemed imminent. Confronted by the chaotic spectacle, Del Valle became enraged. With tears in his eyes, he ran frantically among the fleeing men shouting: "All paratroopers back to the line [to] die there!" His action had the desired effect. Emboldened by their leader's resolve, the paratroopers rallied and launched a counterattack that succeeded in briefly disrupting the enemy advance. Seizing the opportunity, Del Valle then retreated with his troop and the two tanks in the direction of Girón.[145]

* * * *

Pandemonium erupted within Girón when reports began circulating that Castro's forces had broken through Oliva's defenses. Unable to raise Oliva, whose field radio batteries had been depleted, Pepe San Román had no choice but to take the information at face value. He ordered all available personnel, mainly headquarters staff, to take up defensive fighting positions with whatever weapons were at hand.[146]

Attorney Penabaz, head of the brigade's legal department,[147] was asleep after coming off a guard duty shift. "Wake up!" one of his fellow attorneys told him. "The enemy is in sight and we'll have to fight hand to hand with the infantry." He jolted out of bed and looked for his Browning automatic rifle, but it was missing. Outside an M-35 gun truck was in position underneath a tree, and a defensive circle was forming around the command post. One of the men in the circle, another of Penabaz's attorneys, smiled at him broadly holding the "missing" BAR in his hands. Such small levities aside, the small band of defenders realized that their prospects were grim. "Boys, we are going to show those dogs how the men of the 2506 die," hollered out staff officer José Andreu trying to steel the men for what was to come.[148]

San Román, meanwhile, sent out frantic radio messages about the dire situation.

> 11:00 A.M. FIGHTING ON BEACH[.] SEND ALL AVAILABLE AIRCRAFT NOW. PEPE.[149]
>
> 11:07 A.M. WE ARE OUT OF AMMO AND FIGHTING ON BEACH. PLEASE SEND HELP WE CANNOT HOLD. PEPE.[150]

Admiral Clark, monitoring the transmissions from aboard the *Essex*, cabled Dennison at 11:09 a.m. with a rash idea. He suggested to his superior that the presence of two FAR planes (possibly Del Pino and Fernández) "circling near one of our destroyers" was justification for him to launch an airstrike.[151]

Another telegram from San Román followed at 11:17 a.m.

> IN WATER OUT OF AMMO[.] ENEMY CLOSING IN, HELP MUST ARRIVE IN NEXT HOUR. PEPE.[152]

Admiral Dennison ignored Clark's airstrike suggestion but, pursuant to a conversation he had had with Burke an hour earlier,[153] issued him new orders at 11:24 a.m.

> 1. DISPATCH 2 DD [DESTROYERS] TO TAKE STATION OFF BLUE BEACH TO DETERMINE WHETHER THERE IS ANY CHANCE FOR EVACUATION.
>
> 2. PROVIDE AIR COVER TO PROTECT DDS.
>
> 3. FLY RECCO [reconnaissance] OVER BEACH TO DETERMINE SITUATION.
>
> 4. REPORT IMMEDIATELY BY FASTEST POSSIBLE MEANS RESULTS [OF] OBSERVATIONS.
>
> 5. CEF SHIPS HAVE BEEN ORDERED TO MOVE INTO BLUE BEACH.
>
> 6. FINAL INSTRUCTIONS ON EVACUATION WILL FOLLOW.[154]

Back in Girón, the reports that Oliva's defenses had collapsed were proven false when a runner brought a message from him asking San Román to send reinforcements. Although the situation was difficult, the message said, the position west of town was being held. The false alarm in Girón had lasted about a half hour,[155] but the ripples it had caused in navy circles vis-à-vis immediate evacuation continued to propagate.

At 11:32 a.m. Dennison cabled further directives to Clark:

1. PROVIDE CONTINUOUS AIR COVER OVER BEACHES TODAY TO PRO-
TECT CEF FROM AIR ATTACK.
2. PROTECTION FROM GROUND ATTACK NOT AUTHORIZED.[156]

Thus, whereas his earlier message authorized air cover for the navy destroyers, this one seemed to indicate that *all* brigade elements—air, sea, and land—were to be protected from air attack. This implication would be dispelled twenty-five minutes later, but it was another of the unfathomable miscommunications and missteps that occurred throughout the entire operation.

CIA headquarters was obviously taken in by Dennison's telegram, for at 11:38 a.m. it dispatched the following message to JMTIDE:

1. COMPLETE NAVY PROTECTION HAS BEEN GRANTED FOR THE
MAXIMUM NUMBER OF B-26 STRIKES, UPON RECEIPT THIS MESSAGE
UNTIL DARKNESS TONIGHT. REQUEST YOU MOUNT THE MAXIMUM
NUMBER SORTIES FOR THIS PERIOD.
2. ENTIRE B-26 FORCE IS TO CONCENTRATE UPON SUPPORT BEACH-
HEAD. FRIENDLY TASK FORCE AT BLUE BEACH THROUGHOUT
AFTERNOON.[157]

Within the JCS, there was evident and justifiable concern about the potential repercussions of what Dennison had implied in his message. At 11:57 a.m. a cable from the joint chiefs addressed to both Denni-son and Clark unequivocally clarified the matter: "FLY AIR COVER FOR DESTROYERS, CEF SHIPPING AND OWN AIR RECONNAISSANCE."[158] This caveat removed all possible misunderstandings about the extent of the air cover. Yet, shockingly enough, CIA headquarters did not countermand their orders for additional B-26 strikes based on the premise of "COMPLETE NAVY PROTECTION."

* * * *

Samuel Rodiles knew that he was in a difficult position. Bunched up with his men opposite the enemy's left flank, he had nothing with which to counter the firepower of the brigade tanks and heavy weapons. Seeking to improve matters, he sent two messengers to commander Ameijeiras in the rear asking for bazooka support. Ameijeiras received the request and gave orders for a bazooka platoon to follow one of the messengers back to Rodiles.[159] But the bazooka men never got to him. They suffered heavy casualties on the way from the white phosphorus rounds that Oliva ordered the 81 mm mortars to begin firing around 11:30 a.m.[160]

As at Caletón, the white phosphorus proved extremely effective. "Most of the casualties we suffer are the result of mortar fire," Ameijeiras noted. "The 81 mm ones cause us more damage than the 106 mm [4.2-inch] ones do. They have good artillery spotting for fire adjustments."[161] The spotting was done from atop the water tower at Girón, where an observer with binoculars and a radio was perched. From there he "commanded a view of the entire road," said a militiaman fighting nearby.[162]

Ameijeiras and the infantry with him, a couple of miles to the rear, were pinned down not only by the mortar bombardment but also by treetop-level .50 caliber machine gun fire (apparently from an M-35 gun truck). As those in the foreground sought shelter behind the idle T-34s, they found themselves caught in a crossfire between the enemy and their own men farther back. "Today we lost our voice," wrote Ameijeiras, "from screaming and passing the word to the comrades far from the tanks to cease firing." Those with more initiative among the PNR men attempted to take out the enemy machine gun using grenade launchers. But others, according to Ameijeiras, became so shocked that "[they] don't fire a single shot . . . [and] sometimes they are killed doing nothing." The high-shooting .50 machine gun was eventually silenced by two blasts from one of the T-34s lurking in the rear. Following Ameijeiras's instructions, the tank rotated its turret in the direction of the incoming rounds and fired—all the while resolutely staying put.[163]

NOON—4:00 PM

Fortunately for the brigade B-26 pilots, JMTIDE was not taken in by head-quarters' misunderstanding that "COMPLETE NAVY PROTECTION" had been granted for further airstrikes. The response that Thorsrud wired back to Washington at 12:07 p.m. was blunt: "SITUATION FOR AIR SUPPORT BEACHHEAD COMPLETELY OUT OF OUR HANDS. THIS MORNING'S EFFORT EXTENDED US TO THE LIMIT."[164]

Although no more B-26s would be sent to Cuba, just as Thorsrud's cable was being transmitted another run to the beach by the brigade ships was getting under way. Both Lynch and Ryberg would later claim that they boldly decided to head back on their own initiative.[165] However, the navy's morning cable traffic clearly indicates that the ships received orders to do so and no doubt were informed that they would now receive air protection.[166] This aptly explains the abrupt change in the crew's disposition to venture back. "[E]ven the ones that were trying to mutiny were ready to go," according to frogman Andy Pruna.

At one point, as *Blagar, Barbara J,* and the three LCUs steamed toward the coast, navy destroyers *Eaton* and *Murray* passed close by headed in the same direction. "Those destroyers are not going in for nothing," Pruna remembered thinking. "[I]t is a wonderful sight. Everybody is ready to die. Everybody is ready to go."[167] In reality, however, the ships were not undertaking some last-minute cavalry-style charge to save the day. Their assigned mission was to evacuate as many invaders as possible before the beachhead collapsed entirely.[168]

The 12:06 p.m. report to Dennison based on the latest reconnaissance flight from the *Essex* was grim, if again imprecise:

AREA HELD BY CEF APPEARS TO BE ONE QUARTER TO ONE HALF MILE ALONG THE BEACH TO A DEPTH OF ABOUT ONE QUARTER [sic][.] UNDER ARTILLERY FIRE WITH TANKS AND VEHICLES TO BOTH EAST AND WEST.[169]

Actually, there were only trucks no less than five miles east of Girón. The militia infantry at Caleta Buena was dug in and not engaged in any offensive actions, just as Castro wanted. The lack of any apparent opposition in that direction was to be the lure that would drive the enemy into the snare he was preparing for them. "You are staying nice and quiet over there, nice and quiet?" he asked roguishly when Tomassevich, who had joined up with Pupo, reported in from Yaguaramas just before noon. "Set up a trap," Castro told him, "so that when they flee in that direction you can capture them all, because that's where they are going to head." When Tomassevich complained that he and Pupo had no antitank weapons except for a defective bazooka, Castro promised to send them some. Just over a half hour later he had arranged for bazookas to be flown in by helicopter. Two antitank guns were also dispatched by way of the track that connected Yaguaramas and Caleta Redonda ("Green Beach," where the Third Battalion was to have landed) on the coast. "Hurry up," Castro exclaimed into the phone about the delivery of the weapons, "because those people are retreating."[170] Of course, the planned trap could only work if the invaders were not evacuated by sea first. That prospect greatly concerned *El Comandante* and presciently so, for at 12:55 p.m. the following message was being relayed to San Román: "PEPE HANG ON[.] EVACUATION ON WAY."[171]

* * * *

A truck from Girón arrived at Oliva's position with bazooka and .50 caliber ammunition. Oliva also received a message from San Román stating that he could not send him the reinforcements he had requested as there were none available. Nevertheless, the message continued, the deputy brigade commander was ordered to "hold his position by any means." "[A]s long as that position was held," San Román still thought, "everything was all right."[172]

By 12:30 p.m., under the hail of withering fire thrown at them over the last hour, Castro's infantry retreated or at least halted its attempts to advance. By then, the Second Battalion's 81 mm mortars, which had been firing continuously over the previous hour, had begun to overheat (accounts say "melt").[173] "They fired at us relentlessly!" reflected one of the PNR soldiers. "[T]he sun became overcast by so much flying shrapnel. Everything around us was riddled with bullet holes."[174] The havoc unleashed on them proved too much for some who opted to surrender. They felt betrayed by their commander who had sent them to be slaughtered, Oliva heard from two militiamen who gave themselves up.[175]

Through it all, the T-34s in the rear with Ameijeiras stayed put, their crews evidently reluctant to meet the same fate that their fellow tankers had met earlier. Castro, upon hearing of this, told Martínez at Australia to send word for the uncooperative tankers to rejoin the fight. "Give those people an opportunity to fight again because we lack [tank] crews to be fucking around!"[176]

The brigade's Sixth Battalion had borne the brunt of the enemy assault and suffered casualties not only from the ground fighting but from FAR air attacks as well. Among the injured was the battalion's second-in-command, Félix Urra, who had been thrown more than twenty yards from his foxhole by the explosion of a plane-dropped bomb.[177] At 1:30 p.m., in anticipation of renewed assaults, Oliva deemed it was time to bring the Second Battalion infantry reserves into the line of battle.[178]

* * * *

Del Valle decided to make his last stand at a three-way junction four miles west of San Blas and five miles from Girón. At this intersection, just east of Helechal, the road from San Blas turns sharply southward toward the coast and intersects a byway to Cayo Ramona, about a mile and a half to the west.

Only the paratroopers and the two tanks were with Del Valle at this new position. The Third Battalion, along with the Fourth Battalion company assigned to the northern sector, had kept going south in the direction of Girón.[179]

From San Blas, the advance of Castro's forces continued. Scattered groups of scouts preceded the main column of armored vehicles followed by infantry. Commander Félix Duque, however, decided to race ahead of them all upon hearing rumors that the forces advancing from Soplillar were in Cayo Ramona. Accompanied by an army captain, he headed there directly in a jeep.[180]

In fact, Castro's forces had not reached Cayo Ramona. *Dentista* Borges and the men of Battalion 111 had been journeying there along a backtrail since the previous day. In a peculiar turn of events, while the militiamen had been making their way east, they had come within shooting range of Tomás Cruz's paratroopers. Cruz and his men had earlier left their hideout between Pálpite and Playa Larga and were trying to reach Girón by way of the same backtrail. When the militia convoy happened to stop near where the paratroopers were lurking, some in the small band raised their weapons to fire. However, Cruz hurriedly motioned them to stop. Trooper Roberto de los Heros was especially disappointed when Castro's men soon moved on unmolested. In his view, another auspicious opportunity to engage the enemy had been squandered. Cruz argued that opening fire would get them all killed because the militia would return fire, but De Los Heros found the argument wholly ridiculous. As he saw it, they had parachuted down precisely to shoot at militiamen and, if the militiamen shot back, it was par for the course.[181] Battalion 111 had ultimately been stopped about a mile from Cayo Ramona by mortar fire from brigade defenders there and the brief intervention of a brigade tank. Borges thereupon halted his advance and went to Central Australia to report on the situation. He was told that the army's Second Column was being sent to reinforce him.[182]

Unaware of any of this, Duque and his driver neared the curve just before Helechal. Seeing tanks in the distance, the pair assumed they were theirs and drove toward them waving.[183] Much too late they realized that they had strayed into Del Valle's battleline and were taken prisoner. The captain accompanying Duque was visibly shaken, but Duque himself remained calm and defiant. "Men, you don't know what's coming towards you," he told Del Valle and the other paratroopers around him. "I have 5,000 men and 14 tanks. You'd better surrender. You know you're going to lose this war." Del Valle, however, was not taken aback by the attempted intimidation. "You don't know what Del Valle can do with 100 paratroopers," he retorted with characteristic cockiness. Some of those gathered around listening to the conversation became incensed at Duque's haughty attitude. One smacked him on the lip and others called for shooting or hanging the "communist pig." "I'm a socialist but I'm not a communist," Duque pleaded. Del Valle intervened and personally drove the two captives to Girón.[184]

Arriving in Girón, Del Valle briefed San Román on the situation in the north. The Third Battalion had fled the battlefield, Del Valle told him, and were not reinforcing the paratroopers around Helechal. The brigade commander forthwith dispatched orders for his brother to relieve Noelio Montero as commander of the Third Battalion "and fight until you don't have anything left to fight with." Upon receiving the orders, Roberto San Román turned over command of the Heavy Weapons Battalion to one of his subordinates and went to find the runaway infantrymen. The Third Battalion men, and their Bon-Blin companions, were apparently cooling their heels just north of Girón. "I wish you luck," Montero told the younger San Román upon being relieved, "but there is nothing else to do here." The troop was then told to prepare to go to Helechal, where they would rejoin Del Valle's paratroopers.[185]

* * * *

Unlike Félix Duque's impulsive jaunt to the south, the advance of Castro's forces from San Blas was a deliberate affair. Castro had wanted the advance to be preceded by air and artillery bombardment of the area around Helechal–Cayo Ramona despite knowing that Battalion 111 may be nearby. However, Curbelo, and apparently Miret as well, had resisted doing so exactly out of fear of hitting friendly units.[186] Curiously, the prospect of causing civilian casualties was, from all indications, never expressly a matter of concern.

Victor Dreke and a scouting party had entered Bermejas, a small hamlet less than two miles from San Blas, sometime before 2:00 p.m. Save for some sporadic shooting from scattered stragglers, they had not met any resistance. Behind Dreke's party advanced the main assault column in staggered fashion, as dictated by the confines of the road. In the vanguard were three "tanks" (although apparently two T-34s and an SU-100 tank destroyer) commanded by Joel Pardo along with two infantry platoons and a bazooka squad. The rest of the column remained 700 feet to the rear, ready to move forward as needed.[187]

By 2:00 p.m. Dreke and his scouts were nearing Helechal, some two and a half miles beyond Bermejas. The group halted just short of the sharp left curve ahead but, seeing no sign of enemy activity, decided to proceed. Hardly fifty feet farther down the road, they came under intense firing and several of the men were hit. Dreke himself received multiple wounds and was carried away in a jeep.[188]

Pardo's armored vehicles sped to the scene and proceeded toward the curve in single file. The T-34s blasted away at the opaque thicket around them, their turrets sweeping the countryside as they went. In rapid sequence, the lead tank, the "larger one" (apparently the SU-100) behind it, and then the one bringing up the rear were struck by exploding projectiles.[189] None of the vehicles were put out of action, however, notwithstanding the dramatic visuals created by the shells exploding against the hulls. As at Caletón, the brigade defenders evidently yet again lacked armor piercing shells. Few were the times when a lucky hit with a high explosive round would severely damage an armored vehicle or harm the crew inside.

The infantry marching with the tanks joined the fray, and a fierce exchange of fire broke out between the opposing forces just as the trucks with the men from the Third and Fourth Battalions were arriving. The side of one of the trucks "looked like a colander" to one of the brigade soldiers surveying the spectacle after he managed to jump off and take cover.[190] Swarms of bullets flew in both directions. A bazooka man firing on the brigade position was killed when one of his rockets was struck and exploded.[191]

As the offensive continued, the brigade defenders began to lose ground and fell back to a new position some 700 feet to the south. Much to their relief, Castro's forces did not pursue them and a temporary lull ensued while both sides took a respite from the fighting. The hiatus was short-lived, however. Just twenty minutes later the advancing juggernaut was on the move again. Machine gun fire from the T-34s sliced through the trunk of a palm tree next to where a paratrooper rested. "[T]he tanks would advance," said combatant William Selva, "firing their main guns intermittently at the flanks and anywhere else that seemed suspicious while systematically machine-gunning anything within range."[192]

The new brigade battleline quickly lost cohesion when large numbers of men broke formation and ran for their lives. "[W]hen we pulled out, we didn't do so under orders; we pulled out of our own accord," noted paratrooper Antonio Fernández. Even the 4.2-inch mortar position to the rear was abandoned. Roberto San Román, with only about forty men left, also decided to retreat. In the pell-mell that followed, paratrooper Fernández observed, "nobody knew who was on whose side." A brigade tank fired at him and others as they ran. Apparently the same tank also mistakenly blasted the truck in which the younger San Román was attempting to flee. The truck's driver and another man were killed while San Román himself was severely wounded. Still able to walk, however, he started on the five-mile trek south to Girón. At one point, a jeep with Del Valle aboard passed by and stopped. The vehicle was so overloaded with men that hardly any part of it was visible. Somehow they managed to make room for San Román and drove on south.[193]

By 3:00 p.m. Castro's forces were in full possession of Helechal, although at least one brigade soldier refused to give up the fight. Equipped with a sniper rifle, the brave man kept shooting at the enemy from the bushes. It took a concerted effort, including the intervention of a tank, to eliminate the obstinate holdout.[194]

The road from the north into Girón was now open, but Castro's troops did not press their attack. "The offensive was stopped momentarily in order to regroup the forces," said Selva. Not knowing what lay west of them on the road to Cayo Ramona, two of the armored vehicles were posted facing in that direction while another guarded the road toward Girón. Within minutes, men were seen coming from the west, and Commander Saborit stepped in to take charge of the situation. He ordered that no one was to fire until he gave the word and sent a scouting party to investigate. It turned out to be the infantry troops from Battalion 111 and the Second Column.[195] They had finally reached their destination, although, as had happened at Playa Larga, too late to block the enemy's retreat to Girón as Castro had intended.

* * * *

"The fighting had become difficult," admitted Adolfo Colombié, one of the PNR combatants who hours earlier had advanced behind tanks on Oliva's position west of Girón. "But when the artillery arrived," the seriously wounded soldier recalled, "everything turned in our favor."[196] The new arrivals were, in fact, four SU-100 tank destroyers, or self-propelled guns, commanded by Fermín Tobar. They were the same vehicles at the vanguard of the bus column carrying Battalion 123 that had been attacked from the air the previous day. One of the two damaged in the attack had since been repaired and put back into service.

Tobar saw the three destroyed T-34s burning in the distance and decided not to close in. He ordered his unit to stop some distance away and open fire with their 100 mm guns in the direction of the enemy. However, the dense vegetation obscured where their shells were landing, so he climbed on top of his vehicle and determined where they should shoot. For some twenty minutes they pounded away at the brigade position.[197]

Stealthily the tank destroyers then began moving toward the front line, using the hulks of the shattered T-34s as cover. From behind the wrecked vehicles, one of the SU-100s scored a direct hit on a brigade M-41 tank and set it ablaze.[198] Tank commander Elio Alemán was killed, but somehow the rest of the crew managed to escape. The burning wreck now posed an imminent danger to the two flanking M-41s loaded with ammunition. When Oliva shouted for someone to drive the fiery menace away, Jorge Álvarez—the tank driver who had rammed the T-34 at Caletón—sprang into action despite having been wounded. He had been peering out the hatch when Alemán's tank next to him was hit, and flying shrapnel had sliced off the top of his right ear lobe. With blood streaming down his face, Álvarez got into the flaming tank and drove it to the rear near where the mortars happened to be. The alarmed mortar men yelled at him to get it out of there, so off he went again. Using the tank's fire extinguisher system, the brave driver subsequently managed to put out the flames. Oliva, who had "thought that man would never come back," was surprised to see Álvarez return to his tank fifteen minutes later. On the spot he promoted him to the rank of captain. "It was illogical," Oliva knew, but at the time it was the only thing he could think of to recognize such an act of bravery.[199]

On the heels of the SU-100 assault, "our offensive picked up steam," declared Rodiles. Arriving militia reinforcements from Battalions 180 and 227 joined what now became close quarters combat. Rodiles was soon in possession of the positions that marked the left flank of the brigade defenses—exactly where Carbó's group had been repelled that morning. "There we found a number of dead militiamen, some inside the rocky foxholes and others on the road [nearby]."[200] Oliva realized what was happening and ordered the Second Battalion's G Company, under Pedro Ávila, to stop the enemy incursion. Into the thick tangle of seagrape and underbrush went the company's men. But it was difficult for them to make out the enemy fighters, mere dark silhouettes moving through the dense vegetation; their shouts of "Fatherland or Death!" interspersed with rapid gunfire. "They had guts," declared one of the brigade soldiers, who themselves also proved their mettle. "They were very brave and they stopped the advance," Oliva said of Ávila's men.

With the immediate threat of being outflanked over, Oliva decided to draw back his lines 200 yards into prepared foxholes. G Company, however, was still fighting on the left flank and could not disengage from the enemy without some rearguard action. Oliva ordered Rodolfo Díaz, in command of the company of M-41s, to go and cover their pullout with his tank. Díaz, after twice being issued the command, hesitantly complied but was unable to locate the group of fighters and came back. Ávila radioed Oliva asking about the whereabouts of the promised armored support and was told to throw a grenade to indicate his location. Upon seeing the explosion, the tank ventured out again.[201] It does not appear that Díaz and his crew ever actually saw or opened fire on the enemy. According to Rodiles, "[t]hey could not see us, but we could see the upper part of the tank's turret and antenna." Still, the sight of the encroaching M-41 shook up Rodiles enough that he gave orders for his men to retreat toward the beach, thus allowing G Company to pull out.[202]

Withdrawing to the last line of defense on the western margins of Girón could hardly have seemed very comforting to Oliva's men. By then the brigade mortars were out of ammunition and stopping another enemy assault would likely be impossible.[203] Fortunately for those preparing to fight the last act of a last stand, the enemy (who had suffered on the order of one hundred casualties) did not advance on them. Castro's men were ordered to hold their positions in anticipation of an all-out air attack on Girón that was to take place at 3:30 p.m.[204]

Upon hearing of the coming airstrike, Efigenio Ameijeiras, although still a good two miles rearward of the front line, decided to head back to Punta Perdiz. There, he and his female secretary—"the only woman within that hell"—settled into a cabin surrounded by rock walls that provided "a natural shelter right on the seashore." "A military engineer could not have built a better shelter than that," remarked Ameijeiras of his safe haven six miles away from the fighting.[205]

* * * *

The sight of navy jets overhead sometime before two o'clock again briefly raised the hopes of the brigade men at Girón. Some boasted to Félix Duque, imprisoned there since shortly after his capture, that these were the "reinforcements" they had been promised.[206] Once more, however, the jets did nothing.

For Pepe San Román, it may have been the final straw. Even before learning of the enemy breakthrough at Helechal or the precarious situation of Oliva's position, he had come to the hard-fought realization that further resistance was futile under the circumstances. Just before 2:17

p.m., the distraught brigade commander sent out what would be his last cable.

AM DESTROYING ALL EQUIPMENT AND COMMUNICATIONS[.] TANKS ARE IN SIGHT[.] I HAVE NOTHING LEFT TO FIGHT WITH. AM TAKING TO WOODS[.] I CANNOT WAIT FOR YOU.[207]

San Román then spoke on the radio to Lynch aboard the *Blagar* and informed him that the enemy tanks were already very close to Girón and that he was ordering a retreat. Lynch implored him to hold on, that they were "coming with everything" and would arrive in three to four hours. "You won't be here in time," San Román replied, signing off with these final parting words: "Farewell friends. I'm breaking this radio right now." Aboard the brigade ships men began to cry as the news spread.[208] Many surely cried out of sadness but others perhaps from the relief felt at the end of a harrowing ordeal. "HQ was notified," wrote Lynch, "and the convoy reversed course as there was no need now for going in."[209]

At CIA headquarters, news of the invasion's denouement also had a sobering effect. "Never before had I seen a room filled with men in tears," remarked E. Howard Hunt, who was among those present.[210] The somber atmosphere notwithstanding, within less than an hour project staff were already taking steps to remove and dismantle all assets related to the operation. JMTIDE was ordered to "stand down all air activity" and prepare to disperse everything at the base. The brigade ships were similarly instructed to disperse at sea and proceed to various ports.[211]

Any lingering doubt San Román may have harbored about quitting the fight would surely have been dispelled when heavy artillery shelling of the Girón area began anew around 3:00 p.m. In response to a request from Fernández four hours earlier, a truck had finally arrived bringing replenishment ammunition for the 122 mm artillery guns. Thereupon, he and artillery chief Roberto Milián initiated a systematic barrage that swept back and forth across enemy-held territory. Gun after gun in each of four six-gun batteries boomed in sequence, raining down a total of 720 shells with every sweep of a rectangular area 0.6 miles deep and 0.1 miles across. "We deemed," Fernández wrote, "that all of the enemy's armaments and positions lay inside this rectangle . . . being saturated by our [artillery] fire."[212]

Paratroopers and men from the Heavy Weapons Battalion began streaming into Girón from the north in concert with the artillery barrage lines creeping across the settlement. "Houses began to fly through the air as if they were made out of paper," observed attorney Penabaz. "There was screaming and confusion," and the spectacle unfolding before his eyes made him realize that "it was all over."[213]

One of the exploding shells badly wounded Harry Williams and the two other men with him as they walked into town from the western battle line to look for mortar ammunition. Such was the force of the blast that William was thrown high into the air and broke both feet and some ribs when he landed back down. He could not move his left arm and had shrapnel fragments embedded throughout his body plus large perforations in his chest and neck.

San Román was still at the command post when a jeep carried in the three injured men. Williams, "bleeding all over, as if he had exploded inside," impassionedly told him, "I may not see it, but I'm sure we will win. Beat them! Beat them!"[214] However, the die was cast, and even as Williams spoke, San Román must have been in the final stages of preparing his exit. He dispatched messengers to his commanders on the north, west, and east ordering a retreat into the swamps until reinforcements came.[215] Just what reinforcements he expected would come, San Román would elucidate many years later. As he bitterly explained then: "Such was my faith [in the Americans] that, even after three days of hearing lies, . . . I ordered my battalion commanders to break off combat with the enemy and retreat into the swamp in company-size units. They were to avoid contact with the enemy 'until the arrival of Uncle Sam.'"[216]

All the prisoners being held in Girón were released, including Félix Duque. The soldiers who had been guarding him, recognizing his high status, asked him to lead them safely across enemy lines so they could surrender.[217]

Soon San Román himself departed the place where he had lovingly kissed a handful of Cuban soil upon arriving two days earlier. Along with Artime, staff officers, and forty-six other men, he now headed into the wilderness of the Zapata Swamp.[218] In a peculiar twist of irony, just as San Román was leaving Girón sensing imminent collapse, Castro, sensing imminent victory, was again leaving Havana for the area. After inquiring about the number of large Stalin tanks in the theater of operations, he and his entourage left unannounced for Covadonga shortly past 2:43 p.m.[219]

* * * *

A little before 3:00 p.m., navy destroyers USS *Eaton* and *Murray* took up station near the coast to determine, as ordered, if there was any possibility of evacuating personnel from the beach.[220]

"Look, captain, two ships," a militiaman said to Fernández, pointing to the sea from their location two and a half miles from Girón. The brigade men inside Girón saw them too. "Here are the Americans. They have come to save us," shouted out Máximo Cruz, peering out from the infirmary where he had been taken severely wounded.[221] Frantic brigade soldiers, making out to sea in any boat they could find along the town's shore, were also elated by what they saw.[222]

The spectacle of boats dotting the water between shore and ships confused Fernández, who took it to signify the landing of additional troops. He quicky dispatched a message to Castro via Central Australia asking for reinforcements. The captain then arranged for a newly arrived battery of 85 mm guns—and whatever other guns could be brought to bear—to open fire but *only* on the boats, not the destroyers. Despite what others around him counseled, Fernández was ever mindful that "[f]iring on the ships could have led to an attack by the United States."[223]

Per the orders issued by the JCS to Admiral Dennison at 1:12 p.m., the destroyers were to "TAKE PERSONNEL OFF THE BEACH AND FROM WATER TO THE LIMIT OF THEIR CAPABILITY." However, they were only authorized to "RETURN . . . FIRE TO PROTECT THEMSELVES." How to deal with the reasonably foreseeable scenario that boats packed with evacuees would themselves receive fire from shore was not addressed by the orders. Dennison had relayed the JCS directives to Admiral Clark at 1:45 p.m. and instructed him to comply with them.[224]

Just before 3:20 p.m., twenty minutes after the firing from shore had started, the destroyer task unit reported being "straddled by [a] shore battery." Rather than return fire, as authorized to do, the ships were instead ordered by Clark to withdraw "at full speed."[225] The final report Clark received from the destroyers less than half an hour later stated that they "SAW NOTHING TO INDICATE ANY CHANCE OF EVACUATION.

BEACH APPEARS COMPLETELY HELD BY LIGHT CASTRO FORCES."[226] It is
hard to fathom how the identity of the men on the beach, not to mention those on the outgoing boats, could have been misinterpreted. The
Eaton (flagship of the destroyer task unit) had been provided beforehand
with descriptions of the brigade uniforms and those worn by Castro's
troops.[227]

To the brigade men in Girón, the sight of the American vessels leaving at full speed was the ultimate act of betrayal. "In the wake of that
ship goes two hundred years of infamy," one of them proclaimed as he
watched the rearmost destroyer sail away. Others shot their weapons
toward the ships and, intentionally or not, those aboard the fleeing boats
got caught in the line of fire.[228] To Fernández, on the other hand, the
departure of the ships brought a moment of sheer elation. "I sensed the
war was over and felt an enormous silence in my head, as if I were floating on air, from the relief I experienced." The time it had taken for the
U.S. Navy vessels to turn tail and leave would prove for him "perhaps the
most stressful minutes I have lived through."[229]

Things only got worse for those seeking to make their escape by sea
when arriving FAR planes began attacking the fleeing boats and the men
along the shoreline. The JCS orders allowed for air cover to be provided
to the "CEF BOATS AND CRAFT" involved in the evacuation. However, those
same orders also put Admiral Clark "IN FULL CHARGE" of the rescue operation, and he had taken it upon himself to disallow any such aerial protection. He informed Dennison of that decision at 2:57 p.m., that is, even
before receiving the inaccurate "final report" from the destroyers about
the situation ashore. Given "the apparently hopeless situation on the
beach," Clark reported, he had ordered both his air and surface units to
fire only in self-defense.[230]

Looking down from their T-33s on the many vessels in the water, Del
Pino and Prendes initially thought—as Fernández had—that a landing
of reinforcements was taking place. Del Pino could not figure out, however, why the destroyer he could see in the distance was not firing on
them. "Why is it not protecting the new landing?" he wondered. Finally it
dawned on him that the boats as well as the destroyer were not approaching but heading away from the coast. He radioed Prendes and both
agreed that they were witnessing an exodus by sea.[231] Unlike the crews
of the American destroyers, the two pilots had no problem identifying
the brigade soldiers. "There are so many mercenaries that they look

like ants," thought Prendes at the time. He could also see artillery shells hitting the town. "In a few minutes the place has turned into a hell for them," he noted gleefully. The two jets dove and strafed the men onshore and in boats until they ran out of ammunition.[232] Two Sea Furies then arrived and continued the merciless attack. "Pieces [of the boats] would fly in the air," described Bourzac, one of the Sea Fury pilots. "[Many of those aboard] threw themselves into the sea. . . . You could see large numbers of people swimming, and then you would go here and there and hit everything." The FAR aviators spotted two navy jets flying near Girón, but the American aircraft did nothing to interfere.[233]

"It has been a fortunate afternoon for Del Pino and me. Without doubt, a very fruitful afternoon for us," reflected Prendes as the pair flew back to San Antonio, mindful that their prey had been sitting ducks abandoned to their fate.[234]

4:00 PM—10:00 PM

From the front lines, Rodiles could see that the artillery bombardment was being concentrated too far into Girón rather than on the enemy positions facing him. Artillery chief Milián took the matter in hand when a messenger from Rodiles reached him. He set off in his transceiver-equipped jeep toward the front and, as close as he dared go, got out and climbed up a tree. The enemy positions were still not visible to him, but at least he could see where his own front line was located. Up and down the tree he went several times, radioing back corrections to his guns.[235]

By 4:15 p.m. the brigade's last remaining line of defense ceased to be when Oliva ordered his 300 men back to Girón. It was a decision he made on his own because the message from San Román to disperse had never reached him. The runner carrying it had been knocked unconscious by an artillery shell blast.

As the deputy brigade commander walked east with his troop, a soldier drove up in a jeep and informed him that Pepe San Román had left. "That's impossible," he told the news bearer, and they hurriedly drove back together to the command post. Arriving there, Oliva saw for himself that only burned maps and destroyed radio equipment remained. Someone then told him that San Román had left in a boat. In actuality, it was Roberto San Román, along with Del Valle, who had fled out to sea, but Oliva took the news at face value. He would not learn the truth until weeks later. Tearing off his shirt in a fit of rage and shaking his fist toward the sea, he told the men around him that he would not abandon them. Nineteen-year-old Amado Gayol, one of Del Valle's paratroopers, drew his pistol to shoot himself. He thought this the best way of sparing his parents the despairing news of his capture and execution. But Oliva stopped him. "No. You're a man. Not like those at sea," he scolded the distraught teenager.[236]

Soon the situation in Girón became completely chaotic. The artillery shelling continued, and the sight of smashed buildings and battered trees added to the demoralized and bewildered mood of the men. At least one man, Vicente León—head of the brigade's "Operation 40" counterintelligence unit—did apparently take his own life rather than face capture. Still, others desperately clung to the hope that they had been pulled into

Girón as part of some masterful plan of the Americans to wipe out the encroaching enemy from the air.[237]

However, it was not American but FAR planes that were on their way, intent on dealing the brigade a final blow. Every available plane and pilot had taken to the air: two or three T-33s, two Sea Furies, and two B-26s. The B-26 flown by Carreras experienced an onboard fire and returned to base, but all the others went on.[238] Sixty miles out from Girón, the approaching pilots could see the pillars of smoke and dust being thrown up by the artillery shelling.[239] Just after 5:00 p.m.—almost two hours later than anticipated—the planes went on the attack with 500-pound bombs, rockets, and bullets.[240] From his perch up in the sky, Prendes described the hell below:

> I confess that I would not have liked to be down there after the planes systematically worked the place over. . . . The destruction was almost total, and that without taking into account what our artillery was doing. From the air we could see the targeted shelling. Hundreds of high-caliber projectiles were exploding everywhere around Girón on the ground and [also] the sea, sending up big jets of water.[241]

Oliva and a column of men were proceeding eastward out of Girón when the air strike came. They quickly scattered helter-skelter under the force of the attack. It was every man for himself from then on.[242]

* * * *

At 5:30 pm, with the air assault over, Castro's forces entered Girón unopposed.[243] The last remnant of the beachhead established barely three days earlier had finally been seized. At that same hour, the CRC members who had hoped to be there, heading a provisional government, were instead in Washington helplessly seeking help for the now hopeless invasion.[244]

Castro himself, after first stopping at Covadonga, was just then arriving at Helechal, where Pedro Miret had emplaced his artillery guns.[245] "Why don't you fire on Girón?" Castro asked him. Miret replied that he thought that the town had already been taken, but Castro ignored the warning and urged him to fire every round he had on it. "We are going to have a hell of a time using up those shells afterward if we don't," he said to the artillery chief "almost jokingly," thought Miret. As the heedless artillery bombardment of reoccupied Girón began, Castro, accompanied by his escort, returned to Covadonga to eat.

On the way back to Helechal about an hour later, Castro's entourage ran into some former prisoners of the brigade making their way north from Girón. Reasoning that the invaders must be trying to escape on boats if they were releasing prisoners, Castro sent a message ahead ordering Miret to start firing toward the sea. Fernández, shortly after 6:00 p.m., had already dispatched an official notification to Central Australia announcing the fall of Girón. Evidently, however, the news had not reached Covadonga by the time Castro had left there around 6:30 p.m.[246]

Darkness had already fallen by the time *El Comandante* reached Helechal, where he issued orders for an armored advance on Girón. "Under the circumstances, what we wanted was for the tanks to continue on, but they had to move down a single road. So I placed . . . one [military] commander in each [of three] tank[s] and told them: 'You have to move forward at full speed firing your main guns . . . and running over any obstacles you encounter.'"[247] Joel Pardo in the lead tank was ordered by Castro not to stop until "his tank treads had become wet on the beach." He was then to fire tracer shells high into the air to indicate the all-clear.[248]

Castro's troops in Girón, not knowing that friendly tanks were coming from the north, became alarmed when they heard them approaching. Rodiles thought the whole thing strange when he was informed. He placed three armored vehicles facing the road from Helechal but, suspecting the advancing tanks might be friendlies, had the crews try to communicate with them. It was a great relief when Pardo confirmed his identity via the radio. Still, Rodiles gave the tank commander a harsh scolding for his reckless act when he arrived. Pardo, however, protested that he was on a mission from Castro to reach the shoreline and fire tracers. "Alright, go do what Fidel told you," Rodiles said to the vexed tanker.[249]

Back in Helechal, even after the agreed-upon all-clear signal was given, Castro hesitated to venture south. He was waiting for the heavy IS-2 Stalin tanks to arrive. However, after waiting for a while he "became a bit impatient" and opted for an SU-100 tank destroyer, in which he finally left for Girón. Upon arriving there, he went to the shore and busied himself writing a press release by flashlight about the defeat of the invasion. Ironically, for all of Castro's concerns for his safety, Miret had not been told to stop shelling the area. When an artillery round exploded nearby, a messenger was quickly dispatched to Helechal with word to cease the artillery fire.

Castro's writing by flashlight near the shore would subsequently get distorted into the first of many myths about his heroics during the invasion. Some published accounts described how *El Comandante* had shrewdly stood at the water's edge, flashlight in hand, signaling the ships offshore. His daring plan, it was reported, was to shell them when they came in thinking that "mercenaries" were signaling for rescue. "[W]e didn't see it and it never happened," admitted José Ríos, a member of Castro's bodyguard escort who was with him. In fact, Castro did not linger at Girón for long. Within an hour of his arrival, he returned to Covadonga for another meal and to spend the night at a private home there.[250]

At 9:00 p.m., close to the time of Castro's arrival at Girón, the CIA, through Len Jones, was releasing the last "CRC Bulletin." The communique rivaled its predecessors in the magnitude of lies and distortions it contained:

> *The Revolutionary Council wishes to make a prompt and emphatic statement in the face of a recent astonishing public announcement from uninformed sources. . . .*
>
> *The recent landings in Cuba have been constantly though inaccurately described as an invasion. It was, in fact, a landing mainly of supplies and support for our patriots who have been fighting in Cuba for months and was numbered in the hundreds, not the thousands.*
>
> *Regretfully, we admit tragic losses in today's action among a small holding force which courageously fought Soviet tanks and artillery while being attacked by Russian MiG aircraft—a gallantry which allowed the major portion of our landing party to reach the Escambray mountains.*
>
> *We did not expect to topple Castro immediately or without setbacks. And it is certainly true that we did not expect to face, unscathed, Soviet armaments directed by Communist advisers. We did and survived!*
>
> *The struggle for the freedom of six million Cubans continues!*[251]

As John Kennedy himself posited just over a year after the invasion, the greatest enemy of the truth in the long run proved to be not the *lie*, "deliberate, contrived, and dishonest," but the *myth*, "persistent, persuasive, and unrealistic."[252]

PART III

EPILOGUE

10

Aftermath

On the morning of April 20, a C-46 cargo plane headed out over the sea from JMTIDE. On board were boxes filled with propaganda leaflets that were to have been dropped over Cuba immediately after the D-Day airstrikes. Eleven million such leaflets had remained stored in Puerto Cabezas since the cancellation of the raids. Now, as the boxes tumbled out of the plane and released their contents, the leaflets delivered their message to an empty sea: "Cubans, you will be free!"[1]

In the afternoon of the same day, a convoy of armored vehicles escorting Fidel Castro arrived at a point on the coast near the stranded *Houston*. From there, first from a T-34 and subsequently from a SU-100, *El Comandante* took great pleasure in firing on the deserted and silent ship.[2] He did so even as dismayed army soldiers aboard two yachts approached the vessel to board it following his orders.[3] Militiamen engaged in onshore mop-up operations also found themselves in the line of fire and dove into abandoned enemy foxholes seeking cover. A third shot fired from the SU-100 scored a direct hit on the stranded ship. "[L]ike a small child," observed one of the bystanders, Castro popped out of the vehicle and jubilantly exclaimed, "It was I that hit it."[4] Decades later he would continue to proclaim publicly that at the time there remained enemy soldiers on the *Houston*, despite it being well established that there was no one left aboard. A photographer on the scene snapped the now-famous photo of Castro as he leaped from the T-34 before boarding the SU-100 with its longer-range gun.[5] The image appears on the country's "Victory of Playa Girón Commemorative Medal" as well as on any number of printed media, including a Topps American Pie trading card (#117). It has proven invaluable in reinforcing the perception that *El Comandante* led the battle right from the front. Even the very SU-100 from which he fired on the ship is prominently displayed outside Havana's Museum of the Revolution. Perched atop a concrete plinth, a bronze plaque attests to "Fidel's" feat aboard the vehicle.

In contrast to such sideshows, in its wake the invasion left much more weighty realities. A total of 183 combatants are estimated to have been killed in action between April 17 and 19. Of those, 115 were from among Castro's men and 68 from the brigade side, including the four American airmen. Publications from Cuba have admitted to as many as 800 total wounded among the country's forces (with no fewer than 23 of those acknowledged to have later died from their injuries). On the brigade side, less than 60 men were wounded in action.[6]

At a press conference on April 21, a chastened President Kennedy refused to discuss what had happened in Cuba. His refusal, he insisted, was "not to conceal responsibility because I'm the responsible officer of the Government . . . but merely because I do not believe that such a discussion would benefit us during the present difficult situation."[7] The very next day he appointed a committee under General Maxwell Taylor to elucidate "the lessons which can be learned from the recent events in Cuba." In addition to Taylor, the committee included his brother, Attorney General Robert Kennedy, Admiral Arleigh Burke, and Allen Dulles.[8] Dulles's days with the CIA were numbered, however. Within a year of the Bay of Pigs operation, he, along with Cabell and Bissell, had all been ousted from the agency.[9]

In Cuba, the roundup of brigade fugitives from the Zapata swamp region extended into May. Although some 100 managed to elude their pursuers, a total of 1,206 men (including Pepe San Román, Oliva, and Artim) were captured.[10] Of those who had escaped by boat, several succumbed during their ordeal at sea. Among them was Alejandro del Valle, who perished along with another nine of the twenty-two men aboard a small sailboat that drifted through the Caribbean for half a month. Forty-three *Houston* survivors were rescued by brigade frogman teams led by Lynch and Robertson. For some days, operating from navy vessels, these teams undertook search and rescue missions along and near the west coast of the Bay of Pigs.[11] Against all odds, other survivors managed to make it to safety inside Cuba. Luis Iglesias, the Fifth Battalion deserter, and Pedro Vera, commander of the failed paratroop drop south of Central Australia, were separately able to reach Havana. There they found asylum in foreign embassies and eventually returned to the United States.[12]

Those rounded up were gathered in Girón and then transported to Havana. In one particularly deplorable act of contempt for the invaders, 149 of them were packed shoulder to shoulder into a sealed truck trailer. Ten of the men would be dead by the time they reached the capital city after traveling for eight hours under such conditions.[13]

In late April, a select set of those captured were interrogated on live TV. Over the course of four days, they were prodded before the cameras to denounce the United States, repent for their actions, and confess their misconceptions about the Cuban Revolution. On day five Castro himself took the stage in Havana's Sports Palace before an assembly of all the prisoners. Using his renowned oratorical skills, he engaged in cat-and-mouse discussions with several of the men, including Tomás Cruz, the hesitant leader of the Pálpite paratroopers. Upon seeing Cruz, an Afro-Cuban, among the group, Castro had derisively asked him, "You, what are you doing here?" Cruz, however, proved to be more than the cocky *El Comandante* had bargained for. Castro's question, he told him, "perhaps referred to the color of my skin, given that since becoming a prisoner that recrimination has been hurled at me almost constantly. Thank God I've never had any complexes. . . . It's true that there were different social strata for black people in Cuba. But I can also tell you that I grew up among whites, and they were almost always like brothers to me." In the ensuing repartee, Castro reminded Cruz that before the Revolution he would not have been allowed to go swimming at the exclusive Havana Nautical Club. "I didn't come to Cuba to go swimming," the paratrooper shot back. "Didn't you swim in the sea at Girón?" retorted Castro, trying to regain the upper hand. But Cruz followed through with a sharp jab: "No sir, because I came by parachute."[14] Cruz's verbal counterpunches became lore in the Cuban exile community. Ironically, many of the paratroopers under his command had been members of just the type of all-white private clubs *El Comandante* had brought up.[15]

Toward the end of the almost four-hour-long session, Castro, in a backhanded way, did acknowledge the ordeal the brigade men had endured. Their experience, he told them, had entailed "a hell of effort, and of sacrifices and of privations, of thirst and of hunger." Nevertheless, he patronizingly added, the experience had provided them "an opportunity to know the truth."[16]

Seeking to resolve the prisoner situation, on May 17, 1961, Castro made a public offer to the United States to release them in exchange for five hundred bulldozers, valued at approximately $28 million.[17] Ten months later, with no satisfactory response from the Americans to the offer, the Cuban press announced that the invaders would be put on trial. The proceedings began on March 29, 1962, and lasted four days.[18] On April 7, a verdict was issued. All the accused were stripped of their Cuban citizenship and individual monetary fines imposed on them. The amounts ranged from $500,000 to $25,000 depending on the defen-dant's deemed "level of responsibility" and the "importance of the economic interests he had come to recover." The total sum amounted to $62 million. If the money was not paid, the verdict stipulated, forced labor sentences of up to thirty years would be imposed on the prisoners. A separate trial had been held the previous September for fourteen "of the most notable henchmen and assassins of the [Batista] tyranny" who had participated in the invasion. Five of them received death sentences, and the others, including the Fifth Battalion's Ricardo Montero, thirty-year prison terms.[19]

Castro, like the men of the brigade, had come to develop a special respect and admiration for Erneido Oliva. After the trial was over, he issued Oliva a furlough to go dine with representatives of the Cuban Families Committee (CFC) in Havana. The CFC, consisting of relatives of the imprisoned men, was the official body negotiating for their release.[20]

Four months after the bulk verdict was issued, Castro entered into negotiations with American attorney James B. Donovan, who, at the behest of Robert Kennedy, was representing the CFC. By September 1, Castro and Donovan had agreed on payment of almost $3 million in cash for sixty wounded prisoners released "on credit" five months earlier. The others would be freed in exchange for food and pharmaceutical products with a world market value equal to the amount of their combined fines. On December 21, a final agreement was signed between the parties, and the remaining 1,113 prisoners subject to the April 7 judgment returned to the United States in time for Christmas.[21]

Following their return to the United States, many former brigade members joined the U.S. military, and a good number of them fought against the communists in Vietnam.[22] Oliva would go on to achieve the rank of major general in the District of Columbia National Guard.[23] Others became CIA covert force operatives helping to counter Castro-sponsored insurgencies around the world. From 1964 to 1967, former brigade members fought in the Congo and helped to derail the pro-Marxist operation there led by Ernesto "Che" Guevara and Victor Dreke.[24] Che's subsequent capture and elimination in Bolivia owed much to another former member of the brigade, Félix Rodríguez. As part of the infiltration teams, Rodríguez had been unable to play a significant role in the invasion. Afterward, however, he joined the CIA to continue a personal war, as he put it, "against Castro and everything he stood for."[25]

11

Flotsam and Jetsam

Over the years and decades after the invasion, many were the personal tragedies and fateful ironies that followed in its wake. Among the most poignant was the fate of Pepe San Román. He became a man haunted by guilt, sorrow, and a sense of betrayal. The affections of his former soldiers filled him with pride, he professed eighteen years later. Yet he also felt shame and guilt at having led them into battle without guarantees from the Americans. His postinvasion life descended into a black hole of chronic depression and economic hardship that ended his marriage. In 1989, alone in the mobile home where he lived, San Román took his own life.[1]

Much different were the circumstances of Rafael del Pino, who wrote a book detailing his exploits as a FAR pilot during the invasion and achieved national hero status in Cuba. During Castro's 1975–1977 military intervention in Angola, Del Pino was given overall command of the Cuban air contingent in the country. Despite being promoted to brigadier general in 1983, he grew discontented and clandestinely defected to the United States with his family four years later.[2] The general and his kin were admitted into the Federal Witness Protection Program when he testified before the U.S. Congress about Cuba's involvement in drug trade activities. Under assumed identities, they settled into a comfortable, government-subsidized existence somewhere within the very country the former Castro loyalist had once so professedly reviled.[3]

Del Pino was neither the only nor the first FAR pilot who, having fought against the invasion, later parted ways with Castro's Revolution. In 1962, Jacques Lagas, who had grown disaffected with the political climate of the island, returned to his native Chile and wrote a book about his experiences.[4] Douglas Rudd emigrated to the United States in 1990 after twenty-five years of virtual house arrest in Cuba for supposed security breaches following his resignation from the FAR. Ironically, he died in Miami two years later while visiting the home of former rival pilot Eduardo Ferrer.[5] In 1994 Álvaro Prendes also departed Cuba for Miami after he dared pen a letter to *El Comandante* asking for democratic changes on the island.[6]

The life trajectories of lesser characters in the invasion saga are no less remarkable. Valerio Rodríguez, the wounded thirteen-year-old literacy teacher who shocked Artime with his Marxist zeal, is still hailed in Cuban state-controlled publications as a paragon of Revolutionary virtue.[7] However, such writings conveniently leave out that in 1969, after his father's fishing boats were confiscated by the government, Valerio was jailed for attempting to leave the island. This he was finally able to do in 1980 during the Mariel boatlift to the United States, where he settled and became a successful businessman.[8]

More spectacular were the sordid falls from grace that befell some of the personages involved. José Miguel Battle, whose bravery under fire had made possible the evacuation of brigade men from the Muñoz Canal, became a hero to the Cuban exile community. Building on that reputation, he rose to infamy as *El Padrino* (the Godfather) of the Cuban mafia in the United States. Through violence, corruption, and accommodation with the Italian mafia, by the 1980s the "Corporation" run by Battle had grown into a nationwide, muti-million-dollar criminal enterprise. He died three years after his arrest in 2004 before he could start serving a twenty-year prison sentence.[9] No less scandalous was the post-invasion metamorphosis from CIA operative to convicted criminal of E. Howard Hunt. His name will forever be inextricably linked to the Watergate break-ins that led to the resignation of President Richard Nixon. For his role in the burglary of the Democratic National Committee's headquarters—a mini Bay of Pigs fiasco in its planning and execution—Hunt would serve thirty-three months in prison.[10] Across the Florida Straits, a harsh fall from grace also befell national hero Efigenio Ameijeiras, chief of the PNR at the time of the invasion. Ameijeiras's Revolutionary accomplishments reached back to the days of the war against Batista. During 1963–1964 he also commanded the Cuban contingent fighting for pro-Marxist Algeria against Morocco. Nonetheless, in 1966, while serving as vice-minister of the armed forces, Ameijeiras was imprisoned and expelled from the central committee of the Cuban Communist Party for unspecified "moral offenses."[11]

As for the man whose removal from power had been the focal point of the invasion, master Machiavellian Fidel Castro, he continued to rule Cuba for another forty-five years. *El Comandante's* rule thus not only outlasted John Kennedy but seven subsequent American administrations as well. In 2006, due to ill health, he turned the reins over to his younger brother Raúl. Unto his death ten years later, at age ninety,[12] the elder Castro continued to promote the perception that he had commanded the forces opposing the invasion right from the battlefield. As early as 1963, he described to visiting American dignitary John Nolan Jr. how, immediately upon being woken and notified of the landings, "he hurried to the Bay of Pigs." "Shortly after he arrived, he received a message . . . that another landing was being made simultaneously in Pinar del Rio." "He hurried there only to find that this was a false report," then quickly returned to the Bay of Pigs "where the battle raged."[13]

The spartan command post at Central Australia, where Castro actually spent only a few hours, has been turned into the Museo Comandancia de las Fuerzas Armadas Revolucionarias (Revolutionary Armed Forces's Command Center Museum). Restored in 2016, the historic landmark "is known foremost," according to the official propaganda, "because the leader of the Cuban Revolution, Fidel Castro, commanded from there the operations of the Girón saga."[14] Given the officially sanctioned storyline, it is not surprising that neither the exact location nor any photograph of Castro's Point One headquarters, where he spent most of the battle, has ever been published. In contrast to the rustic building at Central Australia, Point One was situated in the swanky Havana neighborhood of Nuevo Vedado. The upscale dwelling it occupied, nestled within a walled, wooded compound on the banks of the Almendares River, had been the former residence of an exiled businessman.[15]

However contrived, the mythmaking proved effective and enduring. "No commander since Erwing Rommel in World War II," posits one admiring academic, "came so close to his troops in combat, and no ruler since Napoleon led and inspired his soldiers by personal example."[16]

In the wake of the invasion's defeat, Castro may have taken a special glee in his American nemesis's Bay of Pigs humiliation. Kennedy now faced a similar indignity to what he himself had experienced less than two years earlier after his failed invasion of the Dominican Republic. Indeed, the parallels between the two operations are striking. The Castro-sponsored "internationalist mission,"[17] intended to depose Dominican strongman Rafael Trujillo, had been carried out in the name of an opposition group (the Dominican Liberation Movement) exiled in Cuba. The Dominican Liberation Army (DLA) that undertook the operation consisted of 198 combatants, including twenty-two Cuban nationals, although Castro had publicly avowed no direct Cuban involvement. Weapons and tactical training were provided to the DLA at a camp in the western hills of Cuba. The strategy for the operation assumed that a focus of resistance on Dominican soil would be joined by civilian, military, and other opposition forces. No effort was made to contact underground elements within the country for the sake of secrecy, although invasion rumors were rampant within Dominican exile communities. Trujillo knew of the invasion and had prepared his defenses. Three landings, one by air (from a transport plane bearing Dominican Air Force insignia) and two by sea, were planned to take place at different places in the country. The three forces were to converge and consolidate in the uplands once on land. After an inauspicious June 13 start from eastern Cuba, on June 19 the two yachts carrying the DLA sea forces sailed away to their destination. They were escorted to within some sixty miles of the Dominican coast by three Cuban navy frigates. Engaged almost immediately by the vastly superior air, land, and naval forces of Trujillo, the amphibious forces were neutralized in short order. The airborne force, which had landed on June 14, met the same fate. Only six of the men that participated in the invasion survived, the rest being either killed in combat or executed after capture.[18] In the aftermath of the disaster, Castro, like Kennedy for the Bay of Pigs failure, bore the brunt of much criticism from the defeated exiles. "Fidel Castro sold us out like pigs, he betrayed us, he did not support us when we most needed it," declared Dominican exile leader and invasion organizer Julian Hernández. "On the very day that the invasion was launched," Hernández added, "Fidel had already started to pull back. . . . [He] realized that the Movement was not communist and from then on started to withhold support." A similar view is shared by Francisco Medardo, one of the few survivors of the expeditionary force: "Fidel Castro left us on our own." "Where's the support Fidel promised us?" Medardo would often hear his commander ask during the fighting.[19]

12

Reckoning

Why did the Bay of Pigs operation fail? Over the decades since the invasion, the reasons for its demise have been the subject of numerous deliberations and discussions. Still, the subject remains a contentious one.

The Taylor Committee presented its findings in a secret report issued in June 1961 that was subsequently declassified piecemeal between 1977 and 2000.[1] Among its conclusions were that "the impossibility of running Zapata as a covert operation under CIA should have been recognized and the situation reviewed." Responsibility for failing to do so was not assigned solely to the CIA, however, but to "all agencies in the Government." This implicitly included the Kennedy administration and its "changing ground rules laid down for non-military considerations."[2] However, in the opinion of CIA historian Jack Pfeiffer, the report did not find the CIA blameless enough. In 1984 he issued a scathing internal review characterizing the investigation as a whitewash shepherded by Taylor and Robert Kennedy to exculpate the president and his advisers.[3]

On a parallel track with the Taylor Committee's inquiry, Dulles instructed the CIA's inspector general (IG), Lyman Kirkpatrick, to conduct his own survey of the agency's role in the operation. The secret report he issued in October 1961 found fault with just about every aspect of the agency's project organization and execution. Nine specific areas of failures and inadequacies were identified: (1) recognition of the agency's limitations, (2) advisement of policymakers, (3) inclusion of exile leaders, (4) support for internal Cuban resistance, (5) military and civilian intelligence, (6) project organization, (7) staffing, (8) assets, and (9) planning.[4] In January of 1962, Bissell took it upon himself to write an internal rebuttal to the IG's survey. He objected to the "black picture of the Agency's role in the operation" painted by the report and, as the operation's mastermind, said he felt "wounded by it." In Bissell's view, "a large majority of the conclusions reached in the Survey are misleading or wrong." The CIA's new director, John McCone, ordered that Bissell's rebuttal be permanently attached to the IG's survey in the official record. Both reports were then kept secret for over thirty years despite repeated requests from an open-government advocacy group. It was not until 1998 that the documents were declassified.[5]

No less contentious than these views-from-above are those of the individuals who fought in and against the invasion. Reflecting on the event, former militiaman Rodolfo Carnota grandiloquently posited why his side had won: "The courage of the Cuban man entrenched itself doggedly and impenetrably in defense of his ideals before the despicable invader who sought to advance and seize that beloved piece of the fatherland."[6] Glaringly missing from Carnota's florid diatribe was any acknowledgment of the simple truth that the foes he had faced were fellow Cubans. From the other side, exile B-26 airman Esteban Bovo expressed his views on the conflict as follows: "In every victory, there are casualties, but to kill people over a predestined loss? That's shameful. After all, those men were Cubans just like us."[7] In truth, however, neither the CIA planners nor President Kennedy believed that the invasion as planned amounted to "a predestined loss," as misguided and naïve as the whole enterprise may seem in hindsight. During his meeting with the distraught CRC members at the fiasco's conclusion, Kennedy explained that on April 13 he had sought reassurances from the CIA that the brigade could win without American military assistance. The president then showed them a response on that date from Marine Colonel Hawkins, paramilitary staff section chief at the CIA, who was visiting the exile units in Puerto Cabezas. Hawkins wrote glowingly of his "confidence in the ability of this force to accomplish not only initial combat missions but also the ultimate objective of Castro's overthrow." The opposing forces in Cuba, the colonel was convinced, would "melt away from Castro, who they have no wish to support." Based on this assessment, Kennedy told the exile leaders, he had given the go-ahead for the invasion.[8]

However misplaced, the CIA's belief in ultimate success persisted even as it readily consented to politically motivated White House demands for militarily inadvisable operational changes. "At some point we should have cried 'enough,'" admitted David Atlee Phillips, one of the

CIA officers who planned the operation. It was, he said, a fault shared by Dulles, Bissell, and "all of us."[9]

One major concession had been staging limited airstrikes on April 15 to help overcome Kennedy's objections to the "too spectacular" aspects of the Trinidad Plan.[10] Following the invasion's collapse, Bissell—who once described himself as a "man-eating shark"[11]—set out to minimize his share of responsibility by rewriting history. Alas, despite solid documentary evidence to the contrary, much of his version of events has been widely embraced across the Bay of Pigs literature. As told by Bissell to author Peter Wyden, when he received approval from Kennedy on April 14 for the next day's airstrike, the president, "almost as an afterthought," asked how many aircraft would be involved. When he replied "sixteen," Kennedy reportedly expressed his disapproval and said that he only wanted a "minimal" number. It was this conversation, Bissell reportedly told Wyden, that led him to reduce the number of aircraft to six. In his own memoirs, Bissell similarly describes this last-minute change forced on him by Kennedy, although therein he correctly sets the number of participating aircraft at eight. Tellingly, he never once mentioned such a chain of events in his 1961 testimony before the Taylor Committee.[12] As previously described, the finalized Zapata Plan, about which Kennedy had been briefed on April 12, specifically called for a *limited* airstrike on D-2. Thus, it is inconceivable that on April 14 Bissell had intended to use all sixteen aircraft available at JMTIDE. Indeed, the CIA's own official history of the Bay of Pigs air operations (declassified in 2011, seventeen years after Bissell's death[13]) indicates that a total of six B-26s had been scheduled to participate in the strike as of April 12. Then, on April 14, under pressure from JMTIDE, Bissell relented and allowed two more to participate.[14]

Others in the CIA also engaged in the postinvasion blame-shifting game. The circumstances surrounding Nino Díaz's aborted diversionary landing on D-2 have been widely and unfairly distorted. Based on the CIA's testimony, the Taylor Commission concluded that "[t]he landing failed to take place, probably because of weak leadership on the part of the Cuban officer responsible for the landing."[15] But in fact, Díaz's actions were exactly in accord with what was specified in the "Operation Mars" plan formulated by the agency. The plan unequivocally stated that the diversionary landing was to begin after a commando team ashore signaled the all-clear. If there was a "lack of acknowledgment from the reception detail on land," another attempt to land was to be made on the following night. If there was still no signal, Díaz was to take his ship and "proceed to a pre-assigned position" from which he was to "contact the rear support base and await instructions."[16] That is exactly what Nino Díaz did when the commandos failed to show. Yet the CIA's representations to the Taylor Committee were patently disingenuous: "The leader [Díaz] was never informed that there would be a reception party. . . . The validity of the reasons given by Díaz [i.e., no signal from shore] for not conducting the landing are questionable."[17]

A very prominent Achilles heel in the execution of the operation, aside from its deficient logistics, was the flawed intelligence it was founded upon. Fundamental tenets about the realities the invaders would encounter proved to be wholly invalid. Yet, despite clear evidence that this was so, the Taylor Committee concluded that "[a]lthough the intelligence was not perfect, particularly as to the evaluation of the effectiveness of the T-33s, we do not feel that any failure of intelligence contributed significantly to the defeat."[18] This egregious conclusion is, to all appearances, a testament to Dulles's influence on the panel.

"I suspect," McGeorge Bundy declared to the Taylor Committee, "that one reason for the later decision not to launch an air strike on the morning of D-Day was that [the T-33 threat] was never put forward as significant."[19] However, the CIA had also underestimated the capabilities of Castro's Sea Furies, which, as it happened, were the aircraft responsible for sinking the *Río Escondido* and disabling the *Houston*. Dean Rusk's testimony before the committee got to the heart of the matter. According to Rusk, when Cabell and Bissell met with him on April 16 about the cancelation of the D-Day sorties, both "indicated that the air strikes would be important, not critical. I offered to let them call [*sic*] the President, but they indicated they didn't think the matter was that important. . . . I believe that Castro turned out to have more operational air strength than we figured." This belief is entirely consistent with the low overall operational effectiveness attributed by the CIA to Castro's air force per the Operation Pluto Plan itself. Both Cabell and Bissell acknowledge their refusal at the time to talk to Kennedy directly as Rusk had offered them the opportunity to do.[20]

Chief of Air Operation Thorsrud, speaking sixteen years after the events, stated that after the D-Day airstrikes were canceled, "[e]veryone knew that the operation didn't have a prayer."[21] Yet such keen prescience was not readily evident on April 17, 1961. Thorsrud's reply to headquarters about the reassignment of the B-26s to a strictly air support role was decidedly less categorical than his retrospective assertion.

BELIEVE . . . CHANGE WILL NOT AFFORD AS MUCH PROTECTION AS ORIGINAL STRIKE PLAN. THE ONLY REAL OFFENSIVE DANGER TO THE BRIGADE IS ENEMY FIGHTERS AND BOMBERS WHICH ARE BETTER HIT ON THEIR HOME FIELD—NOT (REPEAT NOT) OVER THE BEACHHEAD.[22]

The CIA planners seriously erred not only in underestimating Castro's air (and ground) capabilities but also in predicting the amount of popular support the invaders would receive within Cuba. Indeed, the IG inquiry harshly criticized the agency for failing "to collect adequate information of the strengths of the Castro regime and the extent of opposition to it." Moreover, it concluded that the agency "failed to evaluate the available information correctly."[23]

As memorialized in the Operation Pluto Plan, the CIA had projected that the invasion force "would receive the immediate support of 25% of the population." It is true that, in the days following the April 15 bombings, tens of thousands of potential anti-Castro sympathizers were jailed. However, it certainly would have been impossible to detain the nearly two million people that this percentage signified.[24] Moreover, the agency was completely off the mark in its prediction that disaffected elements would double the brigade's number within twenty days of landing and double it again within thirty.[25] Those projections may perhaps have been the basis for the additional men that Miró Cardona would later say he had been promised (albeit falling short of the ten to thirty thousand he variously claimed). Their origin of these men had not been explained, he admitted, but he "assumed they would come from the United States Army."[26]

After the debacle, however, many of the CIA principals involved sought to obfuscate or flatly deny the agency's faux pas in its popular support predictions. "No one, right up to the level of Allen Dulles," wrote Bissell in his memoirs, "expected a mass uprising the minute the men hit the beach." But, he added, "[after three of four days] if aircraft had been operating out of the beachhead and had successfully prevented Castro's forces from destroying it, there was a very real possibility, we hoped, that significant defections would begin." Bissell further mused that "it is at least possible that the original plan to land at Trinidad, a city of twenty thousand, would have provided the large uprising needed to support the troops."[27] This pipe dream about the Trinidad Plan ignored, of course, that Castro and his advisers were not blind to the tactical advantages of the area and had ensured that it was "well defended." While the landings at the Bay of Pigs had met with only limited initial opposition, at Trinidad the invaders would have faced strong resistance right from the outset.[28] Dulles himself was more categorical on the matter of uprisings when he wrote: "I know of no estimate that a spontaneous uprising of the unarmed population of Cuba would be touched off by the landing."[29] Equally unequivocal was E. Howard Hunt: "[A] mass popular uprising had never been expected or contemplated."[30]

A contrastingly honest appraisal of the importance placed on popular support, reflective of what had been emphasized in the March 16 presidential briefing, was offered by Colonel Hawkins. As he wrote in a Memorandum for the Record (May 5, 1961):

> The ultimate success of strike operations against Cuba in causing the overthrow of Castro depended upon the precipitation by these operations of large-scale uprisings among the people of Cuba and widespread revolt within the ranks of Castro's armed forces. The invasion force was never intended to overthrow Castro by itself, and no representations were ever made by the Central Intelligence Agency that the force had such a potential.[31]

Hawkins's views were echoed by Marine General Shoup of the JCS before the Taylor Committee. "The mission was to get some well-trained military people into Cuba, who could gather into their fold and equip all the people that were just waiting for a chance to get at Castro[.] [T]hen these military people could develop a real military organization and increase their strength to the extent that the whole Castro regime would fall apart." In response to whether popular support from uprisings was expected, his point was cogent (if numerically inaccurate): "Well, it's obvious we wouldn't be taking 30,000 [sic] additional rifles if we didn't think there was going to be somebody to use them." When asked if he would send 1,200 Marines to hold out against thousands of Castro's troops, his reply was equally on point. "No, I wouldn't, unless 1,200 Marines are going to be assisted by 30,000 Cubans."[32]

The men of the brigade certainly expected massive support from both civilians and Castro's military, as a sampling of testimonies from their televised interrogations in Havana reveal. "I came thinking that we would be welcome by the Cuban population and thus not have to fight against any Cuban." "We expected that the whole island was up in flames and that the militia would join with us." "I believed that when our force landed in Cuba, we would, in effect, be an army of occupation."[33] "I thought that after the first combats we would be joined, as we had been told, by the militia and the Rebel Army."[34]

These expectations were certainly shared by CRC president José Miró Cardona, as he proclaimed on the Spanish-language radio program Voice of Free Cuba on April 11, 1961. "Fidel Castro knows that there is no way out for him," he told the audience. "He knows that the whole of the Cuban people is against him; that any militia and Rebel [Army] soldiers he may have are acting under coercion and terror."

That the Kennedy administration betrayed the invaders by withholding military support is a view held by many to this day. Yet Miró Cardona himself publicly declared during his radio appearance that he understood the administration's ground rules regarding American intervention and was more than willing to go along with them. One of the program's hosts brought up President Kennedy's statements, as reported in that day's *New York Times*, that anti-Castro Cubans would not receive U.S. military support. After confessing to not yet having read the statements, the man who was to preside over a provisional government in Cuba indicated that "we are perfectly in agreement" with Kennedy's position. "I have already said," he expounded, "that there is to be no government-in-exile but a republic-in-arms. At that time . . . we will request that western democratic governments extend us moral and material support. That will be a different time under different circumstances. It will then not be a revolutionary organization receiving military assistance but a government in charge of a territory."[35] Thus, at least in public, the preinvasion views of CRC and the Kennedy administration were in agreement. When Kennedy again pledged no U.S. military intervention the following day in a press conference, he added: "[A]s I understand it, this Administration's attitude is so understood and shared by the anti-Castro exiles from Cuba in this country."[36]

As it happened, however, the besieged beachhead was never consolidated, and the question of whether the United States would have provided military support or even recognized a provisional government in Cuba will forever remain elusive. Incredibly, it was not until early April that the legality of recognizing such a government was raised with the State Department by Arthur Schlesinger. A memorandum dated April 7 containing the State Department's determination did not reach Schlesinger until April 17, the first day of the Bay of Pigs invasion. As conveyed by Schlesinger to Kennedy:

> *The memorandum makes clear that the United States can not, under international law, recognize an insurrectionary group which has control of only a relatively small area in Cuba. The tests for recognition include possession of the machinery of state, administering the government with the assent of the people and without substantial resistance, and capacity to discharge international obligations. Obviously the Revolutionary Council will not meet these tests until it is established in Habana [sic] and until fighting has substantially ceased. Recognition of the insurgents at an earlier stage would probably constitute a casus belli.*[37]

Given that the American proxy invasion was in itself a prima facie "act of war," this splitting of hairs so late in the game is truly astonishing.

In the final analysis, notwithstanding his pledge not to do so, the president could have indeed opted to unleash the American military on Cuba when the invasion faltered. There were foreboding ramifications to, as Robert Kennedy put it, "the U.S. having been beaten off with her tail between her legs."[38] Even as the elder Kennedy doled out vague promises about Cuba's future to the exile leaders that April 19,[39] an alarmed attorney general prepared a portentous memorandum to his brother about the situation. Sending American troops into Cuba "might have to be reconsidered," the younger Kennedy reckoned, as "something forceful and determined must be done." His reasoning was uncannily prescient: "The time has come for a showdown for in a year or two years the situation will be vastly worse. If we don't want Russia to set up missile bases in Cuba, we had better decide now what we are willing to do to stop it."[40]

Robert Kennedy's perceptive warning proved for naught, as it failed to stir the president to decisive action. Instead, half a year later, he authorized Operation Mongoose, which primarily amounted to a series of ineffective hit-and-run attacks against the island.[41] This was followed in

February 1962 by a presidential proclamation expanding the U.S. trade embargo with Cuba.[42]

Emboldened by Kennedy's seeming weakness and lack of resolve, on September 7, 1962, Khrushchev authorized sending Cuba atomic bombs, nuclear warheads, and tactical missiles capable of carrying them. In the ensuing U.S.–U.S.S.R. showdown the following month over the delivery of these weapons to the island, the world would come closer to nuclear Armageddon than at any other time.[43] Many laud the Kennedy administration's handling of the Cuban Missile Crisis, dramatically portrayed in the 2000 film *Thirteen Days*, as a showcase of brinkmanship and good judgment. However, as incisively noted more than three decades after the invasion by then Division General Enrique Carreras: "If they hadn't failed at Girón, there would never have been an October [Missile] Crisis."[44]

APPENDIX A

Missions Undertaken April 17–19 by the Fuerza Aérea Revolucionaria (FAR)

APRIL 17

PILOT	AIRCRAFT TYPE (FLT. PILOTS)	DEPARTURE	REMARKS	SOURCES
GUSTAVO BOURZAC	Sea Fury (w/ Carreras and Silva)	5:40 AM	Second to hit *Houston* with rockets. Falsely claims to have sunk a "ship" before attacking the *Houston*.	Carreras 2008, 99–101 Otero et al. 1961, 102–3 USDOS 1997, Doc. 231, 591 Lagas 1964, 81
=	**Sea Fury (solo)**	**9:00 AM (estimated)**	**Attacks shipping off the Girón coast. Despite contradictions among sources, it is during this flight that he apparently engaged in a dogfight with Mario Zúñiga's B-26.**	**Ferrer 1975, 189** **Casaus 2012, 157–58** **(See related entries in appendix B)**
=	Sea Fury (w/ Del Pino and Silva)	~Noon	Fires rockets on landing craft off Girón and is hit by antiaircraft fire.	Sánchez 1979, 165-66 Casaus 2012, 154–55 Del Pino 1969, 79
ENRIQUE CARRERAS	**Sea Fury (w/ Bourzac and Silva)**	**5:40 AM**	**First to hit Houston with rockets at 6:30 AM.**	**Carreras 2008, 99–101** **Otero et al. 1961, 102–3** **USDOS 1997, Doc. 231, 591** **Lagas 1964, 81 (wrongly states Carreras flew a T-33)**
=	(Sea Fury) (solo)	9:00 AM (estimated)	Hits *Río Escondido* with rockets causing it to explode and sink at 9:30 AM. His plane is subsequently damaged by B-26 flown by Mario Zúñiga and pursued by B-26 flown by Matías Farías.	Carreras 2008, 102–5 Otero et al. 1961, 96–97 USDOS 1997, Doc. 198, 435 Ferrer 1975, 188 (misidentifies *Río Escondido* as *Houston*) CSG 1961, annex 28 (See related entries in appendix B)

APRIL 17

PILOT	AIRCRAFT TYPE (FLT. PILOTS)	DEPARTURE	REMARKS	SOURCES
RAFAEL DEL PINO	T-33 (w/ Silva and Bourzac)	~Noon	Shoots down Raúl Vianello's B-26. Makes uncorroborated claim that he subsequently attacked a ship off the coast of Girón.	Otero et al. 1961, 102 Del Pino 1969, 78–79 Ferrer 1975, 192 (wrongly credits kill to Prendes) (See related entries in appendix B)
"	**T-33 (w/ Prendes and Rudd)**	**3:00 PM (estimated)**	**Attacks José Crespo's B-26, which is subsequently mortally damaged by Rudd. Also attacks land positions at Playa Larga.**	**Del Pino 1969, 86, 91–92** **Otero et al. 1961, 101** **Ferrer 1975, 193** **(Also see related entries in appendix B)**
ALBERTO FERNÁNDEZ	T-33 (solo)	8:00 AM (estimated	Attacks grounded *Houston*. Fires three rockets at ship; a fourth fails to fire.	Otero et al. 1961, 104–5 Casaus 2012, 88 Gónzalez Lalondry 1995, 109
"	**T-33 (solo)**	**9:00 AM**	**Shoots down Matías Farías's B-26 at ~9:30 AM (est.).**	**Otero et al. 1961, 105** **Fontaine 2014, 68** **CSG 1961, annex 28** **Lagas 1964, 88** **(See related entries in appendix B)**
WILLY FIGUEROA	T-33 (w/ Ulloa)	6:45 AM (estimated)	Is arrested after returning to base for abandoning Ulloa and not engaging in combat.	Fontaine 2014, 64 Lagas 1964, 104 Prendes 1982, 50 Del Pino 1969, 72, 93 Carreras 2008, 102 (does not mention Figueroa and wrongly states that Ulloa flew with Fernández)

APRIL 17

PILOT	AIRCRAFT TYPE (FLT. PILOTS)	DEPARTURE	REMARKS	SOURCES
JACQUES LAGAS	B-26 (solo)	9:00 AM (estimated)	Attacks shipping off the coast of Girón. Dogfights with Matías Farías's B-26 (both pilots make exaggerated claims).	Lagas 1964, 84, 86–87 CSG 1961, annex 28 Otero et al. 1961, 103–4 (See related entries in appendix B)
"	**B-26 (solo)**	**12:10 PM (estimated)**	**Takes off after L. Silva's FAR B-26. Claims over two hours into flight he attempts to intercept but loses enemy B-26 flying east (possibly Crispín García's).**	**Otero et al. 1961, 104** **Lagas 1965, 91, 94–95** **(See related entries in appendix B)**
ÁLVARO PRENDES	T-33 (solo)	8:30 AM	Hits landing craft off Girón with rockets and strafes it. Damaged by antiaircraft fire.	Prendes 1982, 91, 95–98 Otero et al. 1961, 99 (makes claim of downing B-26 excluded in Prendes 1982)
"	**T-33 (solo)**	**~Noon**	**Damages left engine of Antonio Soto's B-26. Loses sight of the damaged bomber in the clouds.**	**Prendes 1982, 102, 106–7** **(See related entries in appendix B)**
"	T-33 (w/ Del Pino and Rudd)	3:00 PM (estimated)	Shoots down Osvaldo Piedra's B-26 at ~3:30 PM.	Johnson 1964, 124–25 Del Pino 1969, 86 Carreras 2008, 109 Otero et al. 1961, 100–101, 105 Prendes 1982, 123–29 (wrongly places this event on the 18th and conflates it with the attack by brigade planes on MNR Battalion 123. Mistakenly identifies B-26 pilot as R. Vianello) Ferrer 1975, 193 (mistakenly attributes Piedra's shootdown to Del Pino) (See related entries in appendix B)

APRIL 17

PILOT	AIRCRAFT TYPE (FLT. PILOTS)	DEPARTURE	REMARKS	SOURCES
DOUGLAS RUDD	Sea Fury (w/ Del Pino and Prendes)	3:00 PM (estimated)	Mortally damages José Crespo's B-26 after it is first attacked by Del Pino. Breaks off the pursuit of Crespo's aircraft when two U.S. Navy Skyhawks appear.	Johnson 1964, 124–25 Del Pino 1969, 86, 91 Carreras 2008, 109 Otero et al. 1961, 101, 105 Wyden 1979, 241 (See related entries in appendix B)
LUIS SILVA	**B-26 (w/ Carreras and Bourzac)**	**5:40 AM**	**Strafes small boats off Playa Larga and then proceeds to strafe landing crafts off coast of Girón.**	**Carreras 2008, 99, 101** **Otero et al. 1961, 102** **Lagas 1964, 81** **USDOS 1997, Doc. 110, 251–52, and Doc. 109, 241** **Lynch 1998, 107**
"	B-26 (w/ Del Pino and Bourzac)	~Noon	Is downed by antiaircraft fire from retreating ships off the Girón coast. B-26 lacked a working bombsight.	Otero et al. 1961, 102 Del Pino 1969, 78–79 Lagas 1964, 90
CARLOS ULLOA	**Sea Fury (w/ Figueroa)**	**6:45 AM (estimated)**	**Crashes off coast of Girón while pursuing C-46 (piloted by Mario Tellechea) returning from paratroop drop. Either stalls or is brought down by antiaircraft fire from the brigade ships.**	**Fontaine 2014, 64** **Ferrer 1975, 204** **USDOS 1997, Doc. 109, 242 (places the shootdown at 8:00 AM, but this time is incompatible with other lines of evidence)** **Carreras 2008, 102 (does not mention Figueroa and wrongly states that Ulloa flew with Fernández)**
Unknown	T-33(s)	Mid-AM (estimated)	FAR jets apparently attack friendly forces occupying Playa Larga around 10:15 AM, as reported by José Fernández to Havana.	Sánchez 1979, 197

APRIL 18

PILOT	AIRCRAFT TYPE (FLT. PILOTS)	DEPARTURE	REMARKS	SOURCES
GUSTAVO BOURZAC	**Sea Fury (w/ Rudd)**	**Early PM (estimated)**	**Attacks various parts of the beachhead including the Girón airstrip.**	**Selva 1987, 115–16, 193 Prendes 1982, 120**
ENRIQUE CARRERAS	Sea Fury (?) (w/ Lagas)	~06:15 AM	Attacks the stranded *Houston* with bombs and rockets.	Carreras 2008, 111–12 Casaus 2012, 130
"	**B-26 (w/ Lagas)**	**~4:00 PM**	**Aborts allegedly due to a machine gun mechanical problem.**	**Lagas 1964, 115, 117**
"	??	Late PM	Reportedly attacks the Girón airstrip and at ~6:30 PM overflies two American warships approaching the coast.	Carreras 2008, 112–13
RAFAEL DEL PINO	**T-33 (w/ Prendes)**	**6:15 AM (estimated)**	**Bombs the Girón airstrip.**	**Del Pino 1969, 97, 100**
ALBERTO FERNÁNDEZ	T-33 (w/ Guerrero)	~6:15 AM	Attacks Playa Larga.	Carreras 2008, 111 Casaus 2012, 130
"	**T-33 (solo)**	**5:00 PM (estimated)**	**Arrives after enemy aerial attack on Bn 123 and sees burning buses.**	**Casaus 2012, 154**
ÁLVARO GALO	B-26 (solo)	AM (estimated)	Flies on a mission out of San Antonio after arriving in a B-26 from Santiago de Cuba on 4/17. His plane is fired upon but not hit by Prendes, who mistakes Galo's B-26 for an enemy bomber. At some point Galo goes into hiding on 4/18 and is arrested for cowardice.	Prendes 1982, 113, 143 Lagas 1964, 104 Carreras 2008, 102

APRIL 18

PILOT	AIRCRAFT TYPE (FLT. PILOTS)	DEPARTURE	REMARKS	SOURCES
ERNESTO GUERRERO	Sea Fury (w/ Fernández)	~6:15AM	Flies on a mission out of San Antonio after arriving from Santiago de Cuba on 4/17. Attacks Playa Larga and subsequently experiences onboard emergency due to damage from ground fire. Is relieved from duty due to the emotional breakdown he suffers as a result.	Carreras 2008, 102, 111–12 Lagas 1964, 108 Casaus 2012, 130 Otero et al. 1961, 113–14 (mistakenly places the event on the 19th and identifies Guerro's plane as a T-33)
JACQUES LAGAS	**B-26 (w/ Carreras)**	**4:00 PM**	**Aborts after takeoff due to onboard fire.**	**Lagas 1964, 115–17**
ÁLVARO PRENDES	T-33 (w/ Del Pino)	6:15 AM (estimated)	Bombs the Girón airstrip.	Del Pino 1969, 97–100 (Prendes 1982 does not mention this flight)
"	**T-33 (solo)**	**AM (estimated)**	**Seeks enemy planes. Momentarily confuses Galo's B-26 as enemy plane and fires on it but misses.**	**Prendes 1982, 112–13**
"	T-33 (solo)	AM (estimated)	Destroys truck carrying troops on eastern outskirts of Girón.	Prendes 1982, 116–17
"	**T-33 (solo)**	**Early PM (estimated)**	**Strafes the woods around Soplillar (unaware that area was occupied by Castro's forces since the previous day).**	**Prendes 1982, 120–21**
DOUGLAS RUDD	Sea Fury (w/ Bourzac)	Early PM (estimated)	Destroys brigade truck on San Blas–Girón road with rockets and subsequently continues to Girón.	Selva 1987, 115–16, 193–94 Prendes 1982, 120 Del Pino 1969, 100–101
Unknown	**Sea Fury and B-26 (?)**	**Mid-PM**	**Militia Bn 144 at Caleta del Rosario is inadvertently attacked at 3:00 PM by FAR aircraft.**	**Núñez Jiménez 2018, chap. 21 Otero et al. 1961, 194–95**

APRIL 19

PILOT	AIRCRAFT TYPE (FLT. PILOTS)	DEPARTURE	REMARKS	SOURCES
GUSTAVO BOURZAC	Sea Fury (w/ Fernández and Rudd)	8:15 AM (estimated)	Attacks Girón and surrounding area; destroys truck.	Prendes 1982, 140 MGBA ~1961, pdf: 26
	Sea Fury (w/ Del Pino, Fernández, and Bourzac)	**Late AM**	**Covers entire area of operations. Perhaps one of two aircraft reported circling near a navy destroyer just after 11:00 AM.**	**Prendes 1982, 143–44** **Del Pino 1969, 109** **USDOS 1997, Doc. 144, 293n5**
=	Sea Fury (w/ Rudd)	2:40 PM (estimated)	Strafes boats escaping from Girón and the men who jump overboard.	Otero et al. 1961, 109 (wrongly states that Guerrero rather than Bourzac flew with Rudd) Del Pino 1969, 111 Casaus 2012, 198 Lagas 1964, 128
=	**Sea Fury (w/ Del Pino, Prendes, Carreras, Rudd, Lagas, and [?] Fernández)**	**~4:50 PM**	**Attacks Girón as part of air strike by multiple aircraft.**	**Lagas 1964, 129** **Prendes 1982, 163** **Del Pino 1969, 112** **Carreras 2008, 117*** **Casaus 2012, 199****
ENRIQUE CARRERAS	T-33 (w/ Prendes)	6:30 AM	Claims that he and Prendes each shot down a B-26 east of Girón, but actually there was only one "kill" between them (R. Shamburger's plane).	Fontaine 2014, 171 Carreras 2008, 115–16 Prendes 1982, 135 (See related entries in appendix B)
=	**B-26 (w/ Del Pino, Prendes, Rudd, Lagas, and [?] Fernández)**	**~4:50 PM**	**Takes off to participate in multiaircraft strike on Girón but aborts due to onboard fire.**	**Carreras 2008, 117–19*** **Del Pino 1969, 112** **Lagas 1964, 129** **Prendes 1982, 163** **Casaus 2012, 199****
=	Sea Fury (solo)	6:00 PM (estimated)	Claims to have attacked Girón in a returning Sea Fury after his aborted B-26 mission. If true, his attack must have come after Girón was already occupied by Castro's troops.	Carreras 2008, 119

APRIL 19

PILOT	AIRCRAFT TYPE (FLT. PILOTS)	DEPARTURE	REMARKS	SOURCES
RAFAEL DEL PINO	**T-33 (w/ Prendes)**	**8:55 AM (estimated)**	**Strafes Girón and surrounding areas.**	**MGBA ~1961, pdf: 26** **Prendes 1982, 138, 140** **Fontaine 2014, 174–75** **(Flight not mentioned in Del Pino 1969)**
"	T-33 (w/ Fernández, Rudd, and Bourzac)	Late AM	Covers entire area of operations. Perhaps one of two aircraft reported circling near a navy destroyer just after 11:00 AM.	Prendes 1982, 143–44 Del Pino 1969, 109 USDOS 1997, Doc. 144, 293n5
"	**T-33 (w/ Prendes)**	**3:00 PM (estimated)**	**Strafes brigade soldiers attempting to escape in boats.**	**Prendes 1982, 158–60** **Del Pino, 110–11** **Otero et al. 1961, 109****
"	Sea Fury (w/ Prendes, Carreras, Rudd, Lagas and [?] Fernández)	~4:50 PM	Attacks Girón as part of airstrike by multiple aircraft.	Lagas 1964, 129 Prendes 1982, 163 Carreras 2008, 117* (excludes Del Pino as a participant) Casaus 2012, 199** Del Pino 1969, 112
ALBERTO FERNÁNDEZ	**T-33 (w/ Rudd and Bourzac)**	**8:15 AM (estimated)**	**Attacks Girón and surrounding areas.**	**Prendes 1982, 140** **MGBA ~1961, pdf: 26**
"	T-33 (w/ Del Pino, Rudd, and Bourzac)	Late AM	Covers entire area of operations. Perhaps one of two aircraft reported circling near a navy destroyer just after 11:00 AM.	Prendes 1982, 143–44 Del Pino 1969, 109 USDOS 1997, Doc. 144, 293n5
"	**T-33 (w/ Del Pino, Prendes, Carreras, Rudd, and Lagas) (?)**	**~4:50 PM**	**May have participated in multiaircraft airstrike on Girón.**	Lagas 1964, 129 **Prendes 1982, 163 (has Fernández flying a Sea Fury)** **Del Pino 1969, 112** **Carreras 2008, 117*** **Casaus 2012, 199****

APRIL 19

PILOT	AIRCRAFT TYPE (FLT. PILOTS)	DEPARTURE	REMARKS	SOURCES
JACQUES LAGAS	B-26 (solo)	5:30 AM	Bombs and strafes along road from San Blas to Girón. Receives friendly antiaircraft fire. Destroys truck traveling on road.	Lagas 1964, 122, 124–26
"	**B-26 (solo)**	**1:00 PM**	**Bombs and strafes supposed mortar positions south of Girón airstrip. Sees American destroyers offshore. Must be "Castro B-26 orbiting over beach" reported by USS Essex at 1:57 PM.**	**Lagas 1964, 127–28** **USDOS 1997, Doc. 152, 300**
"	B-26 (w/ Del Pino, Prendes, Carreras, Rudd, and [?] Fernández)	4:50 PM	Attacks Girón as part of an airstrike by multiple aircraft. Drops bombs in very center of Girón and receives enemy ground fire that shatters his cockpit windshield.	Lagas 1964, 129, 135–36 Prendes 1982, 163 Del Pino 1969, 112 Carreras 2008, 117* Casaus 2012, 199**

APRIL 19

PILOT	AIRCRAFT TYPE (FLT. PILOTS)	DEPARTURE	REMARKS	SOURCES
ÁLVARO PRENDES	**T-33 (w/ Carreras)**	**6:30 AM**	**Claims that he and Carreras each shot down a B-26 east of Girón, but actually there was only one kill between them (R. Shamburger's plane).**	**Fontaine 2014, 171** **Prendes 1982, 135** **Carreras 2008, 115–16** **(See related entries in appendix B)**
=	T-33 (w/ Del Pino)	8:55 AM (estimated)	Strafes Girón and surrounding areas.	MGBA ~1961, pdf: 26 Prendes 1982, 138, 140 Fontaine 2014, 174–75 (Flight not mentioned in Del Pino 1969)
=	**T-33 (solo)**	**Late AM**	**Bombs airfield. Misses runway on first two passes and is hit by ground fire on third one, rupturing the plane's hydraulic tank.**	**Prendes 1982, 143–44, 148–49, 151**
=	T-33 (solo)	Early PM (estimated)	Drops a bomb near Girón airstrip. Also claims bombing and strafing the stranded *Houston* to silence a .50 caliber machine gun aboard, but the ship was vacant by then.	Prendes 1982, 155–56 Gónzalez Lalondry 1995, 121, 161
=	**T-33 (w/ Del Pino)**	**3:00 PM (estimated)**	**Strafes brigade soldiers attempting to escape in boats. Observes artillery shells falling on Girón.**	**Prendes 1982, 158–60** **Del Pino, 110–11** **Otero et al. 1961, 109****
=	T-33 (w/ Del Pino, Bourzac, Rudd, Carreras, Lagas, and (?) Fernández	~4:50 PM	Attacks Girón as part of airstrike by multiple aircraft.	Lagas 1964, 129 Carreras 2008, 117–19* Prendes 1982, 163 Del Pino 1969, 112 Casaus 2012, 199**

APRIL 19

PILOT	AIRCRAFT TYPE (FLT. PILOTS)	DEPARTURE	REMARKS	SOURCES
DOUGLAS RUDD	**Sea Fury (w/ Fernández and Bourzac)**	**8:15 AM (estimated)**	**Attacks Girón and surrounding areas; destroys truck.**	**Prendes 1982, 140** **MGBA ~1961, pdf: 26**
"	Sea Fury (w/ Del Pino, Fernández, and Bourzac)	Late AM	Covers entire area of operations. Perhaps one of two aircraft reported circling near a navy destroyer just after 11:00 AM.	Prendes 1982, 143–44 Del Pino 1969, 109 USDOS 1997, Doc. 144, 293n5
"	**Sea Fury (w/ Bourzac)**	**2:40 PM (estimated)**	**Attacks escaping boats off Girón. Sees two American jet planes flying nearby.**	**Otero et al. 1961, 109 (wrongly states that Guerrero rather than Bourzac flew with Rudd)** **Del Pino 1969, 111**
"	Sea Fury (w/ Del Pino, Prendes, Carreras, Bourzac, Lagas, and [?] Fernández)	~4:50 PM	Attacks Girón as part of air strike by multiple aircraft.	Lagas 1964, 129 Prendes 1982, 163 Del Pino, 112 Carreras 2008, 117* Casaus 2012, 199**

*Gives incongruous takeoff time. **Gives incongruous over-target time.

Sources Cited

Carreras Rolas, Enrique. *Por el dominio del aire.* 1995 1st ed. La Habana: Editora Política, 2008.

Casaus, Víctor. *Girón en la memoria.* Colección Premio Casa de las Américas, 1970 1st ed. La Habana: Centro Cultural Pablo de la Torriente Brau, 2012. http://www.centropablo.cult.cu/libros/giron-en-la-memoria/.

Cuba Study Group (CSG, Taylor Committee). "Paramilitary Study (Taylor Report), Part III— Annexes." John F. Kennedy Presidential Library and Museum, Boston.

Del Pino, Rafael. *Amanecer en Girón.* La Habana: Instituto del Libro, 1969.

Ferrer, Edward B. *Operación Puma.* Miami: International Aviation Consultants, 1975.

Fontaine Ortiz, Elvin. *Fidel desde el Punto Uno a Playa Girón.* La Habana: Editorial de Ciencias Sociales, 2014.

González Lalondry, Luis. *Bahía de Cochinos.* Miami: Vanguardia, 1995.

Johnson, Haynes. *The Bay of Pigs.* New York: Norton, 1964.

Lagas, Jacques. *Memorias de un capitán rebelde.* 4th ed. Santiago de Chile: Editorial del Pacifico, 1964.

Lynch, Grayston L. *Decision for Disaster.* Washington, DC: Brassey's, 1998.

Marina de Guerra de la Brigada de Asalto (MGBA) 2506. "Documentos confidenciales." Unpublished c. 1961 report on Asoc. Veteranos Bahía de Cochinos website, accessed December 28, 2020. http://bayofpigs2506.com/nueva%20pagina%20relatos%20ineditos.html.

Núñez Jiménez, Antonio. *En marcha con Fidel—1961.* 1998 1st ed. Amazon Digital Services LLC (Kindle), 2018.

Otero, Lisandro, Edmundo Desnoes, and Ambrosio Fornet, eds. *Playa Girón: derrota del imperialismo.* Vol. 1 of 4. La Habana: Ediciones Revolución, 1961.

Prendes, Alvaro. *En el punto rojo de mi kolimador: Cronicas de un aviador.* 1974 1st ed. La Habana: Editorial Letras Cubanas, 1982.

Sánchez, Miguel Ángel. *Girón no fue sólo en abril.* La Habana: Editorial ORBE, 1979.

Selva Álvarez, William A. *Girón: testimonio de una victoria.* La Habana: Editorial de Ciencias Sociales, 1987.

U.S. Department of State (USDOS). *Foreign Relation of the United States, 1961–1963, Volume X, Cuba, January 1961–September 1962.* Washington, DC: U.S. Government Printing Office, 1997.

Wyden, Peter. *Bay of Pigs.* New York: Simon & Schuster, 1979.

APPENDIX B

B-26 Missions Undertaken April 17–19 by the Brigade Air Force

APRIL 17

PILOT/Crewmate	DEPARTURE	ARRIVAL	REMARKS	SOURCES
RENÉ GARCÍA Luis Ardois	**2:45 AM**	**5:30 AM (estimated)**	**Jointly attack and disable *El Baire* north of Isle of Pines just after 6:00 AM and then go to beachhead and join in escorting paratroop planes.**	**Ferrer 1975, 187** **G. Ponzoa rpt. in Penabaz 1983, 156** **G. Herrera rpt. in Penabaz 1983, 162–63**
MARIO CORTINA Salvador Miralles	"	"		
JOAQUIN VARELA Tomás Afont	3:15 AM	6:00 AM (estimated)	Both escort paratroop C-46 and attack along road south of Central Australia. Varela departs area before Herrera due to a drop tank fuel transfer problem.	Ferrer 1975, 187 G. Herrera rpt. in Penabaz 1983, 160–63 G. Ponzoa rpt. in Penabaz 1983, 156
GONZALO HERRERA Ángel López	"	"		
MARIO ZÚÑIGA Oscar Vega	**3:45 AM**	**6:30 AM (estimated)**	**Flies cover over brigade ships. Damages Sea Fury piloted by Enrique Carreras and then dogfights with another flown by Gustavo Bourzac. Lands in Grand Cayman due to low fuel.**	**Ferrer 1975, 188–90** CSG 1961, annex 28 (time of Faría's shootdown reported as 10:30 AM but consistent with 9:30 AM EST) (See related entries in appendix A)
MATÍAS FARÍAS Eddy González	"	"	**Flies cover over beachhead. Pursues Carreras's plane after it is damaged by Zúñiga and stays over area after latter departs. Dogfights with B-26 flown by Jacques Lagas and is shot down by a T-33 piloted by Fernández. Farías survives a crash landing on the Girón airstrip that kills his crewmate.**	
GUSTAVO PONZOA Rafael García	7:00 AM	9:45 AM (estimated)	Flies cover over brigade ship for almost 2.5 hours. Fires on arriving T-33 before departing.	G. Ponzoa rpt. in Penabaz 1983, 156–57 USCIA 1961, Attachment C USDOS 1997, Doc. 109, 243
IGNACIO ROJAS Esteban Bovo	"	"	Unable to release a wing fuel tank upon arriving over the brigade ships, diverts to Cienfuegos airport and bombs it before returning to Nicaragua.	

PILOT/Crewmate	DEPARTURE	ARRIVAL	REMARKS	SOURCES
RAÚL VIANELLO Demetrio Pérez	**10:00 AM**	**12:15 PM (estimated)**	**Attacks area around Central Australia and is subsequently shot down by a T-33 piloted by Rafael del Pino. Crewman Pérez was rescued by a U.S. Navy destroyer, but Vianello was lost and presumed dead.**	**USCIA 1961, Attachment C** Ferrer 1975, 191–92 (wrongly attributes kill to A. Prendes) G. Ponzoa rpt. in Penabaz 1983, 157 Wise and Ross 1964, 58–60
ANTONIO SOTO Benito González	=		**Attacks Soplillar-Pálpite area. Damaged by a T-33 flown by Álvaro Prendes and makes emergency landing in Grand Cayman.**	**Castro 2011, 14–15** Carré 1975, 149, 159 (See related entries in appendix A)
MIGUEL CARRO Eduardo Barea	11:30 AM	ABORTS	Although accounts are muddled, it appears that Carro took off at the same time as García in a B-26 armed only with machine guns. His mission was to escort a C-46 flown by Eduardo Ferrer that was to land supplies at the Girón airstrip. However, Carro aborted in flight due to a mechanical problem with his plane's machine guns.	USCIA 1961, Attachment C Ferrer 1975, 192, 195–96, 200, 205 Selva 1987, 75–76 Pfeiffer 1979, 313–15 Trest and Dodd 2001, 123
CRISPÍN GARCÍA Juan M. González	=	2:15 PM (estimated)	Attacks Castro units south of Covadonga. Diverts to Key West due to low fuel after Ferrer's C-46 fails to appear. Crashes on return trip to Nicaragua that same night with loss of both airmen.	
JOSÉ CRESPO Lorenzo Pérez	**12:15 PM (estimated)**	**3:05 PM**	**Attacks Castro units north of Caletón. Attacked by T-33 flown by Rafael del Pino and mortally damaged by Sea Fury piloted by Douglas Rudd. Goes down at sea on the way back to Nicaragua with loss of both airmen.**	**Johnson 1964, 124–25** Ferrer 1975, 193 (mistakenly reverses the roles of Del Pino and Prendes) (See related entries in appendix A)
OSVALDO PIEDRA José Fernández	=		**Attacks Castro units north of Caletón. Shot down by T-33 flown by Álvaro Prendes.**	

APRIL 17

PILOT/Crewmate	DEPARTURE	ARRIVAL	REMARKS	SOURCES
JOAQUÍN VARELA Tomás Afont	5:07 PM	7:50 PM (estimated)	Attempts to attack San Antonio airbase but blackout and heavy haze preclude success. Mistakenly drops bombs and rockets on nearby illuminated chicken farm.	USCIA 1961, Attachment C (a second entry for another flight by Valera and Afont at 5:10 AM on 4/18 is ostensibly an erroneous duplicate) Carreras 2008, 110
MARIO CORTINA Salvador Miralles	5:30 PM	8:15 PM (estimated)	Attempts to attack San Antonio airbase but blackout and heavy haze preclude success.	Del Pino 1969, 101–3 Prendes 1982, 109–10
IGNACIO ROJAS Esteban Bobo	ABORTS		Destined for attack on San Antonio airbase.	Wise and Ross 1964, 63 (erroneously states Varela did not drop ordnance)
MIGUEL CARRO Eduardo Barea	ABORTS		Destined for attack on San Antonio airbase.	

APRIL 18

PILOT/Crewmate	DEPARTURE	ARRIVAL	REMARKS	SOURCES
GONZALO HERRERA **Ángel López**	**1:30 AM**	**4:01 AM**	**Attempts to attack José Martí International Airport but blackout and heavy haze preclude success. On own initiative, diverts to and bombs the Batabanó naval base.**	**USCIA 1961, Attachment C** **G. Herrera rpt. in Penabaz 1983, 152–53**
CONNIE SEIGRIST Gustavo Villoldo	2:07 PM	4:50 PM	Attack convoy of vehicles, including buses carrying Militia Battalion 123, advancing from Playa Larga to Girón.	USCIA 1961, Attachment C G. Ponzoa rpt. in Penabaz 1983, 158
DOUG PRICE Alberto Pérez Sordo	=	=		Pino 1983, 128 (erroneously states that only three of the B-26s attacked the convoy)
GUSTAVO PONZOA Rafael García Pujol	=	=		Villaraus 2008, 286, 288–89
RENÉ GARCÍA Luis Ardois	=	=		Ferrer 1975, 208–9
MARIO ZÚÑIGA Manuel Villafaña	=	=		
ANTONIO SOTO Benito Gónzalez	=	=		

APRIL 19

PILOT/Crewmate	DEPARTURE	ARRIVAL	REMARKS	SOURCES
DALTON LIVINGSTON [Unnamed Cuban] **THOMAS "PETE" RAY** Leo F. Baker	3:15 AM (estimated) =	6:00 AM	Attacks Castro's forces north of San Blas. **Attacks Central Australia at 6:00 AM and is shot down by antiaircraft fire.**	**Persons 1990, 90–91 (contradictory takeoff information given but 3:15 AM consistent with narrative, known arrival time, and chain of events; see table note) Pfeiffer 1979, 359** Otero et al. 1961, 221–22 Fontaine 2014, 169–70 Casaus 2012, 178, 185–86
GONZALO HERRERA	3:30 AM (estimated)	6:15 AM (estimated)	Flies mission alone after crewmate leaps out of aircraft prior to takeoff. Attacks troops west of Girón and his B-26 is damaged by antiaircraft fire.	Persons 1990, 90–91 (contradictory takeoff information given but 3:30 AM consistent with narrative, known arrival time, and chain of events; see table note)
BILLY GOODWIN [Unnamed American]	=	=	Attacks troops east of Girón along coastal trail. Because of a machine gun malfunction, could only use his eight underwing rockets, one of which misfires.	Ferrer 1982, 213 (takeoff [Nicaraguan?] time given as 2:30 AM) Dille 1962, 72
RILEY SHAMBURGER Wade Gray	4:00 AM	6:45 AM (estimated)	**Shot down at 6:50 AM (by T-33 flown by either Prendes or Carreras) while initiating attack on troops east of Girón along coastal trail.**	USCIA 1961, Attachment C Persons 1990, 90–92 (see table note) Pfeiffer 1979, 358 (Also see related entries in appendix A)
JOSEPH SHANNON [Unnamed American]	4:00 AM	6:45 AM (estimated)	Attacks troops east of Girón along coastal trail. Witnesses T-33 shootdown of Shamburger's B-26 but (despite claims by Carreras and Prendes) **he himself eludes the fighters.**	
CONNIE SEIGRIST [?]	5:30 AM	ABORT	Abort mission on the way to Cuba after learning of Shamburger's shootdown.	Pfeiffer 1979, 380
DOUG PRICE [?]	=	=		Persons 1990, 93 (see table note)

Note: Persons (1990, 154) admittedly uses unique aliases in his book for most of the American air personnel involved in the invasion. Cross-referencing of sources cited herein allows them to be identified as follows: "Bill Peterson" = Dalton Livingston, "Connie" = Connie Seigrist, "Don Gordon" = Billy Goodwin, "Hal McGee" = Joseph Shannon, "Larry" = Garfield Thorsrud, "Vic" = Doug Price.

Sources Cited

Carré Lazcano, Elio. *Girón: una estocada a fondo*. La Habana: Imprenta Federico Engels de la Empresa de Medios de Propaganda, 1976.

Carreras Rolas, Enrique. *Por el dominio del aire*. 1995 1st ed. La Habana: Editora Política, 2008.

Casaus, Víctor. *Girón en la memoria*. Colección Premio Casa de las Américas, 1970 1st ed. La Habana: Centro Cultural Pablo de la Torriente Brau, 2012. http://www.centropablo.cult.cu/libros/giron-en-la-memoria/.

Castro, Fidel. "La batalla de Girón (Segunda Parte)." *Cuba Debate*, May 25, 2011. http://www.cubadebate.cu/la-batalla-de-giron/segunda-parte-1/.

Cuba Study Group (CSG, Taylor Committee). "Paramilitary Study (Taylor Report), Part III—Annexes." John F. Kennedy Presidential Library and Museum, Boston.

Del Pino, Rafael. *Amanecer en Girón*. La Habana: Instituto del Libro, 1969.

Dille, John. "We Who Tried." *Life*, May 10, 1963.

Ferrer, Edward B. *Operación Puma*. Miami: International Aviation Consultants, 1975.

Fontaine Ortiz, Elvin. *Fidel desde el Punto Uno a Playa Girón*. La Habana: Editorial de Ciencias Sociales, 2014.

Johnson, Haynes. *The Bay of Pigs*. New York: Norton, 1964.

Otero, Lisandro, Edmundo Desnoes, and Ambrosio Fornet, eds. *Playa Girón: derrota del imperialismo*. Vol. 1 of 4. La Habana: Ediciones Revolución, 1961.

Penabaz, Manuel. *La trampa*. Miami: Zoom, 1983.

Persons, Albert C. *Bay of Pigs: A Firsthand Account of the Mission by a U.S. Pilot in Support of the Cuban Invasion Force in 1961*. 1968 1st ed. Jefferson, NC: McFarland, 1990.

Pfeiffer, Jack B. *Official History of the Bay of Pigs Operation*. 5 vols. Central Intelligence Agency, 1979. https://www.cia.gov/readingroom/collection/bay-pigs-release.

Pino Machado, Quintín. *La batalla de Girón*. La Habana: Editorial de Ciencias Sociales, 1983.

Selva Álvarez, William A. *Girón: Testimonio de una victoria*. La Habana: Editorial de Ciencias Sociales, 1987.

Trest, Warren A., and Donald Dodd. *Wings of Denial*. Montgomery, AL: NewSouth Books, 2001.

U.S. Central Intelligence Agency (CIA). *Plan de Operación Pluto*. Washington, DC: CIA FOIA Document Number 0000135658, 1961. https://www.cia.gov/readingroom/docs/DOC_0000135658.pdf.

U.S. Department of State. *Foreign Relation of the United States, 1961–1963, Volume X, Cuba, January 1961–September 1962*. Washington, DC: U.S. Government Printing Office, 1997.

Villaraus Gallo, Felipe J. *Huellas y caminos*. Miami: Ahora Printing, 2008.

Wise, David, and Thomas B. Ross. *The Invisible Government*. New York: Random House, 1964.

ACKNOWLEDGMENTS

This book would clearly not have been possible without the considerable body of personal recollections and documents preserved and disseminated over the years by various entities and individuals. I am especially indebted to the digital curation work of Vicente Blanco Capote at the Bay of Pigs Veterans Association in Florida. I also gratefully acknowledge Elvin Fontaine Ortiz's invaluable published collection of day-by-day, time-labeled Point One transcriptions which provided a robust framework for chronological correlations of events.

It has been a pleasure to work with the Stackpole Books team in making this book a reality. I extend a special thanks to Dave Reisch, Senior Acquisitions Editor, for his support and early appreciation of my work several weeks ahead of another publisher. I am also most grateful to Patricia Stevenson for deftly managing the book's production through its final hurdles.

The influence of my late parents, José and Zoila, has been a constant companion to me on this project and, as always, a wellspring of motivation. Their legacy endures. To my darling Teresa, who has cajoled, encouraged, advised, and supported me throughout the development of this book, my everlasting and loving thanks.

NOTES

Abbreviations used:

AVBC   Asociación de Veteranos de Bahía de Cochinos—Brigada 2506
CSG   Cuba Study Group (Taylor Committee)
USCIA   U.S. Central Intelligence Agency
USDOS   U.S. Department of State
MGBA   Marina de Guerra de la Brigada de Asalto 2506
FRUS   *Foreign Relations of the United States*

Author's Note

1. International Humanitarian Law Databases, "Protocol Additional to the Geneva Conventions of 12 August 1949," accessed May 25, 2022, https://ihl-databases .icrc.org/applic/ihl/ihl.nsf/vwTreaties1949.xsp.

Preface

1. Valdés, "Autobiography," 17, 19–22.
2. Rodríguez, *Batalla*, 75.
3. Gobierno de Cuba, "Discursos de Fidel Castro," speech of April 19, 1986.
4. R. Miller, *Closing*, 194.
5. E.g., Alonso, *Año 61*, 94.

Introduction

1. Szulc, *Fidel*, 193–94, 458; Geyer, *Guerrilla Prince*, 160–209.
2. Brown, *Cuba's Revolutionary World*, 47–67.
3. Geyer, *Guerrilla Prince*, 191. A facsimile of the Castro's handwritten note is included in the photographic appendix to Zaldívar and Etcheverry, *Una fascinante historia*.
4. Geyer, *Guerrilla Prince*, 257–58.
5. Smith, *Fourth Floor*, 100.
6. USDOS, *FRUS, Vol. VI*, Doc. 486, 861–63.
7. Zucker, "Refugee Resettlement," 156.

Chapter 1

1. USDOS, *FRUS, Vol. X*, Doc. 109, 238–39; Lynch, *Decision*, 41, 62–63, 69; Pérez San Román, *Respuesta*, 13; USCIA, "Pluto," 1–2, 6; Wyden, *Bay of Pigs*, 77–78. Codenames were assigned to the ships as follows: *Atlántico*: TIBURÓN, *Caribe*: SARDINA, *Houston*: AGUJA, *Río Escondido*: BALLENA (Martínez, *Historia*, 44). The estimated number of troops within each unit and the overall total are based on personnel rosters from the following sources:

a. AVBC, "General Index," published 2011, http://bayofpigs2506.com/pagina%20indice%20general.html, sublink: "Brigada, Miembros; Miembros de la Brigada de Asalto 2506."

b. AVBC, "Miembros de la Brigada," published 2011, http://bayofpigs2506.com/MIEMBROS%20DE%20LA%20BRIGADA.pdf.

c. El *Nuevo Herald* (newspaper), "Base de datos de los veteranos de Bahía de Cochinos" (lookup database), published April 14, 2011, https://c0dzk099.caspio.com/dp/ce401000d69ebaaeb4cb43849383.

2. USDOS, *FRUS, Vol. X*, Doc. 109, 238–39; USCIA, "Pluto," 6, Anexo C, C-1; Lynch, *Decision*, 34, 92; Belen Jesuit School, accessed June 1, 2020, http://wolverines.belenjesuit.org/wom/jorgejones-letter.jpg; César, *San Blas*, 126. The *Lake Charles* was assigned the codename ATÚN (Martínez, *Historia*, 44). Battalion tallies from sources listed in note 1.

3. USDOS, *FRUS, Vol. X*, Doc. 109, 239; USCIA, "Pluto," 6, Anexo C, C-1; Lynch, *Decision*, 92. Battalion tallies from sources listed in note 1.

4. Johnson, *The Bay of Pigs*, 94.

5. USDOS, *FRUS, Vol. X*, Doc. 9, 12, USCIA, "Pluto," 6. The codenames for the LCIs were *Blagar*: MARSOPA; *Barbara J*: BARRACUDA (Martínez, *Historia*, 44). The CIA also chartered two additional ships (the *Oratava* and *La Playa*) from the United Fruit Company for follow-up delivery of supplies and equipment after the assault phase (Hawkins, "Record of Paramilitary Action," 14, 30–31).

6. Lynch, *Decision*, 54–55, 66–67.

7. Lynch, *Decision*, 66, 69; Pérez San Román, *Respuesta*, 17; USDOS, *FRUS, Vol. X*, Doc. 109: 238–39. Troop tally from sources listed in note 1.

8. Johnson, *Bay of Pigs*, 32–39, 41, 54–55, 98; Wise and Ross, *Invisible Government*, 27; Carbonell, *Russians Stayed*, 89–90; Hawkins, "Record of Paramilitary Action," 9.

9. Johnson, *Bay of Pigs*, 55; Triay, *Bay of Pigs*, 63.

10. Johnson, *Bay of Pigs*, 99; Hawkins, "Record," 2–3; Cullather, *Operation PBSUCCESS: The United States and Guatemala, 1952–1954*, 1, passim.

11. Pfeiffer, *Official History*, vol. 1, 107.

12. Wise and Ross, *Invisible Government*, 23–25, 27–28; Johnson, *Bay of Pigs*, 44–45, 55–57; Pfeiffer, *Official History*, vol. 1, 20; Oliva, "Bay of Pigs Experience," chap. 7, section 42.

13. Lynch, *Decision*, 24.

14. Lynch, *Decision*, 24; Johnson, *Bay of Pigs*, 55.

15. Machado, *Cuba*, chap. 5.

16. Johnson, *Bay of Pigs*, 56.

17. USDOS, *FRUS, Vol. X*, Doc. 231, 581, passim.

18. Johnson, *Bay of Pigs*, 99; Posada, *Los Caminos del guerrero*, 65. The numbers of Seventh Battalion and Homestead recruits are derived from source (b) in note 1.

19. Oliva, "Bay of Pigs Experience," chap. 7, sec. 42; Johnson, *Bay of Pigs*, 34, 83–84. The number of men assigned to the First Battalion is derived from source (b) in note 1.

20. Pfeiffer, *Official History*, vol. 1, 101–2, 107; Ferrer, *Operación Puma*, 62.

21. Numbers are derived from tallies based on personnel rosters from the following source: AVBC, "General index" (see URL in note 1 above), sublink: "Fuerza Aérea, Miembros; Miembros de la Fuerza Aérea de Liberación."

22. Carbonell, *Russians Stayed*, 143–44; Johnson, *Bay of Pigs*, 24, 26, 62, 97.

23. Johnson, *Bay of Pigs*, 74, 77–78; Ferrer, *Operación Puma*, 139; Pfeiffer, *Official History*, vol. 1, 152, 163–66. Pfeiffer (166) erroneously states that "the 160 airborne troops . . . would be flown directly from JMADD to the drop zones in Cuba on D-Day." As described by Ferrer, one of the paratroop transport pilots, they flew out from JMTIDE (*Operación Puma*, 178–79).

Chapter 2

1. USDOS, *FRUS, Vol. VI*, Doc. 481, 850–51, and Doc. 486, 861–63; USDOS, *FRUS, Vol. X*, Doc. 58, 137, and Doc. 231, 577.
2. Kennedy had first learned of the plan's existence on November 18, prior to his inauguration (USDOS, *FRUS, Vol. X*, Doc. 231, 580).
3. USDOS, *FRUS, Vol. X*, Doc. 30, 62n1.
4. By this point, the CIA already had a draft Trinidad military operation plan (USCIA, "Plan de Operación 1–200").
5. USDOS, *FRUS, Vol. X*, Doc. 35, 69.
6. USDOS, *FRUS, Vol. X*, Doc. 58, 140–141, Doc. 59, 143, and Doc. 61, 145; Schlesinger, *Thousand Days*, 242. In his memoirs, Bissell recalls the time frame for developing a new plan as four days and comments: "It is hard to believe in retrospect that the president and his advisers felt that the plans for a large–scale, complicated military operation that had been ongoing for more than a year could be reworked in four days and still offer a high likelihood of success. It is equally amazing that we in the agency agreed so readily" (Bissell, *Reflections*, 169).
7. USDOS, *FRUS, Vol. X*, Doc. 61, 145–48; Doc. 65, 159, and Doc. 66, 159.
8. USDOS, *FRUS, Vol. X*, Doc. 62, 149–50.
9. USDOS, *FRUS, Vol. X*, Doc. 66, 159–60.
10. USDOS, *FRUS, Vol. X*, Doc. 74 (March 29), 177, Doc. 80 (April 4), 185–86, Doc. 83 (April 5), 190–91, and Doc. 84 (April 6), 191–92.
11. Bissell, *Reflections*, 173.
12. USDOS, *FRUS, Vol. X*, Doc. 74, 177.

Chapter 3

1. USDOS, *FRUS, Vol. X*, Doc. 93, 216; Pérez San Román, *Respuesta*, 13; Paterson, *Contesting Castro*, 208–9.
2. USCIA, "Pluto," 1–6 passim. Commenting on postinvasion media coverage, CIA operative E. Howard Hunt observes: "Gleeful much was made of exposing the operation's supposed codename: Pluto. CIA files, however, reflect no such project usage" (Hunt, *This Day*, 214). In fact, the name was limited to the military plan. Within the CIA, the program was code-named JMATE (earlier JMARC) (Pfeiffer, *Official History*, vol. 1, 5n**). Within the Pentagon, the JMATE support program was designated "Bumpy Road" (earlier "Crosspatch") (USDOS, *FRUS, Vol. X*, Doc. 76, 181–82).
3. USCIA, "Pluto," Anexo A, A-1.
4. Although neither the accompanying maps or photos are included in the version of the operation plan available from the CIA's website, a reproduction of a captured invasion map is shown in Clark and Waters, *Playa Girón*, 150.
5. USCIA, "Pluto," 3; CSG, "Part III—Annexes," Annex 22, Ops Map 1; Lynch, *Decision*, 41, 92–93, Johnson, *Bay of Pigs*, 115.

6. USCIA, "Pluto," Anexo A, A-1.
7. USCIA, "Pluto," 2; USDOS, *FRUS, Vol. X*, Doc. 231, 596.
8. USCIA, "Pluto," 2, 4–5, Anexo H, H-2-3; USDOS, *FRUS, Vol. X*, Doc. 109, 240.
9. USCIA, "Pluto," 5.
10. USCIA, "Pluto," 4.
11. USCIA, "Pluto," Anexo E, E-1, E-2-1, E-3-1. A common misconception repeated by many authors is that the entire B-26 squadron was to operate from the seized Girón airstrip (e.g., Rasenberger, *Disaster*, 275; Triay, *Bay of Pigs*, 39; Lynch, *Decision*, 42). There were good reasons why the plan called for only two B-26s to do so, at least in the initial phase of the operation (Hawkins, "Record of Paramilitary Action," 23). The 4,000-foot airstrip at Girón was shorter than the 4,500 feet a B-26 nominally needed to land safely (Pfeiffer, *Official History*, vol. 1, 156, 178). Thus, the pilots of the two B-26s that would operate from the strip required specialized short-landing training (155–56, 178n). There were logistical constraints as well. Operating even two B-26s from the beachhead required allocating considerable ship space to the ordnance, parts, equipment, fuel, and ground crews they required (172n, 177).
12. USCIA, "Pluto," 4, Anexo E, E-1-1.
13. USCIA, "Pluto," 3–4; CSG, "Part III—Annexes," Annex 22, Ops Map 1.
14. USDOS, *FRUS, Vol. X*, Doc. 109, 240, and Doc. 110, 249; USCIA, "Pluto," Anexo H, H-3–1.
15. USCIA, "Pluto," 3–4; CSG, "Part III—Annexes," Annex 22, Ops. Map 1.
16. Johnson, *Bay of Pigs*, 116; USCIA, "Pluto," Anexo A, A-2–A-4.
17. USCIA, "Pluto," 1, Anexo E, E-1; Rodríguez and Weisman, *Shadow Warrior*, 67; Johnson, *Bay of Pigs*, 120.
18. USCIA, "Pluto," 5, Anexo A, A-1, A-8, Plan Administrativo, Anexo A, A-10-1 and Anexo F, F-1.
19. USCIA, "Pluto," Anexo A, A-2–A-3.

Chapter 4

1. Silva, "Reconversión," 298–301.
2. Silva, "Reconversión," 10, 94.
3. Silva, "Reconversión," 229.
4. Silva, "Reconversión," 324.
5. Silva, "Reconversión," 315, 349n642.
6. Silva, "Reconversión," 349n642; Páz-Sánchez, *Zona de guerra*, 189–90, 199, 201; Franqui, *Family Portrait with Fidel*, 123, 182. Guilefully, the pivotal role played by Ciutat in shaping the Cuban military is generally understated in publications written in Cuba.
7. Herrera, *Operación Jaula*, 47, 111; Silva, "Reconversión," 316–17; Sánchez, *Girón no fue sólo en abril*, 37. Militia battalions were given three-digit designations with the leftmost digit indicating their province of origin from among the six Cuban provinces existing at the time: 1xx—Havana, 2xx—Matanzas, 3xx—Las Villas, etc. (Rodríguez, *Girón*, 292n29).
8. Silva, "Reconversión," 342.
9. Sánchez, *Girón*, 42, 47; Silva, "Reconversión," 316, 399n728, 470; Mayo, *Niños héroes*, 40–41.
10. Sánchez, *Girón*, 42.

11. USDOS, *FRUS, Vol. X*, Doc. 56, Appendix B, Security, item 8a, 131; Gobierno de Cuba, "Discursos de Fidel Castro," speech of May 19, 1961.

12. Rodríguez, *Girón*, 182; United Nations, *Statement by Raúl Roa*, 519; E. Ferrer, *Operación Puma*, 124.

    Cuban-exile sources claim that a brigade recruit named Benigno Pérez was a Castro spy and that there were possibly others (Tamayo, "The Spy"; Rodríguez and Weisman, *Shadow Warrior*, 60). Pérez was part of the brigade infiltration teams smuggled into Cuba during the second half of March 1961 (ibid.; Méndez, "Preparativos para la invasión"). However, Rodríguez (*Girón*, 181–82) maintains that Cuban intelligence was never successful in infiltrating the training camps. According to him, Pérez was arrested on April 21, married in Cuba after serving fourteen years in prison, and subsequently elected to stay on the island.

13. Gobierno de Cuba, "Discursos de Fidel Castro," speech of December 31, 1960; Silva, "Reconversión," 317, 343, 394n714; Escalante, *Secret War*, 16–29; Sánchez, *Girón*, 99–100; Rodríguez, *Girón*, 128. Trujillo saw his planned 1959 invasion of Cuba as payback for Castro's launching of an expeditionary force against him earlier that year. The would-be invasion supposedly included conspirators inside Castro's inner circle, but they turned out to be double agents who exposed and derailed the entire operation (Escalante, ibid.).

14. Military units defending the Trinidad area remained in placed despite the demobilization of troops in other parts of the country (Rodríguez, *Girón*, 128).

15. Gobierno de Cuba, "Discursos de Fidel Castro," speech of January 20, 1961; Herrera, *Operación Jaula*, 111, 202; Encinosa, *Escambray*, 25–26; García Iturbe, *Hombres de Girón*, 37, 69, passim.

16. Sánchez, *Girón*, 103, 249; *El Avance Criollo*, "Finalizado el entrenamiento"; Hunt, *This Day*, 144; Johnson, *Bay of Pigs*, 62.

17. Sánchez, *Girón*, 103; Szulc, "Anti-Castro Units." An often-repeated myth is that President Kennedy learned of the *Times* story before its publication and urged executives of the newspaper to suppress it (Campbell, *Getting It Wrong*, 68–84).

18. Herrera, *Operación Jaula*, 153–54, 202.

19. Silva, "Reconversión," 570; Sánchez, *Girón*, 99; Guerra, *Revolución cubana*, 113n283; Páz-Sánchez, *Zona*, 201.

20. Rodríguez, *Girón*, 188–90; Gobierno de Cuba, "Discursos de Fidel Castro," speeches of January 20, 1961, March 4, 1961, and April 7, 1961; Otero et al., *Playa Girón*, vol. 1, 443–44; Sánchez, *Girón*, 99; Gómez, *Un batallón*, 19, 100.

21. Sánchez, *Girón*, 101; Núñez, *En marcha con Fidel—1959*, chap. 11; Núñez, *En marcha con Fidel—1960*, chaps. 9–10; Marrero, *Geografía de Cuba*, 490, 492–93.

22. Sánchez, *Girón*, 101. Some sources state that Ciutat, based on the study of possible landing sites, had identified the Bay of Pigs to Castro as the likely target (Silva, "Reconversión," 349; Páz-Sánchez, *Zona*, 202).

Chapter 5

1. Reston, "Top Advisers in Dispute."

2. President's News Conference, April 12, 1961, John F. Kennedy Presidential Library and Museum, https://www.jfklibrary.org/archives/other-resources/john-f-kennedy-press-conferences/news-conference-9.

3. USDOS, *FRUS, Vol. X*, Doc. 92, 213, and Doc. 93, 213–16.

4. Johnson, *Bay of Pigs*, 80–87.

5. USDOS, *FRUS, Vol. X*, Doc. 92, 213; Pfeiffer, *Official History*, vol. 1, 192.

6. Pfeiffer, *Official History*, vol. 1, 189–90, 192–93.

7. Díaz, *Cuba*, 132, 143–44; USCIA, "Plan de Operación Marte," reproduced as appendix 8 in Díaz, 535; Troy, *Zapata*, 97, 128; Hunt, *This Day*, 186. Although the operation plan and Díaz render the name of the beach and its associated river as "Mocambo," the accepted spelling in Cuba is Macambo.

8. Díaz, *Cuba*, 132, 141–42; Lynch, *Decision*, 32–33.

9. Díaz, *Cuba*, 143–44; "Plan de Operación Marte," reproduced as appendix 8 in Díaz, 535; Feeney, "Night," 2; Troy, *Zapata*, 96; Machado, *Cuba*, chap. 11. Castro would later declare that there were already adequate forces in Oriente Province to deal with a landing there. Thus, he argued, such an event would not have resulted in any deviation of resources from western to eastern Cuba and would have been militarily inconsequential (Pino, *Girón*, 284–85).

10. Confusingly, the FAR acronym as used in Cuba at the time was applied to both the air force as well as the whole of the combined armed services or *Fuerzas Armadas Revolucionarias* (Revolutionary Armed Forces). Herein it will be used throughout to refer solely to the air force unless otherwise noted.

11. G. Herrera's and G. Ponzoa's 1961 after-action reports reproduced in Penabaz, *Trampa*, 148 and 153, respectively; Persons, *Bay of Pigs*, 79; Pfeiffer, *Official History*, vol. 1, 217; E. Ferrer, *Operación Puma*, 152, 154.

12. Pfeiffer, *Official History*, vol. 1, 199–200, 203–4; Wise and Ross, *Invisible Government*, 8–9.

13. Unpublished report of G-2 chief quoted in Lussón and Gárciga, *Girón*, 47; G. Herrera's and G. Ponzoa's 1961 after-action reports reproduced in Penabaz, *Trampa*, 149–50 and 153–55, respectively; Sánchez, *Girón*, 110, 112–13; USDOS, *FRUS, Vol. X*, Doc. 103, 227–28; E. Ferrer, *Operación Puma*, 161; 163–64; Prendes, *Punto rojo*, 49.

14. Wise and Ross, *Invisible Government*, 13–14, 16–18; Pfeiffer, *Official History*, vol. 1, 218–20, 239, 248.

15. Prendes, *Punto rojo*, 54n7, Pfeiffer, *Official History*, vol. 1, 209; Otero et al., *Playa Girón*, vol. 1, 451; report of G-2 chief quoted in Lussón and Gárciga, *Girón*, 47; Carreras, *Dominio*, 92–93.

16. Prendes, *Punto rojo*, 49, 54.

17. Sánchez, *Girón*, 116–17; Carreras, *Dominio*, 94.

18. Johnson, *Bay of Pigs*, 94; USDOS, *FRUS, Vol. X*, Doc. 87, 203(source note), Doc. 93, 215, and Doc. 102, 226. Radio Swan had been conceived and constructed specifically for making anti-Castro broadcasts to Cuba. For "A Brief History of Radio Swan" see CSG, "Part III—Annexes," annex 2.

19. César, *San Blas*, 134–36; MGBA, "SS *Atlántico*," Informe #2, pdf: 42; Wyden, *Bay of Pigs*, 80, 134.

20. Johnson, *Bay of Pigs*, 94; Wyden, *Bay of Pigs*, 221–22; USCIA, "Pluto," Anexo A, A-6.

Chapter 6

1. Gobierno de Cuba, "Discursos de Fidel Castro," speech of April 16, 1961; Otero et al., *Playa Girón*, vol. 1, 455.

2. Sánchez, *Girón*, 125; Rodríguez, *Girón*, 205–6; Silva, "Reconversión," 317.

3. Otero et al., *Playa Girón*, vol. 1, 478. The Operation Pluto Plan specified that the feint would be carried out "in front of the Cuban coast in the vicinity of LA FE to make the enemy divert his land, naval and aerial forces to said zone" (USCIA, "Pluto," 1). La Fe is located at the head of an embayment near the western end of Cuba, some 150 miles from Havana, in Pinar del Río Province. Apparently, however, the actual operation took place in front of the Santa Fe-Baracoa area, just west of Havana (ibid.; Cuban naval operations report reproduced in Fontaine, *Fidel*, 42–43). In 2011 a Cuban exile who partook in the decoy mission described that rafts with radar reflectors on poles were used to mimic the electromagnetic signature of ships off Cuba's northern coast (Yanez, "Operation Mirage"). However, the technological trick was lost on the Cuban military who apparently lacked radar facilities (Silva, "Reconversión," 520, n943) and relied on visual detection (Cuban naval operations report, Fontaine).

4. USDOS, *FRUS, Vol. X*, Doc. 231, 587; Pfeiffer, *Official History*, vol. 1, 223–25n, 234–35, 303–4, 443–44.

5. USDOS, *FRUS, Vol. X*, Doc. 198, 433; USCIA, "Pluto," Anexo H, H-1-1, H-1-B-2, H-1-C-1; Lynch, *Decision*, 69, 72; J. Cosculluela, "Participación naval del *Blagar*," in César, *San Blas*, 330.

6. González Lalondry, *Bahía de Cochinos*, 82; Johnson, *Bay of Pigs*, 100.

7. Lynch, *Decision*, 69. The brigade emblem consisted of two parts. A golden tab embroidered with "2506" overarched a conoid-shaped patch bearing a Latin cross and Cuban flag. Behind the cross and flag was a verdant field topped by blue sky.

8. USDOS, *FRUS, Vol. X*, Doc. 198, 433; Lynch, *Decision*, 34, 69, 73; USCIA, "Pluto," Plan Administrativo, Anexo A, Apéndice 4.

9. Sánchez, *Girón*, 126; Gárciga, *General Tomassevich*, 136.

10. Wyden, *Bay of Pigs*, 195–97; Hunt, *This Day*, 194–96 (Hunt's version of the events in question is muddled); USCIA, "Pluto," Anexo E: E-1; Hawkins, "Record of Paramilitary Action," 23. Hawkins captures the operational thinking at the CIA regarding the airstrikes as follows: "The landing was to be followed by air attacks on air fields and other military targets at dawn of D-Day, by which time the airfield in the objective area was expected to be in friendly hands. D-Day air attacks were to be represented, if necessary, as coming from the field seized in Zapata" (23).

11. USDOS, *FRUS, Vol. X*, Doc. 108, 235.

12. USDOS, *FRUS, Vol. X*, Doc. 64, 158.

13. A common misconception promulgated in the Bay of Pigs literature is that the tail guns were removed from the B-26 bombers because of the fuel requirements of flying to/from Nicaragua (e.g., Johnson, *Bay of Pigs*, 112; Wise and Ross, *Invisible Government*, 40; Higgins, *The Perfect Failure*, 134; H. Jones, *The Bay of Pigs*, 34, 126; Wyden, *Bay of Pigs*, 252; Rasenberger, *Disaster*, 191). However, as explained by Gar Thorsrud, in charge of the B-26s at JMTIDE: "There were some questions later in the game . . . why didn't you have a tail gun? a tail-turret? Well, that went out years ago as far as a tail-turret on those [B-26] aircraft" (Pfeiffer, *Official History*, vol. 1, 45). The Cuban invasion B-26s were obtained from U.S. Air Force inventory (Pfeiffer, *Official History*, vol. 1, 43) where the aircraft had been repurposed after the Korean War as "a counterinsurgency bomber and reconnaissance plane" without a tail-turret ("Gallery of USAF Weapons—Bombers; B-26 Invader," *Air Force Magazine and Space Digest*, September 1962, 222).

14. Hawkins, "Record of Paramilitary Action," 33–34; USDOS, *FRUS, Vol. X*, Doc. 108, 235–36; Cabell's handwritten note (May 1961?) quoted in Pfeiffer, *Official History*, vol. 1, 292; Cabell, *Man of Intelligence*, 388; Bissell, *Reflections*, 184.
15. USCIA, "Pluto," Anexo A: A-2–A-4.
16. Wise and Ross, *Invisible Government*, 54; Hunt, *This Day*, 200–201 (Hunt's version of the events in question is again especially muddled); Phillips, *Night Watch*, 110n; Johnson, *Bay of Pigs*, 120; Rodríguez and Weisman, *Shadow Warrior*, 86–88.
17. Hawkins, "Record of Paramilitary Action," 42.
18. USDOS, *FRUS, Vol. X*, Doc. 109, 240, and Doc. 198, 433; USCIA, "Pluto," Anexo A: A-1; Johnson, *Bay of Pigs*, 103; Zayas-Bazán, *My Life*, 92; USDOS, *FRUS, Vol. X*, Doc. 109, 240.
19. USDOS, *FRUS, Vol. X*, Doc. 198, 433; Lynch, *Decision*, 73.
20. USDOS, *FRUS, Vol. X*, Doc. 109, 239.
21. Lynch, *Decision*, 47, 83–84, 187.
22. USDOS, *FRUS, Vol. X*, Doc. 109, 239–40; MGBA, "Documentos," pdf: 8.
23. Rodríguez, *Girón*, 274–75; Carré, *Girón*, 85.
24. Carré, *Girón*, 86–87, 90.

Chapter 7

1. Pfeiffer, *Official History*, vol. 1, 277; Hawkins, "Record of Paramilitary Action," 2, 34.
2. USDOS, *FRUS, Vol. X*, Doc. 109, 240; Carré, *Girón*, 90–91. Lynch purports, thirty-seven years after the event, that a beach-marking light aboard the frogmen's boat malfunctioned and gave them away (Lynch, *Decision*, 85). This is not corroborated by any other account, including his 1961 after-action report (USDOS, *FRUS, Vol. X*, Doc. 109). It appears more likely that what was seen from shore was a positioning light. Every ship carried one of a different color so it could be located and identified in the dark (MGBA, "Documentos," pdf: 66).
3. USDOS, *FRUS, Vol. X*, Doc. 109, 240; MGBA, "Documentos," pdf: 8.
4. Carré, *Girón*, 92; Johnson, *Bay of Pigs*, 104; USDOS, *FRUS, Vol. X*, Doc. 109, 240; MGBA, "Documentos," pdf: 8.
5. USDOS, *FRUS, Vol. X*, Doc. 109, 240; MGBA, "Documentos," pdf: 8; Carré, *Girón*, 92; Sánchez, *Girón*, 129; César, *San Blas*, 334.
6. USDOS, *FRUS, Vol. X*, Doc. 109, 240, Triay, *Bay of Pigs*, 106; Zayas-Bazán, *My Life*, 93.
7. MGBA, "Documentos," pdf: 66.
8. Carré, *Girón*, 87; Sánchez, *Girón*, 131.
9. Pino, *Girón*, 69; Sánchez, *Girón*, 131.
10. Johnson, *Bay of Pigs*, 108.
11. Johnson, *Bay of Pigs*, 104; MGBA, "Documentos," pdf: 31; Wise and Ross, *Invisible Government*, 50.
12. Fontaine, *Fidel*, 49–50, 53; González Pérez, "Girón desde el mar," 31.
13. USDOS, *FRUS, Vol. X*, Doc. 110, 250; Troy, *Operation Zapata*, 184.
14. Lynch, *Decision*, 50.
15. USDOS, *FRUS, Vol. X*, Doc. 110, 250; MGBA, "Documentos," pdf: 31, 71; Johnson, *Bay of Pigs*, 106.
16. Johnson, *Bay of Pigs*, 106; Hawkins, "Record of Paramilitary Action," 27.

17. Iglesias, *Escape*, 12.
18. Wyden, *Bay of Pigs*, 134.
19. Wyden, *Bay of Pigs*, 222; Johnson, *Bay of Pigs*, 106.
20. Carré, *Girón*, 87.
21. Sánchez, *Girón*, 131.
22. Triay, *Bay of Pigs*, 100; Dille, "We Who Tried," 33; Johnson, *Bay of Pigs*, 106.
23. Lynch, *Decision*, 60–62.
24. MGBA, "Documentos," pdf: 31, 52; Johnson, *Bay of Pigs*, 108.
25. Johnson, *Bay of Pigs*, 106–7.
26. USDOS, *FRUS*, Vol. X, Doc. 110, 251; Troy, *Operation Zapata*, 184–85; MGBA, "Documentos," pdf: 71; Sánchez, *Girón*, 131; Carré, *Girón*, 86. The left side of the beach was eventually marked with a blinking flashlight pointed toward the sea (Troy, 184).
27. Pino, *Girón*, 69.
28. Sánchez, *Girón*, 130.
29. J. Coscuella, "Participación naval del *Blagar*," in César, *San Blas*, 335.
30. USDOS, *FRUS*, Vol. X, Doc. 109, 240–41.
31. Troy, *Operation Zapata*, 21; USDOS, *FRUS*, Vol. X, Doc. 231, 599.
32. USDOS, *FRUS*, Vol. X, Doc. 109, 241, and Doc. 198, 434.
33. Johnson, *Bay of Pigs*, 104.
34. Dille, "We Who Tried," 23.
35. Johnson, *Bay of Pigs*, 105; Wise and Ross, *Invisible Government*, 58; Wyden, *Bay of Pigs*, 141. Pérez San Román (*Respuesta*, 18) and Pfeiffer (*Official History*, vol. 1, 322) state that the bulldozer/motor grader was aboard the *Lake Charles*, but the Administrative Plan attachment to the Operation Pluto Plan shows that the D-6 tractor, equipped with a 7.8-foot blade, was carried aboard LCU #3 (USCIA, "Pluto," Plan Administrativo, Anexo A, A-4-1, A-5-1, and Tabla D [mislabels the LCU as #2]). Castro's troops came across the bulldozer on April 20 after following its tracks believing they had been made by a small tank (Fontaine, *Fidel*, 228).
36. Wyden, *Bay of Pigs*, 141. The CIA's Photo Intelligence Division was overseen by renowned photoreconnaissance pioneer Arthur Lundahl (140).
37. Johnson, *Bay of Pigs*, 105; Dille, "We Who Tried," 33.
38. USDOS, *FRUS*, Vol. X, Doc. 109, 241.
39. Sánchez, *Girón*, 131.
40. Rodríguez, *Girón*, 276.
41. Johnson, *Bay of Pigs*, 107; USDOS, *FRUS*, Vol. X, Doc. 110, 250; Wise and Ross, *Invisible Government*, 53.
42. Johnson, *Bay of Pigs*, 108.
43. MGBA, "Documentos," pdf: 71; USDOS, *FRUS*, Vol. X, Doc. 110, 251.
44. González Lalondry, *Bahía de Cochinos*, 91. Carmenates's body was subsequently taken to the *Barbara J* and later buried at sea (MGBA, "Documentos," pdf: 32, 72).
45. MGBA, "Documentos," pdf: 71–72.
46. Sánchez, *Girón*, 131–32; Andrés García Suárez, interview with Ramón González Suco, *Vanguardia*, March 1963, reproduced in *5 de Septiembre*, May 4, 2020, https://www.5septiembre.cu/les-di-el-alto-gritamos-patria-o-muerte-y-disparamos/.
47. Fontaine, *Fidel*, 52; Carré, *Girón*, 89.

48. Milagros Gálvez Aguilera, historical report quoted in Fontaine, *Fidel*, 50.
49. Ferrer, *Operación Puma*, 182–83; USDOS, *FRUS, Vol. X*, Doc. 231, 591.
50. USDOS, *FRUS, Vol. X*, Doc. 109, 241; Lynch, *Decision*, 88; Zayas-Bazán, *My Life*, 94.
51. USDOS, *FRUS, Vol. X*, Doc. 198, 434; Hawkins, "Record of Paramilitary Action," 34.
52. Lynch, *Decision*, 88.
53. USDOS, *FRUS, Vols. X/XI/XII, Microfiche Supplement*, Doc. 261.
54. Pfeiffer, *Official History*, vol. 1, 279.
55. Johnson, *Bay of Pigs*, 107–8.
56. MGBA, "Documentos," pdf: 31, 52, 71–72.
57. Johnson, *Bay of Pigs*, 105, 107.
58. Troy, *Operation Zapata*, 184–85; Fontaine, *Fidel*, 235; USDOS, *FRUS, Vol. X*, Doc. 110, 250–51; MGBA, "Documentos," pdf: 31, 34, 37; O. Inguanzo, "Participación naval del *Barbara J*," in César, *San Blas*, 368; Johnson, *Bay of Pigs*, 108.
59. Johnson, *Bay of Pigs*, 108; Wyden, *Bay of Pigs*, 222.
60. García Iturbe, *Hombres de Girón*, 105.
61. Rodríguez, *Girón*, 267; Sánchez, *Girón*, 136–37.
62. Geyer, *Guerrilla Prince*, 170–72; Fontaine, *Fidel*, 53.
63. Fontaine, *Fidel*, 54–56.
64. Gárciga, *General Tomassevich*, 136; Gómez, *Un batallón que permanece*, 19, 100.
65. Selva, *Girón*, 43, 48; García Iturbe, *Hombres de Girón*, 152.
66. G. Ponzoa's 1961 after-action report reproduced in Penabaz, *Trampa*, 158; Pfeiffer, *Official History*, vol. 1, 380; Wise and Ross, *Invisible Government*, 54.
67. See appendix B; Pfeiffer, *Official History*, vol. 1, 279.
68. USDOS, *FRUS, Vol. X*, Doc. 198, 434, and Doc. 109, 241.
69. Colloquially, the Playa Larga–Caletón area is sometimes collectively referred to as Playa Larga.
70. Johnson, *Bay of Pigs*, 122.
71. Sánchez, *Girón*, 136; USDOS, *FRUS, Vol. X*, Doc. 110, 251; Wyden, *Bay of Pigs*, 226.
72. Sánchez, *Girón*, 136–37; Rodríguez, *Girón*, 269; Chávez et al., *Girón*, 297.
73. Otero et al., *Playa Girón*, vol. 4, 166–67.
74. Johnson, *Bay of Pigs*, 122; Rodríguez, *Girón*, 268.
75. Sánchez, *Girón*, 139–40.
76. Fontaine, *Fidel*, 61.
77. Sánchez, *Girón*, 135.
78. Báez, *Secretos de generales*, 378.
79. Fernández, *Hombre afortunado*, 135; Sánchez, *Girón*, 134; Fontaine, *Fidel*, 84; Silva, "Reconversión," 229.
80. Fernández, *Hombre afortunado*, 44.
81. Clark and Waters, *Playa Girón*, 111.
82. Silva, "Reconversión," 344.
83. Sánchez, *Girón*, 134.
84. USDOS, *FRUS, Vol. X*, Doc. 109, 241; Troy, *Operation Zapata*, 297; J. Cosculluela, "Participación naval del *Blagar*," in César, *San Blas*, 337; Dille, "We Who Tried," 23; Johnson, *Bay of Pigs*, 108–9. There is contradiction between accounts about whether dawn coincided with high or low tide. However, NOAA tide predictions leave no doubt that on April 17, 1961, low tide occurred locally just after 6:00 a.m.

85. Sánchez, *Girón*, 144; Pino, *Girón*, 112.
86. Sánchez, *Girón*, 135–36.
87. Fontaine, *Fidel*, 56; Geyer, *Guerrilla Prince*, 31, 39–40.
88. USDOS, *FRUS, Vol. X*, Doc. 111, 257–58.
89. Cabell, *Man of Intelligence*, 390–91; USDOS, *FRUS, Vol. X*, Doc. 108, 237.
90. USDOS, *FRUS, Vol. X*, Doc. 111, 258n3.
91. Padrón and Betancourt, *Batista*, 71–72, 176, 184, 187.
92. Fontaine, *Fidel*, 62–63.
93. Fontaine, *Fidel*, 63, 92–93.
94. Guerra, *Revolución cubana*, 93, 95–96, 113n283. Castro's predilection for placing close allies from M-26-7 in key positions was demonstrated early on. Manuel Urrutia, a former judge under Batista who had publicly sided with Castro, barely served six months as new president of Cuba before being ousted. He was replaced with Osvaldo Dorticós, a member of M-26-7's top leadership cadre and an unconditional Castro loyalist (H. Thomas, *Cuban Revolution*, 158, 251, 455–56; Guerra, 113n283).
95. Rivas, *Playa Girón*, 28–31.
96. Suárez, *Aviones volaron*, 30. Del Pino (*Amanecer*, 75–76) identifies the metal employed as lead, but Carreras (*Dominio*, 82) agrees with Suárez (ibid.), an aviation technician at the time, that it was silver.
97. Del Pino, *Amanecer*, 63.
98. Casaus, *Girón*, 124.
99. Martínez, *Historia*, 295.
100. Carreras, *Dominio*, 81.
101. Carreras, *Dominio*, 90. Acosta's flight was apparently motivated by U.S. Navy ships reportedly engaged in deception maneuvers off the coast of Baracoa to draw attention away from the Nino Díaz expedition (Wyden, *Bay of Pigs*, 172n†).
102. See appendix A. Ironically, Martín Klein, "the best combat pilot our Air Force had" (Del Pino, *Amanecer*, 37), had been shot down and killed in a Cessna three months earlier by friendly antiaircraft fire (Suárez, *Aviones volaron*, 54).
103. Lagas, *Memorias*, 81.
104. USDOS, *FRUS, Vol. X*, Doc. 109, 241; J. Cosculluela, "Participación naval del *Blagar*," in César, *San Blas*, 336.
105. USCIA, "Pluto," Anexo C, C-1-1; USDOS, *FRUS, Vol. X*, Doc. 109, 241; César, *San Blas*, 148.
106. Iglesias, *Escape*, 8. Such was the resentment of many of the brigade men toward the Batista elements of Montero's battalion that in Guatemala their part of the camp had been dubbed "Esbirrilandia" ("Henchmanland") (ibid.).
107. Padrón and Betancourt, *Batista*, 268.
108. Johnson, *Bay of Pigs*, 108; Troy, *Operation Zapata*, 185; USDOS, *FRUS, Vol. X*, Doc. 110, 251.
109. Placer, "La contribución de la Marina de Guerra Revolucionaria," 29–30; González Pérez, "Girón desde el mar," 30; Otero et al., *Playa Girón*, vol. 1, 116–22, 127–28.
110. Lagas, *Memorias*, 90, 108.
111. Casaus, *Girón*, 81–82.

112. Carreras, *Dominio*, 100; Johnson, *Bay of Pigs*, 122; USDOS, *FRUS, Vol. X*, Doc. 110, 251–51, and Doc. 109, 241; Lynch, *Decision*, 107.

113. Carreras, *Dominio*, 100.

114. G. Herrera's 1961 after-action reports reproduced in Penabaz, *Trampa*, 160–61; USDOS, *FRUS, Vol. X*, Doc. 110, 252. As Herrera's formation approached the coast, it had come under fire from brigade ships off Girón. The firing ceased after he identified who they were, but, in his words, "They almost shot us down" (Herrera, ibid.).

115. USDOS, *FRUS, Vol. X*, Doc. 110, 252.

116. Johnson, *Bay of Pigs*, 108; Dille, "We Who Tried," 33; USCIA, "Pluto," Plan Administrativo, Anexo A, A-8-2 and Anexo D, D-2; CSG, "Part III—Annexes," Annex 24, "Supplies on the Houston" sheet.

117. Dille, "We Who Tried," 33; De Castroverde, *Patria*, 243.

118. USDOS, *FRUS, Vol. X*, Doc. 198, 434, and Doc. 109, 241; USCIA, "Pluto," Anexo A, Plan Administrativo, Anexo A, Apéndice 5, Table C. The unloading succession (i.e., LUCs #2, #3, and #1, in that order) specified for the LCUs in the operation plan (USCIA, "Pluto," Plan Administrativo, Anexo A, A-4-1) was presumably followed.

119. Dille, "We Who Tried," 33. Dille states that Álvarez's was the first tank to disembark and did so under air attack. However, this conflicts with other lines of evidence. For example, Lynch's 1961 after-action report describes the first air attack as taking place after the first LCU had unloaded its vehicles and departed the beach (USDOS, *FRUS, Vol. X*, Doc. 109, 241).

120. Triay, *Bay of Pigs*, 90; César, *San Blas*, 144; Troy, *Operation Zapata*, 290; U.S. Dept. of the Army, *Field Manual*, 3–4; Johnson, *Bay of Pigs*, 111; Penabaz, *Trampa*, 211.

121. Fernández, *Hombre afortunado*, 137–39. In another source (Fontaine, *Fidel*, 85), Fernández is quoted as stating that he had received instructions from Castro to go to Central Australia after he had already left Matanzas.

122. Sánchez, *Girón*, 142; Fernández, *Hombre afortunado*, 138–39.

123. Sánchez, *Girón*, 145.

124. Wise and Ross, *Invisible Government*, 56–57.

125. Rodríguez, *Girón*, 273, 290; Chávez et al., *Girón*, 295; Johnson, *Bay of Pigs*, 123; Sánchez, *Girón*, 145–46.

126. Sánchez, *Girón*, 145; Rodríguez, *Girón*, 271; Mayo, *Niños héroes*, 343–44; Otero et al., *Playa Girón*, vol. 1, 394; "El ultimo amanecer de Cira García," Cubainformación, April 17, 2022, Género, https://cubainformacion.tv/genero/20220417/96731/96731-el-ultimo-amanecer-de-cira-garcia; Wise and Ross, *Invisible Government*, 56–57; Triay, *Bay of Pigs*, 98.

127. Rodríguez, *Girón*, 271.

128. Rodríguez, *Girón*, 272; Johnson, *Bay of Pigs*, 123.

129. De Castroverde, *Patria*, 249; G. Herrera's 1961 after-action report reproduced in Penabaz, *Trampa*, 161; Sánchez, *Girón*, 149; Fernández, *Hombre afortunado*, 141; Rodríguez, *Girón*, 284.

130. G. Herrera's 1961 after-action report reproduced in Penabaz, *Trampa*, 161–62.

131. De Castroverde, *Patria*, 249–50; Dille, "We Who Tried," 33. The missing paratrooper, Germán Koch, was killed per source b in note 1, chapter 1.

132. USDOS, *FRUS, Vol. X*, Doc. 109, 241; Lynch, *Decision*, 107; Carreras, *Dominio*, 101; Troy, *Operation Zapata*, 290.

133. Dille, "We Who Tried," 33; Penabaz, *Trampa*, 130–34, 212–13.
134. Johnson, *Bay of Pigs*, 111; USDOS, *FRUS, Vol. X*, Doc. 109, 241; Dille, "We Who Tried," 33.
135. USDOS, *FRUS, Vol. X*, Doc. 109, 241; MGBA, "Documentos," pdf: 12; Pfeiffer, *Official History*, vol. 1, 330; Penabaz, *Trampa*, 213; Johnson, *Bay of Pigs*, 112 (conflates elements of the first attack on the Girón ships with those of a later occurrence). The friendly fire incident involving the C-54 was apparently a repetition of a similar one reported by Gonzalo Herrera (1961 after-action report reproduced in Penabaz, *Trampa*, 161).
136. USDOS, *FRUS, Vol. X*, Doc. 109, 241; Penabaz, *Trampa*, 213; MGBA, "Documentos," pdf: 12; Pfeiffer, *Official History*, vol. 1, 330.
137. Triay, *Bay of Pigs*, 90; Troy, *Operation Zapata*, 290.
138. Selva, *Girón*, 45, 47–48.
139. Selva, *Girón*, 49–53.
140. Clark and Waters, *Playa Girón*, 150, lámina 14 (reproduction of captured brigade tactical map); USCIA, "Pluto," 3.
141. Dille, "We Who Tried," 33; Villaraus Gallo, *Invasión*, 75; Johnson, *Bay of Pigs*, 114; Wise and Ross, *Invisible Government*, 55–56; Pfeiffer, *Official History*, vol. 1, 325.
142. E. Ferrer, *Operación Puma*, 184; E. Ferrer, *Operation Puma*, 168–69.
143. Troy, *Operation Zapata*, 24, 296; Triay, *Bay of Pigs*, 94.
144. Viana, *Por ti murieron*, 17–18; Johnson, *Bay of Pigs*, 115; César, *San Blas*, 157; Otero et al., *Playa Girón*, vol. 4, 112.
145. Rodríguez, *Girón*, 284–85; Fontaine, *Fidel*, 78.
146. USDOS, *FRUS, Vol. X*, Doc. 110, 253, Doc. 109, 248, and Doc. 231, 591; CSG, "Part III—Annexes," Annex 28 (report of M. Farías), 2. See appendix B.
147. Carreras, *Dominio*, 101; Johnson, *Bay of Pigs*, 113; USDOS, *FRUS, Vol. X*, Doc. 231, 591, Doc. 109, 248, and Doc. 110, 253; D. Sánchez, *Funny Thing*, 144.
148. González Lalondry, *Bahía de Cochinos*, 107–9.
149. USDOS, *FRUS, Vol. X*, Doc. 109, 242, and Doc. 110, 253; González Lalondry, *Bahía de Cochinos*, 105.
150. G. Herrera's 1961 after-action reports reproduced in Penabaz, *Trampa*, 162.
151. Sánchez, *Girón*, 149–50; Carré, *Girón*, 104, 106.
152. Rodríguez, *Girón*, 282–83; Arturo, "Medio siglo después," 58–59; Casaus, *Girón*, 67–68.
153. Sánchez, *Girón*, 150; Dille, "We Who Tried," 33; Johnson, *Bay of Pigs*, 114.
154. Sánchez, *Girón*, 150; Rodríguez, *Girón*, 282. Masiques, quoted in Carré (*Girón*, 108–9), incongruously places this event in a different context.
155. Johnson, *Bay of Pigs*, 111; Meyer and Szulc, *Cuban Invasion*, 126; Elliston, *Psywar*, 49.
156. Wise and Ross, *Invisible Government*, 51–52; Schlesinger, *Thousand Days*, 279; Carrillo, *Cuba*, 119.
157. USDOS, *FRUS, Vol. X*, Doc. 109, 242; Johnson, *Bay of Pigs*, 113–14.
158. USDOS, *FRUS, Vol. X*, Doc. 109, 242; César, *San Blas*, 145; J. Cosculluela, "Participación naval del *Blagar*," in César, *San Blas*, 340; E. Ferrer, *Operación Puma*, 204; Prendes, *Punto rojo*, 50. E. Ferrer (185) relates his own encounter with a FAR B-26 as he returned to JMTIDE, but his account is not supported by other lines of evidence.

159. Prendes, *Punto rojo*, 50; Lagas, *Memorias*, 104; Del Pino, *Amanecer*, 93.
160. Selva, *Girón*, 53, 55, 57–58. Selva mistakenly implies (57) that this was the first news Castro had received about the paratroop drops.
161. García Iturbe, *Hombres de Girón*, 89–90; Casaus, *Girón*, 96–98.
162. Rodríguez, *Girón*, 279; Sánchez, *Girón*, 155; Fontaine, *Fidel*, 64.
163. Sánchez, *Girón*, 155; Rodríguez, *Girón*, 291.
164. Clark and Waters, *Playa Girón*, 114; Mera, *Combatientes*, 3–4; Sánchez, *Girón*, 159; Rodríguez, *Girón*, 292.
165. De Castroverde, *Patria*, 251; Sánchez, *Girón*, 160; Fernández, *Hombre afortunado*, 143; Rodríguez, *Girón*, 292.
166. Wise and Ross, *Invisible Government*, 54.
167. Fernández, *Hombre afortunado*,143; Rodríguez, *Girón*, 292.
168. De Castroverde, *Patria*, 251.
169. Fontaine, *Fidel*, 64–65; Sánchez, *Girón*, 144.
170. Fontaine, *Fidel*, 121–22.
171. Fontaine, *Fidel*, 88; Otero et al., *Playa Girón*, vol. 1, 145; Rodríguez, *Girón*, 292; Fernández, *Hombre afortunado*, 143. One of the six companies of the Militia Leaders' Battalion did not arrive at the theater of operations until after 3:00 p.m. (Castro, "Batalla de Girón," 19).
172. Otero et al., *Playa Girón*, vol. 1, 145–46; CSG, "Part III—Annexes," Annex 28 (report of M. Farías), 2.
173. De Castroverde, *Patria*, 251–52.
174. Fontaine, *Fidel*, 68.
175. Fontaine, *Fidel*, 65.
176. Prendes, *Punto rojo*, 95–98. Prendes's account, published twenty-one years after the event, erroneously describes the ships at the time as being located some sixty miles from the coast and steaming to the southeast.
177. Penabaz, *Trampa*, 214; Dille, "We Who Tried," 34; César, *San Blas*, 145.
178. USCIA, "Pluto," Plan Administrativo, 1, Anexo A, A-2 and Apéndice 2; MGBA, "Documentos," pdf: 11, 56; Johnson, *Bay of Pigs*, 113; Hawkins, "Record of Paramilitary Action," 29; USDOS, *FRUS, Vol. X*, Doc. 238, 613; CSG, "Part III—Annexes," Annex 24 ("Supplies on *Río Escondido*" and "Supplies on the *Atlántico*" sheets). Although a "radio trailer" is erroneously listed among the vehicles carried aboard LCU #2 in "Pluto," Plan Administrative, Anexo A, A-4-1, it is described merely as "communications equipment" in CSG, "Part III—Annexes," Annex 24 ("Supplies on 3 LCU's" sheet).
179. See appendix A.
180. Otero et al., *Playa Girón*, vol. 1, 96.
181. Wyden, *Bay of Pigs*, 229–30; MGBA, "Documentos," pdf: 17; USCIA, "Pluto," Plan Administrativo, Anexo A, A-6-5; Johnson, *Bay of Pigs*, 113.
182. USDOS, *FRUS, Vol. X*, Doc. 109, 242; Wyden, *Bay of Pigs*, 230.
183. Otero et al., *Playa Girón*, vol. 1, 96; E. Ferrer, *Operación Puma*, 188-89 (Ferrer's account mistakes the *Río Escondido* for the *Houston* and erroneously places the encounter just after the arrival of Zúñiga and Farías over Cuba); Beerli, "Transmittal of Documents," Attachment C (mission NT-26-19); CSG, "Part III—Annexes," Annex 28 (report of M. Farías), 2. The portrayal herein of these air encounters is the most logical and coherent one that can be synthesized from often contradictory sources. Compare, for example, the account by

pilot Carreras quoted in Otero et al. (*Playa Girón*, vol. 1, 96–97) with his later account in Carreras (*Dominio*, 103–5). Although Carreras does not mention it in any of his accounts, he evidently radioed San Antonio for help. At 9:20 a.m. Point One was notified that "two enemy B-26 are pursuing one of our jets [*sic*]. Another [*sic*] jet has already taken off to assist" (Fontaine, *Fidel*, 68). Evidently, the T-33 flying off to assist was flown by Alberto Fernández. See appendix A.

184. E. Ferrer, *Operación Puma*, 189. See appendix A.
185. E. Ferrer, *Operación Puma*, 189; Beerli, "Transmittal of Documents," Attachment C (mission NT-26-19).
186. CSG, "Part III—Annexes," Annex 28 (report of M. Farías), 2; Lagas, *Memorias*, 86–89; Otero et al., *Playa Girón*, vol. 1, 105; E. Ferrer, *Operación Puma*, 190.
187. USDOS, *FRUS, Vol. X*, Doc. 198, 435. San Román would later contend (Johnson, *Bay of Pigs*, 105; Pérez San Román, *Respuesta*, 18) that, immediately after occupying Girón, the airstrip was found to be usable, with none of the obstacles reported by CIA photo analysts. If that is so, however, one wonders why it apparently took until 9:30 a.m. to report its readiness. In any case, after the sinking of the *Río Escondido* and subsequent developments, the plan to operate B-26s from the Girón strip became untenable (Pfeiffer, *Official History*, vol. 1, 322–23).
188. Troy, *Operation Zapata*, 191; USDOS, *FRUS, Vol. X*, Doc. 112, 259; G. Ponzoa's 1961 after-action reports reproduced in Penabaz, *Trampa*, 157.
189. MGBA, "Documentos," pdf: 11.
190. USCIA, "Pluto," Plan Administrativo, Anexo A, Apéndices 1–2. Calculated percentage based on cargo weights reported in ibid., Apéndices 6, 8–9 and 11.
191. Johnson, *Bay of Pigs*, 113–14.
192. Selva, *Girón*, 61–62.
193. Villaraus, *Huellas y caminos*, 262.
194. Johnson, *Bay of Pigs*, 114–15, 128; USCIA, "Pluto," 3, 5; Selva, *Girón*, 67; Villaraus, *Huellas y caminos*, 262.
195. Selva, *Girón*, 63–64.
196. Johnson, *Bay of Pigs*, 116–17. Although the boy involved in the discussion with Artime is not named, there can be no doubt based on the information given that it was Valerio Rodríguez.
197. Johnson, *Bay of Pigs*, 115–16, 124; USDOS, *FRUS, Vol. X*, Doc. 109, 247.
198. Fontaine, *Fidel*, 68.
199. Fernández, *Hombre afortunado*, 143–44; Fontaine, *Fidel*, 88; Castro, "Batalla de Girón," 13.
200. Sánchez, *Girón*, 163.
201. Fontaine, *Fidel*, 72, 88.
202. Rodríguez, *Girón*, 293; Castro, "Batalla de Girón," 14; Fernández, *Hombre afortunado*, 144; Otero et al., *Playa Girón*, vol. 1, 270. There is some discrepancy between accounts as to which company of the Militia Leaders' Battalion was sent to Soplillar.
203. Johnson, *Bay of Pigs*, 116, 142; Sánchez, *Girón*, 206; Fontaine, *Fidel*, 156; Troy, *Operation Zapata*, 292.
204. Fontaine, *Fidel*, 122; Sánchez, *Girón*, 189.
205. G. Ponzoa's 1961 after-action reports reproduced in Penabaz, *Trampa*, 156–57; Beerli, "Transmittal of Documents," Attachment C (mission NT-26-22); USDOS, *FRUS, Vol. X*, Doc. 109, 243. Pfeiffer (*Official History*, vol. 1, 320–21n**)

describes air photo verification of the bomb damage at the Cienfuegos airport
but dismisses Lynch's account of the circumstances leading to it. Instead, citing
the mission summary report (Beerli, ibid.), he identifies Antonio Soto as the
pilot responsible. However, as Soto left Nicaragua at 10:00 a.m. (and was later
involved in other events; see appendix B), he could not possibly have been over
Cienfuegos at the time the attack occurred.

206. Sánchez, *Girón*, 164, 169–70; Waters, *Escambray*, 10, 101; Fontaine, *Fidel*, 90.
207. Selva, *Girón*, 66–67; Wyden, *Bay of Pigs*, 104, 252–53.
208. Selva, *Girón*, 67–68. Félix Duque (quoted in Carré, *Girón*, 99) offers a version of
events that, as is typical of his accounts, conflates and/or distorts incidents and
facts.
209. Johnson, *Bay of Pigs*, 123.
210. Tally of fatalities derived from sources listed in note 1, chapter 1.
211. Dorschner and Fabricio, *Winds of December*, 207–10 passim.
212. Iglesias, *Escape*, 15-16, 71.
213. García Iturbe, *Hombres de Girón*, 95; Rodríguez, *Girón*, 291; Fontaine, *Fidel*, 115;
Chávez et al., *Girón*, 148–49; Sánchez, *Girón*, 172.
214. The convoy, as Pérez remembered, included a tank (Wise and Ross, *Invisible Government*, 59). However, there is clear evidence that no Castro tanks were in
the area at the time.
215. Wise and Ross, *Invisible Government*, 59.
216. Castro, "Batalla de Girón," 14–15; Carré, *Girón*, 149, 159.
217. Prendes, *Punto rojo*, 106–7.
218. Beerli, "Transmittal of Documents," Attachment C (mission NT-26-24); see note
205 above regarding the Cienfuegos bombing.
219. Del Pino, *Amanecer*, 77–78.
220. Wise and Ross, *Invisible Government*, 59–60; E. Ferrer, *Operación Puma*, 206.
221. USDOS, *FRUS, Vol. X*, Doc. 109, 243, and Doc. 110, 254.
222. Otero et al., *Playa Girón*, vol. 1, 102; Del Pino, *Amanecer*, 74, 78; Chávez et al.,
Girón, 254.
223. MGBA, "Documentos," pdf: 32; Del Pino, *Amanecer*, 78–79; Lagas, *Memorias*, 90;
USDOS, *FRUS, Vol. X*, Doc. 109, 243, and Doc. 110, 254 (the 3:30 p.m. incident time estimated by Rip Robertson does not reconcile with other lines of
evidence).
224. Del Pino, *Amanecer*, 79.
225. Fontaine, *Fidel*, 74.
226. MGBA, "Documentos," pdf: 32; USDOS, *FRUS, Vol. X*, Doc. 110, 254.
227. Gárciga, *General Tomassevich*, 137 (Tomassevich, quoted herein, mistakenly
switches the names of Covadonga and Yaguaramas in his narrative); Sánchez,
Girón, 164.
228. Dille, "We Who Tried," 69; Triay, *Bay of Pigs*, 95.
229. Johnson, *Bay of Pigs*, 126–27; Triay, *Bay of Pigs*, 95; Dille, "We Who Tried," 69.
230. Sánchez, *Girón*, 163–64; Pino, *Girón*, 99.
231. Fontaine, *Fidel*, 102–3; Lisanka, "Pasajes de una victoria," 12; Guerra, *Revolución
cubana*, 113n283.
232. Sánchez, *Girón*, 164; Gárciga, *General Tomassevich*, 137.
233. Selva, *Girón*, 75, 78–82.

234. Otero et al., *Playa Girón*, vol. 1, 385; García Iturbe, *Hombres de Girón*, 52–53.
235. Beerli, "Transmittal of Documents," Attachment C (listed under missions NT-25-25 and NT-26-26. Notice matching takeoff times for Crispín and Carro); E. Ferrer, *Operación Puma*, 192, 195, 200; USDOS, *FRUS, Vols. X/XI/XII, Microfiche Supplement*, Doc. 264, item 1c.
236. García Iturbe, *Hombres de Girón*, 54–55; Otero et al., *Playa Girón*, vol. 1, 170, 385; Carré, *Girón*, 100.
237. Chávez et al., *Girón*, 135; Otero et al., *Playa Girón*, vol. 1, 387; Sánchez, *Girón*, 222; Selva, *Girón*, 88–89.
238. Troy, *Operation Zapata*, 291; Otero et al., *Playa Girón*, vol. 4, 110; Selva, *Girón*, 83; Carré, *Girón*, 132; Viana, *Por ti murieron*, 20; Johnson, *Bay of Pigs*, 126.
239. E. Ferrer, *Operación Puma*, 192; Beerli, "Transmittal of Documents," Attachment C (mission NT-25-25).
240. Sánchez, *Girón*, 163; Fontaine, *Fidel*, 89, 101; Fernández, *Hombre afortunado*, 144; Rodríguez, *Girón*, 294.
241. Castro, "Batalla de Girón," 25.
242. Fontaine, *Fidel*, 72–73, 75.
243. Johnson, *Bay of Pigs*, 124.
244. Johnson, *Bay of Pigs*, 123–24 (erroneously identifies the militia unit as Battalion 339); Triay, *Bay of Pigs*, 98.
245. Dille, "We Who Tried," 69.
246. Castro, "Batalla de Girón," 19.
247. Johnson, *Bay of Pigs*, 124–25.
248. Otero et al., *Playa Girón*, vol. 1, 147; Johnson, *Bay of Pigs*, 125; Fontaine, *Fidel*, 100.
249. Triay, *Bay of Pigs*, 99.
250. Otero et al., *Playa Girón*, vol. 1, 148.
251. Otero et al., *Playa Girón*, vol. 1, 147.
252. E. Ferrer, *Operación Puma*, 193; Prendes, *Punto rojo*, 123–29; Otero et al., *Playa Girón*, vol. 1, 100–101; Del Pino, *Amanecer*, 90.
253. E. Ferrer, *Operación Puma*, 206.
254. Del Pino, *Amanecer*, 90–91; Otero et al., *Playa Girón*, vol. 1, 101.
255. Wyden, *Bay of Pigs*, 240–41.
256. Otero et al., *Playa Girón*, vol. 1, 101; Del Pino, *Amanecer*, 91.
257. E. Ferrer, *Operación Puma*, 202–3, 206.
258. USDOS, *FRUS, Vol. X*, Doc. 198, 435.
259. General Cabell asserts in his memoirs (Cabell, *Man of Intelligence*, 393) that the strikes were to be at dawn on April 18 as "a night attack was infeasible." He also claims that he himself instigated the "about-face" vis-à-vis attacking the airfields by appealing yet again to the administration. His time frame for the airstrike is unquestionably in error, and the claim that the mission was allowed due to his insistence is neither supported by the record nor contextually credible. Other than Cabell's claim, there is no indication that any administration official was consulted again prior to the issuance of the attack order by CIA headquarters.
260. Beerli, "Transmittal of Documents," Attachment C (mission NT-26-27). In what is an evident error, the JMTIDE flight information report records that Varela took off again for San Antonio at 5:10 a.m. on April 18 (NT-26-26). See appendix B.

261. Fontaine, *Fidel*, 84, 105.
262. Geyer, *Guerrilla Prince*, 109; Penabaz, *Trampa*, 90, 92.
263. Fontaine, *Fidel*, 99; Báez, *Secretos de generales*, 379; Sánchez, *Girón*, 171.
264. Báez, *Secretos de generales*, 378; Sánchez, *Girón*, 227; Carré, *Girón*, 116.
265. Báez, *Secretos de generales*, 378–79.
266. Fontaine, *Fidel*, 99–100, 107–8, 113.
267. Fontaine, *Fidel*, 106; Rodríguez, *Girón*, 297.
268. Fontaine, *Fidel*, 109; Fernández, *Hombre afortunado*, 145.
269. Johnson, *Bay of Pigs*, 125–26.
270. Johnson, *Bay of Pigs*, 125–26; González Lalondry, *Bahía de Cochinos*, 35, 120–21, 123, 125.
271. Johnson, *Bay of Pigs*, 126; Casaus, *Girón*, 238; Sánchez, *Girón*, 140, 186; García Iturbe, *Hombres de Girón*, 88, 105; Martínez, *Historia*, 265–66.
272. Selva, *Girón*, 84–85.
273. Sánchez, *Girón*, 170, 222; Troy, *Operation Zapata*, 291; Otero et al., *Playa Girón*, vol. 1, 251–52, 254–55, 266; Selva, *Girón*, 96–97; Villaraus, *Huellas y caminos*, 262–63; Carré, *Girón*, 132; Casaus, *Girón*, 107.
274. Dille, "We Who Tried," 69.
275. Johnson, *Bay of Pigs*, 131; Sánchez, *Girón*, 170.
276. Triay, *Bay of Pigs*, 95. It is likely that the tank, apparently the one commanded by Rodolfo Díaz (César, *San Blas*, 146), developed mechanical problems and returned to Girón, where it was present on April 18 (César, 155).
277. Triay, *Bay of Pigs*, 95; Dille, "We Who Tried," 70; Johnson, *Bay of Pigs*, 131.
278. Johnson, *Bay of Pigs*, 129–30; Zayas-Bazán, *My Life*, 95–96.
279. USDOS, *FRUS, Vol. X*, Doc. 116, 263, and Doc. 231, 592; Lynch, *Decision*, 120, 122.
280. Johnson, *Bay of Pigs*, 128; Oliva, "Bay of Pigs Experience," chapter 7, section 42.
281. Johnson, *Bay of Pigs*, 128; Sánchez, *Girón*, 184; Alonso, *Año 61*, 94; Martínez, *Historia*, 265.
282. González Lalondry, *Bahía de Cochinos*, 126.
283. Johnson, *Bay of Pigs*, 138.
284. Beerli, "Transmittal of Documents," Attachment C (mission NT-26-33); Del Pino, *Amanecer*, 101–3; Prendes, *Punto rojo*, 109–10; Casaus, *Girón*, 160–62 (erroneously places the event on April 18); Carreras, *Dominio*, 110–11.
285. Del Pino, *Amanecer*, 103.
286. Fontaine, *Fidel*, 113, 116; Fernández, *Hombre afortunado*, 146.
287. Fontaine, *Fidel*, 113.
288. Fontaine, *Fidel*, 113–14, 118.
289. Fontaine, *Fidel*, 115–17; Fernández, *Hombre afortunado*, 147; Núñez, *En marcha con Fidel—1959*, chapter 35.
290. Fontaine, *Fidel*, 117.
291. Báez, "El pueblo derrota la invasión," 56.
292. USDOS, *FRUS, Vol. X*, Doc. 109, 243, Doc. 110, 255, and Doc. 116, 263; USCIA, "Pluto," 5, Plan Administrativo, 1.
293. Troy, *Operation Zapata*, 188; MGBA, "Documentos," pdf: 4; USDOS, *FRUS, Vol. X*, Doc. 109, 243, and Doc. 110, 255.
294. USDOS, *FRUS, Vol. X*, Doc. 109, 243–44, and Doc. 110, 255; Johnson, *Bay of Pigs*, 129–30.

295. Sánchez, *Girón*, 182–83; Johnson, *Bay of Pigs*, 133; Rodríguez, *Girón*, 298; Carré, *Girón*, 149–50; Fontaine, *Fidel*, 116.
296. González Lalondry, *Bahía de Cochinos*, 126, 128–29, 133.
297. Dille, "We Who Tried," 70; Viana, *Por ti murieron*, 20–21.
298. Selva, *Girón*, 97–98; unpubl. rpt. of A. Velaz (G-2) quoted in Lussón and Gárciga, *Girón*, 105.
299. Johnson, *Bay of Pigs*, 131; Dille, "We Who Tried," 70; Villarauso, *Huellas y caminos*, 260, 264; English, *Corporation*, 28, 32–33, 39.

Chapter 8

1. R. Milián's 1961 after-action report reproduced in Sánchez, *Girón*, 256.
2. Johnson, *Bay of Pigs*, 134; Oliva, "Bay of Pigs Experience," chapter 12, section 75; Triay, *Bay of Pigs*, 101.
3. Rodríguez, *Girón*, 298.
4. Carré, *Girón*, 149–50.
5. Oliva, "Bay of Pigs Experience," chapter 12, section 75; Triay, *Bay of Pigs*, 106; Johnson, *Bay of Pigs*, 134.
6. Wise and Ross, *Invisible Government*, 64; Atienza Pérez, "Batalla de Playa Larga," 19.
7. Otero et al., *Playa Girón*, vol. 4, 167.
8. Báez, *Secretos de generales*, 380; Fernández, *Hombre afortunado*, 147; Castro, "Batalla de Girón," 27; Fontaine, *Fidel*, 117, 119.
9. Carré, *Girón*, 155–56, 159–61; Pavón, "Historia de El Combatiente," 21–22; Rodríguez, *Girón*, 302; Báez, *Secretos de generales*, 381. López Cuba and the crew of the lead tank claimed that, in addition to the track damage, a projectile perforated their tank's gun, making it unusable. However, no damage to the gun is discernable in a published up-close photograph of the tank taken after the battle (Pavón, ibid., 19).
10. Lisanka, "Pasajes de una victoria," 15; Sánchez, *Girón*, 185; Oliva, "Bay of Pigs Experience," chapter 7, section 76.
11. López Cuba claims that the engine of the third tank was stalled when he climbed aboard it (Báez, *Secretos de generales*, 381).
12. Rodríguez, *Girón*, 303; J. R. Fernández's 1961 after-action report quoted in Lussón and Gárciga, *Girón*, 108; Pino, *Girón*, 148.
13. Triay, *Bay of Pigs*, 99, 101.
14. Otero et al., *Playa Girón*, vol. 1, 149–50; Rodríguez, *Girón*, 302; Martínez, *Historia*, 266.
15. Sánchez, *Girón*, 186.
16. J. R. Fernández's 1961 after-action report quoted in Lussón and Gárciga, *Girón*, 109; Rodríguez, *Girón*, 302; Báez, *Secretos de generales*, 96; Sánchez, *Girón*, 185.
17. Johnson, *Bay of Pigs*, 135; J. R. Fernández's 1961 after-action report quoted in Lussón and Gárciga, *Girón*, 108.
18. González Lalondry, *Bahía de Cochinos*, 134, 139–40.
19. Fontaine, *Fidel*, 136–37.
20. Johnson, *Bay of Pigs*, 130.
21. Johnson, *Bay of Pigs*, 132–33; Triay, *Bay of Pigs*, 90–91.
22. De Castroverde, *Patria*, 253.
23. Johnson, *Bay of Pigs*, 133; Triay, *Bay of Pigs*, 90–91.

24. Otero et al., *Playa Girón*, vol. 1, 252; Selva, *Girón*, 99–100; García Iturbe, *Hombres de Girón*, 156.

25. Johnson, *Bay of Pigs*, 131.

26. Sánchez, *Girón*, 189.

27. Fontaine, *Fidel*, 118, 138; Guerra, *Revolución cubana*, 113n283.

28. E.g., Johnson, *Bay of Pigs*, 110; Wyden, *Bay of Pigs*, 258; Pino, *Girón*, 112; Rasenberger, *Disaster*, 273.

29. Báez, "El pueblo derrota la invasión," 56. The segment in Báez's article reporting on the phone conversation is tellingly omitted from the piece reproduced in Otero et al., *Playa Girón*, vol. 1, 316–20.

30. Gobierno de Cuba, "Discursos de Fidel Castro," speech of April 19, 1986.

31. Fontaine, *Fidel*, 138.

32. Penabaz, *Trampa*, 92.

33. Johnson, *Bay of Pigs*, 135; Báez, *Secretos de generales*, 96; Sánchez, *Girón*, 186.

34. Sánchez, *Girón*, 187.

35. Fontaine, *Fidel*, 117–18.

36. Pavón, "Historia de El Combatiente," 22–23; Báez, *Secretos de generales*, 381.

37. Sánchez, *Girón*, 186.

38. Johnson, *Bay of Pigs*, 135; Dille, "We Who Tried," 69.

39. Johnson, *Bay of Pigs*, 135–36; Pavón, "Historia de El Combatiente," 22; H. Ferrer, "Misión cumplida," 33; Báez, *Secretos de generales*, 381; Lisanka, "Pasajes de una victoria," 15; Fontaine, *Fidel*, 121.

40. Dille, "We Who Tried," 70; Johnson, *Bay of Pigs*, 135; Oliva, "Bay of Pigs Experience," chapter 12, section 76.

41. G. Herrera's 1961 after-action reports reproduced in Penabaz, *Trampa*, 152; Beerli, "Transmittal of Documents," Attachment C (mission NT-26-33); Wise and Ross, *Invisible Government*, 64.

42. G. Herrera's 1961 after-action reports reproduced in Penabaz, *Trampa*, 152–53; Beerli, "Transmittal of Documents," Attachment C (mission NT-26-33).

43. Johnson, *Bay of Pigs*, 131–32. Although their radio had been damaged the day before and could not reach San Blas (Triay, *Bay of Pigs*, 95), apparently it was still capable of shorter-range communications.

44. Johnson, *Bay of Pigs*, 132; Sánchez, *Girón*, 190.

45. Johnson, *Bay of Pigs*, 132.

46. Triay, *Bay of Pigs*, 101; Oliva, "Bay of Pigs Experience," chapter 12, section 75.

47. Johnson, *Bay of Pigs*, 136, 138; Oliva, "Bay of Pigs Experience," chapter 12, sections 75 and 76.

48. Fontaine, *Fidel*, 139.

49. Lisanka, "Pasajes de una victoria," 15; Johnson, *Bay of Pigs*, 136–37.

50. Sánchez, *Girón*, 195; Triay, *Bay of Pigs*, 102.

51. Otero et al., *Playa Girón*, vol. 1, 158; Johnson, *Bay of Pigs*, 137; Sánchez, *Girón*, 196.

52. Oliva, "Bay of Pigs Experience," chapter 12, section 76; Johnson, *Bay of Pigs*, 137. Johnson (ibid.) provides a slightly different version of the exchange between Oliva and the surrendering tank crewman.

53. Oliva, "Bay of Pigs Experience," chapter 12, section 76; Sánchez, *Girón*, 185. The total crew complement of a T-34/85 tank was five (Báez, *Secretos de generales*, 378). Sánchez (ibid.) states that three of the tank's crew had managed to escape and

two were taken prisoner, but Oliva (ibid.) asserts that a total of three crewmen (commander, gunner, and driver) were captured.

54. Oliva, "Bay of Pigs Experience," chapter 12, section 76.
55. Oliva, "Bay of Pigs Experience," chapter 12, section 76; Johnson, *Bay of Pigs*, 137. The reckoning by brigade attestants as to the number of enemy tanks destroyed during the battle is itself highly inflated. They range from "five or six" (Johnson, 138) to "nine" (Oliva) with "several" others reported to have been abandoned.
56. Oliva, "Bay of Pigs Experience," chapter 12, section 76; Johnson, *Bay of Pigs*, 138.
57. Oliva, "Bay of Pigs Experience," chapter 12, section 76; Johnson, *Bay of Pigs*, 138; Penabaz, *Trampa*, 226.
58. Johnson, *Bay of Pigs*, 138–39.
59. Rodríguez, *Girón*, 310.
60. Johnson, *Bay of Pigs*, 138; García Iturbe, *Hombres de Girón*, 107; Lynch, *Decision*, 98.
61. González Lalondry, *Bahía de Cochinos*, 135, 142–44.
62. Otero et al., *Playa Girón*, vol. 1, 294.
63. J. R. Fernández's 1961 after-action report quoted in Lussón and Gárciga, *Girón*, 110; Fernández, *Hombre afortunado*, 148; Otero et al., *Playa Girón*, vol. 1, 158.
64. J. R. Fernández's 1961 after-action report quoted in Lusson and Gárciga, *Girón*, 108–10.
65. Fernández, *Hombre afortunado*, 149, 151, 153; Báez, *Secretos de generales*, 96–97; Núñez, *En marcha con Fidel—1961*, 170.
66. Fernández, *Hombre afortunado*, 149–50.
67. Otero et al., *Playa Girón*, vol. 1, 214, 493; Sánchez, Girón, 206.
68. Otero et al., *Playa Girón*, vol. 1, 184–85, 187, 188–89; Sánchez, *Girón*, 196; Pérez, "Un battallón," 24.
69. Lagas, *Memorias*, 109.
70. *Verde Olivo*, "Aquellos artilleros de Girón," 25–26. Notwithstanding its indirectness, Oropesa's admission stands out as a rare exception to the numerous accounts published over the years in Cuba. These continue to categorically identify the attacking plane(s) as enemy aircraft or fail to mention the incident altogether: e.g., Fernández, *Hombre afortunado*, 151n61; Mayo, *Niños héroes*, 171, 189, 257, 317.
71. Carreras, *Dominio*, 111.
72. Carreras, *Dominio*, 111–12; Casaus, *Girón*, 130–31.
73. Otero et al., *Playa Girón*, vol. 1, 294, 303–4; Sánchez, *Girón*, 196.
74. Rodríguez, *Girón*, 310; Otero et al., *Playa Girón*, vol. 1, 187; Pérez, "Un battallón," 23; Sánchez, *Girón*, 196; Fernández, *Hombre afortunado*, 151.
75. USDOS, *FRUS, Vol. X*, Doc. 117, 264.
76. Khrushchev and Talbot, *Khrushchev Remembers*, 491.
77. USDOS, *FRUS, Vol. X*, Doc. 117, 264–65.
78. Bonafede, "3 Beachheads Secured"; Buchanan, "Giant Pincer."
79. Jones, "Joy, Worry"; Southworth, "Able-Bodied Cubans"; Deal and Buchanan, "Crash Boats"; *Miami Herald*, "Cuba Tells U.N."; *Miami Herald*, "Observation Post" (editorial cartoon).
80. *New York Times*, "Havana Normal"; Pino, *Girón*, 94–95, 114.
81. Rodríguez, *Girón*, 206.
82. Wise and Ross, *Invisible Government*, 64–65.
83. *New York Times*, "Havana Reported Calm."

84. Rodríguez, *Girón*, 310; Otero et al., *Playa Girón*, vol. 1, 184; Sánchez, *Girón*, 195; Pino, *Girón*, 118.

85. Sánchez, *Girón*, 196.

86. Rodríguez, *Girón*, 304–5; Núñez, *En marcha con Fidel—1961*, 184; Fontaine, *Fidel*, 140; Fernández, *Hombre afortunado*, 150.

87. Troy, *Operation Zapata*, 291–92.

88. Troy, *Operation Zapata*, 291–92; Johnson, *Bay of Pigs*, 116, 142.

89. USDOS, *FRUS, Vol. X*, Doc. 198, 436.

90. Martínez, *Historia*, 255, 277; Dille, "We Who Tried," 71.

91. Johnson, *Bay of Pigs*, 139.

92. Triay, *Bay of Pigs*, 91.

93. Otero et al., *Playa Girón*, vol. 1, 270.

94. Fernández, *Hombre afortunado*, 150.

95. Sánchez, *Girón*, 163.

96. Carré, *Girón*, 133.

97. García Iturbe, *Hombres de Girón*, 40.

98. Carré, *Girón*, 133; Otero et al., *Playa Girón*, vol. 1, 243.

99. Carré, *Girón*, 54, 135–37.

100. Penabaz, *Trampa*, 226.

101. USDOS, *FRUS, Vol. X*, Doc. 198, 436.

102. USDOS, *FRUS, Vol. X*, Doc. 198, 436; Pfeiffer, *Official History*, vol. 1, 328–29.

103. Troy, *Operation Zapata*, 95, 128.

104. Pfeiffer, *Official History*, vol. 1, 314. For unknown reasons, on the return trip to Nicaragua the men flew the B-26 that had diverted to Key West on April 15 rather than the one in which they had landed (ibid., 313–14). In November 1961 the wreckage of their plane was found deep in the jungles of Nicaragua near a village some 150 miles east of JMTIDE. They had apparently lost their way flying by night and crashed in the remote area (315; Trest and Dodd, *Wings of Denial*, 123).

105. Pfeiffer, *Official History*, vol. 1, 157, 346–47n***.

106. Johnson, *Bay of Pigs*, 141–42; Pérez San Román, *Respuesta*, 27–28.

107. USDOS, *FRUS, Vol. X*, Doc. 125, 278.

108. Fontaine, *Fidel*, 122, 156.

109. Sánchez, *Girón*, 189, 199; Fontaine, *Fidel*, 122, 155–56; Rodríguez, *Girón*, 315.

110. Sánchez, *Girón*, 199–200.

111. See appendixes A and B. It is possible that the B-26 was the one flown by Álvaro Galo, which may have been in the area at the time. Reportedly, the peasant argued to Pupo that the attacking plane belonged to the enemy because it had "a bluish cross underneath" (Sánchez, *Girón*, 200). However, brigade planes bore no such "cross" and the added detail seems apocryphal.

112. Casaus, *Girón*, 114; García Iturbe, *Hombres de Girón*, 40; Otero et al., *Playa Girón*, vol. 1, 243.

113. Johnson, *Bay of Pigs*, 145–46.

114. Casaus, *Girón*, 116.

115. Johnson, *Bay of Pigs*, 139.

116. Sánchez, *Girón*, 196–97.

117. Fernández, *Hombre afortunado*, 153.

118. Pérez, "Un battallón," 24; Mayo, *Niños héroes*, 344; Dille, "We Who Tried," 70; Alonso, *Año 61*, 100.
119. Johnson, *Bay of Pigs*, 142–43.
120. USDOS, *FRUS, Vol. X*, Doc. 116, 263.
121. Lynch, *Decision*, 122.
122. Johnson, *Bay of Pigs*, 143.
123. Pfeiffer, *Official History*, vol. 1, 341.
124. Johnson, *Bay of Pigs*, 143.
125. Johnson, *Bay of Pigs*, 144; Penabaz, *Trampa*, 226.
126. Unpubl. rpt. of A. Velaz (G-2) quoted in Lussón and Gárciga, *Girón*, 120; Selva, *Girón*, 105–6; Carré, *Girón*, 134.
127. Otero et al., *Playa Girón*, vol. 1, 252; Selva, *Girón*, 106.
128. Otero et al., *Playa Girón*, vol. 1, 253.
129. Casaus, *Girón*, 133, 137–38; Selva, *Girón*, 114.
130. Selva, *Girón*, 107–8.
131. The first name is rendered as "Diósmedes" in Selva, *Girón*, 114.
132. Casaus, *Girón*, 138. Sánchez (*Girón*, 222n226) provides another account of a friendly fire incident among militiamen of Battalion 113 resulting from mortars with improperly set elevation angles.
133. Casaus, *Girón*, 139–41.
134. Casaus, *Girón*, 141; Otero et al., *Playa Girón*, vol. 1, 253.
135. Johnson, *Bay of Pigs*, 144–45.
136. Fontaine, *Fidel*, 145–46, 173; Sánchez, *Girón*, 200, 211; Guerra, *Revolución cubana*, 113n283.
137. Fontaine, *Fidel*, 145–46; Sánchez, *Girón*, 200; Carré, *Girón*, 115–16; Pino, *Girón*, 134.
138. Fontaine, *Fidel*, 143–44; Sánchez, *Girón*, 197–98.
139. Fernández, *Hombre afortunado*, 150; Rodríguez, *Girón*, 304; Núñez, *En marcha con Fidel—1961*, 186.
140. Fontaine, *Fidel*, 147.
141. Fontaine, *Fidel*, 147–48.
142. USDOS, *FRUS, Vols. X/XI/XII, Microfiche Supplement*, Doc. 253.
143. Pfeiffer, *Official History*, vol. 1, 341, 349.
144. USDOS, *FRUS, Vol. X*, Doc. 120, 273.
145. USDOS, *FRUS, Vol. X*, Doc. 120, 273.
146. Pfeiffer, *Official History*, vol. 1, 345; G. Ponzoa's 1961 after-action reports reproduced in Penabaz, *Trampa*, 158 (Ponzoa evidently conflates the orders he received based on this cable with the sighting of vehicles upon arriving over Cuba).
147. USDOS, *FRUS, Vol. X*, Doc. 109, 244; Handleman, "Real Story," 41.
148. USDOS, *FRUS, Vol. X*, Doc. 120, 273; Wise and Ross, *Invisible Government*, 66.
149. Troy, *Operation Zapata*, 301; unpubl. rpt. of A. Velaz (G-2) quoted in Lussón and Gárciga, *Girón*, 120; Triay, *Bay of Pigs*, 96; Johnson, *Bay of Pigs*, 145.
150. Carré, *Girón*, 134.
151. Carré, *Girón*, 134; Selva, *Girón*, 111.
152. Selva, *Girón*, 111–12.
153. Johnson, *Bay of Pigs*, 145; Pérez San Román, *Respuesta*, 28.
154. César, *San Blas*, 155; Prendes, *Punto rojo*, 120; Selva, *Girón*, 193n14.

155. Selva, *Girón*, 115–17, 193–94n14; Del Pino, *Amanecer*, 100–101.
156. Selva, *Girón*, 115–16, 193n14.
157. See note 1 (source a) in chapter 1.
158. Sexto, "Memoria en vivo," B8–B9; Otero et al., *Playa Girón*, vol. 1, 181, 215; *Radio Llanura*, "Identifican nueva víctima."
159. Rodríguez, *Girón*, 226; Triay, *Bay of Pigs*, 108.
160. Sexto, "Memoria en vivo," B8–B9; Otero et al., *Playa Girón*, vol. 1, 181, 215; *Radio Llanura*, "Identifican nueva víctima."
161. Fontaine, *Fidel*, 149–50.
162. Fontaine, *Fidel*, 150–51; Gárciga, *General Tomassevich*, 138.
163. Fontaine, *Fidel*, 217.
164. Fontaine, *Fidel*, 152.
165. Otero et al., *Playa Girón*, vol. 1, 209; Fontaine, *Fidel*, 122, 156.
166. Johnson, *Bay of Pigs*, 146.
167. USDOS, *FRUS, Vol. X*, Doc. 125; 278.
168. Pfeiffer, *Official History*, vol. 1, 370n*.
169. G. Ponzoa's 1961 after-action reports reproduced in Penabaz, *Trampa*, 158; Villaraus, *Huellas y caminos*, 286; Pfeiffer, *Official History*, vol. 1, 345–47n***, 355; Trest and Dodd, *Wings of Denial*, 80.
170. Fontaine, *Fidel*, 148–49.
171. Fontaine, *Fidel*, 149–50; Sánchez, *Girón*, 202; Carré, *Girón*, 116, 118.
172. Fontaine, *Fidel*, 153.
173. Fontaine, *Fidel*, 153.
174. César, *San Blas*, 162; Carré, *Girón*, 134; Sánchez, *Girón*, 222.
175. Viana, *Por ti murieron*, 23–24; Franqui, *Family Portrait with Fidel*, 123; Johnson, *Bay of Pigs*, 148; Selva, *Girón*, 120; César, *San Blas*, 162.
176. Triay, *Bay of Pigs*, 96; Troy, *Operation Zapata*, 296; César, *San Blas*, 162; Selva, *Girón*, 121; Fontaine, *Fidel*, 18; Martínez, *Historia*, 280.
177. Johnson, *Bay of Pigs*, 146; Triay, *Bay of Pigs*, 96; Viana, *Por ti murieron*, 24.
178. Dille, "We Who Tried," 34; César, *San Blas*, 148; Penabaz, *Trampa*, 200.
179. Fontaine, *Fidel*, 154; Fernández, *Hombre afortunado*, 153; Sánchez, *Girón*, 202; Rodríguez, *Girón*, 318.
180. Fernández, *Hombre afortunado*, 154.
181. Sánchez, *Girón*, 202; Fernández, *Hombre afortunado*, 154; Rodríguez, *Girón*, 317; J. R. Fernández's 1961 after-action report quoted in Lussón and Gárciga, *Girón*, 118; Casaus, *Girón*, 144.
182. Fontaine, *Fidel*, 156.
183. Fontaine, *Fidel*, 148.
184. Prendes, *Punto rojo*, 120–21.
185. Núñez, *En marcha con Fidel—1961*, chapter 21 (Kindle). In a rare admission, longtime Castro loyalist Núñez Jiménez concedes in the 2018 Kindle edition of his book that the aerial attack was a friendly fire incident. This admission is omitted from both the 1998 and the 2004 printed editions.
186. Otero et al., *Playa Girón*, vol. 1, 195.
187. Núñez, *En marcha con Fidel—1961*, chapter 21 (Kindle); Otero et al., *Playa Girón*, vol. 1, 194; Martínez Sánchez, *Girón*, 27.
188. Núñez, *En marcha con Fidel—1961*, chapter 21 (Kindle).

189. Núñez, *En marcha con Fidel—1961*, chapter 21 (Kindle); Otero et al., *Playa Girón*, vol. 1, 194.
190. Carré, *Girón*, 118; USDOS, *FRUS, Vol. X*, Doc. 127, 279.
191. One (flown by Lagas) experienced an onboard fire and the other (flown by Carreras) reported a machine gun malfunction. See appendix A.
192. Rodríguez (*Girón*, 317) claims that the plan was for the men to travel ten miles by bus (the span reconnoitered for enemy forces) and then proceed on foot. This is not at all credible, however, as walking the remaining eleven miles to Girón would have ruled out capturing it by 6:00 p.m. as Castro had demanded.
193. Casaus, *Girón*, 144.
194. Casaus, *Girón*, 144, 146; Carré, *Girón*, 167; Rodríguez, *Girón*, 317.
195. Carré, *Girón*, 167–68.
196. USDOS, *FRUS, Vol. X*, Doc. 122, 275–76.
197. Wyden, *Bay of Pigs*, 214.
198. USDOS, *FRUS, Vol. X*, Doc. 121, 274–75 (text, and notes 3 and 5).
199. USDOS, *FRUS, Vol. X*, Doc. 124, 277.
200. Wyden, *Bay of Pigs*, 130–31, 245.
201. León, *Testimonio*, 331; Báez, *Secretos de generales*, 387. The date given by León for invasion-related events is systematically one day behind the actual date.
202. Johnson, *Bay of Pigs*, 147–48.
203. Dille, "We Who Tried," 72.
204. USDOS, *FRUS, Vol. X*, Doc. 127, 279.
205. USDOS, *FRUS, Vol. X*, Doc. 125, 278, and Doc. 127, 279.
206. Pfeiffer, *Official History*, vol. 1, 371.
207. G. Ponzoa's 1961 after-action reports reproduced in Penabaz, *Trampa*, 158; J. R. Fernández's 1961 after-action report quoted in Lussón and Gárciga, *Girón*, 118; Villaraus, *Huellas y caminos*, 285–86, 288 (erroneously gives date as April 19). Ponzoa (ibid.) claims that two hours before departing Nicaragua (i.e., at noontime) they had been informed of the caravan. This seems to represent a conflation on his part stemming from the airstrike order to "destroy tanks and vehicles on approaches beachhead" (Pfeiffer, *Official History*, vol. 1, 345) that had arrived at JMTIDE just before noon.
208. García, *Hombres de Girón*, 68–69; J. R. Fernández's 1961 after-action report quoted in Lussón and Gárciga, *Girón*, 118–19; Rodríguez, *Girón*, 318.
209. Villaraus, *Huellas y caminos*, 286, 288; G. Ponzoa's 1961 after-action reports reproduced in Penabaz, *Trampa*, 158.
210. Sánchez, *Girón*, 203; Casaus, *Girón*, 147; Carré, *Girón*, 166.
211. Casaus, *Girón*, 146–47, 149; Encinosa, *Unvanquished*, 48; García Iturbe, *Hombres de Girón*, 69–70.
212. Villaraus, *Huellas y caminos*, 288; G. Ponzoa's 1961 after-action reports reproduced in Penabaz, *Trampa*, 158; Casaus, *Girón*, 149–50; García Iturbe, *Hombres de Girón*, 70.
213. Mayo, *Niños héroes*, 206, 400. Curiously, the survivors of the incident insist that U.S. Navy jets were responsible for the strafing attack.
214. García Iturbe, *Hombres de Girón*, 70–71; Otero et al., *Playa Girón*, vol. 1, 248.
215. Villaraus, *Huellas y caminos*, 289.
216. G. Ponzoa's 1961 after-action reports reproduced in Penabaz, *Trampa*, 158.
217. Villaraus, *Huellas y caminos*, 289; Pfeiffer, *Official History*, vol. 1, 347.

218. García Iturbe, *Hombres de Girón*, 70.
219. J. R. Fernández's 1961 after-action report quoted in Lussón and Gárciga, *Girón*, 119.
220. Casaus, *Girón*, 154.
221. G. Ponzoa's 1961 after-action reports reproduced in Penabaz, *Trampa*, 159.
222. Rodríguez, *Girón*, 319.
223. Chávez et al., *Girón*, 299–313 ("Tabla resumen").
224. Casaus, *Girón*, 150.
225. Sánchez, *Girón*, 204.
226. Fernández, *Hombre afortunado*, 154; Sánchez, *Girón*, 205.
227. Fernández, *Hombre afortunado*, 155.
228. USDOS, *FRUS, Vols. X/XI/XII, Microfiche Supplement*, Doc. 254.
229. USDOS, *FRUS, Vols. X/XI/XII, Microfiche Supplement*, Doc. 255.
230. Pfeiffer, *Official History*, vol. 1, 343n**.
231. USDOS, *FRUS, Vols. X/XI/XII, Microfiche Supplement*, Doc. 254.
232. Selva, *Girón*, 105, 121. Selva mistakenly places the initial bombardment by Pedro Miret's 122 mm artillery before noon (106).
233. Martínez, *Historia*, 280; unpubl. rpt. of A. Velaz (G-2) quoted in Lussón and Gárciga, *Girón*, 120; Fontaine, *Fidel*, 146; Dille, "We Who Tried," 71.
234. Dille, "We Who Tried," 71; César, *San Blas*, 156, 163; Bolet, *Dark Nights*, 108–9.
235. Schlesinger, *Thousand Days*, 276.
236. USDOS, *FRUS, Vol. X*, Doc. 130, 281–84.
237. MGBA, "Documentos," pdf: 21; USDOS, *FRUS, Vol. X*, Doc. 198, 436.
238. USDOS, *FRUS, Vol. X*, Doc. 109, 244, and *Vols. X/XI/XII, Microfiche Supplement*, Doc. 264, item 1a.
239. Johnson, *Bay of Pigs*, 148–49; USDOS, *FRUS, Vol. X*, Doc. 109, 244.
240. Dille, "We Who Tried," 72.
241. MGBA, "Documentos," pdf: 23.
242. Dille, "We Who Tried," 72; Johnson, *Bay of Pigs*, 149–50.
243. León, *Testimonio*, 332. Again, the date given by León for invasion-related events is systematically one day behind the actual date.
244. Sánchez, *Girón*, 225; Fontaine, *Fidel*, 157.
245. USDOS, *FRUS, Vol. X*, Doc. 109, 242–44; Zayas-Bazán, *My Life*, 97.
246. MGBA, "Documentos," pdf: 23.
247. Sánchez, *Girón*, 205; Fernández, *Hombre afortunado*, 154.
248. Carré, *Girón*, 145, 165; Pino, *Girón*, 132.
249. Fontaine, *Fidel*, 238; Pérez, "Un batallón," 21, 24; Sánchez, *Girón*, 211.
250. Sánchez, *Girón*, 206.
251. USDOS, *FRUS, Vol. X*, Doc. 198, 436.
252. MGBA, "Documentos," pdf: 23.
253. Johnson, *Bay of Pigs*, 149.
254. USDOS, *FRUS, Vol. X*, Doc. 198, 437, and Doc. 135, 287.
255. Troy, *Operation Zapata*, 193, 298; Lynch, *Decision*, 127.
256. USDOS, *FRUS, Vol. X*, Doc. 231, 592–93, Doc. 232, 601, and Doc. 116, 263; Wyden, *Bay of Pigs*, 276.
257. Reports are contradictory regarding the arrival of *Caribe* at Point Zulu. Some sources state or imply that it was not there on either the eighteenth or nineteenth (Johnson, *Bay of Pigs*, 129, 162; USDOS, *FRUS, Vol. X*, Doc. 232, 601).

Others differ on the supposed timing of its arrival (Troy, *Operation Zapata*, 192–93; USDOS, *FRUS, Vol. X*, Doc. 109, 243; Lynch, *Decision*, 130). In his 1961 after-action report, Robertson evidently misidentifies the *Atlántico* as the *Caribe* when describing events for the night of the eighteenth (USDOS, *FRUS, Vol. X*, Doc. 110, 255).

258. USDOS, *FRUS, Vol. X*, Doc. 109, 243; Troy, *Operation Zapata*, 193.
259. Johnson, *Bay of Pigs*, 150.
260. Lynch, *Decision*, 127.
261. MGBA, "Documentos," pdf: 21.
262. MGBA, "Documentos," pdf: 23, 27.
263. USDOS, *FRUS, Vol. X*, Doc. 110, 255; Lynch, *Decision*, 127.
264. USDOS, *FRUS, Vol. X*, Doc. 231, 593.
265. MGBA, "Documentos," pdf: 5.
266. USDOS, *FRUS, Vol. X*, Doc. 135, 287; T. Miller. "Destroyers at the Bay of Pigs," 6.
267. E. Ferrer, *Operation Puma*, 216; Persons, *Bay of Pigs*, 89; Pfeiffer, *Official History*, vol. 1, 157, 355. The airstrike on San Antonio planned for sunset/predawn of April 18/19 (USDOS, *FRUS, Vols. X/XI/XII, Microfiche Supplement*, Doc. 253) was never carried out.
268. USDOS, *FRUS, Vols. X/XI/XII, Microfiche Supplement*, Doc. 255.
269. USDOS, *FRUS, Vol. X*, Doc. 115, 262.
270. Persons, *Bay of Pigs*, 90.
271. Unlike the B-26 pilots, the Cuban transport plane crews were said to be "holding up well" (Pfeiffer, *Official History*, vol. 1, 354).

Chapter 9

1. Fontaine, *Fidel*, 112.
2. J. R. Fernández's 1961 after-action report quoted in Lusson & Gárciga, *Girón*, 119; Fontaine, *Fidel*, 142.
3. Sánchez, *Girón*, 209.
4. Johnson, *Bay of Pigs*, 149–50.
5. USDOS, *FRUS, Vol. X*, Doc. 231, 593. Lynch (*Decision*, 127) gives the time the message was received as 2:30 a.m., but Robertson (Troy, *Operation Zapata*, 189) less credibly estimates its arrival at around 4:00 a.m.
6. Rostow, *Diffusion of Power*, 209; USDOS, *FRUS, Vol. X*, Doc. 140, 290(source note).
7. Schlesinger, *Thousand Days*, 277–78; Rostow, *Diffusion of Power*, 209–10; Bissell, *Reflections*, 188–89. Schlesinger and Rostow both indicate that General Lemnitzer was also present at the meeting. Bissell, however, asserts that the general was out of town and that Burke was thus acting as both acting chairman of the JCS and chief of naval operations.
8. U.S. Navy, *Radioman 3 & 2*, 134.
9. Zulu (Z) time is equivalent to Greenwich Mean Time.
10. USDOS, *FRUS, Vols. X/XI/XII, Microfiche Supplement*, Doc. 256; Pfeiffer, *Official History*, vol. 1, chart 1, between 22 and 23.
11. Fontaine, *Fidel*, 169–70. See appendix B.
12. See appendix B. The takeoff times and pilot pairings reported in the CIA's Mission Summaries (Pfeiffer, *Official History*, vol. 1, 380) are contradicted by other compelling evidence as well as common sense. Herrera, for one, is reported to have taken off first at 2:00 a.m. on a single-aircraft flight. This would absurdly

place his arrival time over the beachhead well before sunrise and almost two hours ahead of the subsequent flights. Viewed in the context of what transpired, the muddled information has all the earmarks of a red herring.

13. Persons, *Bay of Pigs*, 90–91.
14. Pfeiffer, *Official History*, vol. 1, 367–68.
15. USDOS, *FRUS, Vol. X*, Doc. 140, 290.
16. Wise and Ross, *Invisible Government*, 170.
17. E.g., Jones, *Bay of Pigs*, 120; Wise and Ross, *Invisible Government*, 70.
18. Bissell, *Reflections*, 189.
19. Cuba is in the Eastern Time Zone, which is one hour ahead of Nicaragua's Central Time Zone.
20. Sánchez, *Girón*, 211.
21. Báez, *Secretos de generales*, 285; Carré, *Girón*, 168–69, 171; Otero et al., *Playa Girón*, vol. 1, 270.
22. USDOS, *FRUS, Vol. X*, Doc. 109, 244.
23. Johnson, *Bay of Pigs*, 150; Pfeiffer, *Official History*, vol. 1, 20.
24. Johnson, *Bay of Pigs*, 155–56.
25. USDOS, *FRUS, Vol. X*, Doc. 109, 244; Pfeiffer, *Official History*, vol. 1, 349; Persons, *Bay of Pigs*, 95–97. American pilot Albert Persons claims that, besides having to instruct rather unenthusiastic Cubans about the F-51, he was to also have flown to the beachhead (Persons, *Bay of Pigs*, 95–98). Pfeiffer gives the number of F-51s delivered as four, E. Ferrer (*Operación*, 212) as three, and Persons (*Bay of Pigs*, 96) as six.
26. USDOS, *FRUS, Vols. X/XI/XII, Microfiche Supplement*, Doc. 264, item 1b.
27. Johnson, *Bay of Pigs*, 156. A second C-46 piloted by César Luaices had also been destined to land at Girón but could not depart JMTIDE in time due to an oil leak. The problem was fixed, and the plane did eventually set out but aborted on the way, as it would have arrived in broad daylight (Villaraus Gallo, *Invasión*, 77; USDOS, *FRUS, Vols. X/XI/XII, Microfiche Supplement*, Doc. 264, item 1b).
28. Lagas, *Memorias*, 122–26.
29. Otero et al., *Playa Girón*, vol. 1, 221; Casaus, *Girón*, 177.
30. Fontaine, *Fidel*, 169.
31. Casaus, *Girón*, 176–77; Otero et al., *Playa Girón*, vol. 1, 177.
32. Casaus, *Girón*, 178.
33. Casaus, *Girón*, 178; Sánchez, *Girón*, 217; Persons, *Bay of Pigs*, 91.
34. Otero et al., *Playa Girón*, vol. 1, 221–22, 324.
35. Pino, *Girón*, 142–43; Trest and Dodd, *Wings of Denial*, 121–22.
36. Pino, *Girón*, 143, 158–59; Fontaine, *Fidel*, 173; Wise and Ross, *Invisible Government*, 81.
37. Trest and Dodd, *Wings of Denial*, 119–20, 122.
38. Dille, "We Who Tried," 73; Viana, *Por ti murieron*, 24; Martínez, *Historia*, 282.
39. Triay, *Bay of Pigs*, 96; USCIA, "Pluto," Anexo E, E-1.
40. Dille, "We Who Tried," 73; Otero et al., *Playa Girón*, vol. 1, 253 (the date of the airstrike is given as the eighteenth but is clearly the nineteenth).
41. Johnson, *Bay of Pigs*, 157; Triay, *Bay of Pigs*, 96; Viana, *Por ti murieron*, 26.
42. Johnson, *Bay of Pigs*, 157; Dille, "We Who Tried," 73.
43. Sánchez, *Girón*, 211, 222.
44. Viana, *Por ti murieron*, 27.

45. Carré, *Girón*, 134.
46. Sánchez, *Girón*, 223; Otero et al., *Playa Girón*, vol. 1, 254.
47. César, *San Blas*, 168; Martínez, *Historia*, 282; Troy, *Operation Zapata*, 296; Triay, *Bay of Pigs*, 96.
48. See appendix B.
49. Dille, "We Who Tried," 72.
50. Sánchez, *Girón*, 206.
51. Persons, *Bay of Pigs*, 91.
52. Dille, "We Who Tried," 72.
53. Otero et al., *Playa Girón*, vol. 1, 188, 229–30 (the date of the airstrike is given as the eighteenth but is clearly the nineteenth); Pérez Guzmán, "Un battallón," 24–25.
54. Pfeiffer, *Official History*, vol. 1, 354.
55. Persons, *Bay of Pigs*, 85.
56. Leyva, "Notas de diario." As many as three other C-54 airdrop missions subsequently aborted on the way to the beach and returned to JMTIDE (USDOS, *FRUS, Vols. X/XI/XII, Microfiche Supplement*, Doc. 264, item 1a; Persons, *Bay of Pigs*, 98).
57. Zumbado and Tacoronte, *¡Coompañíaa teencioón!*, 116.
58. Johnson, *Bay of Pigs*, 149.
59. Carré, *Girón*, 171–72.
60. Pfeiffer, *Official History*, vol. 1, 369–71.
61. See appendix B.
62. Persons, *Bay of Pigs*, 90–91; Pfeiffer, *Official History*, vol. 1, 391.
63. E. Ferrer, *Operación Puma*, 214.
64. Persons, *Bay of Pigs*, 91–92.
65. Persons, *Bay of Pigs*, 93; León, *Testimonio*, 333 (the date given is again one day behind the actual date).
66. Persons, *Bay of Pigs*, 93.
67. Prendes, *Punto rojo*, 133; Carreras, *Dominio*, 114.
68. Persons, *Bay of Pigs*, 92–94; Pfeiffer, *Official History*, vol. 1, 358, 369. The cable reporting the shootdown quoted in Pfeiffer (358) renders Shamburger's words as "We've been jumped."
69. Prendes, *Punto rojo*, 134–35; Carreras, *Dominio*, 115–16.
70. Persons, *Bay of Pigs*, 92, 94; Dille, "We Who Tried," 72.
71. Carreras, *Dominio*, 115–16; Prendes, *Punto rojo*, 135.
72. Dille, "We Who Tried," 72; Johnson, *Bay of Pigs*, 155 (conflates Herrera's attack with that of D. Livingston north of San Blas); E. Ferrer, *Operación Puma*, 97; E. Ferrer, *Operation Puma*, 216.
73. Persons, *Bay of Pigs*, 92 (see table note in appendix B). Presumably, as a pilot, Goodwin used nautical miles for navigation.
74. Persons, *Bay of Pigs*, 92. Almost two decades after the event, Mike Griffin, the commanding officer for the Skyhawk squadron aboard the *Essex*, recalled for author Peter Wyden the instructions he gave his pilots that morning: "We're going to rendezvous with some B-26s and escort them to the beach and wait for them to come out, and if anybody is following them, we'll take action" (Wyden, *Bay of Pigs*, 143). Despite the "to the beach" adjunct, the compelling implication of Griffin's statement is that the navy fliers intended—as they had been

doing—to escort the planes to/from the limits of the exclusion zone. Griffin and his men set off in two sections, inferably of three Skyhawks each, and he allegedly met no B-26s while on patrol. Given Goodwin's encounter with three navy jets, presumably these belonged to the section that did not include Griffin. It is nevertheless puzzling that news of the incident would not have been shared with Griffin. Wyden himself recounts Goodwin's Skyhawk encounter (ibid, 239) but fails to note the apparent disconnect with Griffin's account.

75. Persons, *Bay of Pigs*, 93. See appendix B.
76. USDOS, *FRUS, Vol. X*, Doc. 193, 411.
77. Pfeiffer, Official History, vol. 1, 369.
78. USDOS, *FRUS, Vol. X*, Doc. 140, 290n4.
79. Wyden, *Bay of Pigs*, 299; Madden, "Operation Bumpy Road," 132.
80. Casaus, *Girón*, 169.
81. Sánchez, *Girón*, 211.
82. Fontaine, *Fidel*, 146, 172; Carré, *Girón*, 187; Sánchez, *Girón*, 206, 206n209.
83. Sánchez, *Girón*, 206; Otero et al., *Playa Girón*, vol. 1, 198–99; Fontaine, *Fidel*, 146.
84. Fontaine, *Fidel*, 172–73.
85. Fontaine, *Fidel*, 174 (the 8:30h transcription entry erroneously places the lieutenant in question, A. Ayala, at Covadonga; cf. page 177).
86. MGBA, "Documentos," pdf: 22.
87. Johnson, *Bay of Pigs*, 163–64; Sánchez, *Girón*, 219; Carré, *Girón*, 174; Dille, "We Who Tried," 72.
88. Carré, *Girón*, 172–73, 175–76; Zumbado and Tacoronte, *¡Coompañíaa teencioón!*, 118; Otero et al., *Playa Girón*, vol. 1, 226–27; Báez, *Secretos de generales*, 285.
89. See appendix A.
90. MGBA, "Documentos," pdf: 25.
91. MGBA, "Documentos," pdf: 26.
92. MGBA, "Documentos," pdf: 26.
93. USDOS, *FRUS, Vols. X/XI/XII, Microfiche Supplement*, Doc. 257.
94. Pfeiffer, *Official History*, vol. 1, 390–93.
95. MGBA, "Documentos," pdf: 26.
96. *Newsweek*, "Cuba: Sealing It Off," 57.
97. Hunt, *This Day*, 207; Schlesinger, *Thousand Days*, 278–79.
98. Schlesinger, *Thousand Days*, 279–80.
99. Schlesinger, *Thousand Days*, 280–82; Johnson, *Bay of Pigs*, 30, 97.
100. Schlesinger, *Thousand Days*, 279, 283.
101. Pfeiffer, *Official History*, vol. 1, 374–75.
102. Wise and Ross, *Invisible Government*, 69; Dille, "We Who Tried," 72.
103. Pfeiffer, *Official History*, vol. 1, 371.
104. Wise and Ross, *Invisible Government*, 71.
105. Persons, *Bay of Pigs*, 94–95.
106. Fontaine, *Fidel*, 174.
107. Fontaine, *Fidel*, 168, 176.
108. Selva, *Girón*, 124–25, 129; Otero et al., *Playa Girón*, vol. 1, 391; Casaus, *Girón*, 171; Johnson, *Bay of Pigs*, 158.
109. Viana, *Por ti murieron*, 24; Casaus, *Girón*, 172–73.
110. Martínez, *Historia*, 320.

111. Carré, *Girón*, 186–87; Selva, *Girón*, 125–26; Casaus, *Girón*, 171; Fontaine, *Fidel*, 172.
112. Fontaine, *Fidel*, 181; Carré, *Girón*, 187; Selva, *Girón*, 125–26.
113. Carré, *Girón*, 187-88; Casaus, *Girón*, 170.
114. Casaus, *Girón*, 170–71; García Iturbe, *Hombres de Girón*, 124; Selva, *Girón*, 126; Carré, *Girón*, 187–88.
115. Carré, *Girón*, 139, 188.
116. García Iturbe, *Hombres de Girón*, 124. Although Gutiérrez erroneously places the event on April 18 "after noon," it is clear from his descriptions that he is referring to the friendly fire incident at San Blas.
117. Casaus, *Girón*, 171.
118. Fontaine, *Fidel*, 179.
119. Sánchez, *Girón*, 231.
120. Zumbado and Tacoronte, *¡Coompañíaa teencioón!*, 119.
121. Sánchez, *Girón*, 219.
122. Zumbado and Tacoronte, *¡Coompañíaa teencioón!*, 119–20; Johnson, *Bay of Pigs*, 164.
123. Zumbado and Tacoronte, *¡Coompañíaa teencioón!*, 121–22, 157; Carré, *Girón*, 177; Johnson, *Bay of Pigs*, 164.
124. Sánchez, *Girón*, 220.
125. Zumbado and Tacoronte, *¡Coompañíaa teencioón!*, 127, 134.
126. Zumbado and Tacoronte, *¡Coompañíaa teencioón!*, 128, 140, 157.
127. Carré, *Girón*, 176, 178, 181–82; García Iturbe, *Hombres de Girón*, 131.
128. Dille, "We Who Tried," 72–73; Johnson, *Bay of Pigs*, 164.
129. Carré, *Girón*, 180; Sánchez, *Girón*, 227; Otero et al., *Playa Girón*, vol. 1, 265.
130. Otero et al., *Playa Girón*, vol. 1, 137; García Iturbe, *Hombres de Girón*, 131; Sánchez, *Girón*, 227; Carré, *Girón*, 182.
131. Castro Hidalgo, *Spy for Fidel*, 13–14.
132. Ameijeiras, "Batalla más corta (III)," 39.
133. Carré, *Girón*, 180; Zumbado and Tacoronte, *¡Coompañíaa teencioón!*, 163–64.
134. Zumbado and Tacoronte, *¡Coompañíaa teencioón!*, 164–65; Ameijeiras, "Batalla más corta (III)," 40–41.
135. Johnson, *Bay of Pigs*, 158; Sánchez, *Girón*, 235. Both Johnson's and Sánchez's books are typical of other works of historical synthesis in their many conflations (chronological and geographic) regarding events that occurred between San Blas and Girón. This is not surprising given the fewer primary sources available for this sector of the battle. The version of events presented in this work is proposed as the most compelling interpretation based on intersecting lines of evidence.
136. Carré, *Girón*, 187; Fontaine, *Fidel*, 172, 177, 183.
137. Johnson, *Bay of Pigs*, 146; Casaus, *Girón*, 171; Troy, *Operation Zapata*, 301.
138. Otero et al., *Playa Girón*, vol. 1, 205–6 (the day of the week of the event is erroneously stated as Tuesday rather than Wednesday); Carré, *Girón*, 189.
139. Carré, *Girón*, 189–90, 192; César, *San Blas*, 167.
140. Carré, *Girón*, 191–92.
141. César, *San Blas*, 167; Casaus, *Girón*, 174.
142. Casaus, *Girón*, 175–76.
143. Viana, *Por ti murieron*, 27.

144. García Guerra, *Victoria en la derrota*, 45.

145. Johnson, *Bay of Pigs*, 157–58; Selva, *Girón*, 130; Fontaine, *Fidel*, 182.

146. Johnson, *Bay of Pigs*, 161. San Roman later estimated the beginning of the false alarm as "about twelve o'clock," but his messages indicate it started an hour earlier.

147. The attorneys of the legal department were supposed to serve as judge advocates within the territory seized by the brigade (Penabaz, *Trampa*, 184).

148. Penabaz, *Trampa*, 227–28.

149. MGBA, "Documentos," pdf: 24. The time appearing on the cable is "1916Z" (2:16 p.m., local time). However, this does not make sense given the chronology of subsequent events. Contextually, it seems that 191600Z (11:00 a.m., local time) is what was intended, with 19 representing the date of the message (a format used in other cables).

150. MGBA, "Documentos," pdf: 24.

151. USDOS, *FRUS, Vol. X*, Doc. 144, 293n5. See appendix A.

152. MGBA, "Documentos," pdf: 25.

153. USDOS, *FRUS, Vol. X*, Doc. 147, 295n1.

154. USDOS, *FRUS, Vol. X*, Doc. 145, 293–94.

155. Johnson, *Bay of Pigs*, 161.

156. USDOS, *FRUS, Vol. X*, Doc. 146, 294.

157. Pfeiffer, *Official History*, vol. 1, 372.

158. USDOS, *FRUS, Vol. X*, Doc. 147, 295.

159. Carró, *Girón*, 177–78, 181; Ameijeiras, "Batalla más corta (III)," 30.

160. Ameijeiras, "Batalla más corta (III)," 39, 41; Johnson, *Bay of Pigs*, 164–65.

161. Ameijeiras, "Batalla más corta (III)," 39–40.

162. Zumbado and Tacoronte, *¡Coompañíaa teencioón!*, 158.

163. Ameijeiras, "Batalla más corta (III)," 40.

164. USDOS, *FRUS, Vol. X*, Doc. 150, 298.

165. Lynch, *Decision*, 131; Troy, *Operation Zapata*, 193.

166. USDOS, *FRUS, Vol. X*, Doc. 145, 294, and Doc. 147, 295.

167. Johnson, *Bay of Pigs*, 162.

168. Hawkins, "Record of Paramilitary Action," 38; USDOS, *FRUS, Vol. X*, Doc. 151, 299.

169. USDOS, *FRUS, Vol. X*, Doc. 149, 298.

170. Fontaine, *Fidel*, 157, 180–83; León, *Testimonio*, 333–34 (the date given is again one day behind the actual date).

171. MGBA, "Documentos," pdf: 26.

172. Johnson, *Bay of Pigs*, 161, 165.

173. Johnson, *Bay of Pigs*, 164–65.

174. Otero et al., *Playa Girón*, vol. 1, 137.

175. Johnson, *Bay of Pigs*, 165.

176. Fontaine, *Fidel*, 184.

177. Penabaz, *Trampa*, 228.

178. Johnson, *Bay of Pigs*, 165.

179. Viana, *Por ti murieron*, 27, 29; Troy, *Operation Zapata*, 293; César, *San Blas*, 169.

180. Sánchez, *Girón*, 235; Carré, *Girón*, 139.

181. De Castroverde, *Patria*, 260.

182. Otero et al., *Playa Girón*, vol. 1, 215; Sánchez, *Girón*, 224; Fontaine, *Fidel*, 176–77.

183. Carré, *Girón*, 139.
184. Johnson, *Bay of Pigs*, 158; Viana, *Por ti murieron*, 18–19; Triay, *Bay of Pigs*, 96.
185. Johnson, *Bay of Pigs*, 158; César, *San Blas*, 169; Troy, *Operation Zapata*, 293.
186. Fontaine, *Fidel*, 179–80, 183; Martínez, *Historia*, 281.
187. Sánchez, *Girón*, 235; Fontaine, *Fidel*, 184–85; Selva, *Girón*, 131.
188. Fontaine, *Fidel*, 195–96; Sánchez, *Girón*, 235.
189. Casaus, *Girón*, 172; Johnson, *Bay of Pigs*, 159; Selva, *Girón*, 132, 137; Pino, *Girón*, 165; Carré, *Girón*, 193; García Iturbe, *Hombres de Girón*, 156–57.
190. Johnson, *Bay of Pigs*, 159; César, *San Blas*, 169–70.
191. Selva, *Girón*, 135–36.
192. Selva, *Girón*, 136–37; Viana, *Por ti murieron*, 29.
193. Johnson, *Bay of Pigs*, 159–60; Selva, *Girón*, 138; Otero et al., *Playa Girón*, vol. 4, 105, 112–13; Troy, *Operation Zapata*, 301.
194. Selva, *Girón*, 138–39.
195. Selva, *Girón*, 138, 140–41; García Iturbe, *Hombres de Girón*, 157.
196. García Iturbe, *Hombres de Girón*, 135, 147.
197. Carré, *Girón*, 166, 179.
198. Sánchez, *Girón*, 232; Carré, *Girón*, 179.
199. Johnson, *Bay of Pigs*, 165; Dille, "We Who Tried," 73; Oliva, "Bay of Pigs Experience," chapter 13, section 87.
200. Carré, *Girón*, 184–85; Pérez, "Un battallón," 25; Otero et al., *Playa Girón*, vol. 1, 183, 270–71.
201. Johnson, *Bay of Pigs*, 165–66.
202. Carré, *Girón*, 184; Otero et al., *Playa Girón*, vol. 1, 183; Johnson, *Bay of Pigs*, 166.
203. Johnson, *Bay of Pigs*, 166.
204. Ameijeiras, "Batalla más corta (III)," 42; Fontaine, *Fidel*, 184; Carré, *Girón*, 179, 185; Zumbado and Tacoronte, *¡Coompañíaa teencioón!*, 172.
205. Ameijeiras, "Batalla más corta (III)," 40–41.
206. USDOS, *FRUS, Vol. X*, Doc. 152, 300; Wyden, *Bay of Pigs*, 260–61.
207. MGBA, "Documentos," pdf: 28 (misspellings corrected); USDOS, *FRUS, Vol. X*, Doc. 153, 300.
208. Johnson, *Bay of Pigs*, 168 (erroneously places the time of the cable and the subsequent conversation with Lynch after 4:30 p.m.); USDOS, *FRUS, Vol. X*, Doc. 109, 244–45
209. USDOS, *FRUS, Vol. X*, Doc. 109, 245.
210. Hunt, *This Day*, 209.
211. Pfeiffer, *Official History*, vol. 1, 375; USDOS, *FRUS, Vol. X*, Doc. 154, 301.
212. Penabaz, *Trampa*, 229; Sánchez, *Girón*, 231, 238; J. R. Fernández's 1961 after-action report quoted in Rodríguez, *Girón*, 327–28.
213. Penabaz, *Trampa*, 229.
214. Johnson, *Bay of Pigs*, 167.
215. Johnson, *Bay of Pigs*, 168; Dausá, *Luchas y combates*, 62.
216. Pérez San Román, *Respuesta*, 28.
217. Selva, *Girón*, 141–42; Carré, *Girón*, 207; Otero et al., *Playa Girón*, vol. 4, 35, 160.
218. Johnson, *Bay of Pigs*, 104, 168; Penabaz, *Trampa*, 229.
219. Fontaine, *Fidel*, 185, 188–89.
220. Sánchez, *Girón*, 243; USDOS, *FRUS, Vol. X*, Doc. 145, 293–94.

221. Sánchez, *Girón*, 240; J. R. Fernández's 1961 after-action report quoted in Rodríguez, *Girón*, 327; Johnson, *Bay of Pigs*, 171.

222. Prendes, *Punto rojo*, 159–60; Dille, "We Who Tried," 74; Viana, *Por ti murieron*, 37–38.

223. Sánchez, *Girón*, 243; Clark and Waters, *Playa Girón*, 129–30.

224. USDOS, *FRUS, Vol. X*, Doc. 151, 299, 299n1.

225. USDOS, *FRUS, Vol. X*, Doc. 155, 301n1.

226. USDOS, *FRUS, Vol. X*, Doc. 155, 301.

227. Wyden, *Bay of Pigs*, 129; Johnson, *Bay of Pigs*, 162–63.

228. Johnson, *Bay of Pigs*, 171.

229. Fernández, *Hombre afortunado*, 165.

230. USDOS, *FRUS, Vol. X*, Doc. 151, 299, and Doc. 153, 300n1.

231. Del Pino, *Amanecer*, 110–11; Prendes, *Punto rojo*, 159. Del Pino (111–12) claims that neither he nor Prendes understood what was happening until, back on land, Curbelo figured it out from their reports. However, Prendes (162) compellingly affirms that they both sized up the situation while flying over the beach.

232. Prendes, *Punto rojo*, 160; Del Pino, *Amanecer*, 111.

233. Del Pino, *Amanecer*, 111; Casaus, *Girón*, 198; Otero et al., *Playa Girón*, vol. 1, 109. See appendix A.

234. Prendes, *Punto rojo*, 160.

235. Otero et al., *Playa Girón*, vol. 1, 271–72; Sánchez, *Girón*, 228–29.

236. Johnson, *Bay of Pigs*, 169, 171, 192, 249–50.

237. Johnson, *Bay of Pigs*, 168–69; Carbonell, *Russians Stayed*, 141–42, 157; Encinosa, *Unvanquished*, 51.

238. See appendix A.

239. Del Pino, *Amanecer*, 113.

240. Lagas, *Memorias*, 129; Prendes, *Punto rojo*, 164.

241. Prendes, *Punto rojo*, 164–65.

242. Johnson, *Bay of Pigs*, 172; Dille, "We Who Tried," 76.

243. Carré, *Girón*, 202; Fernández, *Hombre afortunado*, 158; Sánchez, *Girón*, 243–44. Sánchez (242) relates a tale about Fernández and two others being injured by enemy fire as they entered Girón in a jeep. Rodiles, however, reveals that the three were injured when their vehicle flipped over after falling into a bomb crater. The latter's account of the accident is omitted from the printed version of *Secretos de Generales* by Luis Báez but appears on the online version of that book (http://www.granma.cu/granmad/secciones/50_granma-80_fidel/secretos_de_generales/art12.html). Fernández himself also refers to being "wounded in an accident" (Sánchez, ibid., 243).

244. Wise and Ross, *Invisible Government*, 72; Carrillo, *Cuba*, 157.

245. Fontaine, *Fidel*, 188, 193–94. Miret's account in Fontaine (193) mistakenly refers to the location as San Blas.

246. Fontaine, *Fidel*, 188, 190, 192–93; Sánchez, *Girón*, 242.

247. Fontaine, *Fidel*, 206.

248. Carré, *Girón*, 204.

249. Carré, *Girón*, 202–4; Báez, *Secretos de generales*, 286.

250. Fontaine, *Fidel*, 205–6, 209–11, 213, 223.

251. Meyer and Szulc, *Cuban Invasion*, 140.

252. JFK Commencement Address at Yale University, June 11, 1962, https://www.jfklibrary.org/archives/other-resources/john-f-kennedy-speeches/yale-university-19620611.

Chapter 10

1. Wise and Ross, *Invisible Government*, 73; Phillips, *Night Watch*, 130–31.
2. Sánchez, *Girón*, 245–46.
3. Fontaine, *Fidel*, 232–33.
4. Lussón and Gárciga, *Girón*, 194, 200–201.
5. Gobierno de Cuba, "Discursos de Fidel Castro," speech of April 19, 1986; Pino, *Girón*, 178; Lussón and Gárciga, *Girón*, 196, 199.
6. Fontaine (*Fidel*, 247) cites the 800 wounded number. The other figures mentioned in the text are based on Chávez et al., *Girón*, 299–313 passim; Álvarez, *Héroes eternos*, passim; AVBC, "Mártires y Heridos—Brigada 2506," published 2011 (http://bayofpigs2506.com/pagina%20heridos%20de%20la%20brigada.html), and the sources cited in note 1, chapter 1.
7. President's News Conference, April 21, 1961, UC Santa Barbara, https://www.presidency.ucsb.edu/documents/the-presidents-news-conference-213.
8. USDOS, *FRUS, Vol. X*, Doc. 230, 575.
9. Hinckle and Turner, *Fish Is Red*, 111–12.
10. Lussón and Gárciga, *Girón*, 231; Pérez-Cisneros et al., *After the Bay of Pigs*, 188, 209–14; Johnson, *Bay of Pigs*, 186–87, 189, 214, 264.
11. Johnson, *Bay of Pigs*, 199–201; USDOS, *FRUS, Vol. X*, Doc. 109, 245–46, and Doc. 110, 256–57.
12. Iglesias, *Escape*, 82–88; Lynch, *Decision*, 99 (Lynch misidentifies Vera's first name as "Reuben").
13. Johnson, *Bay of Pigs*, 185, 187–89.
14. Otero et al., *Playa Girón*, vol. 4, 23–24, 455–58; Johnson, *Bay of Pigs*, 206–7, 210–11.
15. De Castroverde, *Patria*, 243.
16. Otero et al., *Playa Girón*, vol. 4, 525.
17. Johnson, *Bay of Pigs*, 229; Pérez-Cisneros et al., *After the Bay of Pigs*, 25.
18. Johnson, *Bay of Pigs*, 265–66, 277.
19. Martínez, *Historia*, 391–411, 429; Pérez-Cisneros et al., *After the Bay of Pigs*, 40, 214.
20. Johnson, *Bay of Pigs*, 245, 283.
21. Kornbluh, *Bay of Pigs Declassified*, 328–30; Johnson, *Bay of Pigs*, 312–13; Pérez-Cisneros et al., *After the Bay of Pigs*, 188, 209. Six prisoners had been released earlier after family members paid their individual fines (Pérez-Cisneros et al., 211).
22. Dille, "We Who Tried," 32–33; Rookes, *God and the CIA*, 61.
23. McDonald, "Gen. Erneido Oliva."
24. Rookes, *God and the CIA*, 26–40, 45–58, 61; Waters, *Escambray to the Congo*, 121.
25. Rodríguez and Weisman, *Shadow Warrior*, 10, 87–88, 155–56, 160–69.

Chapter 11

1. Pérez San Román, *Respuesta*, 23–24; MacPherson, "Last Casualty."
2. Del Pino, *Proa a la libertad*, 168–69, 334–35, 374, 378; Del Pino, *Años de la guerra*, 463–64.

3. U.S. Congress, *War on Drugs*, 18–19; Correa, "Antiguos enemigos."

4. Lagas, *Memorias*, 289–93.

5. Rudd, "My Own T-Shirt Hero;" MacPhail, "Bay of Pigs."

6. Correa, "Antiguos enemigos."

7. E.g., Rodríguez, *Girón*, 275.

8. Zayas-Bazán, *My Life*, 229–30.

9. English, *Corporation*, 13, 56, 138, 507, 511, 516; President's Commission on Organized Crime, *Organized Crime and Gambling*, 101–9, 145.

10. Graff, *Watergate*, 161–69; Hunt, *American Spy*, 321.

11. Thomas, *Cuban Revolution*, 691.

12. A. Ferrer, *Cuba*, 453, 462.

13. Nolan, "Memorandum to the Attorney General."

14. De Jesús, "Reabre sus puertas."

15. Fontaine, *Fidel*, 18, 33, 60.

16. De la Pedraja, *Wars of Latin America*, 101.

17. Lussón and Gárciga, *Girón*, 230n32.

18. Cordero, "Expediciones de junio de 1959," 97–138; Brown, *Cuba's Revolutionary World*, 52.

19. Ysalguez, *14 de junio*, 107, 120, 124.

Chapter 12

1. USDOS, *FRUS, Vol. X*, Doc. 230, 575; Kornbluh, *ULTRASENSITIVE Bay of Pigs*. The report's sensitive information included disclosures about the American airmen killed during the battle, which the government publicly denied (Wise and Ross, *Invisible Government*, 74–90). Thomas Ray's body, which had been kept frozen in Cuba for eighteen years, was returned to the United States in 1979 at the behest of his family. Officially, however, the participation of the dead American was not publicly acknowledged by the CIA until 1998 (Fineman and Mascarenas, "Secret Death of Pete Ray").

2. USDOS, *FRUS, Vol. X*, Doc. 233, 603.

3. Pfeiffer, *Official History*, vol. 4, 231, 243.

4. Kirkpatrick, "Inspector General's Survey," 99–100.

5. Bissell, "Analysis of the Cuban Operation," 133–34; Kornbluh, *Bay of Pigs Declassified*, 10, 13.

6. Martínez Sánchez, *Girón*, 61, 72.

7. Rivadeneira, *Bay of Pigs*, 18.

8. Schlesinger, *Thousand Days*, 284; Carrillo, *Cuba*, 157; Kenneth Addicott, "Historian's Note," preface to "Record of Paramilitary Action," by J. Hawkins; USDOS, *FRUS, Vol. X*, Doc. 98, 221.

9. Phillips, *Night Watch*, 140.

10. Castro thought the timing of the raid was asinine: "The attack forty-eight hours ahead [of the landings] gave us time. Why they did so is inexplicable" (Gobierno de Cuba, "Discursos de Fidel Castro," speech of April 16, 1996).

11. Thomas, *Very Best Men*, 237.

12. Wyden, *Bay of Pigs*, 170; Bissell, *Reflections*, 183; Troy, *Operation Zapata*, 64–69, 146–47.

13. Pfeiffer, *Official History*, vol. 1, cover page; Bissell, *Reflections*, 246.

14. See discussion in chapter 5.

15. USDOS, *FRUS, Vol. X*, Doc. 231, 586–87.

16. "Operación Marte" plan, reproduced as appendix 8 in Díaz's *Cuba*, 535.

17. "The leader was never informed" comment appears on the online version of USDOS, *FRUS, Vol. X*, Doc. 198 (https://history.state.gov/historicaldocuments/frus1961-63v10/d198) but is not found in the 1997 printed edition. The comment (in parentheses) follows "(1) Friendly beach reception party . . ." in the online version under *Diversionary Landing in Oriente*. Despite the circumstances, Díaz's men disagreed with his decision not to land and openly spurned him when they were taken aboard U.S. Navy ships to Vieques Island, Puerto Rico (Díaz, *Cuba*, 145, 165).

18. USDOS, *FRUS, Vol. X*, Doc. 233, 605.

19. USDOS, *FRUS, Vol. X*, Doc. 201, 457.

20. USDOS, *FRUS, Vol. X*, Doc. 200, 452. Rusk in his testimony must have meant to say "talk" rather than "call," as both Cabell and Bissel indicate that the president was already on the line at the time (Cabell's handwritten note [May 1961?] quoted in Pfeiffer, *Official History*, vol. 1, 292; Cabell, *Man of Intelligence*, 388; Bissell, *Reflections*, 184). CIA historian Jack Pfeiffer, ignoring the damning evidence of the CIA's underestimation of Castro's air force, characterizes Rusk's testimony as "disingenuous" (Pfeiffer, *Official History*, vol. 1, 229).

21. Pfeiffer, *Official History*, vol. 1, 279–80.

22. Pfeiffer, *Official History*, vol. 1, 278.

23. Kirkpatrick, "Inspector General's Survey," 99.

24. USCIA, "Pluto," Anexo A, A-8; Escalante, *Secret War*, 86. Cuba's estimated population at the time was 6,744,000 (American University, *Area Handbook for Cuba*, 63).

25. USCIA, "Pluto," Plan Administrativo, Anexo F, F-1.

26. Troy, *Operation Zapata*, 355–56; Schlesinger, *Thousand Days*, 281.

27. Bissell, *Reflections*, 190.

28. Otero et al., *Playa Girón*, vol. 1, 443; Rodríguez, *Girón*, 128.

29. Dulles, *Craft of Intelligence*, 164.

30. Hunt, *This Day*, 201n*.

31. Hawkins, "Record of Paramilitary Action," 40.

32. USDOS, *FRUS, Vol. X*, Doc. 209, 500–501.

33. Otero et al., *Playa Girón*, vol. 4, 119, 206, 395.

34. Lussón and Gárciga, *Girón*, 320.

35. José Miró Cardona, interview by Diego González and Juan A. Bras, *La Voz de Cuba Libre* radio show, April 9 [*sic*, but April 11 based on internal information], 1961, José Miró Cardona Papers, University of Miami Library, Cuban Heritage Collection, https://digitalcollections.library.miami.edu/digital/collection/chc5122/id/97/rec/11.

36. President's News Conference, April 12, 1961, John F. Kennedy Presidential Library and Museum, https://www.jfklibrary.org/archives/other-resources/john-f-kennedy-press-conferences/news-conference-9.

37. USDOS, *FRUS, Vol. X*, Doc. 114, 260(n1)–61.

38. USDOS, *FRUS, Vol. X*, Doc. 157, 304.

39. Schlesinger, *Thousand Days*, 284.

40. USDOS, *FRUS, Vol. X*, Doc. 157, 302–4.

41. USDOS, *FRUS, Vol. X*, Doc. 270, 666–67; "Minutes of the Meeting of the Special Group (Augmented) on Operation MONGOOSE, 4 October, 1962," Memorandum for Record, https://nsarchive2.gwu.edu//nsa/cuba_mis_cri/621004%20Minutes%20of%20Meeting%20of%20Special.pdf.

42. President John F. Kennedy, Proclamation, "Embargo on All Trade with Cuba, Proclamation 3447," *Federal Register* 27, no. 26 (February 1962): 1085, https://www.federalregister.gov/citation/27-FR-1085.

43. Absher, *Mind-Sets and Missiles*, 34, 69, 86.

44. Waters, *Making History*, 53, 64.

BIBLIOGRAPHY

Absher, Kenneth M. *Mind-Sets and Missiles: A First Hand Account of the Cuban Missile Crisis.* Carlisle, PA: U.S. Army War College Press, 2009. https://press.armywarcollege.edu/monographs/352/.

Alonso, Dora. *El año 61.* La Habana: Editorial Letras Cubanas, 1981.

Álvarez, Justina. *Héroes eternos de la patria.* La Habana: Editora Política, 2006.

Ameijeiras Delgado, Efigenio. "La batalla más corta (III)." *Bohemia,* July 21, 1989, part 3 of 4. https://original-ufdc.uflib.ufl.edu/UF00029010/04085?search=bohemia.

American University. *Special Warfare Area Handbook for Cuba—1961.* Washington, DC: U.S. Government Printing Office, 1962.

Arturo, Héctor. "Medio siglo después." *Verde Olivo,* April 2011. https://www.verdeolivo.cu/sites/default/files/revistas/rvo2011-2.pdf.

Atienza Pérez, Orlando. "La batalla de Playa Larga." In *A los 31 años de la invasión a Bahía de Cochinos,* edited by Sergio Díaz Morejón and Orlando Atienza Pérez, 14–16 and 19–20. Los Angeles: Publicaciones Orsersa, 1992.

Báez, Luis. "El pueblo derrota la invasión." *Bohemia,* April 30, 1961. https://original-ufdc.uflib.ufl.edu/UF00029010/02929?search=bohemia.

———. *Secretos de generales.* La Habana: Editorial SI-MAR S.A., 1996.

Beerli, Stanley W. "Transmittal of Documents." Memorandum to Lt. Colonel B. W. Tarwater, USAF (with attachments), April 26, 1961. https://www.cia.gov/readingroom/docs/DOC_0000252273.pdf.

Bissell, Richard. "An Analysis of the Cuban Operation, 18 January 1962." In Kornbluh, *Bay of Pigs Declassified,* 133–234.

Bissell, Richard M. *Reflections of a Cold Warrior.* With Jonathan E. Lewis and Frances T. Pudlo. New Haven, CT: Yale University Press, 1996.

Bolet, Alberto J. *Dark Nights in the Castle of the Prince.* Miami: Ediciones Universal, 2021.

Bonafede, Dom. "3 Beachheads Secured, Cuba Invaders Push On." *Miami Herald,* April 18, 1961, Street Edition.

Brown, Jonathan C. *Cuba's Revolutionary World.* Cambridge, MA: Harvard University Press, 2017.

Buchanan, James. "Giant Pincer Drives to Cut Cuba in Two." *Miami Herald,* April 18, 1961, Street Edition.

Cabell, Charles P. *A Man of Intelligence: Memoirs of War, Peace, and the CIA.* Edited by Charles P. Cabell, Jr. Colorado Springs, CO: Impavide Publications, 1977.

Campbell, W. J. *Getting It Wrong: Ten of the Greatest Misreported Stories in American Journalism.* Berkeley: University of California Press, 2010.

Carbonell, Néstor T. *And the Russians Stayed.* New York: William Morrow, 1989.

Carré Lazcano, Elio. *Girón: una estocada a fondo.* La Habana: Imprenta Federico Engels de la Empresa de Medios de Propaganda, 1976.

Carreras Rolas, Enrique. *Por el dominio del aire.* 1995 1st ed. La Habana: Editora Política, 2008.

Carrillo, Justo. *A Cuba le tocó perder.* Miami: Ediciones Universal, 1993.

Casaus, Víctor. *Girón en la memoria.* Colección Premio Casa de las Américas, 1970 1st ed. La Habana: Centro Cultural Pablo de la Torriente Brau, 2012. http://www .centropablo.cult.cu/libros/giron-en-la-memoria/.

Castro Hidalgo, Orlando. *Spy for Fidel.* Miami: E. A. Seemann Publishing, 1971.

Castro, Fidel. "La batalla de Girón (Segunda Parte)." *Cuba Debate,* May 25, 2011. http://www.cubadebate.cu/la-batalla-de-giron/segunda-parte-1/.

César Guayanes, Eli B. *San Blas.* Edited by Felipe Villaraus Gallo, 2nd. ed. Miami: Editorial Los Amigos, 2007.

Chávez, Clara E., Dulce M. Medina, and Saúl V. Almohalla. *Girón: biografía de la victoria.* La Habana: Editora Política, 1986.

Clark, Steve, and Mary-Alice Waters, eds. *Playa Girón/Bahía de Cochinos: primera derrota de Washington en América.* New York: Pathfinder, 2001.

Cordero Michel, Emilio. "Las expediciones de junio de 1959." *Clio* 177 (Enero–junio, 2009): 97–150. https://en.calameo.com/read/000530775148e63f3708a.

Correa, Armando. "Antiguos enemigos se unen en grupo militar contra régimen cubano." *El Nuevo Herald,* April 17, 1997.

Cuba Study Group (CSG, Taylor Committee). "Paramilitary Study (Taylor Report), Part III—Annexes." John F. Kennedy Presidential Library and Museum, Boston.

Cullather, Nicholas. *Operation PBSUCCESS: The United States and Guatemala, 1952– 1954.* Publications of the CIA History Staff. Washington, DC: Center for the Study of Intelligence, USCIA, 1994. https://archive.org/details/CIA-Guatemala -Coup-Report/mode/2up.

Dausá, José Enrique. *Luchas y combates por Cuba.* Miami: Ediciones Universal, 2001.

De Castroverde, Waldo. *Que la patria se sienta orgullosa.* Miami: Ediciones Universal, 1999.

De Jesús, Venturas. "Reabre sus puertas Museo Comandancia de las FAR." *Granma,* August 19, 2016. https://www.granma.cu/cuba/2016-08-19/reabre-sus-puertas -museo-comandancia-de-las-far-19-08-2016-23-08-38.

De la Pedraja, René. *Wars of Latin America, 1948–1982: The Rise of the Guerrillas.* Jefferson, NC: McFarland, 2013.

Deal, Charles, and James Buchanan. "Crash Boats Give Keys Martial Air in Invasion's Wake." *Miami Herald,* April 19, 1961, Street Edition.

Del Pino, Rafael. *Amanecer en Girón.* La Habana: Instituto del Libro, 1969.

———. *Proa a la libertad.* México, DF: Editorial Planeta Mexicana, S.A., 1991.

———. *Los años de la guerra.* N.p., 2013.

Díaz, Higinio (Nino). *Cuba: Isla crucificada de América.* Miami: n.p., 2011.

Dille, John. "We Who Tried." *Life,* May 10, 1963.

Dorschner, John, and Roberto Fabricio. *The Winds of December.* New York: Coward, McCann & Geoghegan, 1980.

Dulles, Allen. *The Craft of Intelligence.* 1963 1st ed. Guilford, CT: Lyons Press, 2016.

El Avance Criollo. "Finalizado el entrenamiento" (photo essay). March 10, 1961. https://dloc.com/UF00077417/00038/images.

El Nuevo Herald. "Base de datos de los veteranos de Bahía de Cochinos" (lookup database). Published April 14, 2011; updated August 24, 2018. https://c0dzk099.caspio .com/dp/ce401000d69ebaaeb4cb43849383.

Elliston, Jon, ed. *Psywar on Cuba: The Declassified History of U.S. Anti-Castro Propaganda.* Hoboken, NJ: Ocean Press, 1999.

Encinosa, Enrique. *Escambray: La guerra olvidada.* Miami: Editorial SIBI, 1988.

————. *Unvanquished: Cuba's Resistance to Fidel Castro.* Los Angeles: Pureplay Press, 2004.

English, T. J. *The Corporation: An Epic Story of the Cuban American Underworld.* New York: William Morrow, 2018.

Escalante Font, Fabián. *The Secret War: CIA Covert Operations against Cuba, 1959–62.* Melbourne, Australia: Ocean Press, 1995.

Feeney, Harold. "The Night of the White Horse." *U.S. Naval Intelligence Professionals Quarterly* 11, no. 1 (1995): 1–4.

Fernández, José R. *Un hombre afortunado.* La Habana: Casa Editorial Verde Olivo, 2018. https://www.verdeolivo.cu/sites/default/files/Edici%C3%B3n%20 Verde%20Olivo/libros/un_hombre_afortunado.pdf.

Ferrer, Ada. *Cuba: An American History.* New York: Scribner, 2021.

Ferrer, Edward B. *Operación Puma.* Miami: International Aviation Consultants, 1975.

————. *Operation Puma.* Miami: International Aviation Consultants, 1982.

Ferrer, Harold. "Misión cumplida." *Verde Olivo,* April 2011 (reprint of April 18, 1965 article). https://www.verdeolivo.cu/sites/default/files/revistas/rvo2011-2.pdf.

Fineman, Mark, and Dolly Mascarenas. "Bay of Pigs: The Secret Death of Pete Ray." *Los Angeles Times,* March 15, 1998.

Fontaine Ortiz, Elvin. *Fidel desde el Punto Uno a Playa Girón.* La Habana: Editorial de Ciencias Sociales, 2014.

Franqui, Carlos. *Family Portrait with Fidel.* New York: Vintage Books, 1985.

García Guerra, Oscar. *Victoria en la derrota de Playa Girón.* Miami: Editorial Nuevos Horizontes Internacionales, 1992.

García Iturbe, Néstor. *Hombres de Girón.* La Habana: Editora Historia, 2011.

Gárciga Blanco, José A. *General Tomassevich.* 2009 1st ed. La Habana: Casa Editorial Verde Olivo, 2014.

Geyer, Georgie A. *Guerrilla Prince: The Untold Story of Fidel Castro.* Boston: Little, Brown & Co., 1993.

Gobierno de Cuba. "Discursos e intervenciones del Comandante en Jefe Fidel Castro Ruz, Presidente del Consejo de Estado de la República de Cuba." Accessed 2022–2023. http://www.cuba.cu/gobierno/discursos/.

Gómez Darna, Percy. *Un batallón que permanece.* La Habana: Casa Editorial Verde Olivo, 2006.

González, Lorenzo F. *Para volver a Cuba.* Lulu.com, 2017.

González Lalondry, Luis. *Bahía de Cochinos* [*Sangre en Bahía de Cochinos* (1965); *Prisioneros de Guerra* (1974)]. Miami: Vanguardia, 1995.

González Pérez, Enildo. "Girón desde el mar." *Verde Olivo,* April 2011 (reprint of April 19, 1965 article). https://www.verdeolivo.cu/sites/default/files/revistas/ rvo2011-2.pdf.

Graff, Garrett M. *Watergate: A New History.* New York: Avid Reader Press, 2022.

Guerra Vilaboy, Sergio. *La revolución cubana: un nuevo panorama de su historia (1953–2000).* Uberlândia, Brazil: Navegando, 2021. https://issuu.com/ navegandopublicacoes/docs/e-book_nueva_historia.

Handleman, Howard. "The Real Story of the Bay of Pigs." *U.S. News & World Report,* January 7, 1963.

Hawkins, Jack. "Record of Paramilitary Action against the Castro Government of Cuba, 17 March 1960–May 1961." May 5, 1961, CIA Clandestine Service Historical Paper No. 105. https://www.cia.gov/readingroom/docs/DOC_0001459144.pdf.

Herrera Medina, José R. *Operación Jaula*. La Habana: Casa Editorial Verde Olivo, 2006.

Higgins, Trumbull. *The Perfect Failure: Kennedy, Eisenhower, and the C.I.A. at the Bay of Pigs*. New York: Norton, 1987.

Hinckle, Warren, and William Turner. *The Fish Is Red: The Story of the Secret War against Castro*. New York: Harper & Row, 1981.

Hunt, E. Howard. *American Spy: My Secret History in the CIA, Watergate, and Beyond*. Hoboken, NJ: John Wiley & Sons, 2007.

———. *Give Us This Day*. New Rochelle, NY: Arlington House, 1973.

Iglesias Arencibia, Luis M. *Escape*. Shelbyville, KY: Wasteland Press, 2010.

Johnson, Haynes. *The Bay of Pigs*. New York: Norton, 1964.

Jones, E. V. W. "Joy, Worry Fill Exile Colony." *Miami Herald*, April 18, 1961, Street Edition.

Jones, Howard. *The Bay of Pigs*. New York: Oxford University Press, 2008.

Khrushchev, Nikita Sergeevich. Introduction, commentary, and notes by Edward Crankshaw. Translated and edited by Strobe Talbott. *Khrushchev Remembers*. Boston: Little, Brown, 1970.

Kirkpatrick, Lyman B. "Inspector General's Survey of the Cuban Operation, October, 1961." In Kornbluh, *Bay of Pigs Declassified*, 23–132.

Kornbluh, Peter, ed. *Bay of Pigs Declassified: The Secret CIA Report on the Invasion of Cuba*. New York: New Press, 1998.

———. *The ULTRASENSITIVE Bay of Pigs*. National Security Archive Electronic Briefing Book no. 29. National Security Archive, 2000. https://nsarchive2.gwu.edu/NSAEBB/NSAEBB29/index.html.

Lagas, Jacques. *Memorias de un capitán rebelde*. 4th ed. Santiago de Chile: Editorial del Pacifico, 1964.

León Lima, José A. *Testimonio del chofer y escolta de Fidel*. 2016 1st. ed. La Habana: Casa Editorial Verde Olivo, 2020.

Leyva, René A. "Notas de Diario (1961)." N.p., 1967. AVBC website. Accessed December 2, 2022. http://bayofpigs2506.com/Rene%20Armando%20Leyva%20relato.png.

Lisanka. "Pasajes de una victoria con Fidel." *Bohemia*, April 18, 1986. https://original-ufdc.uflib.ufl.edu/UF00029010/03915?search=bohemia.

Lussón Batlle, Antonio E., and José A. Gárciga Blanco. *Girón: Manos tras la cabeza*. La Habana: Casa Editorial Verde Olivo, 2016.

Lynch, Grayston L. *Decision for Disaster*. Washington, DC: Brassey's, 1998.

Machado, Ramón E. *Cuba, My (Twice) Betrayed Generation*. Kindle ed. Amazon Digital Services LLC, 2014.

MacPhail, Doug. "Bay of Pigs—The Men and Aircraft of the Cuban Revolutionary Air Force." *Latin American Aviation Historical Society*, February 15, 2019. https://www.laahs.com/bay-of-pigs/.

MacPherson, Myra. "The Last Casualty of the Bay of Pigs." *Washington Post*, October 17, 1989.

Madden, John P. "Operation Bumpy Road: The Role of Admiral Arleigh Burke and the US Navy in the Bay of Pigs Invasion." Master's thesis, Old Dominion University, 1988. https://digitalcommons.odu.edu/history_etds/35.

Marina de Guerra de la Brigada de Asalto 2506. "Documentos confidenciales." Unpublished c. 1961 report on Asoc. Veteranos Bahía de Cochinos website.

Accessed December 28, 2020. http://bayofpigs2506.com/nueva%20pagina%20 relatos%20ineditos.html.

Marrero, Leví. *Geografía de Cuba*. Reprint of 1957 ed. Miami: La Moderna Poesía, 1981.

Martínez, Aurelio, ed. *Historia de una agresión*. La Habana: Ediciones Venceremos, 1962.

Martínez Sánchez, Raddy. *Girón: razón de la victoria*. La Habana: Casa Editorial Verde Olivo, 2015.

Mayo, José. *Niños héroes de Playa Girón*. La Habana: Editorial Gente Nueva, 1983.

McDonald, Greg. "Gen. Erneido Oliva: Second in Command at the Bay of Pigs." *AARP Bulletin*, April 15, 2011.

Méndez, José L. "Preparativos para la invasión de Playa Girón (II)." *Cuba Debate,* March 23, 2011. http://www.cubadebate.cu/opinion/2011/03/23/preparativos-para-la-invasion-de-playa-giron-ii/.

Mera Piñera, Magda. *Combatientes jovellanenses en Girón. [Monografía 1233].* Jovellanos, Cuba: Universidad de Matanzas "Camilo Cienfuegos," 2012. http://monografias.umcc.cu/monos/2012/CUM%20Jovellanos/mo1233.pdf.

Meyer, Karl E., and Tad Szulc. *The Cuban Invasion: The Chronicle of a Disaster*. New York: Praeger, 1962.

Miami Herald. "Cuba Tells U.N. U.S. Backs Rebels." April 18, 1961, Street Edition.

Miami Herald. "Observation Post." April 18, 1961, Street Edition.

Miller, Robert H. *Closing the Circle*. CognitioBooks.com, 2017.

Miller, Terry. "Destroyers at the Bay of Pigs Invasion." *The Tin Can Sailor,* January-February-March, 2011 (National Association of Destroyer Veterans).

New York Times. "Havana Normal, Broadcasts Say." April 19, 1961.

New York Times. "Havana Reported Calm." April 19, 1961.

Newsweek. "Cuba: Sealing It Off." May 8, 1961.

Nolan, John. "Memorandum to the Attorney General on Castro's Statements and Notes on Cuban Trip, April 5–9, 1963." National Security Archive, George Washington University, Washington, DC. https://nsarchive2.gwu.edu/bayof-pigs/19630400b.pdf.

Núñez Jiménez, Antonio. *En marcha con Fidel—1959*. 1998 1st ed. Amazon Digital Services LLC (Kindle), 2018.

———. *En marcha con Fidel—1960*. 1998 1st ed. Amazon Digital Services LLC (Kindle), 2018.

———. *En marcha con Fidel—1961*. 1998 1st ed. La Habana: Editorial de Ciencias Sociales, 2004.

———. *En marcha con Fidel—1961*. 1998 1st ed. Amazon Digital Services LLC (Kindle), 2018.

Oliva, Erneido A. "The Bay of Pigs Experience." Unpublished memoir excerpts posted on April 2011 on the Cuban-American Military Council website. http://www.camcocuba.org (site discontinued).

Otero, Lisandro, Edmundo Desnoes, and Ambrosio Fornet, eds. *Playa Girón: derrota del imperialismo*. 4 vols. La Habana: Ediciones Revolución, 1961.

Padrón José, L., and Luis A. Betancourt. *Batista: últimos días en el poder*. La Habana, Cuba: Ediciones Unión, 2008.

Paterson, Thomas G. *Contesting Castro: The United States and the Triumph of the Cuban Revolution*. New York: Oxford University Press, 1994.

Pavón, Luis. "Historia de El Combatiente y su dotación." *Verde Olivo,* April, 2011 (reprint of April 18, 1965 article). https://www.verdeolivo.cu/sites/default/files/revistas/rvo2011-2.pdf.

Páz-Sánchez, Manuel de. *Zona de guerra: España y la revolución cubana (1960-1962).* Tenerife, Canary Islands: Centro de la Cultura Popular Canaria, 2001.

Penabaz, Manuel. *La trampa.* Miami: Zoom, 1983.

Pérez-Cisneros, Pablo, John B. Donovan, and Jeff Koenreich. *After the Bay of Pigs: Lives and Liberty on the Line.* Miami: Alexandria Library Publishing House, 2007.

Pérez Guzmán, Francisco. "Un batallón." *Bohemia,* April 17, 1981. https://original -ufdc.uflib.ufl.edu/UF00029010/03658?search=bohemia.

Pérez San Román, José. *Respuesta.* Miami: Carlos Miami Press, 1979. http://bayof pigs2506.com/RESPUESTA%20de%20Jose%20San%20Roman.pdf.

Persons, Albert C. *Bay of Pigs: A Firsthand Account of the Mission by a U.S. Pilot in Support of the Cuban Invasion Force in 1961.* 1968 1st ed. Jefferson, NC: McFarland, 1990.

Pfeiffer, Jack B. *Official History of the Bay of Pigs Operation.* 5 vols. Central Intelligence Agency, 1979. https://www.cia.gov/readingroom/collection/bay-pigs-release.

Phillips, David Atlee. *The Night Watch.* 1977 1st ed. New York: Ballantine Books, 1982.

Pino Machado, Quintín. *La batalla de Girón.* La Habana: Editorial de Ciencias Sociales, 1983.

Placer Cervera, Gustavo. "La contribución de la Marina de Guerra Revolucionaria a la victoria de Girón." *Verde Olivo,* April 2021. https://www.verdeolivo.cu/sites/default/files/revistas/rvo_no.2_2021_especial_giron_con_todo_0.pdf.

Posada Carriles, Luis. *Los caminos del guerrero.* N.p., 1994.

Prendes, Alvaro. *En el punto rojo de mi kolimador: cronicas de un aviador.* 1974 1st ed. La Habana: Editorial Letras Cubanas, 1982.

President's Commission on Organized Crime. *Organized Crime and Gambling. Record of Hearing VII, June 24–16, 1985.* Washington, DC: U.S. Government Printing Office, 1985. https://www.ojp.gov/pdffiles1/Digitization/108890NCJRS.pdf.

Radio Llanura de Colón. "Identifican nueva víctima civil de invasión por Playa Girón." April 17, 2018. Accessed February 7, 2021. https://www.radiollanuradecolon.icrt .cu/identifican-nueva-victima-civil-de-invasion-por-playa-giron/.

Rasenberger, Jim. *The Brilliant Disaster.* New York: Scribner, 2011.

Reston, James. "Top Advisers in Dispute on Aid to Castro's Foes." *New York Times,* April 11, 1961.

Rivadeneira, Ken, ed. *Bay of Pigs: The Men Behind the Invasion.* Spanish-English ed. Miami: HCP/Aboard Publishing, 2011.

Rivas, Santiago. *Playa Girón: The Cuban Exiles' Invasion at Bay of Pigs 1961.* Latin America @ War Series no. 2. Solihull, England: Helion, 2017.

Rodríguez, Félix I., and John Weisman. *Shadow Warrior.* New York: Simon and Schuster, 1989.

Rodríguez, Juan Carlos. *Girón: la batalla inevitable.* Edición ampliada. La Habana: Editorial Capitán San Luis, 2005.

Rookes, Stephen. *For God and the CIA.* Warwick, England: Helion, 2020.

Rostow, W. W. *The Diffusion of Power.* New York: Macmillan, 1972.

Rudd Fernández, Clive. "My Own T-Shirt Hero: The Forgotten Story of a Bay of Pigs Pilot." *Havana Times,* July 22, 2014. https://havanatimes.org/features/my-own -t-shirt-hero-the-forgotten-story-of-a-bay-of-pigs-pilot/.

Sánchez, Desi. *A Funny Thing Happened on My Way to Freedom.* Cheyenne, WY: Stratton Press, 2018.

Sánchez, Miguel Ángel. *Girón no fue sólo en abril.* La Habana: Editorial ORBE, 1979.

Schlesinger, Arthur M. *A Thousand Days.* Boston: Houghton Mifflin, 1965.

Selva Álvarez, William A. *Girón: Testimonio de una victoria.* La Habana: Editorial de Ciencias Sociales, 1987.

Sexto, Luis. "La memoria en vivo." *Bohemia,* April 12, 1996. https://original-ufdc.uflib .ufl.edu/UF00029010/04367?search=bohemia.

Silva Ardanuy, F. M. "Reconversión de Ejército Rebelde a Ejército Regular al servicio de la República de Cuba (1956–1970)." Doctoral diss., Universidad Pablo de Olavide (Seville, Spain), 1980. https://www.latinamericanstudies.org/book/reconversion.pdf.

Smith, Earl E. T. *The Fourth Floor: An Account of the Castro Communist Revolution.* New York: Random House, 1962.

Southworth, George. "Able-Bodied Cubans Swamp Anti-Fidel Recruiting Office." *Miami Herald,* April 18, 1961, Street Edition.

Suárez Isaac, René. *Y los aviones volaron.* La Habana: Casa Editorial Verde Olivo, 2010.

Szulc, Tad. "Anti-Castro Units Trained to Fight at Florida Bases." *New York Times,* April 7, 1961.

———. *Fidel: A Critical Portrait.* 1986 1st ed. New York: Perennial, 2002.

Tamayo, Juan O. "The Spy Who Betrayed the Brigade." *El Nuevo Herald,* April 17, 2011.

Thomas, Evan. *The Very Best Men: The Daring Early Years of the CIA.* 1995 1st ed. New York: Simon & Schuster, 2006.

Thomas, Hugh. *The Cuban Revolution.* New York: Harper & Row, 1977.

Trest, Warren A., and Donald Dodd. *Wings of Denial.* Montgomery, AL: NewSouth Books, 2001.

Triay, Victor Andrés. *Bay of Pigs.* Gainesville: University Press of Florida, 2001.

Troy, Thomas F., ed. *Operation Zapata: The Ultrasensitive Report and Testimony of the Board of Inquiry on the Bay of Pigs* (with introduction by Luis Aguilar). Frederick, MD: University Publications of America, Inc., 1984.

United Nations. *Statement before UN General Assembly by Raúl Roa.* UN General Assembly 15th Session, Official Records, 7 October 1960, 517–19. New York: United Nations, 1960. https://ask.un.org/faq/75009.

U.S. Central Intelligence Agency. "Plan de Operación 1–200." Washington, DC: CIA FOIA Document Number 0000135730, 1961. https://www.cia.gov/readingroom/docs/DOC_0000135730.pdf.

U.S. Central Intelligence Agency. "Plan de Operación Pluto." Washington, DC: CIA FOIA Document Number 0000135658, 1961. https://www.cia.gov/readingroom/docs/DOC_0000135658.pdf.

U.S. Congress. *War on Drugs in the Western Hemisphere: Fact or Fiction? Hearing before the Subcommittee on the Western Hemisphere of the Committee on International Relations, House of Representatives, One Hundred Fourth Congress, Second Session, June 6, 1996.* Washington, DC: U.S. Government Printing Office, 1996.

U.S. Department of the Army. *Field Manual FM-23-92, 4.2-Inch Mortar M30.* Washington, DC: U.S. Government Printing Office, 1961.

U.S. Department of State. *Foreign Relations of the United States, 1958–1960, Cuba, Volume VI.* Washington, DC: U.S. Government Printing Office, 1991.

U.S. Department of State. *Foreign Relation of the United States, 1961–1963, Volume X, Cuba, January 1961–September 1962.* Washington, DC: U.S. Government Printing Office, 1997.

U.S. Department of State. *Foreign Relations of the United States, Cuba 1961–1962; Volumes X/XI/XII, Microfiche Supplement.* Washington, DC: U.S. Government Publishing Office, 2021. https://history.state.gov/historicaldocuments/frus1961-63v10-12mSupp.

U.S. Navy. *Radioman 3 & 2, NAVPERS 10228-C.* U.S. Navy Training Publication Center, 1961.

Valdés, José A. "Autobiography." Unpublished manuscript, [1982?], paper copy.

Verde Olivo. "Aquellos Artilleros de Girón." April 2011 (reprinted April 17, 1966 article). https://www.verdeolivo.cu/sites/default/files/revistas/rvo2011-2.pdf.

Viana, Renato. *Los que por ti murieron.* Miami[?]: n.p., 1961.

Villaraus Gallo, Felipe J. *Huellas y caminos.* Miami: Ahora Printing, 2008.

———. *Invasión: Bahía De Cochinos, Cuba.* Waddy, KY: Wasteland Press, 2011.

Waters, Mary-Alice, ed. *From the Escambray to the Congo: In the Whirlwind of the Cuban Revolution—Interview with Víctor Dreke.* New York: Pathfinder, 2002.

———. *Making History: Interviews with Four Generals of Cuba's Revolutionary Armed Forces.* New York: Pathfinder, 2000.

Wise, David, and Thomas B. Ross. *The Invisible Government.* New York: Random House, 1964.

Wyden, Peter. *Bay of Pigs.* New York: Simon & Schuster, 1979.

Yanez, Luisa. "Operation Mirage, Fighters Scored a Small Win Against Che." *Miami Herald,* April 15, 2011.

Ysalguez, Hugo A. *El 14 de junio: La raza inmortal.* 1980 1st ed. Santo Domingo, RD: Editora Búho, 2013.

Zaldívar Diégues, Andrés, and Pedro Etcheverry Vázquez. *Una fascinante historia: La conspiración trujillista.* La Habana: Editorial Capitán San Luis, 2010.

Zayas-Bazán, Eduardo. *My Life.* Miami: Alexandria Library Publishing House, 2021.

Zucker, Norman L. "Refugee Resettlement in the United States: The Role of the Voluntary Agencies." *Michigan Journal of International Law* 3, no. 1 (2021): 155–77. https://repository.law.umich.edu/mjil/vol3/iss1/8.

Zumbado, H., and A. Tacoronte. *¡Coompañíaa teencioón!* La Habana: Editorial Arte y Letra, 1976.

INDEX

AANG. *See* Alabama Air National Guard
Acevedo, Luis, 51, 96
Acosta, Orestes, 56, 265n101
Afont, Tomás, 92, 246, 248
Alabama Air National Guard (AANG), 157, 171
Alejos, Roberto, 7
Alemán, Elio, 197
Almeida, Juan, 22, 35, 50, 53, 75, 82, 132, 138, 145, 175
Alonso, José, 46
Álvarez, Jorge, 60, 111, 197, 266n119
Ameijeiras, Efigenio, 132–33, 154, 163, 184, 189, 192, 198, 218
Andreu, José, 187
Aragonés, Emilio ("Fatman"), 132, 175–76, 180, 182, 189
Arbenz, Jacobo, 7
Artime, Manuel, 8, 46, 71, 79–80, 126, 129, 200, 212, 218, *p1*
Assault Brigade 2506. *See* Brigade 2506
Atienza, Orlando, 104
Atlántico (freighter), 5, 30, 48, 60, 63, 77, 85, 96, 100, 130, 155–56
Ávila, Pedro, 96, 104, 197–98

B-26 aircraft (brigade): 12, 27, 34–35, 130, 158, 162, 171, 174, 188, 190, 223, 225; American pilots flying, 134, 139, 146, 157, *p6*; canceled of D-Day airstrikes by, 47–48; casualties among pilots of, 84, 90–91, 126, 165–67, 172; color scheme of, 64, *p3*; encounters with FAR planes, 59, 77–78, 84, 90–91, 172; fake defector and, 28–29; Girón airstrip and, 16, 78, 258n11; lack of tail guns on, 35, 261n13; missions flown by, 28–29, 50, 58–59, 62–64, 67–70, 74–78, 81–85, 87–88, 90–91, 98, 112, 139, 146–48, 161, 165–69, 172–73; pilot training for, 8–9. *See also* appendixes A and B
B-26 aircraft (Castro). *See under* Fuerza Aérea Revolucionaria
Babiney strongpoint, 65–66; attacks by Castro's forces on, 85–86, 95; Castro's forces overrunning of, 108, 112–13, 124–25, 128
Bacallao, Valentín, 46
Báez, Luis, 100, 109

Baire (Cuban patrol boat). *See* Cuban (Castro) patrol boats
Baker, Leo, 161, 166–67, 250, *p6*
Barbara J (LCI), 6, 37, 43–44, 47–49, 51, 59, 67–69, 85, 96, 100, 130, 155–56, 190; drifting boats towed by launches from, 48, 59; FAR attack damage of, 69, 78, 100; invasion plans for, 16–17
Barnes, Tracy, 36
Base Trax (JMTRAV), 7, 9, 164. *See also* Guatemala, training camps in
Batista, Fulgencio, ix, 1, 6, 21, 56–57, 82, 90, 99, 106, 137, 214, 218
Battle, José Miguel, 102, 218
Battle of the Rotonda, x. *See also* Caletón (Triangle)
Bay of Pigs: Castro and, 23, 53; invasion area encompassing, 5, 12–13, 15–17, 51; population in area of, 18, 23
Beerli, Stanley, 161
Berle, Adolf, 178–79
Bissell, Richard, 12, 14, 22, 35–36, 41, 55, 160–361, 179, 212, 221, 222–25; Cuban mass uprisings and, 225–26; direct appeal to Kennedy rejected by, 36; rewriting of history by, 223
Blagar (LCI): 34, 36–37, 41–42, 46, 48, 63–64, 72, 77–78, 82, 85, 96, 100, 107, 126, 129–30, 139, 153, 155–57, 160, 190, 199; brigade commander raises Cuban flag on, 34, *p1*; command ship role of, 6; invasion plans for, 16–17
Blue Beach. *See* Girón
Borges, Luis ("*Dentista*"), 99, 118, 192–93
Borrego, Félix, 90
Bourzac, Gustavo, 58–59, 68, 77–78, 85, 98, 136, 203, 232, 236, 238
Bovo, Esteban, 222, 246
Bravo, Flavio, 87, 104, 106, 110, 114, 133
Brigade 2506, 5–6; air resupply of, 88, 91, 135, 164–65, 170, 151, 164, 170; anticipated population joining, 17–18, 51, 227; C-46 aircraft of, 8, 47, 59, 62, 64, 72, 88, 91, 135, 155, 162, 164–65, 211, 282n27; C-54 aircraft of, 8, 47, 151, 157–58, 162, 164, 169–70, 267n135, 283n56; capture of, 212, *p9*; casualties sustained by, 212; emblem of, 261n7; F-51 (Mustang) aircraft and,

301

Moya, Rolando, 42–43
MSTS. *See* Military Sea Transportation Service
Muñoz Canal strongpoint, 65, 67, 79, 87–88;
    attacks by Castro's forces on, 88, 94–95,
    101–2, 108; brigade soldiers evacuated
    from, 102, 108, 218; Castro's forces
    occupying, 108, 123, 131, 150
Murray USS, 30, 84, 190, 201
Mustang F-51, 134–35, 164–65
Mustelier, Mariano, 37, 41–42, 45

napalm, 55, 126, 147, 148–49, 157–58, 167,
    169–70
Navarro, Manuel, 164–65
Nixon, Richard, 218
Nolan, John, Jr., 219

Oliva, Erneido, 5–6, 34, 43, 77, 214, *p2*;
    admiration for, 116, 130, 214; brigade
    withdrawal suggestion of, 126–27, 129–30;
    capture of, 212; Girón western defenses
    and, 152, 159–60, 176, 182, 186, 188–89,
    191–92, 196–98, 204; Playa Larga defenses
    and, 48–49, 80, 83, 89–90, 93–94, 96–97,
    101, 106–7, 109, 111, 113–16, 130; retreat
    from Girón lead by, 204–5; San Román, J.,
    fly-out order to, 164–65; withdrawal from
    Playa Larga by, 124–26, 132–33, 143
Olivera, Filiberto, 75, 86–87, 108, 168, 182;
    offensive from Covadonga led by, 53,
    occupation of San Blas by, 180
Operación Jaula (Operation Cage), 21–22
Operación Marte (Operation Mars), 27, 223,
    260n7. *See also* Díaz, Higinio ("Nino")
Operation Mongoose, 228
Operation Pluto Plan, 15–18, 30, 33, 35,
    224–25; B-26 operations under, 16, 35; CIA
    codename and, 257(ch. 3)n2; Cuban exiles
    in the dark about, 15, 26; ship codenames
    for, 255(ch. 1)n1, 256n2; U.S. Navy decoy
    mission for, 33, 261n3
Oropesa, Enrique, 118, 275n70
Ortiz, Amparo, 61

Padrón, Adolfo, 167
Pálpite, 62–63, 69–70, 73–76, 80–81, 84,
    89–90, 93, 99, 101, 104, 106, 107, 110, 114,
    117, 119, 123, 192, 213; Castro's views on
    importance of, 69, 81; invasion plans for
    area of, 59–60
Pardo, Joel, 180–81, 184–85, 194, 206
Pardo Llada, José, 92
PBSUCCESS, 7, 44

Pedro Vera, 70, 212
Penabaz, Manuel, 63, 76–77, 186–87, 200
Pérez, Benigno, 259n12
Pérez, Bienvenido, 54, 99
Pérez, Demetrio, 83–84, 247
Pérez, Gastón, 28
Persons, Albert, 282n25
Pfeiffer, Jack, 161–62, 170–71, 221, 269n205,
    291n20
Phillips, David A., 36, 222–23
Piedra, Osvaldo, 90–91, 234, 247
Pino, Néstor, 95–96, 112–13, 128
Playa Larga, 5, 23; advance of Castro's forces
    from, 141–42, 144, 146–47, 152, 154, 169;
    Almeida and, 35; amphibious landings
    and, 36–37, 43–45, 47–49, 55, 57–59, 63,
    67–68, 80; brigade defenders pull back
    to, 114; brigade withdrawal from, 124;
    Castro and, 49, 55, 61, 75, 80–81, 89, 93,
    106, 109, 114, 137–38; Castro's forces
    advance toward, 99, 110, 113–14, 118–19,
    123; Castro's forces encirclement attempts
    of, 81, 117–18, 124, 132–33; faulty CIA
    intelligence about, 30–31; 5th Battalion
    and, 80, 83, 93, 101, 116–17; invasion plans
    for, 6, 16–17; Oliva in, 48–49, 77, 80, 83,
    93, 97, 113–16; paratroopers and, 74–76,
    107, 192; prisoners held in, 62, 116, 119;
    reinforcements from Girón to, 83, 96, 107–
    8, 115–16; shelling of, 103;. *See also* Pálpite;
    Caletón (Triangle); *Houston* (freighter)
Playa Girón. *See* Girón
Playa Macambo, 27, 260n7
Playa Morena, 81, 142, 153
PNR (National Revolutionary Police). *See*
    Policía National Revolucionaria
Point One, 20–21, 49–50, 54–55, 61, 67, 75,
    87, 99, 166, 184, 219
Point Zulu, 34, 130, 155–56, 160; *Caribe* arrival
    at, 280n257; Lynch on *Blagar's* return to,
    281n5
Policía Nacional Revolucionaria (PNR),
    battalion, 19, 132, 154, 163–64, 176,
    183–84, 189, 191, 196; Ameijeiras as head
    of, 132; militia company attached to, 154,
    164, 176, 182–83; Rodiles given command
    of, 163
Ponzoa, Gustavo, 82, 246, 249, 277n146,
    279n207
Posada, Luis, 131
Prendes, Álvaro, 29, 76–77, 84, 90–91, 143,
    172–74, 202–3, 205, 218, 234, 237, 241,
    288n231

ABOUT THE AUTHOR

J. J. Valdés is a writer with over thirty years of experience in historical research for government agencies including the Department of Defense. Born in Cuba, he came to the United States with his family in the 1960s and later attended Boston University and the University of Massachusetts. He is a member of the Conference on Latin American History and the Southern Historical Association. Valdés lives in Estero, Florida.